Engels and the formation of Marxism

Engels
and the formation of Marxism

History, dialectics and revolution

S. H. Rigby

Manchester University Press
Manchester and New York

Copyright © S. H. Rigby 1992, 2007

The right of S. H. Rigby to be identified as the author of this work has been asserted by him in accordance with the Copyright, Designs and Patents Act 1988.

Published by Manchester University Press
Oxford Road, Manchester M13 9NR, UK
and Room 400, 175 Fifth Avenue, New York, NY 10010, USA
www.manchesteruniversitypress.co.uk

Distributed exclusively in the USA by
Palgrave, 175 Fifth Avenue, New York NY 10010, USA

Distributed exclusively in Canada by
UBC Press, University of British Columbia, 2029 West Mall,
Vancouver, BC, Canada V6T 1Z2

British Library Cataloguing-in-Publication Data
A catalogue record for this book is available from the British Library

Library of Congress Cataloging-in-Publication Data
A catalog record for this book is available from the Library of Congress

ISBN 13: 978 0 7190 7774 6

First published in hardcover by Manchester University Press 1992

First digital paperback edition published 2007

Printed by Lightning Source

CONTENTS

PREFACE—*page vi*
ABBREVIATIONS—*vii*

INTRODUCTION Making sense of Engels—*1*

PART ONE The flight from Hegel:
Engels and the genesis of Marxism

CHAPTER ONE Hegelian liberalism—*12*
CHAPTER TWO Hegelian socialism—*29*
CHAPTER THREE Engels' epistemological break—*47*
CHAPTER FOUR Historical materialism—*64*
CHAPTER FIVE Communism: practical materialism—*84*

PART TWO The return to Hegel:
Engels and dialectical materialism

CHAPTER SIX Dialectical materialism—*96*
CHAPTER SEVEN Dialectical materialism: an assessment—*122*
CHAPTER EIGHT Was Marx an 'Engelsist'?—*144*
CHAPTER NINE Historical materialism: an assessment—*164*
CHAPTER TEN Scientific and critical Marxism: an assessment—*206*

CONCLUSION Engels without myth—*235*

BIBLIOGRAPHY—*241*
NAME INDEX—*253*
SUBJECT INDEX—*255*

PREFACE

Engels is perhaps the most neglected, and certainly the most unfashionable, of the major socialist thinkers. Yet many of the most problematical aspects of Marxist theory, such as dialectics, materialism, base and superstructure, scientific socialism and gender, are dealt with most explicitly in the classic texts of Marxism by Engels rather than by Marx himself. This present work is not intended as an account of Engels' life, which readers can easily find elsewhere (Carlton; Carver, 1989; Gemkow *et al*; Henderson, 1976; Ilyichov *et al*; Kapp; Mayer; Whitfield). Rather, it offers an interpretation of Engels' social theory, politics and philosophy. Its purpose is to assess Engels' contribution to the genesis of Marxism in the period before 1848; to ask how far Engels departed from this paradigm in the years after 1848; and to examine the degree to which Marx himself shared Engels' intellectual trajectory.

My aim has certainly not been to defend Engels, but neither has it been to debunk him. Rather, it has been to engage with his thought ⁄ and with the justifications and criticisms of it offered by more recent writers ⁄ as a means of assessing the strengths and weaknesses of historical materialism, of dialectical materialism, and of scientific and critical Marxism. I write not as a Marxist, nor as a professional Marxclogist, but rather as an historian who wishes to arrive at a workable social theory which will generate hypotheses which can be tested against empirical evidence. I hope that the critique of historical materialism offered in the present work will reveal the extent to which my engagement with Engels' works has altered my own previous opinions (Rigby, 1987), even if this has been in ways which Engels himself would have been unlikely to condone. Unfortunately, this book was completed before the publication of J. D. Hunley, *The Life and Thought of Friedrich Engels: a Reinterpretation* (New Haven, 1991).

Thanks are owed to a number of friends and colleagues who criticised earlier drafts of this book: Rob Lapsley and Penny Watson suggested a number of improvements to the Introduction; David Lamb kindly commented on my summary of Hegel's thought; Jon Dyson's thoughts on Marx's 'golden chains' of the proletariat form the basis of my critique of Engels' theory of revolution; R. C. Nash and Ann Hughes offered extremely helpful advice on my assessment of Engels' historical materialism. In particular, I would like to thank Rosalind Brown⁄Grant, who read and corrected the entire text, and John Breuilly, who read the work in typescript and whose perceptive comments forced me to make a number of changes to its argument and presentation. They are all, of course, absolved of responsibility for the final outcome.

ABBREVIATIONS
All works published in London unless otherwise specified

AD	F. Engels, *Anti-Dühring* (Peking, 1976)
Cap. I-III	K. Marx, *Capital volumes I-III* (Harmondsworth, 1976-81)
CM	K. Marx and F. Engels, *The Communist Manifesto* (Harmondsworth, 1970)
CPE	K. Marx, *A Contribution to the Critique of Political Economy* (1971)
CW	K. Marx and F. Engels, *Collected Works volumes 1-42* (Lawrence and Wishart, 1975-87)
CWCE	*The Condition of the Working Class in England* (1972; Introduction by E. J. Hobsbawm)
DN	F. Engels, *Dialectics of Nature* (Moscow, 1964)
EMC	W. H. Chaloner and W O. Henderson, eds, *Engels as a Military Critic* (Manchester, 1959)
EN	*The Ethnological Notebooks of Karl Marx* (ed. L. Krader; Assen, 1972)
FIA	K. Marx, *The First International and After* (ed. D. Fernbach; Harmondsworth, 1974)
Gr.	K. Marx, *Grundrisse* (Harmondsworth, 1974)
GRCR	F. Engels, *Germany: Revolution and Counter-Revolution* (1969)
MEGA	Karl Marx and Friedrich Engels, *Gesamtausgabe* (vols 1-, Berlin 1975)
OB	K. Marx and F. Engels, *On Britain* (Moscow, 1953)
OFPPS	F. Engels, *The Origin of the Family, Private Property and the State* (Moscow, 1968)
OMC	F. Engels, *On Marx's Capital* (Moscow, 1972)
OTU	K. Lapides, ed. *Marx and Engels on the Trade Unions* (New York, 1987)
PCEF	K. Marx, *Pre-capitalist Economic Formations* (ed. E. J. Hobsbawm, 1975)
PWG	F. Engels, *The Peasant War in Germany* (Moscow, 1977)
RE	K. Marx, *The Revolutions of 1848* (ed. D. Fernbach; Harmondsworth, 1973)
RFH	F. Engels, *The Role of Force in History* (1968)
SC	K. Marx and F. Engels, *Selected Correspondence* (Moscow, 1975)
SFE	K. Marx, *Surveys From Exile* (ed. D. Fernbach, Harmondsworth, 1973)
SW	K. Marx and F. Engels, *Selected Works* volume I (Moscow, 1962); volume II (Moscow, 1949)

Abbreviations

TORR   K. Marx and F. Engels, *Correspondence 1846-1895* (ed D. Torr; London, 1936)
TSV   K. Marx, *Theories of Surplus Value* (three parts, 1969-72)
WLC   K. Marx, *Wage Labour and Capital* (Moscow, 1970)
WPP   K. Marx, *Wages, Prices and Profit* (Moscow, 1970)

INTRODUCTION

Making sense of Engels

> The Bible is a large book in which men find different things
> in different ages in different circumstances (Hill, 1969: 142).

Perhaps the main difficulty in attempting to examine Engels' contribution to the formation of Marxism is that the very obviousness of Engels' historical existence as a real person who had thoughts and intentions tends to encourage a particular way of reading his texts. If Engels was a real person who attempted to express his meaning through certain works, it is easy to assume that his works must, therefore, provide a direct access to that original meaning. In effect, Engels' texts record and transmit his meaning to the reader, even though, of course, the reader may then choose to disagree with Engels' argument. This transmission of meaning may be summarised in the following form:

Engels I (the real-life Engels) ⟶ Engels' works ⟶ The reader

In fact, it could be argued that the process of deriving meaning from Engels' works is the direct opposite of their apparent process of transmission. If we examine the *reception* of Engels' texts then we must begin with the reader who actually sets to work on the text and who begins with specific biases, questions and assumptions. It is the reader who actively interprets the text and thus, in a sense, constructs Engels' 'meaning':

The reader ⟶ Engels' works ⟶ Engels II/ III/ IV etc.
(interpretations produced by specific readers)

Engels I was a real person who lived, breathed, wrote books, devoted his life to political agitation, enjoyed good wine and so on. Engels II (or III or IV) is not a real person but is rather the outcome of textual interpretation. Engels II/ III/IV does not pre-date the text as a real person, rather 'he' is the product of our encounter with the texts which bear his name. Of course, it could be argued that Engels I is also the product of textual interpretation since we can only know about the life of Engels through specific texts such as letters, newspapers, memoirs and so on. However, whilst it is possible, through the procedures which historians have agreed upon for assessing the reliability of such sources, to establish the factual outline of Engels' life which creates the apparent obviousness of Engels I (he was born in 1820, died in 1895 and so on), we have no such agreed procedures with which to choose between conflicting interpretations of Engels' works.

Naturally, all readers believe that the interpretation of Engels which they derive from his works (Engels II, III, IV, etc.) coincides with the original intentions of Engels. Yet this would only be the case if readers were essentially passive in their reception of the meaning which the author originally embodied within the text, and which the text faithfully reproduces. Yet, in fact, readers are far from passive in their relationship with the text. Indeed, given the variety of readings to which Marx and Engels are now open, it would be easier to argue that, in the dialectic whereby readers obtain meanings from texts and texts constrain the meanings open to readers, it is the reader who has the upper hand.

This is notoriously the case in the interpretation of Marx's works where, despite, or perhaps because of, a mountain of interpretation, the most fundamental questions remain open to debate. His thought is said to display an underlying unity between the *Paris Manuscripts* (1844) and *Capital* volume I (1867) (Avineri, 1971: 3; Maguire: x; Kolakowski I: 263; Howard: 134; Hyppolite: xii), or, alternatively, to be comprised of up to four different approaches, marked by one or more fundamental breaks (Althusser, 1977: ch.2; Benton, 1977: 150/3; Callinicos, 1987a: 43/5; Adamson, 1981). Marx was either an existentialist humanist or a structuralist anti-humanist (Fromm: 71; Althusser, 1977: ch.7). He became more positivist in his later writings Lichtheim, 1971a: 236, 243; McLellan, 1976: 423), or was never a positivist (Thomas, 1976: 3/4). He was always essentially an Hegelian; broke sharply with Hegelianism; broke sharply with Hegelianism but then returned to it; became progresively less Hegelian; or, alternatively, progressively more Hegelian, as time went by (Kolakowski I: 263; Althusser, 1977: 33/8; Althusser, 1971: 90/1; Cornu: v; Lowith: 92; Hyppolite: 96/7, 128; Kain). Thus with every book and article which is published about Marx, we seem to be ever further removed from an understanding of him.

In 1899, Bernstein claimed that 'today ... one can prove everything out of Marx and Engels.' Given the number of varieties of Marxism which have flourished in the twentieth century, his comment is now more valid than ever. To expound the views of Marx and Engels is thus to develop them in some specific way. Marx and Engels are thus 'neither more nor less than they appear in their books' (Bernstein: 25/6; Jordan: xi; Croce: 80). The problem is that, just as the theological radicals of the Reformation claimed merely to be returning to the original purity of Holy Scripture, so many readers pass off their developments of Marx and Engels simply as returns to Marx and Engels' own original intentions (Meikle, 1986: 40). It is thus futile to claim that

'Marx was eminently capable of saying what he meant' for himself (Slaughter: 45), since today, Marx, like Engels, cannot speak for himself, but only through our readings of his texts.

A recognition of the active role which readers have in creating meaning might seem to imply the view that reading involves nothing more than a 'monumentally egotistic and finally tedious projection' of the reader's own thoughts on to an author (Aers: 6-7). Marx and Engels' works would then become nothing more than a mirror for the reader: if a humanist looked in, you wouldn't expect a structuralist to peer out. As a result, we would seem to be left with a total relativism, where all interpretations of Marx and Engels works are equally valid. However, an acknowledgement of the fact that Marx and Engels' works are open to a number of legitimate readings does *not* mean that any reading is as valid as any other. Certain readings, for instance the claim that Marx never used the phrase 'scientific socialism' and the deduction that, indeed, 'he could not have used it', *can* be refuted by textual evidence (Thomas: 1; FIA: 337; Rubel and Manale: 305, 317-18; MEGA 27/1: 541-2). That there are innumerable correct readings of Marx and Engels does not mean that there are no incorrect ones (Sayer: ix).

This active role of the reader in determining the meaning of a text is nowhere more apparent than in the case of Engels' works, where the range of interpretations and assessments on offer is, amazingly, even greater than that for Marx's works. For some writers, Engels was an inferior philosopher, a determinist, a positivist and a mechanistic materialist, who ignored the specificity of the social world in his reduction of the universe to matter in motion. Yet, for others, Engels was a genius who offered a critique of mechanistic materialism and positivism and who consciously rejected reductionism. (Levine, 1975: xiv; Levine, 1984: 103-6; Avineri, 1971: 65-70; Benton, 1979: 119; Jones, G. S., 1982: 294; Timpanaro: 68).

Engels has been seen as the founder of an anti-empirical Marxism based on *a priori* laws of matter, and also as a brilliant historian whose intellectual strength lay in empirical studies, and who demanded that all history be studied afresh rather than being compressed into some ready-made schema (Gorman; Abrams: 63). For some commentators, Engels' later works reveal that he had never freed himself from the Hegelianism of his youth; for others his Hegelianism was purely verbal rather than substantial (Lichtheim, 1978: 296; Benton, 1979: 119). Politically, Engels has been seen as increasingly reformist in his later years - but also as a lifelong opponent of reformism (Levine, 1975: ch. 11; Thomas: 6; Fetscher: 216-17; Draper: 25; Henderson, 1976 II: 664, 667).

Given this total lack of agreement about the nature of the thought of either Marx or Engels, it is hardly surprising that there is no agreement about the nature of the intellectual relationship betwen them. Engels himself, of course, regarded his later works, such as *Anti-Dühring* (1878), as accurately representing the thought of Marx (AD: 8/9). The world communist parties have traditionally followed this line, arguing that the works of Marx and Engels together form a perfect whole. 'Silly bourgeois ideologists' might attempt to show that Engels' works diverge from Marx's but the unequivocal and verifiable facts 'speak for themselves' in showing the unity of the thought of the two men (Gemkow: 7; CW 25: xviii).

It is not only orthodox communists who have adopted this interpretation. Krieger, for instance, described Marx and Engels as 'the most harmonious intellectual duet in the history of western culture', whilst writers such as Evans, Hobsbawm, Wood and Weiss have warned against the tendency to overemphasise the differences between the two (Krieger, 1967: xiii/xiv; Evans, 1975: 19/21, 78/9; PCEF: 53; Wood, A. W,. 1981: 159; Weiss: 15/30). Engels *is* often given credit for his role in the genesis of Marxism in the 1840s; whilst Bernstein even went so far as to argue that Engels' famous letters of the 1890s revealed a more subtle and developed form of historical materialism than the strict economic determinism of the 1859 'Preface', Marx's most explicit statement of his social theory (Nova: 23/4; Carlton: 57/8; Henderson, 1976 I: 73, 128; Mayer: ch. 8; Jordan: 320; Howard: 84; Jones, G. S., 1977: 102; Loewenstein: 57; Adamson, 1981: 401; Bernstein: 7/12).

In general, however, the dominant tendency in the twentieth century has been to divorce the works of Marx from those of Engels, invariably to the latter's disadvantage. Engels' later works may have provided an introduction to Marxism for thinkers such as Kautsky and Plekhanov, Lenin and Mao, but 'Western' (or 'Critical') Marxism has based itself on a critique of the 'Scientific' Marxism which it traces back to *Anti-Dühring*. By 1914, the foundations of this critique of Engels had already been established. Writers such as Gentile, Sorel, Andler, Masaryk, Brzozowski, Szabó, Arturo Labriola and Mondolfo argued that Engels had failed to appreciate Marx's achievement and had transformed Marxism from a critique of political economy, based on the concept of revolutionary praxis, to a passive materialistic science, which counterposed the social primacy of the productive forces to Marx's own emphasis on class (Jacoby: 52/8).

Similarly, Gramsci criticised those who assumed that Marx and Engels held identical views on all subjects; whilst Lukács argued that Engels had ignored the revolutionary dialectic of subject and object and that he had illegitimately extended the dialectic to the realm of nature. Of the founding fathers of western Marxism, only Korsch stressed that Marx himself had shifted to a more 'scientific' Marxism after the defeat of the 1848 Revolution although, like Fischer, he blamed the worst excesses of dialectical materialism on Kautsky rather than on Engels (Gramsci: 385/6; Lukács: 3, 24; Korsch 1938: 168, 186; Vajda: 131/4; Fischer: 85).

Making sense of Engels

The discovery of Marx's early writings, particularly the *1844 Manuscripts* (first published in 1932), further encouraged the tendency to divorce the works of Marx and Engels. Marx the scientific economist, who established the laws of motion of capitalist society, was replaced by Marx the philosophical humanist, whose early critique of alienation and theory of praxis formed the basis of his later thought. Writers such as Sartre, Schmidt and Colletti continued to reject Engels' universal laws of the dialectic and argued that he and Marx had possessed 'profoundly different ways of seeing the world' (Sartre: 27-34; Schmidt, 1971: ch. 1; Colletti, 1973: 24).

It is not only revolutionary Marxists who wish to distinguish Marx and Engels' contributions to the formation of Marxism. The academic literature on Marx now 'threatens to drown both the theory and its students.' However, one straw for the drowning scholar to clutch at has been the certainty that Engels' later works have 'only the remotest connection with Marx's viewpoint', and that they created a new theory which was incompatible with the Marxism of the 1840s and which distorted Marx's own views on science, epistemology and socialism. Above all, Engels lacked the concept of praxis and instead adopted a mechanistic and deterministic philosophy which led, apparently, to both the failures of reformism and to the revolutionary excesses of the Bolsheviks. Since Marx's views form a consistent whole and are incompatible with those of Engels, it is possible to *deduce* that *if* Marx had read Engels' *Anti-Dühring*, he would have disagreed with it (Lictheim, 1978: 296; Miller, J.: ch. 5; Fetscher: 162-79; Avineri, 1971: ch. 3; Thomas: 1-23; Walton and Gamble: 75).

This rare consensus amongst Marxologists about the divergences between the thought of Marx and Engels is disrupted only by disagreement as to *when* such differences became apparent. For Fetscher, Engels' dialectical materialism emerged in opposition to Marx's historical materialism in 1878; for Schmidt, Levine and Carver, the two men's opinions diverged after 1858-59; whilst for Lichtheim and Andler, such differences were apparent as early as the 1840s (Fetscher: 162; Schmidt, 1971: 52; Carver, 1984a: 261-79; Levine, 1984: 21; Lichteheim, 1971a: 54; Jacoby: 55).

In 1970, Timpanaro argued that those writers who divorce Marx from Engels eventually come to find much of the later Marx too 'Engelsian', obliging such writers to identify some 'real' Marx in the *1844 Manuscripts* or the *Theses on Feuerbach* (1845) (Timpanaro: 77). His argument was soon to be confirmed with the appearance of the works of Norman Levine, the most systematic and comprehensive exponent of the view that Engels' later works distort and vulgarise the outlook which Marx had developed in the 1840s. In *The Tragic Deception*, Levine argued that, after 1878, Engels ignored the key concepts developed by Marx in the 1840s: praxis, alienation and species-being (since Marx's works form a consistent whole it is, Levine assumes, fair to represent his views from his early works, particularly the *1844 Manuscripts*). The result was that Engels lapsed into a mechanistic materialist view of the universe, a technological determinist account of historical change, a parliamentarian and reformist political strategy, and a vision of the communist future as one enormous factory, where the productive forces had been liberated, rather than human alienation transcended (Levine, 1975).

Levine's later *Dialogue Within the Dialectic* argued that central to the differences betwen Marx and Engels were their different understandings of Hegel's dialectic. Engels' misappropriation of Hegel proved disastrous, since the dialectic is the central unifying principle in Marx's thought: a principle of more importance than his history, philosophy, politics, economics or sociology. For Levine, Marx took from Hegel an emphasis on praxis, on subjective agency, and so created historical materialism; whereas Engels interpreted the dialectic in terms of a law-bound evolutionary process and so invented dialectical materialism. Levine believes that whilst Marx 'assigned' Engels the task of producing a philosophy of nature, Marx himself would not have accepted the dogmatic and deterministic materialism which Engels produced, with its necessitarian and mechanistic laws of the dialectic at work in both nature and society. Even Engels' achievement in editing volumes two and three of *Capital*, was double-edged as in his creation of three volumes, rather than Marx's intended two, Engels transformed *Capital* from a work of critique, an economic justification of the political demands of the working class, into a scientific treatise about the laws of social evolution and the inevitable collapse of capitalism (Levine, 1984; see also Hook, 1934: 35; Rubel, 1977: 47-8).

Terell Carver's analysis of the intellectual relationship between Marx and Engels is far more reasonable in tone than Levine's denunciation. Yet, paradoxically, he argues that Levine's own critique of Engels does not go far enough since it continues to interpret Marx's thought through the paradigm established in Engels' 1859 review of Marx's *Critique of Political Economy*. It is this review, with its emphasis on Marx's scientific, materialist and dialectical method, which Carver sees as the birthplace of dialectical materialism - Engels' own philosophical invention which was opposed to the historical materialism which he had helped Marx to create in the 1840s. Engels was thus forgetful of his own achievement. He came to regard Marx as an academic historical scientist who established the laws of evolution of society, rather than as a revolutionary thinker whose main priority was the transformation of capitalist society. Carver emphasises that Marx did *not* endorse Engels' laws of the dialectic outlined in *Anti-Dühring*. Indeed, there is no proof that Marx had even read the entire text of Engels' work. In the absence of positive proof that Marx agreed with Engels, we must assume that he disagreed with him, since Engels' views were out of line with the opinions which Marx had expressed elsewhere (Carver, 1976; 1980; 1983; 1984a; 1985: 172-3; 1989: 259).

That the readers of a text do not have direct access to its author's intentions, and are themselves obliged to deduce such intentions in order to understand it, can be seen from the variety of interpretations of Engels' claim that his works were an accurate representation of Marx's own opinions. Evans and Schmidt, for instance, claim that Marx and Engels were not themselves aware of any substantial differences between them on matters of theory. Similarly, Gramsci, Lichtheim and McLellan argue that it was Engels' characteristic modesty which led him to emphasise his secondary role in his partnership with Marx, and thus, inadvertently, to pass his own views off as those of Marx (Evans, 1975: 19-21; Schmidt, 1971: 207; Lichtheim, 1978: 296; McLellan, 1977a: 65; Nova: 90).

Carver, on the other hand, offers a more Machiavellian interpretation of Engels' motives. In the first edition of *Anti-Dühring* (1878), Engels did not formulate his general views on dialectics; he was 'canny enough to avoid creating disagreement with Marx.' Only in 1885, two years after Marx's death, did Engels introduce such non-Marxist material into the 'Preface' of the second edition of the book. Engels' post-1883 accounts of how *Anti-Dühring* was written claimed an ever-larger role for Marx and thus 'gave the reader the impression that Marx approved his work as an expression of "their" outlook whilst avoiding the statement that Marx agreed explicitly to any such thing' (Carver, 1980: 353-63; 1983: 125; SC: 14).

One alternative to merely emphasising the differences of opinion between Marx and Engels would be to show that, although the two men differed in their views on philosophy and the natural sciences, their ideas on social theory and history, which, after all, constitute 'the source of all [Marxism's] value and its justification', were 'virtually identical'. Anderson even ventured the 'scandalous opinion' that 'Engels's historical judgements are nearly always superior to those of Marx', even though Engels was inferior in his grasp of general theory (Leff: 7; Anderson, 1979: 23; Ross Gandy: vii; Bak: 89).

Yet even here there is no unanimity of opinion. Kain argues that Marx and Engels' essential differences lie in their versions of historical materialism, rather than in their interpretation of Hegel's dialectic. Engels has thus been criticised for propounding a unilinear social evolutionism, whereas Marx is held to have been aware of the multilinear nature of social development. For Cohen, Marx and Engels rightly claimed that society's evolving productive forces determine the nature of its relations of production; for Avineri and Colletti, on the other hand, Marx rejected such productive force determinism to which Engels, however, did mistakenly adhere. According to Colletti, it was Engels who most frequently used the metaphor of society's economic 'base' determining its political and ideological superstructure; a metaphor which, with its overtones of economic determinism, rarely occurs in the works of Marx. Carver agrees that as Engels' philosophical views diverged from Marx's after 1859, so did the content of his historical studies (Kain: 109; Shanin, 1981: 119; Levine, 1975: ch. 10; Cohen, 1978: 145; Avineri, 1971: 153-4; Colletti, 1972: 65; Carver, 1983: 142).

We have seen that the process of reading Marx is an active one, in which Marx's works are used as building blocks that limit, but do not directly determine, the nature of the reader's construction of meaning. Marx is thus regularly modernised (as, for instance, an existentialist or a structuralist) and purified of those elements which the reader finds unacceptable. Like other contemporary intellectual heroes, he thus seems always to have singlehandedly 'anticipated and surpassed the most significant theoretical trends of recent decades' (Shepherd: 91). 'In all of these operations there is a need for somebody on whom everything which Marxists, at that particular moment, are asking to get rid of can be dumped. That somebody is Friedrich Engels' (Timpanaro: 73-4).

Psycho-analysts would, of course, find this a familiar psychological defence mechanism: we divide the world into good and bad objects; the good objects we perceive as idealised unities whose qualities have to be 'introjected' into ourselves; the bad objects ('the bad breast') we perceive as fragmented and, having projected on to them all that we find threatening, have to reject and expel them (Segal: 64-5, 78, 116; Klein, 1980: 2-6, 62-3; Klein, 1981: 262, 285, 291). Thus, we are told, again and again, that Marx's works form a coherent and consistent unity. It is Engels - whose views are a 'false synthesis' of Comte and Hegel, a 'contradictory mixture' of pragmatism, positivism, mechanical materialism and emergent evolutionism - who has to be expelled from Marxism. (For Marx as a unity see the references cited above and Schmidt, 1972: 33-5; for the divided Engels see Thomas: 11; Levine, 1984: 84; Colletti, 1972: 26.)

This book argues that such attempts to counterpose the views of Marx and Engels are essentially a strategy designed to forestall a confrontation with the problems which lie within Marx's works themselves. It is not our intention to deny that Engels' thought was 'dramatically contradictory', but rather to show that similar antinomies are also to be found in the thought of Marx. Of course, this argument involves yet another claim about the 'real nature' of Marx's works, even though it replaces the orthodox emphasis on coherence with an emphasis on contradiction. This way of reading Marx and Engels does, however, offer two advantages. Firstly, a recognition of the contradictory discourses present within their texts allows us to explain why they have been open to such widely divergent interpretations; it means that we need not simply reject previous interpretations as mistaken, but, rather, can see them as aspects of a broader totality.

Secondly, accepting that Marx and Engels' works are open to a variety of legitimate interpretations has the further advantage of allowing us to turn our attention away from the impossible task of deciding which reading represents their 'real meaning'. Instead, we can concentrate on the more important issue of deciding which reading of Marx and Engels is the most useful for our practice as historians, social theorists, political activists and so on. We should not, however, confuse the claim that *we* find a particular reading of Marx and Engels to be the most useful, with the claim that this was, therefore, Marx and Engels' own, consciously-intended meaning.

Thus an acknowledgement of the active role of the reader does not mean that all reading of Marx and Engels is equally valid or that attempting to interpret their texts is futile. What it does mean is that we must abandon the search for Marx and Engels' (or anyone else's) single, unitary meaning. This approach obviously owes much to Althusser's call for a 'symptomatic reading' of Marx and Engels which would locate the contradictory discourses which are to be found within their texts. Where it differs from Althusser is in its rejection of the assumption that Marx's works necessarily progressed towards an ever more 'Marxist' position which turns out to be yet another reading of Marx's 'real meaning'. Thus, if there are differences of emphasis between Marx and Engels, they express difficulties which lie at the heart of Marxism, rather than showing that one man was a 'real Marxist' (and thus correct) whilst the other was not. Our aim is not to rescue Engels, but rather to show that it is futile to denigrate him as a means of avoiding the problems posed by Marx's own works. We have been taught to 'read for the best Marx'; we must now learn to avoid reading for the worst Engels (Althusser and Balibar: 32-4; Althusser, 1971: 90; Gouldner: 274-5; Stanley and Zimmermann, 229; Croce: 77-81; Johnson, R., 1982).

PART ONE

The flight from Hegel:
Engels and the genesis of Marxism

CHAPTER ONE

Hegelian liberalism

Now I'll study Hegel over a glass of punch
(Engels, November 1839. CW 2: 487).

HEGEL AND THE YOUNG HEGELIANS

According to Lichtheim, Engels was a lifelong prisoner of the Hegelian system which he encountered in his youth (Lichtheim, 1978: 296). Even if we do not accept this judgement, there is no doubt that some knowledge of Hegel's thought, and of its development by his Young Hegelian successors, is crucial for an understanding of Engels' intellectual development from the orthodox Hegelianism of his youth, through his break with idealism and the creation of historical materialism in the mid-1840s, to his return to Hegel in the years after 1858.

According to Hegel, previous philosophical systems were never entirely wrong, rather they expressed some one-sided truth about the world which had to be subsumed within some higher, more embracing account of reality. Thus from Plato, Hegel took the belief that reality is essentially ideal in nature. Spirit, or self-conscious reason, is the only true reality; the material world is thus subordinate to the world of Spirit. Yet, unlike Plato, Hegel did not accept that the ideal 'forms' which constitute reality were fixed, eternal and perfect. Instead, he adopted the Aristotelian picture of reality as the progressive unfolding of an essential inner nature: being is movement. World history consists of the unfolding of Spirit's potential until it has fully realised its essence and reached its final goal (or 'Idea'): freedom. The Idea is thus not something which has existed for all time, but is rather a goal which is arrived at via the purposive activity of Spirit (Hegel, 1956: 19; 1971: 68, 83; 1971: 85; 1988: 43-8, 87-8; Marcuse: 121-2).

Since Spirit, as self-conscious reason, constitutes true reality, it follows that reason is the substance of the universe. Nature, for instance, embodies reason in the sense that it is subject to universal laws; it is a rational structure which is produced by divine wisdom in its quest to create an absolutely rational world for itself (Hegel, 1956: 11; 1988: 24; Cohen, 1978, ch. 1; Findlay: 272).

For Hegel, Spirit is not only sovereign in the realm of nature but also in the realm of active mind, of human consciousness. Indeed, since Spirit is self-conscious reason, and reason is perfectly free, self-conditioning thought, it follows that Spirit finds its truest embodiment in free human activity. Nevertheless, such freedom does not simply exist; rather it progresses through the march of human history towards the 'Idea' of Spirit. History thus consists of the growth of freedom and reason in human affairs; it is Spirit's struggle to impose itself on the world and to overcome all restraints on its full development. For Hegel, this potential for freedom is an essence which must be realised since it is the absolute and final goal of Spirit, a goal which was implicit in the very beginning of the whole teleological process of Spirit's development. Thus, whilst nature is cyclical in its development, human history is a progressive evolution towards the fulfilment of reason and freedom. Nature is thus the realm of peace, human history the realm of consciousness, will and struggle. History is not simply a series of accidents. Rather, it is 'a rationally based succession of phenomena', a necessary chain of connections: the Idea is thus 'an organic system, a totality including in itself a wealth of stages and features' (Hegel, 1956: 16-21; 1988: 20, 23-4, 31, 53, 55, 74-6).

Hegel thus rejected the orthodox Christian vision of God as a perfect and self-sufficient being, separate from the creation which he brought into being through an act of free will. In the Hegelian system, the creation was not some arbitrary act of God but was rather a necessary expression of his nature; it is the means through which God fully realises his essence: 'without the world, God is not God' (Taylor, 1979: 38). Unlike the self-sufficient God of orthodoxy, Spirit needs the universe in order to embody and express its true nature. Finite mind thus shares in the nature of the infinite. Indeed, for Hegel, it is through finite mind that Spirit comes to a consciousnes of its own nature. The long history of philosophy is the progress of Spirit coming to an ever more adequate understanding of itself, absolute knowledge finally being attained when Spirit sees reality as it is really is, i.e. as it is revealed by Hegel's own philosophy: 'Hegel speaks of Spirit confident that Spirit speaks through him' (Hegel, 1956: 78; Lowith: 9; Inwood: 2). Hegel thus rejected the 'unhappy consciousness' of 'dualist' religion in which humanity alienates its own spiritual qualities from itself and projects them on to a separate divine being. Rather, he believed that through reason, which man shares with God, man comes to self-consciousness and is reconciled with God (Hegel, 1988: 28; Singer: ch. 4).

Spirit's development is described by Hegel as 'dialectical' in nature, in other words, it is a teleological progression towards the increasingly adequate expression of its Idea. Through a dialectical development the Idea 'assumes successive forms which it successively transcends.' Each stage of the progression 'negates' the previous one but, for Hegel, this does not mean that the previous stage is annulled. Rather, it is transcended so that its positive features are retained in the succeeding higher stages through which the Idea 'gains an affirmative, and in fact, a richer and more concrete shape' (Hegel, 1956: 63). We can now see why, for Hegel, 'the truth is the whole' since, in his system, the Absolute is not eternally given, but is instead the product of a series of changes; changes which can only be fully understood when they are seen as stages of the realisation of the total process (Hegel, 1971: 81, 112).

Hegel believed in the universality of change but he did not regard such change as a mere random flux. Rather, 'everything around us may be viewed as an instance of dialectic' where change takes the form of ordered progression through which Spirit develops and perfects its powers, an inner self-movement through which each stage necessarily overcomes the inadequacies of the previous one. Hegel's dialectic is thus based upon the 'absolute method' of 'triplicity', of the progression from some initial simple unity, through a stage of separation and particularity, to reach a third and final stage which both transcends the previous stages whilst preserving their positive aspects within a higher and differentiated unity (Hegel, 1956: 63; 1971: 68, 83, 107; 1987: 118; 1988: 83; MacGregor: 16; George: 124; Norman and Sayers: 36-42).

Through what necessity is Spirit obliged to progress through this ordered development towards its Idea? Hegel's answer lies in the centrality of contradiction to existence. For formal logic, contradictions are a blemish which have to be removed from thought; formal logic emphasises identity, fixed categories and, through the law of non-contradiction, forbids contradictory statements about the world. Hegel offered an alternative, 'dialectical' logic which, he claimed, could grasp reality in the totality of its interrelationships and its inner movement. In this alternative logic, contradiction is more important than identity since contradiction is the 'root of all movement, it is only so far as something has contradictions that it moves'. Since, for Hegel, being is motion and motion is the 'immediate form of existence of contradictions', it follows that all reality is necessarily contradictory (Hegel, 1969: 439-40; 1988: 58).

In addition to this 'temporal' dialectic which allows us to grasp *change* over time, Hegel also offers a 'conceptual' dialectic which supposedly allows us to grasp the *structure* of reality. This synchronic dialectic is a means of dealing with oppositions such as those between mind and matter, the particular and the universal, subject and object, and so on. Dualist philosophy presents each side of such oppositions as self-sufficient in its nature, enjoying a real, but independent, existence. In contrast, a reductionist understanding of such oppositions denies the reality of one side of the opposition. Dialectical thought, unlike reductionism, accepts the reality of both sides of the opposition but, unlike dualism, would deny their autonomous existence and insists, instead, on their reciprocal interdependence and mutual constitution. Thus we can only fully understand the nature of each side of an opposition when we see it as a moment of the totality; in the conceptual, as in the temporal, dialectic, the truth is the whole (Norman and Sayers: 29-31; Lapsley and Westlake: 53-4). Hegel argued that this 'identity' or interdependence of opposites also meant that, despite the claims of formal logic, contradictions do exist in reality. Nevertheless, as we shall see, it is not clear that what he calls 'contradictions' are, in fact, logical contradictions and so contrary to formal logic.

Since, for Hegel, Spirit creates itself through its own labour, through its struggle to realise its own essence by imposing itself on the world, the dialectic between subject and object was, inevitably, of particular importance to him. Just as absolute Spirit can only arrive at a self-consciousness of its own nature through the existence of something outside itself (human consciousness), so human finite spirit (or human subjectivity), through its encounter with the outside world, proceeds via the logically necessary stages which culminate in its own freedom and self-consciousness. Thus Hegel did not see knowledge as simply the product of the application of a dialectical methodology to a specific subject-matter from the outside but rather saw knowledge itself as dialectical in nature as it progressed through its inherent contradictions (Hegel, 1971: 88-92; 1988: 41-2; Lamb, 1980: 30; Taylor, 1975: 129).

Perhaps Hegel's philosophy can be be understood through looking at his application of it to actual human history. His account of the development of the state, for instance, is a classic example of the temporal dialectic at work. For Hegel, history is, in the broadest sense, the work of God but, in practice, it is the state, 'the divine idea as it exists on earth', which is 'the basis and the centre of the other concrete elements in the life of a people - of Art, of Law, of Religion, of Science' (Hegel, 1956: 39, 49). Spirit is at work in history, Spirit is self-conscious reason whose Idea is freedom. It follows that it is the state which is the embodiment of rationality and the realm where freedom exists, it is freedom's 'objective form.' A truly rational state would be one in which the state's interest, society's universal interest and the individual citizen's interest all coincided. Freedom is thus actualised through the citizen's membership of a rational, self-conscious community. This does not necessarily mean that any given state is rational at any particular time, nor that all states are equally rational. On the contrary, the truly rational state is the outcome of a dialectical process whereby the inadequacies of each stage of development are necessarily overcome and so lead inexorably to the complete embodiment of reason (Hegel, 1956: 36-9, 109-10; 1979: 155, 160, 164, 279, 285).

The state's development towards this final goal takes the familiar form of the 'dialectical three-step.' In the Ancient Greek world, there was a simple unity between the individual and society through the citizen's membership of the *polis*; social harmony was produced by the absorption of the individual by the universal. The Middle Ages gave expression to the second stage of the temporal dialectic, the age of particularity where individual social ties (such as those between lord and vassal or ruler and subject) were paramount. The one-sidedness of each of these first two stages of development had necessarily to be overcome by a new unity, which preserved their positive features whilst transcending their incompleteness.

The result was the modern state which allows a return to the social unity and harmony of the *polis* whilst preserving the positive benefits of individuality passed on by the Middle Ages. The modern state is thus a differentiated unity with which the individual citizen rationally identifies because it offers a community based on freedom for all. Hegel's vision of world history is thus one of a progression towards a realm of freedom, reason and self-consciousness which establishes the harmony of man and man, of individual and community, and of the citizen and the state. It was a vision which was to have a decisive impact on the political philosophy of Marx and Engels (Hegel, 1956: 106-7, 109-10; Singer: ch. 2-3; Norman and Sayers: 40-2).

THE YOUNG HEGELIANS

Even before Hegel's death in 1831, the ambiguous implications of his system had become apparent. For some conservatives, Hegelianism offered a means of providing Christianity with a rational basis with which to strengthen its position in the modern world. Yet other writers questioned whether, in practice, Hegel's philosphy *did* preserve the content of Christianity since his thought could also be seen as a critique of the dualist separation of man and God found in orthodox Christianity. By the end of the 1820s, Feuerbach was arguing that each form of religion was based on a prior philosophical outlook but that the religious form corresponding to Hegel's new philosophy had yet to be created. Feuerbach thus outdid his master by arguing that Hegel's break with dualism had not gone far enough. He sought to develop Hegel's thought through to its logical conclusion and to break with the compromise which Hegel had reached with the existing form of religion (Toews: ch. 6).

Strauss, like Feuerbach, both developed and criticised Hegel's philosophy of religion in his *Life of Jesus* (1835). For Strauss, the Bible expressed a vital truth but it did so in mythical or allegorical form. The truth which Christianity revealed was not an historical truth about an individual who lived in the past, but a philosophical truth about the situation of humanity. Christ's importance lay in his symbolising the essential unity between God and Man, that both share a common nature in Spirit: 'God does not remain as a fixed and immutable infinite outside and above the finite.' Man considered purely as a finite creature has no truth, God shut up in his infinitude has no reality. Thus 'the infinite spirit is only real when it discloses itself in finite spirits.' Strauss's argument was taken to its logical conclusion by Engels' friend, Bruno Bauer, who, by 1841, had passed beyond Strauss's pantheistic unity of God and his creation to explicit atheism, an atheism which, he claimed, was implicit in Hegel's system itself (Toews: ch. 8/9; Stepelevich: 44/5; 180/1; Hook, 1936: 77/125).

Despite his radicalism, Bauer continued to work within the framework of the Hegelian system, conceiving of humanity in terms of culture, spirit and consciousness. It was to be Feuerbach who provided the way out of Hegelian idealism. His *Essence of Christianity* (1841) argued that, if the only spirit with real existence is human reason, the idea of a divine being must be the result of a projection of human powers on to an imaginary object. Thus it is not God who creates man, rather it is man who creates God. Through religion, man inverts reality so that his own subjectivity becomes a predicate of God and he denies his own powers by ascribing them to God: 'To enrich God, man must become poor, that God may be all, man must be nothing.' Feuerbach rejected this alienation of human powers through religious belief, along with any belief in Reason as a self-sufficent entity which realises itself through humanity. Reason is the goal of history, not in the sense of the logical and necessary unfolding of an idea, but in the practical sense that human history consists of the growth and actualisation of human powers. He thus called for an end to both theology and speculative idealism and, in his *Provisional Theses for the Reformation of Philosophy* (1843), argued for a materialist, 'anthropological' outlook based on the understanding of man as a natural, sensual being (Stepelevich: 139, 150, 154, 167; Toews: ch. 10; Hook, 1936: ch. 7; McLellan, 1980: 85/116).

However, whilst Feuerbach dismissed Hegelian idealism as the last refuge of theological thought, the more orthodox Hegelians, such as Bauer, attempted to salvage Hegel's method. They agreed that the content of Hegel's system was explicitly conservative, but claimed that his dialectical method, with its emphasis on change and the primacy of reason, was implicitly radical in nature. Whilst Hegel himself had claimed to be an orthodox Lutheran, the Young Hegelians argued that his system led logically to pantheism or even atheism (Brazill: 18).

The Young Hegelians found a similar contradiction at work between Hegel's personal political views and the logical implications of his philosophy. For Hegel, the state is the embodiment of the Idea and, as such, the state could contain 'nothing except what is an expression of rationality.' By 1821, Hegel had decided that the embodiment of reason in political form had been achieved by the contemporary Prussian state. He argued, however, that whilst philosophy could discern the 'cunning of reason' at work in human history, it could only do so retrospectively: 'The owl of Minerva spreads its wings only with the falling of dusk.' Since philosophy can only be wise *after* the event, it cannot allow us to prescribe future practice (Toews: 62; Hegel, 1979: 12/13, 285).

The Young Hegelians accepted Hegel's belief that the state should be fully rational, they simply disagreed with his claim that this stage of political development had already been achieved. For them, the contemporary state was irrational and had thus inevitably to fall 'before the force of the mind.' Whilst Hegel devoted himself to studying the *past* development of Reason, the Young Hegelians sought to actualise it in the *future* (Stepelevich: 183-5; Sayers, 1987: 150).

For the Young Hegelians, it was thus the duty of philosophers to criticise the irrationality of existing political institutions so that the community could achieve the complete realisation of freedom. Writers such as Ruge argued that a state which truly embodied freedom and reason would necessarily involve popular sovereignty and the rule of law (Brazill: ch. 6; Hook, 1936: ch. 4). Hegelian philosophy could thus be used to undermine the foundations not only of established religion but also of the contemporary state. It provided the philosophical basis for a humanism which aimed to overcome both the religious alienation involved in subjecting oneself to the creation of one's own mind, and the political alienation involved in subjection to monarchical despotism. In the place of such alienation, the unity of man and man would be created in a self-conscious community based on freedom and reason. Such ideas were to have a decisive importance in Engels' own development from liberalism to communism.

ENGELS AND YOUNG GERMANY

The intellectual development of the young Engels ran along broadly similar lines to that of the young Marx: politically, from radical liberalism through humanist socialism to the position set out in *The Communist Manifesto*; philosophically, from Hegelianism to the historical materialism outlined in *The German Ideology*. Yet this progression was to prove more difficult for Engels than for Marx, entailing, as it did, a break with the conservative beliefs of his Pietist family. This does not mean, however, that Engels' political views can be dismissed as merely a product of his personal conflicts with his family. If we want to, we can see *The Condition of the Working Class in England* as his revenge against his capitalist father but, nevertheless, not every rebellious child ends up producing such a masterpiece (Henderson and Chaloner: xxvii). Engels himself was certainly aware of the intergenerational nature of contemporary political conflict, but he also stressed that such conflict was historically specific in its content: it was in his and Marx's native Rhineland, with its social and economic mobility and its receptiveness to modern ideas, rather than in the untroubled towns of the interior, that the 'disagreeable process' of the breakup of the traditional German family was most advanced (CW 2: 135, 165).

Engels' conflicts with his father date to before his fifteenth birthday but, at first, they do not seem to have involved any break with his family's religious or political beliefs. In 1842, Engels senior claimed that when his son was confirmed at the age of seventeen (i.e. 1837/38), he had been motivated by feelings of genuine piety; certainly a poem written by Engels shortly before this date testifies to his orthodox piety with its prayer to Jesus to 'Step down from heaven and save my soul for me' (CW 2: 555, 582, 586).

It is only from March 1839, when Engels published his 'Letters from Wuppertal', that the extent of his break with his family becomes apparent. The 'Letters', written whilst Engels was working in Bremen, were a comprehensive attack on the morals and piety of his own class. They portrayed the twin-towns of Barmen and Elberfeld as inhabited by a drunken and degraded population whose condition was the result, first and foremost, of its employment in factory work. In particular, Engels emphasised the reckless way in which the employers ran their factories, exploiting cheap child labour, choking their employees wuth dust and fumes, and depriving them of all strength and joy in life. The populace found its escape in alcohol and in the bigoted Calvinism of the Pietist church. The manufacturers themselves had flexible consciences: 'causing the death of one child more or less does not doom a pietist's soul to hell, especially if he goes to church twice every Sunday.' Engels even claimed that 'it is a fact that the pietists among the factory owners treat their workers worst of all.' Despite his claim to love Wuppertal, he could find few redeeming features in his home-town (CW 2: 7/27, 31).

Although the 'Letters' make clear Engels' disgust at the social and political life of Wuppertal, they reveal less about his own political views. Nevertheless, three main themes do appear: firstly, his political liberalism, his preference for modern liberal literature and his interest in the Young Germany movement; secondly, his German nationalism, evident in his condemnation of Wuppertal for its lack of traditional German folk-songs and wholesome vigour; thirdly, his abhorrence of Pietist dogmatism. These three themes were to run throughout his letters and journalism during the rest of his stay in Bremen.

The 'Letters from Wuppertal' appeared in the Young Germany journal *Telegraph für Deutschland* in March-April 1839, during which time Engels wrote to his friend Friedrich Graeber: 'I must become a Young German, or rather, I am one already.' Young Germany was a liberal literary movement, inspired by the exiled poets Borne and Heine, whose members included writers such as Gutzkow (editor of the *Telegraph*), Mundt, Beck, Laube and Schuking. For Engels, Young Germany embodied the central 'thoughts' of the nineteenth century: the natural rights of Man; participation by the people in political life; constitutional government; the emancipation of the Jews and of women; and the abolition of the hereditary aristocracy (CW 2: 421/2).

Engels' writings are rather unspecific about the detail of his own liberalism although he certainly favoured the granting of a constitution, the rule of law (which required representative institutions to create such law), the emancipation of women and an open legal system with trial by jury. More obvious was the depth of his anger at the institutions he opposed: despotic government, aristocracy, censorship, and religious mysticism. Engels portrayed himself as a Jacobin, threatening a storm which would shake the political despots, the aristocracies of blood and of money and the religious obscurantists. Nevertheless, like many German liberals, he was, despite his poetic invocations of the power of the sword and the book, rather vague about the precise form that such a storm would take (CW 2: 32, 55-62, 423, 464, 480, 483).

As we shall see, by the end of 1839, Engels was reading Hegel but, at first, his contact with Hegelian philsophy made little difference to his political outlook. On the contrary, Engels found in Hegel a confirmation of the convictions he, along with other German liberals, had already arrived at, namely that historical development would eventually lead to the rule of reason and freedom. In his articles and letters from Bremen he continued to call for an end to despotism, for constitutional government and the emancipation of women.

Engels' liberalism was sharpened and clarified through his attack on the resurgent medievalism of the 1830s and 1840s, with its defence of absolutism, feudalism and Catholicism and its call for an 'organic state', which would emerge out of German history, rather than being imposed through revolutions inspired by foreign political doctrines. He criticised those medievalists and Romantics who sought an impossible return to the social and constitutional arrangements of the pre-Reformation era, a period he characterised as one of servility and ignorance. Against the medievalist idea of government based on the mutual love of king and subject, Engels called for the rule of law; against the desire for a government based on the privileges of hereditary estates, he called for a unified nation of citizens who enjoyed equal rights. The rhetoric of medievalism was, he claimed, merely a cover for aristocratic privilege, whereas Engels favoured an end to such privilege through the abolition of primogeniture and entailment of land. In general, he argued that a genuine 'self-development of the nation', which the organicists claimed to favour, should involve political freedom and self-expression for the nation. It was, he claimed, the liberals, who sought a government based on the people, who were the real defenders of an 'organic state life' (CW 2: 40, 48, 66-9, 99, 136-40, 145-7, 491).

Engels remained rather vague as to how such constitutional government was to be obtained although, as his commemoration of the French Revolution of July 1830 in 1839 and 1840 makes clear, he certainly believed that revolutionary action against despotism was justified. Like other German liberals, Engels relied on the march of Progress to bring about the inevitable victory of reason and freedom rather than specifying exactly how, in practice, despotism could be overcome (CW 2: 111, 135/6, 145, 463/4, 501).

For Engels, literature, along with science and politics, had a crucial role in shaking up traditional German life and spreading new liberal ideas. In literature, as in politics, he championed modernism (including the work of Schiller, Heine, Shelley, Gutzkow, Kuhne and, above all, Borne), and opposed the medievalist and Romantic call for a return to the 'authentic German soul' which, he believed, meant, in practice, militarism, servility, contempt for outsiders and anti/semitism. Engels himself aspired to be a poet, portraying himself as a sparrow singing on the boughs of Borne's great oak/ tree. His poems, with their feathered choirs singing joyfully to the new dawn of freedom, are, however, now only of historical, rather than literary, interest. Engels' literary talents were to find their true expression in history, polemic and acute social observation, rather than in verse (CW 2: 32/3, 109, 111, 472, 494, 497).

Nationalism performed a variety of functions in nineteenth/century Europe. It could, for instance, be adopted by political reactionaries, with their desire for a return to the purity of authentic German pre/Enlightenment culture and the rejection of alien political philosophies (Snyder: ch. 2; Pundt: ch. 5). In Engels' early works, however, nationalism is presented as the natural concomitant of liberalism although, in practice, he had some difficulty in reconciling the two. He looked back with enthusiasm to the German war of liberation against Napoleon as a time when the Germans had asserted themselves as a sovereign nation and when the people themselves were the 'source of state power.' For Engels, national unity was essential if Germany was to obtain constitutional government: 'so long as our Fatherland remains split we shall be politically null, and public life, developed constitutionalism, freedom of the press and all else that we demand will be mere pious wishes.' As a nationalist he bemoaned the loss of Alsace, Lorraine, Flanders, Holland and Belgium, and called for the reconquest of the left bank of the Rhine, the return of Alsace and Lorraine and the 'Germanisation' of Holland and Belgium, even though such policies would inevitably mean war with France. Nevertheless, for Engels, national unity was not an end in itself: 'we are not worthy of the Alsatians so long as we cannot give them what they now have: a free public life in a great state' (CW 2: 139/40, 149/50, 518, 521).

Closely linked with Engels' desire for Germany's political unity was his cultural nationalism. He criticised those German merchants who emigrated to America and then tried to hide their German origins and praised the German peasant who, even in America, 'adhered with iron firmness to his national customs and language.' In his poem on the death of Immermann, Engels vowed 'to be as German and as strong and firm' as Immermann himself whilst elsewhere he called for a popular literature imbued with a 'strong, trusty German spirit' (CW 2: 32, 117, 125).

Nevertheless, he rejected the xenophobia and excessive Germanic purity which 'held that the entire world was created for the sake of the Germans', a view which he associated with a reactionary desire to retreat into the national isolation of the Middle Ages. He hailed the war of liberation against Napoleon yet also criticised those who could not appreciate the 'innumerable seeds of world history which had grown on soil that was not German', such as Napoleon's introduction into Germany of trial by jury and the emancipation of the Jews. Engels was thus caught up in the contradictions of his nationalist liberalism, advocating measures which, as he himself saw, made war with France inevitable, whilst calling for a 'clear, mutual understanding among the European nations' and for 'Love and Peace' to fill the world (CW 2: 62, 140-1, 148-9).

Coming from a family of profound Pietist convictions, religion was inevitably an intensely personal issue for Engels. Yet, given the situation in Germany in the late 1830s and early 1840s, religion could never remain simply a matter of individual conscience. In an age when the Prussian state used Christianity to legitimate its rule and where religion was associated with a reactionary Romanticism, it was impossible to divorce faith from politics. As Engels said, the battle for German public opinion would be fought out in the fields of religion and of politics (CW 2: 33, 48, 64, 480; CW 3: 480).

Engels' Bremen writings emphasise his disillusionment with Pietism's claim to possess a monopoly of truth and salvation, and with its belief in the literal truth of the Bible, and reveal his search for some alternative form of faith. At first he was drawn towards rationalism, a post-Enlightenment form of Christianity which aimed to make religion compatible with science and reason. In his 'Letters from Wuppertal' he claimed that Pietism was 'in most direct contradiction with reason and the Bible' and, by April 1839, was claiming to be a 'supernaturalist' whose awareness of the contradictions of the Bible made it impossible for him to accept its literal truth. Nevertheless, he continued to claim that the liberal politics of Young Germany were compatible with Christianity and wrote that he longed for salvation from sin through God's grace (CW 2: 14, 421-6, 456).

By the summer of 1839, Engels' growing doubts had led him to a profound religious crisis. He was 'threshing around in all sorts of opinions', adopting, and then doubting, rationalism but firm in his rejection of the literal truth of the Bible and its compatibility with science. He argued that the unity of Man and God lay in their common reason: to use reason is to exercise true freedom, dogmatic belief is thus enslavement. He still yearned for communion with God, praying daily, crying as he wrote his letters of spiritual turmoil to his friend, the orthodox Friedrich Graeber. In June 1839, Engels wrote to

Graeber: 'I hope to see a radical transformation in the religious consciousness of the world – if only I were clear about it myself.' Clarity was, however, soon at hand in the form of the works of David Friedrich Strauss. By October, Engels was writing to Graeber, 'I am now an enthusiastic Straussian ... if you can refute Strauss, eh bien, I'll become a pietist once again' (CW 2: 453–63, 471). It was Strauss's Hegelianism that was to resolve Engels' crisis of faith and so lead him from Young Germany to Young Hegelianism.

ENGELS AND YOUNG HEGELIANISM

Engels was aware of contemporary debates around Hegel's philosophy as early as April 1839, but it was his encounter with Strauss' work which put him 'on the straight road to Hegelianism'. By the end of the year, he declared that he was 'on the point of becoming an Hegelian'; his full conversion to what he described as the 'most colossal creation of thought of the nineteenth century' was soon complete. Although he continued to write for the *Telegraph für Deutschland* until the end of 1841, he increasingly distanced himself from Gutzkow and the Young Germans and allied himself with the Young Hegelian movement. By July 1842, he was dismissing sympathy with Young Germany as a pardonable youthful aberration. The choice facing German liberals was now that between Young Germany and Left Hegelianism. Engels did not regard himself as an uncritical follower of Hegel, he criticised the master's 'excessive schematism' and 'brazen style'. Nevertheless, he argued that the way to truth led through Hegel's clouds of speculation and rarefied abstraction (CW 2: 71–93, 99, 102–3, 168, 196–7, 287–90, 435–7, 451–2, 485–90).

From the late 1850s, Hegelian philosophy was to be of vital importance to Engels in providing the basis of a new world outlook, an outlook which stressed the dialectical nature of reality and the need for a dialectical thought which could grasp that reality. However, his first encounter with Hegelianism was of significance to him primarily as a means of resolving his crisis of faith and as a philosophical justification of first his liberal, and then his socialist, politics.

In July 1839, Engels was still coming to terms with the Pietism of his youth, grappling with thorny problems such as the New Testament's contradictory accounts of Joseph's family tree. By October, the existence of such contradictions were no longer a problem for him: 'There lie the four gospels in a crisp and colourful chaos ... in comes David Strauss like a young god and brings the chaos into the light of day and – Adios faith!' From Strauss, Engels took the belief that the historical truth of the Bible and the dogmatic foundations of Christianity had been undermined. What remained was the Bible's 'mythic' content, even if the detail of Strauss's case were to be disproved this fundamental insight would remain. Strauss's argument thus allowed Engels to break totally with a dogmatic Biblical literalism whilst, at first, still claiming to be a Christian committed to the mythical truth of the Bible's content. If Engels' initial break with Pietism involved much spiritual anguish, his development soon became relatively painless and straightforward. Indeed, by early 1840, he was labelling himself a 'pantheist' who accepted the Hegelian principle that 'humanity and divinity are in essence identical' in their common nature of reason; humanity thus issues forth from the divine as the 'conscious links in the great spirit-chain by which eternal matter is confined' (CW 2: 109, 466, 471, 480, 485-90).

The issue of religious faith soon became of minor importance to Engels so that by the time of his *Schelling and Revelation* (written at the end of 1841) he had passed easily from 'pantheism' to atheism, accepting only the reality of nature and the human spirit and rejecting any concept of an extra-mundane or superhuman being. Christianity was thus not a truth given to Man from outside, but was rather a product of human self-consciousness, just like any other belief. In 1843, Engels even claimed to have been the first of the Young Hegelians to allow the charge of atheism, laid against them by their enemies, to be just, although Bruno Bauer could perhaps more rightly have claimed the credit for this step (CW 2: 216, 228; CW 3: 404; Hook, 1936: 89-95).

Years later, when Engels came to give an account of his time as a Young Hegelian, he claimed that the Hegelian system had, with one blow, been destroyed by the appeareance of Feuerbach's *Essence of Christianity* (1841), which rejected the Hegelian emphasis on the primacy of thought and returned to philosophical materialism: 'we all became *at once* Feuerbachians' (SW II: 333). Yet the evidence Engels cites for the importance of Feuerbach is *The Holy Family*, written (almost entirely) by Marx at the end of 1844. Certainly, Engels' *Schelling and Revelation* (1842), a response to Schelling's attack on Hegel delivered at Berlin University from November 1841, does not reveal any break with Hegelianism or turn to materialism even though Engels was, by this date, familiar with Feuerbach's work. On the contrary, his first substantial published work was an explicit defence of the Hegelian system against the criticisms offered by the conservative Schelling.

Hegel had argued against Kant's unknowable 'thing in itself', claiming that the universe is a rational structure and that its true nature, including the existence of God, was open to rational comprehension and demonstration (Arthur: 109-10). Engels followed Hegel in his belief that 'what is reasonable is, of course, also necessary and what is necessary must be, or at least become, real.' Thinking and being necessarily form an identity: 'with thought, real existence is also given.' Once we admit the existence of reason, 'the existence of all its consequences follows of itself.' Thus Hegel's rational categories, driven ever onwards by the motive force of the dialectic, are not only models of reality but are also the generating forces through which the things of this world have been created. The only alternative to reason is to revert to a reliance on mystical revelation which was, Engels claimed, the option chosen by Schelling (CW 2: 187, 200/1, 207/10).

He was to develop this point in satirical form in his *Schelling, Philosopher in Christ* (1842) which, like Bruno Bauer's *The Trumpet of the Last Judgement over Hegel the Atheist and Anti- Christ* (1841), pretended to be the work of an anti-Hegelian Pietist. In this guise Engels ridiculed Schelling by appearing to agree with his orthodox Christian conclusions: 'who would have dared hope that in the year 1842 a philosopher, nay the founder of a new school of blasphemy' would acknowledge the truth of the Virgin birth of Christ and other Christian dogmas (CW 2: 254)?

Like the other Young Hegelians, Engels' believed that Hegel had failed to follow his own philosophy through to its logical conclusions. The Young Hegelians believed that Hegel's 'cautious, even illiberal conclusions' were the result of his accommodation with the reactionary conservative prejudices of the Restoration era, rather than the product of 'pure thought'. Hegel's conclusions were thus in conflict with the independent and free-minded nature of his own philosophy. Ironically, the Young Hegelians accepted the conservative accusation that Hegel was, in effect, 'servile in front and revolutionary behind' (CW 2: 66, 196/7).

In his doctoral thesis (1841), Marx had already criticised those who explained Hegel's conservatism in personal terms and claimed instead that Hegel's accommodation with the Prussian government had its roots in the inadequacies of Hegel's system itself. He developed this criticism in the *1844 Manuscripts* where, under the influence of Feuerbach's materialism, he argued that Hegel's supposed overcoming of religious and political alienation merely took place at the level of thought, reconciling Man with an unchanged reality rather than abolishing the reality which had produced such alienation. Yet, for the Engels of 1842, Feuerbach's work was not a challenge to the Hegelian system but was rather its 'necessary complement' (CW 1: 84; CW 3: 313, 332, 339; CW 2: 237; Arthur: 107/8).

Perhaps the distance between Hegel and Feuerbach was not obvious to Engels because his interpretation of Hegel differed from that offered by Feuerbach, although it should also be emphasised that Feuerbach's own break with Hegel only became fully apparent in his *Provisional Theses*, published the year after Engels' attack on Schelling. Feuerbach's criticism was that Hegel had turned the process of thinking into an independent subject, the Idea, which then externalised itself in the form of the material world. Yet it was precisely this interpretation of Hegel which Engels rejected in 1842, even though, like Marx, he himself was eventually to adopt it. The belief that the Idea was an extra-mundane being, a personal god, was, he claimed, 'a thing which never occurred to Hegel', for whom the absolute did not exist outside of nature and the human mind. We can now see why Feuerbach's claim that 'the secret of theology is anthropology' did not undermine Engels' Hegelianism since, for Engels, Hegel's philosophy already involved the belief that 'reason cannot exist except as mind and that mind can only exist in and with nature' (SW II: 335/6; CW 2: 209, 213, 216, 237/8; Cap. I: 102).

Whether Engels' or Feuerbach's reading of Hegel had the better claim to authenticity is unclear, since Hegel appears to have his cake and eat it by denying the existence of any rational mind apart from finite mind whilst also referring to the workings of infinite mind; perhaps it is simplest to conclude that there are as many versions of Hegel as there are Hegelians (Inwood: 1/6; Findlay: 19/20; MacGregor: 21; Toews: 74; Plamenatz: 144). Certainly, given his interpretation of Hegel, Engels could not, in 1842, see the full implications of Feuerbach's critique. Yet if, as Engels said, 'reason cannot possibly exist except as mind' and mind can 'only exist in and with nature' rather than as a being superior to nature, then, as Schelling pointed out, Logic can never produce being out of itself (CW 2: 209). Ironically, Feuerbach the materialist would have agreed with Schelling's claim (to which Engels took such exception) that reason, or pure thought, 'is simply impotent to prove the existence of anything'. Feuerbach would simply have rejected Schelling's conclusion that reason had therefore to be supplemented by faith. For Feuerbach, the alternative to reason was not revelation but rather empirical research and observation (CW 2: 182/3, 200/1, 207/10; Arthur: 114/15).

Engels' defence of Hegelianism was not the result of any desire to indulge in abstract philosophical speculation but was, he believed, a matter of pressing political urgency since the only alternative seemed to be the reactionary mysticism offered by Schelling. For Engels, the Hegelian discovery that the Idea was nothing but the self-consciousness of humanity and that nature was its rightful home meant that a new era in human history had begun, an age in which the unity of man with his fellow man and of man with nature would replace the alienation of the dualist consciousness within which Schelling was still trapped. Through such rational self-consciousness, the inevitable victory of freedom was guaranteed: 'victory must be ours' (CW 2: 238/40).

In his 'Preface' to *The German Ideology*, Marx was to parody this type of thought as one which attempted to overcome alienation through a change of attitude, as if a drowning man were to attempt to save himself by getting the idea of gravity out of his head. Marx's criticism was not entirely fair since the Young Hegelians did *not* believe in merely changing Man's attitude to an unchanging reality, rather they argued that changing consciousness was a *precondition* for changing reality. As Engels put it, 'thought in its development alone constitutes the eternal and positive whereas the factual, the external aspect of what is taking place, is precisely what is negative, evanescent and vulnerable to criticism.' Thus criticism would not leave the world as it was, its results were 'entirely positive' (CW 5: 24; CW 2: 293).

Certainly, in practice, Engels' critical outlook involved more than a mere change of attitude since he continued to call for the establishment in Germany of a modern state based on universal civic and human rights, the separation of the judiciary and the executive power, the creation of an independent jury system and an end to the censorship laws (CW 2: 260, 302, 305/11, 364/7). Indeed, in a satire on the Young Hegelians written in 1842, Engels portrayed himself as a Jacobin, playing a tune on the guillotine whilst bellowing out the *Marseillaise*. For Engels, critical theory was not an alternative to action. On the contrary, it was the strength of north German liberalism that it proceeded from theory to practice and had thus overcome the dilemma of whether to put liberalism or nationalism first, the dilemma which had plagued the south German liberal tradition (CW 2: 260, 265/7, 278, 302, 305/11, 335, 352, 364/7, 550).

All criticism presupposes, of course, some prior standpoint, some privileged position, from which to criticise. The Young Hegelians found such a standpoint in Hegel's rationalism: if history is a rational process which leads necessarily to freedom, the Young Hegelians could criticise existing reality in the name of History, Reason and the future. The liberal call for a rational and free political constitution was thus not merely a Utopia of theory spun in the critic's brain but was rather the expression of the historical self-development of the nation through which Spirit 'creates for itself its own freedom in the state.' To deny Spirit, freedom and reason is thus to deny our own nature (CW 2: 145, 272/3, 356/7).

Ironically, given his later views, the young Engels attacked those whose politics were based on self-interest and 'envy', rather than on the basis of some 'principle' of free thought which would overcome those who resisted the rational state. Engels, ever optimistic, argued that the rational state would be all the more easily attained in Prussia precisely because the Prussian state was not the product of a long historical evolution but had rather been brought consciously into being. Frederick Willliam IV's reactionary 'Prussian principle' could thus be criticised in the name of the alternative 'principle' of free thought. Prussia's salvation therefore lay 'solely in theory' through which 'eternally young spirit' would become self-conscious of its own nature and thus bring into being its own essence, i.e. freedom (CW 2: 119, 145, 272/3, 356/7; Toews: 46).

In fact, the Young Hegelians' appeal to Reason and its inevitable progression to freedom was not the most secure of standpoints from which to mount their assault on existing reality. As heirs to the Enlightenment, the Young Hegelians found themselves confronted with the problem that, despite the general tendency to appeal to reason, philosophers had proved 'unable to agree as to what precisely those principles were which would be found undeniable by all rational persons' (MacIntyre: 1/6). For Hegel, for instance, the only rational form of the state was a constitution based on the representation of estates whereas for Engels only a state based on universal civil rights was truly rational. In both cases, the label of rationality was, in practice, merely a rhetorical device for signalling an approval which was, in reality, based on other grounds. We can see a similar strategy at work when Engels first condemned Pietism for being against reason and the Bible, and then, in turn, criticised the Bible itself for being irrational (CW 2: 14; CW 3: 399).

The ideal of criticism on the grounds of Reason proved impossible to attain because there can be no such thing as Reason in the sense of some pure, logical thought which would command universal assent and so allow us to criticise or justify political actions. Instead there are only socially and historically specific rationalities which are in conflict with each other. Rationality is thus conditional; at most it only allows us to say 'if we wish to achieve x then we must do y or z, but it does not justify why we chose x as an end in the first place.

Conservative Hegelians had a ready response to this problem: History itself would reveal which historical paths represent the onwards march of Reason and which were historical dead-ends; philosophy could thus only be wise after the event (CW 4: 86; Hegel, 1979: 12-13). This option was not, however, open to the Young Hegelians who did not want to 'let History judge' but rather to inspire people to make history for themselves. In the short term, the Young Hegelians' belief in the necessary working out of the dialectic and their confidence that they represented the self-comprehension of the age served to bolster their faith in the victory of reason and freedom. In the long term, they could only hope that their optimism was justified. The failure of the 1848 Revolution to achieve a liberal constitution for Germany and the eventual imposition of national unity from above were to show that, although he was right to predict that 'the day of the great decision ... is approaching', Engels was wrong to believe that a radical victory was assured (CW 2: 143, 240, 356-7).

In itself, Engels' mistake is not particularly significant; after all, most political thinkers make incorrect predictions about the future. But for the Young Hegelians, the failure to foresee the future was particularly damning, precisely because their criticisms of the present were justified by an appeal to a future which rational necessity had necessarily to bring about. The failure of this predicted future to emerge thus cut the ground from under the Young Hegelians' feet, as they then no longer had any guarantee that they were speaking in the name of Reason. By the time this failure became apparent, Engels had, of course, passed beyond his early liberal Hegelianism. Yet this period is a crucial one in revealing the problems inherent in *any* radical critique of the present made in the name of Reason or by an appeal to the future. As we shall see, such problems were to confront Engels for the rest of his life and, indeed, continue to haunt Marxism to the present day.

CHAPTER TWO

Hegelian socialism

So-called material interests never operate in history as independent powers but always, conciously or unconciously, serve a principle (Engels, 1842. CW 2: 370-1).

ALIENATION AND HUMANISATION

In the 1830s, German liberals had mainly been concerned with the issues of constitutional and political rights, nationalism and religion, rather than with economic and social problems. Indeed, Engels' 'Letters from Wuppertal', with their emphasis on poverty and the consequences of industrialisation, were pioneering works in their raising of the 'Social Question'. It was in the 1840s, as the effects of population growth, urbanisation, industrialisation and proletarianisation became apparent, and a workers' movement emerged, that social issues gained widespread public attention, often via novels such as Eugene Sue's *The Mysteries of Paris* (1843), to which Marx so tediously alluded in *The Holy Family*. (CW 3: 415; Sheehan: ch. 2)

Along with these developments came a growing knowledge of socialist ideas introduced to Germany by writers such as Moses Hess and Wilhelm Weitling, and even through Lorenz von Stein's report on French socialism made for the Prussian government (CW 3: 388, 402, 406). Hess' *The Sacred History of Mankind* (1837) could claim to be the first communist work in German. It offered an Hegelian vision of world history as a three-stage development: from an initial unity, through a necessary phase of human alienation, to communism, which restored the unity of man with man, and of man with God. His *European Triarchy* (1840) secularised this outlook and claimed that it was the growth of industrialisation, with its accompanying polarisation of classes, which made possible a new communist society. It followed that England, where industrialisation was most developed and the gulf between rich and poor most pronounced, would be the first country to experience communist revolution, an idea which Hess developed in his articles for the *Rheinische Zeitung* (McLellan, 1980: 138-44; Avineri, 1985).

It was Hess who converted Engels to communism when the latter visited the offices of the *Rheinische Zeitung* in October 1842. Hess reported of their meeting that 'we talked about questions of the day and he, an out and out revolutionary, parted from me the keenest of communists' (McLellan, 1980: 147). That Hess did not exaggerate the speed of Engels' conversion can be seen by comparing Engels' 'Frederick William IV, King of Prussia', written in October 1842, with his articles on 'The Internal Crises', written in London at the end of November 1842. In the former, Engels wrote as a radical liberal concerned with civic rights, representative government and a free press. In the latter he outlined the class bases of the Whig, Tory and Chartist parties; argued that economic development was creating a class of propertyless and impoverished proletarians; and predicted that, once this class became conscious of its own strength, it would provide the basis for a social revolution against the landed and industrial aristocracies (CW 2: 360-74).

Yet, whilst Engels' politics had altered dramatically, his philosophical outlook remained essentially unchanged. In particular, he retained the Young Hegelian distinction between the political conservatism of the content of Hegel's philosophy and the radicalism of his dialectical method. Like the Young Hegelians, Engels still wished to preserve Hegel's method whilst replacing Hegel's politics with a radical, indeed a communist, content (CW 3: 404-6).

By the time of his 'Outlines of a Critique of Political Economy' (October-November 1843), Engels had accepted Feuerbach's claim that Hegel's Absolute Idea was actually an abstraction of the human consciousness. By transforming a predicate of human existence into its subject, Hegel had turned reality 'on its head', a metaphor with which Marxists have wrestled ever since (CW 3: 427, 486; Cap. I: 103). By 1843, Marx had appreciated the extent of Feuerbach's materialist break with Hegel (McLellan, 1977b: 13). However, for the Engels of 1843, correcting Hegel's inversion of reality did not result in materialism. On the contrary, he criticised materialism, at least in its eighteenth-century form for merely positing Nature, instead of God, as the absolute confronting man. Rather than overcoming the contradiction betwen mind and nature, and between spirit and matter, materialism had merely opposed the abstract subjectivity of Christianity with an equally one-sided objectivity of matter(CW 3: 419, 470). In practice, despite the influence of Feuerbach, Engels continued to work within the assumptions of an Hegelian idealism which saw world history as the logical and necessary working out of a number of 'principles'. He merely rejected the notion that such principles had any existence apart from the individuals who held them; it was not idealism *per se*, but rather *supernatural* idealism, to which he objected.

Engels had, of course, adopted the Hegelian view that world history consisted of the unfolding of a series of 'principles' before he became a communist but, as a radical liberal, had mainly been concerned with the *political* consequences of such principles (CW 2: 359, 361). Now he turned his attention to the *social* arrangements which flowed from the outlook which was dominant in each historical epoch. Following Hegel's analysis, he characterised the outlook of antiquity as 'abstract, universal and material': antiquity knew nothing of the rights of the individual; it followed that this epoch 'could therefore not exist without slavery.' By contrast, the 'Christian-Germanic' outlook had replaced the universality of antiquity with an 'abstract subjectivity and hence arbitariness, inwardness and spiritiualism.' In a classic piece of Hegelian reasoning, Engels argued that this subjectivity, 'precisely because it was abstract and one-sided', was bound to turn at once into its opposite. Thus, in practice, the social consequence of the new principle was feudal serfdom (CW 3: 475-6; Hegel, 1956: 225, 279, 343-4).

The modern world had abolished feudal servitude but this did not mean the end of the Christian principle of subjectivity. On the contrary, subjectivity and particularisation had now been developed to their highest degree through the elevation of egotistical interest to the dominant general principle: 'Once a principle is set in motion, it works by its own impetus through all its consequences.' The result is the 'transformation of mankind into a collection of mutually repelling atoms.' Modern society, in its working out of the principle of individualism, has ended all vestiges of human community, even the family is dissolved as the factory system transforms children into wage-earning boarders in their own homes. Mankind has become a 'horde of ravenous beasts (for what else are competitors?) who devour one another' (CW 3: 421-4, 432, 475-6; Gaskell, 1833: 11, 89-94).

Engels' writings of 1843-44 thus portray a bleak picture of humanity in a state of total alienation. Man had been set in opposition to nature, to his fellow man and to his own essence. Each individual pursues only his own gain at the expense of the rest of society. Buyers and sellers seek to cheat each other through the legalised fraud of the market, an immoral means to an immoral end. Yet, this pursuit of individual interest does not, despite the claims of the economists, mean that society's benefits are maximised. On the contrary, since the general interest lies in social equality, the individual and the general interest are in conflict. Self-interest thus becomes a power over man, setting individual and society against one another (CW 3: 421-4, 432, 475-6, 485).

As Draper has pointed out, the analysis offered by Engels, in his 'Critique of Political Economy', places much emphasis on trade and the market (Draper: 160). Nevertheless, Engels also stressed that it was what he and Marx were later to refer to as capitalism's relations of *production*, based as they are on private property and the division between wage labour and capital, which represent the ultimate alienation of man from his own essence. The labourer is separated from land and from nature, from the principal means of subsistence, from the means of production, and from the product of his own labour. He can survive only by turning himself into an object of huckstering. Society's wealth, which the labourer has himself created, (since, as the economists admit, capital is only stored-up labour), confronts him only as wages. Through private property, the basic form of man's alienation, man himself has been turned into a commodity whose very existence is dependent on the balance of supply and demand produced by competition. Man, once subject to man under slavery and serfdom, has now become 'the slave of things', of capital, of commodities, above all of money. The perversion of the human condition is thus complete: 'the servitude of the modern world, this highly developed, total, universal venality, is more inhuman and more all-embracing than the serfdom of the feudal era' (CW 3: 427-32, 439-40, 476, 485).

The source of Engels' analysis of modern society was, of course, Feuerbach's argument that through religious consciousness man had enslaved himself to the products which he himself had created. Engels' originality lay in applying Feuerbach's critique to the social relations and political economy of capitalism and in offering a social analysis of alienation based on the institution of private property. Nevertheless, he continued to accept the religious framework set out by Feuerbach and even repeated the latter's claim that the desultoriness and hollowness of the modern world 'have their roots in religion' since it was religion which drained man of his substance and 'transfers this substance to the phantom of an other-worldly God'. Universal fragmentation was thus not only the result of private property but was 'the ultimate conseqence of the Christian principle of subjectivity.' Of course, so long as men believed in the phantoms they had themselves created, they could obtain, as in the Middle Ages, 'considerable energy' from their faith. But, in the modern world, man has neither faith nor an understanding of his true reality. He is thus 'bound to despair of truth, reason and nature ... until mankind perceives that the being worshipped as God was its own, as yet unknown being' (CW 3: 461-4, 476).

Engels applied a similar analysis to the modern state which, he argued, also expresses man's alienation from himself since the essence of the state, as of religion, 'is mankind's fear of itself.' The political experience of three thousand years had not educated men but, on the contrary, made them more confused and prejudiced: 'it has made them mad, and the result of this madness is the political condition of present-day Europe.' Pure monarchy, pure aristocracy and pure democracy had all failed but 'instead of concluding from the imperfection or rather inhumanity of all forms of the state that the state itself is the cause of all these inhumanities and is itself inhuman', people had rejected only specific forms of government. Ironically, all three unsatisfactory forms of the state had been combined to produce the modern constitutional monarchy which, with its built-in balance of powers, expressed mankind's fear of itself in its most extreme form (CW 3: 491-2).

Engels thus approved of writers such as Proudhon and Weitling who

Hegelian socialism

argued not for a new form of the government, but rather saw that all forms of the state are based on force. Thus, even in a democracy, the best form of government, 'the force of the majority oppresses the weaknesses of the minority'. Democracy, *political* equality, is merely another form of government, a form which is in contradiction with itself and which, like every other form of government, 'must ultimately break to pieces.' It would then be transformed either into despotism, or into the *genuine* equality of communism and anarchy: 'the rule of nobody, the responsibility of every one to nobody but himself' (CW 3: 393, 399, 413).

Despite the depressing picture of the economic, social, political and religious alienation of modern society which he presented, Engels remained optimistic. The very fact that human alienation had attained its most complete form meant that the underlying principle of the Christian world had reached the limit of its development. Society must therefore collapse under its own weight 'and make way for a humane, rational order.' The total atomisation of social interest is thus 'the last *necessary* step towards the free and spontaneous association of men.' The rule of money has appeared in order to complete the process of human alienation, it is 'an inevitable stage which *has to be passed through* if man is to return to himself, as he is now on the verge of doing' (CW 2: 476).

Engels thus retained the Hegelian picture of world history as a teleological development which necessarily has to include a stage of alienation in order to achieve its final goal of 'the self-understanding and the self-liberation of mankind.' In this perspective history does not represent merely a decline into the total immorality of the present. On the contrary, 'progress is the essence of humanity.' In effect, the Hegelian 'hidden hand of Reason' is at work in history so that even those economists whose systems allow the fullest development of private property, and thus of human alienation, are the unconscious servants of 'mankind's universal progress'. By bringing individualism to its highest pitch, they pave the way 'for the great transformation to which the century is moving ⁄ the reconciliation of mankind with nature and with itself' (CW 3: 420, 424, 469, 499).

Why should history necessarily progress in a teleological manner? Engels again gives an Hegelian answer: history is driven forwards by the need to resolve contradictions. It consists of the development and resolution of the universal antitheses of substance and subject; nature and mind; necessity and freedom. Its events may appear fortuitous but they are, in fact, ruled by 'necessity and inner connection'. The eighteenth century's radical innovations in the realms of science, history, political economy and philosophy had not resolved society's inherent contradictions. On the contrary, such contradictions became more fully developed than ever, and were set against each other in their clearest form. 'The consequence of this clear final evolution of the antitheses was general revolution which spread over various nations': philosophical revolution in Germany; political revolution in France; and, in England, a social revolution, the most universal form of revolution. Yet even the eighteenth century, 'the century of revolution', had, Engels argued, failed to resolve society's contradictions; only now was this task on the verge of completion.(CW 3: 419, 469, 72).

Whilst Engels explicitly argued that 'the inner rottenness of all social institutions' in the modern world had its roots 'in religion itself', in practice, his critique centred not on religion, but on the social relations of capitalist society and its accompanying political economy. For Engels, political economy, the science of enrichment, 'bears on its brow the mark of the most detestable selfishness'. It is a system of hypocrisy which reaches its apogee in Malthus' theory of population, a 'hideous blasphemy against nature and mankind', with its doctrine that the poor are surplus to society's requirements and that 'nothing should be done for them except to make their dying of starvation as easy as possible'. (CW 3: 418-20, 437, 461-2).

However, for Engels, political economy was not only immoral, but also scientifically incorrect. Economists had failed to grasp economic relations in their totality, instead they consistently offered one-sided and partial definitions of their object of investigation. Thus, one school of economists defines value in terms of costs of production, another in terms of utility; rent is explained either by the differential fertility of the soil, or by competition for the use of land. Similarly, capital and labour are presented by political economy as an antithesis rather than as a unity, whilst Malthus' theory involved the opposition between man and nature.

Nor did Engels see such errors as entirely innocent. On the contrary, he anticipated Marx's argument that modern political economy had degenerated from science into ideology : 'the nearer the economists come to the present time, the further they depart from honesty.' They simply cannot afford to understand the true causes of poverty, of a situation where crises of overproduction mean that people starve from sheer abundance. Hence the appearance of Malthus' theory of population which was specifically invented so that political economy could avoid a confrontation with the real origins of poverty and 'surplus population', namely competition and private property (CW 3: 419-20, 424, 428-9, 435-439).

It was not only political economy which foundered on its own antitheses. Even more importantly, Engels believed that capitalism itself embodied a number of antitheses and oppositions: the contradiction between the inherent utility of a commodity and its determination in exchange; the separation of labour from its product, from capital, from land and from the means of production and subsistence; the divorce between the natural and the human sides of production; the 'unhealthy' conflict between supply and demand. As a result of such oppositions, capitalism involved the alienation of man from any authentic human community, from nature, and from his own essence. Only the full unfolding of such contradictions would allow society to pass beyond the economics of private property, since their resolution necessarily involved the transcendence of the underlying principle of the modern world. The chaos of capitalism would then be superseded by the rational, conscious organisation of the economy and the creation of a free, fully human community (CW 3: 420-35, 442, 476).

Engels' vision of the new society which would emerge from the resolution of the oppositions of modern society was obviously influenced by the writings of Utopians, such as Fourier, Saint-Simon and Owen, but it also drew heavily on the Hegelian picture of a humanity which has overcome alienation and been restored to its true essence. But what is the nature of this essence? Here, Engels once more re-cast Hegel's argument in socialist terms. For Hegel, humanity makes itself and becomes conscious of its own nature through its labour, through its encounter with the external world. Although Hegel presented this encounter essentially in terms of intellectual labour, this outlook could also lead to an emphasis on the human spirit's struggle with nature, as in the young Engels' musings on Man's conquest of the Alps and the Rhine (CW 2: 177).

From this positive view of human labour, it was easy for Engels to adopt the socialist argument, derived from Fourier, that 'the essence of the human mind is to be active itself and to bring the body into activity.' It follows that true human labour is not an imposition, but an enjoyment, since through labour man realises his own essence. Similarly, Carlyle had argued that 'man perfects himself by working', and that, through work, man is put into harmony with nature, and with himself. In a rational society there would thus be no need to force people to be active, since the overcoming of the separation between labour and enjoyment would mean that labour would no longer be a toil (CW 3: 386-7, 394-6, 435, 458-9, 476).

Where Carlyle had erred, Engels argued, was in creating a 'religious cult' of work when, in fact, work is a purely human matter. Work embodies the struggle of humanity to overcome nature and the means to its achievement of a 'free, human self-consciousness, the discernment of the unity of man and nature, and the independent creation - voluntarily by its own effort - of a new world based on purely human and moral social relationships.' In a world where man takes himself 'as the measure of all aspects of life', there is no need for recourse to religious superstition. The only real history is thus human history, 'the development of the human species through history, its irresistible progress, its ever-certain victory over the unreason of the individual, its overcoming of all that is apparently supernatural.' Man's task is thus 'to organise the world in a truly human manner according to the demands of his own nature' (CW 3: 463-5).

Engels also stressed that humanity cannot realise its own essence in a society of isolated individuals, rather, as Fourier had argued, the goal of human development is the 'free and spontaneous association of men.' But Fourier had failed to see that the attainment of this fully human community necessarily required the abolition of private property; only through this means could the split between capital and labour, humanity and nature, be overcome. Hegel had portrayed human history as the growth and victory of reason and self-consciousness. For Engels, this meant, in social terms, the end to the chaos and crises of capitalism where production was carried out unconsciously, without planning. At present, the economy appears to proceed like a force of nature which acts without the conscious intentions of human agents. The alternative is to 'carry out production consciously as human beings - not as dispersed atoms without consciousness of your species.' The Hegelian goals of self-understanding and self-consciousness, of reason and the realisation of the individual's freedom through membership of a political community were thus transformed in Engels' writings into a socialist vision of 'a new order to be created by self- conscious man in full freedom' (CW 3: 395, 430, 432-4, 476, 486).

Fleischer has described Marx's outlook in the *Paris Manuscripts* of 1844 as 'anthropological', or 'anthropogenetic', in character. As in Hegel, history is given a universal meaning as a teleological process of humanisation. History is the realisation of an essence inherent in the human species, which necessarily passes through a negative phase of alienation, but whose totality consists in the attainment of freedom and self-consciousness (Fleischer: 12-16). It is, of course, this humanist, democratic Marx of 1844 who is so frequently contrasted with the scientific, authoritarian Engels of the 1870s. Yet, ironically, Engels himself had once adhered to this 'anthropogenetic' outlook which appears in explicit form in his 'Outlines of a Critique of Political Economy' (1843), a work to which Marx refers admiringly in the *Paris Manuscripts* (CW 3: 232, 290, 375-6).

Engels has even been given the credit for developing this outlook before Marx, although it would perhaps be more accurate to say that Marx had arrived independently at a similar position to Engels through his own encounter with Hegelianism, Feuerbachian materialism and Utopian Socialism (Maguire:58-60). It first finds expression in Marx's work as early as his 'On the Jewish Question', an article which was written about the same time as Engels' 'Critique', where he argues that money is the 'estranged essence of man's work and man's existence', an 'alien essence' which Man comes to worship (CW 3: 172, 174). Nevertheless, this perspective is only hinted at in Marx's work; in Engels 'Outline', it is a fully developed outlook, which offers a critique not just of capitalism, but also of the political economy which defends it.

Hegelian socialism

Given the convergence of Marx and Engels' views, Benton's assessment of Marx's *Paris Manuscripts* could equally be applied to Engels' 'anthropogenetic' works of this period: like Marx, Engels provides an 'ethical-philosophical denunciation' of modern society of 'quite exceptional depth and beauty of expression'. Nevertheless, this critique, though it is vigorous and persuasive, does not amount to a scientific theory of the capitalist mode of production; it was soon to be transcended, but never entirely replaced, by a very different mode of analysis (Benton, 1977: 150-3).

ENGELS' SOCIAL THEORY: THE LIMITS OF HEGELIANISM

The limitations of Engels' social theory at this period can be seen in his treatment of the concept of 'alienation'. Wood has usefully distinguished between Marx's employment of alienation as an *explanatory* concept in his early writings, and its use in his later works, where it becomes a descriptive term for the *effects*, such as commodity fetishism, generated by the capitalist mode of production (Wood, A. W., 1981: 7-8). However, confusion arises because Marx and Engels, in their early works, use the term 'alienation' to refer to *both* the social relations of capitalism and to the effects produced by such relations.

Engels argued, for instance, that private property has the effect of turning labour into a commodity, the ultimate form of 'self-alienation'. The social domination of private property makes man into the slave of things, another form of alienation from man's essence. In the same vein, he referred to the true significance of wages under capitalism as hidden, i.e. as 'alienated', and argued that this alienation will only be overcome when private property has been abolished. 'Alienation' functions, in these cases, as a term of critique of the *effects* of the domination of the 'principle' of private property (CW 3: 429-32, 439-40).

Yet, as well as referring to the alienating *effects* of private property, Engels also referred to private property itself as 'the basic form of alienation' since it involves the separation of the labourer from the land, from the means of subsistence, and from the means of production. Alienation, in this sense, is not merely an effect of capitalist social relations; rather it constitutes one of capitalism's essential characteristics. The concept thus has an explanatory power, as when the supremacy of money is said to be the inevitable 'culmination of the process of alienation' (CW 3: 476).

The way is thus opened for an analysis of economic systems in terms of their specific forms of unity and separation of the producer and the means of production, and for a socio-economic explanation of the transition from one economic formation of society to another. This was, of course, the alternative which, having abandoned their anthropogenetic outlook, Marx and Engels were to develop from the time of *The Condition of the Working Class in England* (1845) and *The German Ideology* (1845-46). It was not, however, Engels' main emphasis in the period 1842-44 when he was chiefly concerned to express his moral outrage at the inhuman nature of capitalism, and of the political economy which justified it.

So far we have emphasised the differences between the Hegelian outlook dominant in Engels' humanist writings and the non-Hegelian social theory of the period after *The Condition of the Working Class*. This contrast would seem to imply that Engels' works after 1845-46 are marked by a sharp break with Hegelian idealism. Yet, it could be argued that it was impossible, in practice, for Engels (or, indeed, for anyone else) ever to give a truly Hegelian account of social development, in which case it would hardly be possible for Engels to break with such an account. Marx makes this point in *The Holy Family* where he satirises those speculative philosophers, such as Hegel, for whom reality consisted of abstract ideas, such as 'Fruit', rather than concrete particulars, such as apples, pears and strawberries, which they see as 'mere forms of existence, *modi* of 'Fruit'.' Yet, in order to retain some contact with reality, the philosopher is obliged to return from the abstraction 'Fruit' to the real apples, pears, etc. But 'it is as hard to produce real fruit from the abstract idea 'Fruit' as it is easy to produce this abstract idea from real fruits. Indeed, *it is impossible to arrive at the opposite of an abstraction without relinquishing the abstraction*'. (CW 4: 58-60).

In other words, philosophers can never, in practice, begin their analysis with a concept or principle from which reality may be deduced. Even though idealist thinkers may *present* their argument in this form, their concepts are, in fact, always abstracted from material reality. However, in order to present such concepts as primary, reality itself has to be inverted so that the concepts abstracted from reality are presented as reality's underlying and determining principle. Ironically, Hegel himself had made a similar point using precisely the same example (Hegel, 1988: 18).

We can detect just this process of inversion at work in Engels' historical analysis in the period 1842-44. As we have seen, Engels claimed that the slavery of Antiquity was the *direct* expression of the dominant principle of the age, but that serfdom was the outcome of the dominant principle of the Middle Ages turning into its opposite (CW 3: 475-6). But if a principle can be expressed either directly, *or* through its opposite, then it is impossible to *derive* real history from such 'principles'. In practice, Engels began by making claims about historical reality (slavery was the dominant social relation of Antiquity, serfdom was the dominant social relation of the Middle Ages); he then deduced principles from this reality (e.g. abstract subjectivity was the dominant outlook of the Middle Ages); then, finally, in presenting his argument, he inverted the whole process and presented the principle, which he had abstracted from reality, as its primary cause.

A similar mode of argument is to be found in the analysis of capitalist society which Engels offered during this period. Years later, he was to claim that 'while I was in Manchester it was tangibly brought home to me that the economic facts, which have so far played no role or only a contemptible one in the writing of history, are, in the modern world at least, a decisive historical fact' (SW II: 344). Nevertheless, although Engels' experience of industrial Manchester was to be of decisive importance for his intellectual development, this experience could not be self-interpreting. It did not simply exist in a pure, unmediated form but rather had to be made sense of through some specific perspective. At first, Engels was able to achieve this within a Hegelian framework, where history consists of a series of outlooks or principles.

Thus he presented capitalism not merely as a social relation of production, defined by the separation of the producers from the means of production, but also as the 'highest point of the Germanic and Christian principle of subjectivity and particularisation.' The individualism and atomisation of modern society are thus the ultimate outcome of 'the Christian principle of subjectivity', they are the 'the culmination of the Christian world order.' Private property itself was described by Engels as a 'principle': 'a natural, spiritless principle ... opposed to the human and spiritual principle.' Engels believed, as we have seen, that once such principles were set in motion they would necessarily work their way through all their logical consequences (CW 3: 424, 475-6).

Why had the principle of private property found its ultimate form of development in England? Here, as elsewhere in Engels' work of this period, the influence of Hess was central. In *The European Triarchy*, Hess had distinguished the Germanic principle of contemplation from the Romance principle of action (Avineri, 1985: ch. 3). Following Hess's work, Engels argued that the principle of private property had reached its fullest expression in England because of the English national character, a character which he described in Hegelian terms as the synthesis of two principles: German spirituality and French (or Romance) materialism. Through a typical Hegelian irony, each of these elements had turned into its opposite: Germanic idealism had expressed itself through 'abstract externalism', hence the mercantile spirit of the English; Romance materialism had, in turn, been transformed into 'abstract idealism' and given rise to the inwardness and piety of the national character.

The English thus 'embody both sides of the antithesis', a contradiction which they are unable to resolve and which is the source of their 'everlasting inner restlessness' and 'externalised energy'; an energy which finds its expression in 'colonisation, seafaring, industry and the immense practical activity of the English in general.' The English character is, for this reason, 'more universal' in nature than either the French or the German. As a result, the English had been drawn into a social revolution, the most universal form of revolution, whereas the French had only experienced a political revolution, and the Germans a revolution in philosophy (CW 3: 469-72).

Yet, as Marx's 'fruit' example showed, it is impossible, in practice, to *deduce* reality from abstractions or 'principles'. Material reality has to be smuggled back into the analysis, even though it is *presented* as the expression of underlying ideas, concepts or principles. The strains involved in this process are apparent in the detail of Engels' account of English historical development which, in many respects, anticipated his and Marx's later historical materialism despite being presented within a traditional Hegelian framework. On his arrival in England, Engels had asked 'is there any other country in the world where feudalism retains such enduring power?' But, by 1844, he was arguing that, in England, the defeat of feudalism had been achieved at least forty years previously, and that England's social and economic development was far in advance of the rest of the Continent. The key to this transformation was, Engels claimed, the process of industrialisation which had begun in cotton manufacturing but whose effects were soon felt in other textiles, engineering, chemicals, metallurgy, mining and transport. He described this development of society's productive forces as the 'foundation of every aspect of modern English life, the driving force behind all social development.' Above all, the growth of industry had produced a proletariat and increased the wealth and power of the middle class (CW 2: 371-3; CW 3: 476-88).

Engels argued that each of the main classes of English society was represented by a particular political party: the aristocracy by the Tories; the manufacturers, merchants, tenant-farmers and upper middle class in general by the Whigs; the lower middle class by the Radicals; the working class by the Chartists; whilst the Socialists drew on lower middle class and working-class support. 'The question is now: who then actually rules England?' the answer Engels gave was that 'property rules' since it was property which dominated the all-powerful House of Commons. More specifically, it was the middle-class, the merchants and manufacturers who controlled the elections in the larger towns and some of the smaller towns, who ruled. In order to have political influence, the aristocracy had to act like the property-owning middle class; its power was not exerted directly through the House of Lords, but rather by its control of the election of the Commons' members for the rural areas and small towns. Finally, Engels argued that social theories have specific class bases and that modern political economy functioned as an explicit defence of the system of private property and competition (CW 2: 375, 381; CW 3: 379, 497-8).

It is obvious that, despite the idealist framework within which it was presented, much of Engels' actual historical analysis in the period 1842-44 anticipated the views which he and Marx were to develop later. Indeed, from his emphasis on the growth of the productive forces, his linking of specific social relations with the level of development reached by the productive forces, the characterisation of the state in terms of class power and his analysis of political economy as a class ideology, 'it is clear that a number of basic and enduring Marxist propositions first surface in Engels' rather than Marx's early writings' (Jones, 1977: 102; Rigby, 1987: 75-7).

Thus the genesis of historical materialism did not require a total break with the historical analysis which Engels had previously offered. Rather, it involved bringing his explicit theoretical claims into line with the implications of the historical analysis which he had already arrived at, by stripping this analysis of the shell of Hegelian abstraction within which he had presented it. But this, as we shall see in chapter three, was to be the achievement of the years after Engels' return to Germany.

POLITICAL PHILOSOPHY AND THE GROUNDS OF CRITIQUE

Like his historical studies, Engels' political philosophy of the period 1842 to 1844 was also marked by a dichotomy between its implicit class analysis and the Hegelian framework within which this analysis was explicitly presented. As a radical liberal, Engels had invoked Reason as the basis for his critique of the political institutions of contemporary society. Yet Reason is merely an abstraction which, in practice, has to be filled with a specific content (in Engels' case with a democratic republicanism) in order to fulfil its rhetorical function of providing a standpoint for criticism.

As a communist, Engels offered an even more wholesale condemnation of the modern world but, once more, he had to provide himself with the ground which would legitimise his right to criticise, and so elevate his analysis above the level of mere subjective opinion. He found this ground, as we have seen, in another abstraction, in the human essence. Just as he had once condemned the German state for its 'irrationality', so he now attacked capitalism and its political economy for its 'inhumanity'. On similar grounds, he praised the work of writers such as Carlyle for striking a human chord and for showing traces of 'a human point of view' (CW 3: 437, 444, 475-6).

Yet, in practice, the human essence offered no more secure a basis for criticism than Reason had, since, as Engels himself realised, there was no agreement amongst philosophers on what constituted this essence. Bentham, for instance, had based his theory on the self-interest of the individual. He thus 'grants the right of the species not to the free, self-conscious, creative man, but to the crude and blind man who remains within the confines of the contradictions' of modern society. Whilst Bentham appears to work from the human essence, his theory, in fact, represents 'the highest point of alienation.'

His mistake was to take as his starting-point the condition of Man in his alienated present rather than how he could be in a future where humanity was restored to its own real essence (CW 3: 486).

But by what right could Engels refer to one form of human existence as an alienation and another as the realisation of the species-essence? Why not, along with the political economists, accept the pursuit of individual self-interest as the true human essence, so that anything which interferes with this pursuit, whether feudal privileges or socialist equality, is seen as 'unnatural', i.e. as an alienation? In other words, even if we accepted the legitimacy of political arguments which base themselves on some essence of humanity, why should we accept the specific content, such as the human need for association and creative labour, which Engels ascribed to this abstraction, rather than some other attributes?

One answer to this question would be that, originally, man had *not* been separated from the means of production. Thus to abolish private property is to restore the 'original unity' of the labourer and the means of production, although it is not entirely clear whether this phrase refers to an era before all private property, or merely to the period before the advent of private property in its specifically capitalist form. But why should we value this original state of human existence? Why not regard the subsequent separation of the producers from the means of production as a progression to a higher stage of existence?

Engels' answer was that human history was now 'on the verge' of a new, yet higher, phase of development which would restore the unity of the producers and the means of production: 'the crisis which will destroy the Christian world order can no longer be far away, and indeed the time of this crisis can be predicted with certainty, even if not quantitatively in years, at least qualitatively; for this crisis must begin when the Corn Laws are repealed and the People's Charter introduced.' Thus, just as Engels' liberal critique of German absolutism in the name of Reason necessarily involved an appeal to a predicted future, which would reveal the irrationality of the present, so Engels' denunciation of capitalist alienation required the prediction of imminent and inevitable revolution in order to demonstrate that the principle of subjectivity had ceased to possess any rationality or historical justification. As his critique of Bentham makes clear, he was criticising capitalist society not on the basis of the alienated man of the present, but in the name of a humanity which has been restored to its essence in the communist future (CW 2: 368-74; CW 3: 431, 434, 467, 476, 486).

But why, even if the human capacity for creative labour creates the *potential* for freedom, should the revolutionary abolition of private property be *inevitable*? One answer which Engels offered to this question involved the Hegelian assumption that human history is a rational process in which principles necessarily resolve their internal contradictions and work their way through to their logical consequences. Since political and philosophical revolutions (such as Chartism and Young Hegelianism), are only partial and one-sided in their nature, they inevitably lead to social revolution, the most universal and far-reaching form of revolution. In the modern world, this means the victory of the principle of socialism. Socialism is thus not merely the *outcome* of prior developments; it is history's *goal*, and so determines the course of events leading up to it. Individual men are thus presented as merely the bearers of history's underlying principles, the unconscious agents of a reason which is greater than themselves, their actions thus necessarily bring about history's teleological end even though they themselves are not 'consciously' aware of it (CW 3: 424, 469, 512-13).

However, this Hegelian solution to the problem of *why* socialism should be inevitable, only creates the further problem of why history should constitute a process which necessarily leads in a particular direction? Hegel's answer to this question was that the universe as a whole is a rationally evolving structure which requires the attainment of human freedom and self-consciousnes in order to complete its development. Reason, in effect, is identical with a divine providence at work in history. In presenting history as a logical succession of principles, Engels himself seems to adopt this solution.

Yet, ironically, Engels also explicitly rejected Hegel's reduction of history as the unfolding of a 'logical problem' in this manner. History is the revelation not of God's works, 'but of man and only man.' It 'contains only what is human' and requires us to 'sweep away everything that claims to be supernatural and superhuman.' In each age, Nature, like the Sphinx of Greek mythology, sets humanity a riddle which it must solve or else perish: 'the answer to the riddle today is, as it was in the myth: man.' Hence, to the riddle 'what is God?', the answer is 'God is man', since God is nothing more than the projection of man's own substance on to a phantom of his own making. Only by taking man as 'the measure of all aspects of life' can we arrive at a 'free and human point of view' (CW 3: 449-50, 463-5).

Yet, if history consists of the actions of men, then why should they act to bring about socialism? The answer which Marx and Engels eventually arrived at was, of course, that it was in the interests of a particular group in society to struggle for socialism: the proletariat. Socialism, in this perspective, is not the goal towards which abstractions such as Reason or History strive but is rather the outcome of the concrete struggles of the working class in pursuit of its own interests (see chapters five and ten, below).

At times, Engels seems to anticipate this line of argument in his writings of 1842-44. It was in England, where industrialisation, proletarianisation and the polarisation of society had been taken to their furthest degree, and where economic crises, which ruin the petit bourgeoisie and swell the ranks of the proletariat, become ever more universal, that social revolution was most imminent. Almost half of the country's population consisted of the poor and propertyless whose conditions became daily more precarious and who were at the mercy of the next downturn of trade: 'what is there left for these people to do but to revolt?' Of course, the Continent had also experienced poverty, misery and oppression, but it was only in England, with the existence of a proletariat and a working-class movement, that the 'masses' had begun to 'act as masses' and so had given their condition a 'national and even world-historical importance' (CW 2: 372-4, 378-9; CW 3: 474).

It was true that the English workers' movement had, at first, taken a political form in the struggle for the Six Points of the People's Charter, but politics, even democratic politics, cannot cure social ills. Chartism, Engels concluded, 'must soon be victorious', then the English workers would 'have the choice only between starvation and socialism.' Revolution was thus inevitable since 'fear of death from starvation will be stronger than fear of the law', which had previously held back the English workers from violent insurrection. Once the last purely political remedy has been tried, 'a new element is bound to develop at once, a principle transcending everything of a political nature. This principle is the principle of socialism.' Thus, Engels optimistically concluded, 'the struggle of ... man against humanity must be decided and there is no question as to which side will be victorious' (CW 3: 430, 434, 441, 450, 467, 469, 474, 487, 492-513).

Yet, despite this analysis of the prospects for revolution in England, Engels, at first, explicitly rejected drawing the general conclusion that communism was merely the movement which expressed the class interest of the proletariat. Indeed, he argued the exact opposite in an article written soon after his arrival in England which dealt with the claim that material interest would prevent the workers from turning to revolution since political upheaval would necessarily involve unemployment and starvation. His response to this argument was not to claim that the revolution *was* in the material interests of the workers (although he obviously believed this, in the long term, to be the case). Rather, he argued that 'there is one thing that is self-evident in Germany but which the obstinate Briton cannot be made to understand, namely, that the so-called material interests can never operate in history as independent, guiding aims, but always, consciously or unconsciously, serve a principle which controls the threads of political progress' (CW 2: 370-1).

Engels did go on to argue that 'revolution is inevitable for England, but as in everything that happens there, it will be interests, and not principles that will begin and carry through the revolution; principles can only develop from interests, that is to say, the revolution will be social, not political.' This did not mean, however, that he had abandoned his Hegelian scheme of history as the necessary progress of principles and outlooks. On the contrary, he accounted for this English empiricism and dominance of interest in terms of the English 'national character' which, as we have seen, he believed to have been formed from a synthesis of Germanic idealism and Romance materialism. Hence, as he wrote in August 1844, in England principles have to be turned into interests in order to influence history (CW 2: 370-4; CW 3: 471-4).

He argued that the Germans, by contrast, were a disinterested nation: 'if in Germany principle comes into collision with interest, principle will always silence the claims of interest.' This love of abstract principle would guarantee the success of communism in Germany even though 'it will appear very singular to Englishmen that a party which aims at the destruction of private property is chiefly made up of those who have property; and yet this is the case in Germany' where converts to communism were to be found chiefly amongst the educated and commercial classes (CW 2: 368-9; CW 3: 379-80, 387, 446, 407).

Thus, whilst there was a working-class communist movement in Germany, there also existed a party of philosophical communists, such as Hess, Ruge, Marx and Herwegh. This party argued that political change alone was insufficient to produce human freedom, 'a social revolution based upon common property, was the only state of mankind agreeing with their abstract principles.' For Engels, communism was 'a necessary consequence' of Young Hegelian principles and of German philosophy in general. 'The Germans', Engels explained to the readers of the Owenite *New Moral World* at the end of 1843, 'are a philosophical nation and will not, cannot abandon Communism as soon as it is founded upon sound philosophical principles.' He concluded, as optimistically as ever, 'the Germans must either reject their great philosophers, whose names they hold up as the glory of their nation, or they must adopt Communism... there can scarcely be any doubt as to which side of the question the people will adopt' (CW 3: 401-6).

Engels' analysis of the revolutionary potential of the English proletariat was crucial for the development of Marx's thought (Draper: 149). Yet, it was Marx who was the first to argue, in the 'Introduction' to his 'Contribution to the Critique of Hegel's Philosophy of Law' (1844), that, even in Germany, the prospects of human emancipation lay with the proletariat, the universal class which 'cannot emancipate itself without emancipating itself from all other spheres of society and thereby emancipating all other spheres of society.' Nevertheless, even Marx concluded that 'the only practical possible liberation of Germany is liberation that *proceeds from the standpoint of the theory* which proclaims man to be the highest being for man ... The head of this emancipation is philosophy, its heart is the proletariat' (CW 3: 186-7).

By 1844, when Engels began his intellectual collaboration with Marx, he was already a revolutionary and a communist who had experienced the English labour movement at first hand and who had preceded Marx in the belief that human emancipation required more than a political revolution. Nevertheless, he continued to work within the framework of an Hegelian idealism where historical events were presented as the unfolding of 'History', a teleological meta-subject which progressed inevitably through a logical succession of principles towards its goal of overcoming human alienation. It was this idealism which allowed him to argue that the Germans would adopt communism 'as soon as it is founded upon sound philosophical principles' (CW 3: 406). Marx's 1844 *Manuscripts* rejected such idealism yet even they remained loyal to a teleological outlook which presented history as the story of Man's return to his essence. The partnership of the two men was soon to lead to their adoption of a very different intellectual outlook.

CHAPTER THREE

Engels' epistemological break

History is nothing but the activity of man pursuing his aims (Engels, 1844. CW 4: 93).

ENGELS' BREAK WITH IDEALISM

In his articles on 'The Condition of England', written in spring 1844, Engels presented history as a succession of Hegelian principles which engendered specific social relations. (CW 3: 475-6). By the time of the introduction to his translation of Fourier's 'On Trade', written in the second half of 1845, he was condemning German communism for 'translating into the language of Hegelian logic, propositions that long ago became commonplaces in France and England'. What the French and English had long ago discovered was thus presented in an abstract form as a new discovery: 'I make no exception here of my own writings.' (CW 4: 614-15).

The German Ideology, jointly written with Marx between November 1845 and August 1846, reveals the extent to which Engels had transformed his outlook, rejecting the idealism and teleology of the Hegelian system, and replacing the ethical socialism of his early works with a new political philosophy based on an appeal to class interest. Althusser argues that Marx's works during this period are marked by an 'epistemological break', in which one paradigm was abandoned to be replaced with a new, scientific problematic: historical materialism (Althusser, 1977: 31-7). One certainly need not share Althusser's account of historical materialism to see that the works of this period represent a turning-point in the development of Marx's thought. But what exactly was the nature of this new outlook and what did Engels contribute to its formulation?

Marx and Engels' first joint work, *The Holy Family*, written between September and November 1844, was a lengthy critique of Bruno Bauer and of his fellow Young Hegelian 'Critical Critics' who published in the monthly *Allgemeine Literatur-Zeitung*. In *The Holy Family*, Marx and Engels openly proclaimed their debt to Feuerbach's humanism (CW 4: 93). For this reason Althusser refused to include it within the works of 'the break' which, he argued, involved a rejection of epistemological humanism. Yet, in fact, *The Holy Family* represents a turning-point in Marx and Engels' intellectual development, with its rejection of the teleology of the anthropogenetic outlook, and its hints of the new historical perspective which they were to outline more systematically in *The German Ideology*. Fleischer refers to this new perspective as the 'pragmatological' outlook, where 'history is regarded as the outcome, more blind than the result of any tendency to a specific goal, of the actions of individuals and of groups impelled by their needs in the situations in which they find themselves' (Fleischer: 13).

It was one of the chapters of *The Holy Family* written by Engels which most clearly expressed his and Marx's break with historical teleology. Engels claimed that Young Hegelian 'Critical Criticism', the target of Marx and Engels' polemic, converted human activity into a series of categories and principles such as 'the struggle of history.' Yet, Engels argued, 'History does nothing, it "possesses no immense wealth", it "wages no battles". It is man, real, living man who does all that, who possess and fights; "history" is not, as it were, a person apart, using man as a means to achieve its own aims; history is nothing but the activity of man pursuing his aims.' It was, Engels claimed, Feuerbach's 'brilliant expositions' which had first revealed this truth and broken free of the mysteries of the Hegelian system (CW 4: 93).

For the first time, Engels showed that he had understood the significance of Feuerbach's critique of Hegelianism, a critique which Marx had adopted as early as his *Critique of Hegel's Philosophy of Right* (1843) and which played a key role in his *1844 Manuscripts* (CW 3: 327-9). In this sense, the materialism of *The Holy Family* represents far more of a break in Engels' development than it did for Marx (although, even for the latter, the work did involve a crucial break with historical teleology). Yet this break does not seem to have been a particularly painful one. As we shall see, Engels continued to give a very similar account of historical change to that which he had offered during his time in England, the difference was largely one of presentation, of abandoning the framework of Hegelian idealism within which his analysis had previously been presented and basing it instead on 'real, living man.'

Overall, Engels' role in the writing of *The Holy Family* was a minor one. It is difficult, at times, to disagree with his own assessment of the work: 'The supreme contempt we two evince towards the *Literatur Zeitung* is in glaring contrast with the twenty-two sheets we devote to it', of which Engels himself claimed credit for only one and a half (CW 38: 7, 18, 25, 28). Nevertheless, in its rejection of teleology and idealism, *The Holy Family* represents an important milestone in the evolution of historical materialism and, in its critique of idealism, was a particularly significant stage in the development of Engels' thought.

Although *The Holy Family* invoked Feuerbach in order to criticise German idealism, Marx and Engels were soon, in turn, to arrive at a critique of Feuerbach himself. This critique was to form the foundation of a new historical outlook; an outlook which was first to be applied in Engels' *The Condition of the Working Class in England* (1845), before being set out in a more general form in Marx and Engels' *The German Ideology* (1845-46).

The first sign of this critique of Feuerbach appears in a letter which Engels wrote to Marx in November 1844, shortly after his return to Barmen, following Engels' reading of Max Stirner's *The Ego and His Own* in proof-form. Feuerbach, as we have seen, argued that it was not God who had created Man, but rather Man who had created God, thus alienating his human powers on to an abstraction of his own making. Stirner now out-Feuerbached Feuerbach, by arguing that to subject oneself to the ethical requirements supposedly inherent in the true nature of Man, was also to bow down to a 'spook', to an abstraction: 'God has had to give place, yet not to us, but to – Man.' Stirner offered a nominalist critique of the category of 'Man', arguing that only concrete individuals existed. 'Man' was thus dismissed, along with other 'spooks' such as reason, humanity, love, liberalism, socialism and humanism. (Stepelevich: 337; Stirner: 52-8, 83, 90, 107)

In his letter to Marx, Engels accepted Stirner's demolition of the universal of 'Man', a concept which Feuerbach had arrived at, in idealist fashion, through a critique of theology. Instead of this idealism, Engels argued, 'we must take our departure from empiricism and materialism', and only deduce the general from the particular, from the study of flesh-and-blood individuals, rather than taking such general philosophical categories as the starting point of analysis. Engels was later to repeat this point in his 'Theses on Feuerbach', written in the autumn of 1845, which criticised Feuerbach for arguing that the key task of modern times was the 'humanisation of God' and the 'negation of theology.' (CW 38: 12; CW 5: 12). Stirner's work was thus of vital importance for the development of Marx and Engels' pragmatological outlook, a point which has often been obscured by the fact that so much of *The German Ideology* is devoted to a polemic *against* Stirner's views and by Engels' dismissal of his work as a 'curiosity' in the account of this period which he was to offer forty years later in his *Ludwig Feuerbach* (McLellan, 1980: 134; Paterson: 122; SW II: 332, 349).

Having rejected the concept of 'Man', the way was now clear for Engels to embark upon the empirical study of modern society, a project which was to result in his *The Condition of the Working Class in England*, a work which he was writing by November 1844, had completed by March 1845, and which was published, with a speed which modern authors can only envy, in June of that year. Yet, Engels' journalism and published speeches of this period give little indication of the originality which was soon to be revealed in *The Condition of the Working Class*, indeed, they tend to express exactly the 'utopian socialism' which Engels' book was to criticise.

Thus Engels continued to describe socialism as an 'ideal' which it was the 'duty' of German workers to take seriously. He was determined to show that this ideal was a practicable one, citing communist 'colonies' in America and England as a proof and looking forward to the foundation of such a colony in Germany. He even argued that, in England, socialism might come about by 'setting up a number of colonies and leaving it to every individual whether to join or not.' Such writings presented communism as a rational ethical ideal which should be generally accepted since it is 'an obvious, self-evident truth that the interest, the well-being, the happiness of each individual is inseparably bound up with that of his fellow men. We must all acknowledge that we cannot do without our fellow men.' To act contrary to this truth, to arrange society to suit our immediate individual interest was a 'fundamental mistake'. We must, therefore, 'correct this fundamental mistake, and that is precisely the aim of communism' (CW 4: 215-28, 230-1, 245-6).

Once the defects of capitalism had been eliminated and production was organised by community, it would be a 'trifling matter' to regulate production according to needs, rather than private profit. The workers would, of course, declare themselves for this rational purpose which would benefit all of mankind, but it was also 'self-evident that the better and more intelligent among the rich will declare themselves in agreement with the workers.' Already many educated and prosperous people had declared themselves socialists. Indeed, in Germany, the middle class formed, as yet, the basis of the socialist party since it was 'far more disinterested, impartial and intelligent' than the middle class in England, although, Engels added, this was for the very simple reason that it was poorer than the English middle class (CW 4: 245-7, 252-3).

Engels' arguments, particularly those made at the Elberfeld public meetings in February 1845, should be seen in their context, rather than taken too literally. He was writing and speaking under the threat of arrest and prosecution and also under the influence of self-confessed excitement at speaking before an audience. The composition of his audience should also be borne in mind for, as he wrote to Marx, 'all Elberfeld and Barmen, from the financial aristocracy to the *epicerie*, was represented, only the proletariat being excluded.' Engels certainly tailored his remarks to suit the occasion, emphasising communism as a sensible answer to the extravagances of capitalism with its swindling middlemen, expensive standing armies and conspicuous consumption by the wealthy (CW 38: 4, 10, 22-4; CW 4: 246-51, 264, 701). Despite his claim that proletarian revolution was the 'unavoidable result of our existing social conditions' (CW 4: 227, 230, 256-64), his works of this period do little to prepare one for the political analysis which Engels was even then engaged in writing in his *The Condition of the Working Class in England*.

THE CONDITION OF THE WORKING CLASS IN ENGLAND: THE PRAGMATOLOGICAL OUTLOOK APPLIED

In his 1892 'Preface' to the English edition of *The Condition of the Working Class*, Engels emphasised the differences between his outlook in 1845 and his later views. He argued there that this early work represented only an embryonic form of Marxism which 'exhibits everywhere the traces of the descent of Modern Socialism from one of its ancestors, German philosophy' (CWCE: 26). Yet, to the modern reader, what is most striking is the degree to which *The Condition of the Working Class* breaks with Engels' earlier works and anticipates the outlook which was to be developed in *The German Ideology* and *The Communist Manifesto*.

Engels' later criticism of his work was that his background in German philosophy had produced a form of Utopian socialism which stressed that 'communism is not a mere party doctrine of the working-class, but a theory compassing the emancipation of society at large, including the capitalist class, from its present narrow conditions' (CWCE: 26). This criticism is certainly borne out by the rhetorical prose of Engels' opening dedication, 'To the working-classes of Great Britain', which addressed the English proletariat as 'members of the great and universal family of Mankind who know their interest and that of all the human race to be the same' and whose success in the 'cause of humanity' was certain. In a similar vein, he concluded his work with the claim that 'communism stands, in principle, above the breach between the bourgeoisie and the proletariat' and that 'communism is a question of humanity and not of the workers alone' (CW 4: 298, 301, 581-2).

Yet the whole thrust of Engels' argument in *The Condition of the Working Class* is that, far from Mankind being a single family, the interests of the workers and of the bourgeoisie are 'diametrically opposed', and that the bitterness and conflict between them would grow ever more intense as 'the classes are divided more and more sharply.' In this perspective, socialism is not merely an ethical ideal, it is the means by which the workers will eventually pursue their own class interests and towards which they will be driven by sheer want (CW 4: 298, 583).

It was this outlook which provided the basis for Engels' critique of those Owenite socialists who presented socialism as a matter of 'philanthropy and universal love', and who thus disapproved of class hatred. They failed to see that the transition to communism would only occur when society had developed until 'the point at which this transition becomes both possible and necessary.' The Owenites thus based their political programme on an appeal to Man in the abstract, to individuals divorced from their social situation. In fact, communism was the product of history and of class interest. It was thus necessary to trace the processes which had brought the modern world into being, and to describe the social and economic conditions which would drive the working class towards the abolition of capitalism. It was these two tasks which Engels set out to achieve in *The Condition of the Working Class*. (CW 4: 302-4, 524-6).

Following Hess's example, Engels used England as the paradigmatic example of modern social development, although the detail of his historical analysis was based on Gaskell's *The Manufacturing Population of England* (Gaskell, 1833; CW 4: 366). Nevertheless, in structuring his account of English industrialisation around the growth of the productive forces and the impact of that growth on class structure, politics and ideology, Engels offered a breadth of vision lacking in his sources and established many of the central theses of historical materialism which he and Marx were to soon to set out in a more systematic form.

Engels claimed that, as recently as the mid-eighteenth century, England 'was a country like every other', with small towns, little industry and a thinly scattered, agricultural population. The population consisted mainly of small landowners, the yeomen who inefficiently cultivated their land according to the methods laid down by custom and who enjoyed an effective security of tenure. The textile industry was carried out in the countryside by family labour, in the workers' own homes, with production geared towards the home market. As such families possessed their own plots of land, they were not entirely dependent upon their wages for subsistence (CW 4: 302-3, 307-11, 320).

Yet, Engels argued, England was, by 1844, a country like no other with a huge capital city, vast manufacturing towns, and a large, densely concentrated population, who worked mainly in trade and industry which supplied a world market. This transformation was, Engels claimed, the product of a revolution in industrial techniques, an industrial revolution which had 'altered the whole civil society.' The first stage of this development was the invention of the spinning jenny in 1764 which meant that the supply of yarn outstripped the number of weavers. As a result, weavers' wages rose and many weavers abandoned their smallholdings to live purely on their wages. As this land came on to the market, it was obtained by new tenant-farmers who consolidated their holdings into large farms of fifty to two hundred acres, improved their techniques and undercut the traditional yeomen farmers, who were thus forced into the ranks of the agricultural proletariat. Further technological improvements led to the centralisation of spinning in factories powered, at first, by water but, after 1785, by steam-power. With the invention of the power-loom, factory production soon developed for weaving as well. The result was the cheapening of manufactured commodities and the dominance of English goods in the world market.

This process of industrialisation, involving the mechanisation and centralisation of production, the use of water and steam-power and the intensification of the division of labour, soon spread to other branches of industry: woollens, hosiery, lace, cotton dyeing, linens and silk. There was a similar expansion of production and proliferation of new techniques in the iron-smelting and metal-working industries. This, in turn, necessarily stimulated the production of coal and of iron-ore. Roads, canals and railways were all improved in order to supply raw materials, and to meet the demand for industrial goods. 'Agriculture made a corresponding advance', with the application of science, mechanisation, larger farms and the reclamation of the wastes (CW 4: 307, 320, 324-5).

Engels claimed that it was this revolution in industrial technique which was the cause of England's revolution in social relations. Firstly, population had been concentrated into large towns based on the new industries with their related service industries: building; food and drink; clothing; and so on. Second, and even more importantly, this industrial revolution had given rise to the emergence of new classes for, as Engels said, 'manufacture on a small-scale created the middle-class; on a large-scale, it created the working-class and raised the elect of the middle-class to the throne.' Industrialisation concentrated the ownership of capital into fewer hands and forced the independent workman and the small-scale employer out of the market. The proletariat was thus the product of England's industrial transformation; it was 'called into existence by the introduction of machinery.' As a result, modern society, particularly its great towns, was polarised into two opposing camps: the bourgeoisie and the proletariat; the petit bourgeoisie and independent artisans were in decline and the worker no longer had the prospect of rising into the middle class.

But it was not only in the sphere of industry proper that the process of proletarianisation had occurred. Handicrafts and retail work were also subject to an intensification of the division of labour and the rise of wage-labour. Similarly, in agriculture, there was the growth of large capitalist farms, based on innovation and mechanisation, and employing a rural proletariat. Thus, according to Engels, proletarianisation began with the technical innovations in textiles; spread first to coal and metal-working; then to agriculture; and finally, in capitalism's quest for wage-labour, drew the Irish into its reserve army of labour (CW 4: 307, 320-1, 324-7, 389, 548-9).

In a well-known aphorism in *The Poverty of Philosophy*, Marx said that 'the hand-mill gives you society with the feudal lord; the steam-mill, society with the industrial capitalist (CW 6: 166). His famous 'Preface' to *A Contribution to the Critique of Political Economy* (1859), expressed this claim for the social primacy of the productive forces as a comprehensive theory of social structure, historical change and revolution; a theory whose discovery Marx had specifically claimed as his own (CPE 20; SC: 64). In fact, this emphasis on the primacy of society's productive base was a commonplace of eighteenth-century political economy. It made its first appearance in the writings of Marx and Engels not in Marx's work, but rather in Engels' *The Condition of the Working Class*, where it provided the framework for Engels' account of modern historical development and, as we shall see, the basis for his prediction of imminent social revolution (Rigby, 1987: ch. 5).

The bulk of *The Condition of the Working Class* is, of course, an account of the living and working conditions of the urban and rural proletariat, an account which, as Engels himself put it, amounted to an indictment of 'social murder' against the English bourgeoisie. His conclusion was that English proletariat was 'everywhere living in want and misery under totally inhuman conditions.' Everywhere, 'we find want and disease permanent or temporary, and demoralization arising from the condition of the workers; in all directions slow but sure undermining and final destruction of the human beings physically as well as mentally' (CW 38: 10-11; CW 4: 330, 393-4, 407, 500, 561).

At work, the proletariat faced a life of meaningless, compulsory toil which, whether in the form of the unbroken monotony of factory-production or the physical overwork of mining, resulted in ill-health, physical injury and mental and moral degradation. Cramped slum-housing, poor clothing and adulterated food meant that the workers were physically enfeebled, aged prematurely and died unnecessarily early. With the lack of compulsory education and the spread of child-labour, they endured, from an early age, mental and spiritual deprivation as well as material hardship. Long working hours for parents, inadequate housing, the growth of mechanisation and the consequent employment of women and children had destroyed family life, demoralizing both parents and their neglected children (CW 4: 393-416, 424-5, 442-57, 491-4, 531-8; see Gaskell, 1833: 7-8, 23, 89-96, 147-9).

The growth of female employment had led to a reversal of the sexes' traditional roles, with wives going out to work and husbands staying at home. It could even, on occasion, result in the supremacy of the wife within the household; a supremacy which, Engels argued, only went to show that 'the sexes have been placed in a false position from the beginning. If the reign of the wife over the husband, as inevitably brought about by the factory system, is inhuman, the pristine rule of the husband over the wife must have been inhuman too.' His solution was not to restore patriarchal authority, but rather to introduce a community of possessions so that no family member could claim that they possessed, or contributed, the greater share of the family's income. Women would continue to be responsible for child-rearing and domestic work but this traditional, sexual division of labour would no longer result in their subordination within the family (CW 4: 434-40).

In *The Condition of the Working Class*, Engels no longer invoked a human essence as the telos towards which history progresses but, nevertheless, a conception of authentic human existence remained the basis for his critique of the quality of life in capitalist society. This humanist critique is most apparent in his condemnation of modern working conditions on the grounds that just 'as voluntary productive activity is the highest enjoyment known to us', so compulsory toil is 'the most cruel, degrading punishment. Nothing is more terrible than being constrained to do some one thing every day from morning until night against one's will.' In a well-ordered society, technological improvements would be 'a source of rejoicing.' Yet, in modern society, the fruits of human ingenuity had, for many, become a curse, which offered the prospect either of meaningless and monotonous work, or of low wages and unemployment. Similarly, the squalor of modern town-life meant that the urban population was 'forced to sacrifice the best qualities of their human nature', and to live in conditions unworthy of men and fit only for beasts (CW 4: 364, 381, 414, 428-9).

That capitalism alienates man from his true essence can be seen not only in the inhuman nature of the modern labour-process, and society's inability to provide decent living conditions. It is evident, too, in the loss of all sense of human community, the total atomisation of society and the declaration of a Stirneresque social war of each against all. 'The simple principles, which for plain human beings, regulate the relations of man to man' are thus 'brought into the direst confusion.' Even the bourgeoisie is alienated from its own humanity in such conditions, existing only for the sake of money which it turns into a god and takes as the measure of all things. The employer sees his workers not as fellow human beings with a 'right' to 'independent activity and opinions' and a life worthy of human beings, but merely as 'hands', as abstractions, as economic categories, the relationship between them is 'purely economic' and thus 'has nothing human in it.' Nevertheless, it is the proletarian, stripped of any economic security, subject to the despotism of the employers who, in modern society, is placed 'in the most revolting, inhuman position conceivable for a human being' (CW 4: 329-30, 373, 411-13, 460, 562-4; Marcus: 232; for the workers as 'hands', see also Gaskell, E., 1979: 166-7).

As Marx and Engels based their political philosophy on the revolutionary potential of the proletariat, it was easy for their critics to claim that they had made the proletariat into 'gods' (CW 4: 36-7). This was certainly not the case in *The Condition of the Working Class* which emphasised that the living and working conditions of the proletariat could easily force it into drunkenness, sexual immorality, brutality and crime. Nevertheless, Engels continued to claim that the proletariat was the class which represented England's future and which was in the forefront of English historical development. The workers experienced their social situation as one of loss, were conscious of their loss, and had a clear understanding of the nature of modern society. It is thus the workers who feel 'bound to proclaim that they, as human beings, shall not be made to bow to circumstances, but social conditions ought to yield to them as human beings' (CW 4: 411/5, 420/1, 506).

Having established the inhuman position in which modern society placed the proletariat, Engels concluded that the worker had only two options. The first was to assert his humanity against the class which was responsible for his fate; the second to enjoy life whilst he could and await the next slump. 'To escape despair, there are but two ways open to him; either inward and outward revolt against the bourgeoisie or drunkenness and general demoralization.' As we have seen, some workers opted for the second choice, but Engels remained optimistic that the majority of the proletariat would come to 'demand a position worthy of men' since it 'cannot feel happy' in conditions in which no man or class could 'think, feel and live as human beings.' 'The workers must therefore strive to escape from this brutalizing condition, to secure for themselves a better, more human position; and this they cannot do without attacking the interest of the bourgeoisie which consists in exploiting them.' Naturally, the bourgeoise attempts to defend its own interests, with the inevitable result that the two classes become open enemies (CW 4: 309, 413, 433, 501; Lenin: 49/50).

Engels offered an outline of the history of the working-class movement which was to be adopted by Marx in *The Communist Manifesto*. The first response by the worker to his oppression is an individual one: crime. The bourgeoisie worship money as a god, yet take the proletarian's money from him, and so 'makes a practical atheist of him. No wonder, then, if the proletarian retains his atheism and no longer respects the sacredness and power of the earthly God' of the bourgeoisie. Social opposition to the bourgeoisie developed when the workers began to resist the introduction of machinery through Luddism. Yet, this form of opposition was no more successful than crime in achieving its goal. Temporary victories could be won but eventually the wrong-doers were punished while the machinery was introduced anyway (CW 4: 412, 502/3).

The third stage of development was the spread of trade unions which sought to defend individuals, regulate wages and to offer mutual support, a development which was encouraged by the legalisation of unions in 1824. Engels argued that in the long run such unions were powerless to control wages or to defend their members against unemployment. Yet, although their strikes usually ended disastrously, Engels argued that the workers, rather than admit the loss of all human feeling, were 'compelled' to rebel. The importance of the trade unions lay not in their short-term achievements, but rather in their recognition of the fact that the workers could only defeat the employers by putting an end to the competition amongst themselves. They form the 'military school of the working-men in which they prepare themselves for the great struggle which cannot be avoided' (CW 4: 503/517).

That the history of the trade unions was 'a long series of defeats of the working men, interrupted by a few isolated victories', only went to show the workers that 'something more is needed than Trade Unions and strikes to break the power of the ruling class.' The result was Chartism, the 'compact form' of the workers' opposition to the bourgeoisie. In Chartism, 'it is the *whole* working-class which arises against the bourgeoisie and attacks, first of all, the political power, the legislative rampart with which the bourgeoisie had surrounded itself.' Chartism was thus not merely a political movement, 'Chartism is of an essentially social nature, a class movement.' The demand for a Ten Hours Bill and the repeal of the New Poor Law and the call for workers to have decent wages and secure employment were thus as much a part of the Chartist movement as the 'Six Points' of the People's Charter. For the Chartists, such political reforms were only the means to a broader end: social happiness (CW 4: 505-7, 517-24).

Yet, even Chartism could not solve the economic problems faced by the working class, so long as it clung to reactionary schemes such as the call for a return to a world of peasant smallholders. The workers must, therefore, either accept the logic of the capitalist economy, and 'succumb to the power of competition once more', or 'entirely overcome competition and abolish it.' As we have seen, Engels was critical of Owenite socialism for its failure to realise that class struggle is the means by which socialism will be brought into being. Socialism thus had to fuse with the working-class movement, with Chartism, if it was to have an impact. Already, the Chartist leaders were, in a broad sense, 'nearly all socialists' and the movement as a whole would inevitably be driven towards socialism 'when the next crisis directs the working-men by force of sheer want to social instead of political remedies' (CW 4: 524-6).

Engels' conclusion was that the prediction of the 'speedy collapse' of bourgeois society and the advent of proletarian revolution was thus 'as certain as a mathematical or mechanical demonstration.' Within a time, 'almost within the power of man to predict', revolution must break out. Indeed, Engels *did* attempt to predict the timing of the next revolution for 'prophecy is nowhere so easy as in England, where all the component elements of society are clearly defined and sharply separated.' He claimed that the next economic crisis (which he correctly predicted for 1847) would have the effect of driving the Chartists towards socialism and would see the repeal of the Corn Laws and the enactment of the People's Charter. By then, the workers would have no choice but to wage a social war against the rich: 'a revolution will follow with which none hitherto known can be compared' (CW 4: 323, 524, 580-3).

It may seem, to the reader of *The Condition of the Working Class*, that its final chapter, on 'The attitude of the bourgeoisie towards the proletariat', does not form an integral part of a work which is largely devoted to the history and condition of the working class. Yet, it could be argued that this chapter is the most crucial in the whole work. As we have seen, Engels no longer presented socialist revolution as a goal towards which History inexorably progressed; it was not the goal, but the result, of historical development, the outcome of human actions and interests. He thus considered the possibility of an alternative historical outcome, whereby revolution was averted by middle-class concessions which would ameliorate the poverty faced by the workers. Only if 'the English bourgeoisie does not pause to reflect' on the need for such reforms would revolution be inevitable. It was, therefore, essential for Engels to show that this possible alternative was historically unviable and that the bourgeoisie would not act to save itself.

He thus argued that reforms under capitalism were impossible since the bourgeoisie looked at everything 'through the spectacles of personal selfishness'. 'The prejudices of a whole class cannot be laid aside like an old coat, least of all those of the stable, narrow, selfish English bourgeoisie.' With the classes divided ever more sharply, it was 'too late for a peaceful solution.' Soon the war of the poor against the rich would become 'direct and universal' - 'but then it will be too late for the rich to be beware' (CW 4: 322-3, 407, 421, 580-3).

For Engels, it was, above all, the actions of the state, 'the bourgeoisie as a party', which revealed the inability of the ruling class to save itself through reforms. The state was, Engels claimed, the political means by which 'the bourgeoisie defends its interests'. In parliament, the monarchical and aristocratic elements of the constitution enjoyed a only a 'sham existence'; the propertied middle class were the 'only power' and sought to 'subjugate the proletariat still further', through measures such as the enclosure and private appropriation of common land. Indeed, in general, 'all legislation is calculated to protect those that possess property against those who do not.' 'The English bourgeois finds himself reproduced in his law, as he does in his God.' The sanctity of law provided 'the strongest support of his social position.' Law made by the propertied in parliament, and administered by them, as judges and justices, on the assumption that the interests of their class formed 'the foundations of all good order (CW 4: 322, 514-8, 567-70, 578).

However, the 'most open declaration of war of the bourgeoisie upon the proletariat' was, Engels claimed, repeating the argument of his 'Outlines of a Critique of Political Economy', Malthus' theory of population and the New Poor Law framed in accordance with it. Malthus' theory had declared that 'the right to live, a right previously asserted in favour of every man in the world' was nonsense. Naturally, it had been adopted as the 'pet theory of all genuine English bourgeois ... since it is the most specious excuse for them', with its reassuring implication that all charities and poor-rates were futile since they would do nothing, in the long run, to remove the surplus population who lived in poverty and distress. Never before had the theory 'that the non-

Engels' epistemological break

possessing class exists solely for the purpose of being exploited, and of starving when the property-holders can no longer make use of it' been so blatantly expressed. However, Engels concluded, the English workers had rejected the political economy of the employers and 'have taken it into their heads that they, with their busy hands, are the necessary, and the rich capitalists, who do nothing, the surplus population' (CW 4: 570-8).

THE CONDITION OF THE WORKING CLASS IN ENGLAND: AN ASSESSMENT

An assessment of the social and political theory offered in *The Condition of the Working Class* can wait for the broader judgement of Engels' thought offered in chapters nine and ten, below. Here we need only note some of the empirical weaknesses in Engels' account of English industrialisation and offer some assessment of the contribution of Engels' book to the formation of Marxism.

Empirically, Engels' book can be criticised in a number of ways. In particular, by claiming that England in 1760 was a country like any other, Engels made it impossible for himself to understand the country's unique development. In fact, England in 1760 was not a country just like any other. For Engels, the dynamic behind England's economic development was technological innovation in industry, which only later generated agricultural innovation. Yet, in fact, it was the prior development of agriculture and rural society in the three centuries before 1760 which was the basis of English industrialisation (Jones, 1976: ch. 1-5). As a result, by 1760, peasant smallholders, producing for their own subsistence, were becoming less and less common. They were replaced by the social triangle of agrarian capitalism with great landlords, leasing out their estates to innovating tenant-farmers, who produced for the market on the basis of wage-labour. This system released labour from agriculture so that, by 1700, 40 per cent of England's population was already involved in non-agricultural pursuits (Brenner, 1976: 66).

A second objection which can be raised against Engels' historical account is the degree to which industrialisation, at least in the classic form of factory production based on technological innovation, was actually the key to English economic growth in the period before 1845. In fact, as Engels' own analysis shows, industrialisation was largely confined to the textile industries. Growth in other fields usually took the form of an expansion of craft production on the basis of a proletarianised work-force (as in clothing), or of an intensification of the division of labour (as in pottery), rather than mechanisation proper. The massive expansion of iron and coal production only came after 1830 with the arrival of the railway era whilst, in general, the development of production in large, mechanised factories was the product of the second, rather than the first, half of the nineteenth century. In other words, by 1845 the process of industrialisation, far from being complete, was limited to one, rather unstable, sector of the economy (Hobsbawm, 1972: 68-72). This mistake was to have decisive effects for Engels' assessment of the capacity for capitalism to grow in the future and for his predictions of imminent socialist revolution.

If Engels' account of England's economic development is open to question, then how accurate is his description of working-class living conditions of which, after all, he had been an eye witness for almost two years? The issue of whether working-class standards of living rose or fell during the Industrial Revolution has, of course, been the subject of long debate. Recent contributions to the debate have stressed the lack of improvement in real wages in the period c. 1755-1810/1820 and have continued to disagree about the extent of improvement in the period 1810/20-1850 (Lindert and Williamson, 1983, 1984; Flinn). It would be unwise for a non-specialist to attempt to offer any answer to this problem, although Thompson's argument that there is more to standards of living than money-wages perhaps needs re-emphasising (Thompson, 1972: 351; Hobsbawm, 1979: 119). Here we shall merely note that much of the criticism which has been levelled against Engels' account of social conditions in the Industrial Revolution has been misdirected, and has misrepresented the nature of his indictment of capitalism.

Firstly, because Engels stressed the role of industrialisation in reducing living standards and working conditions, it is easy to counter his arguments with the claim that it was those employed in small workshops, such as the overworked sewing girls of the East End of London, who faced the worst conditions rather than factory workers (Henderson and Chaloner: xiv). Yet Engels himself stressed that it was the non-industrial workers, such as the hand-loom weavers, who were in competition with machine production, who had the 'worst situation'. Similarly, he argued that the dressmakers of the East End were amongst those whose employment involved 'the saddest consequences for the health of the workers' (CW 4: 433, 498).

Nor was Engels' argument essentially concerned with trends in real wages (Henderson and Chaloner: xiv-v), about which, he admitted, 'it is hard to get to the bottom of the matter.' He himself pointed out that the wages paid in mining were relatively high but, having looked at the industry's record of accidents and its horrific effects on health, asked 'whether any pay in money can indemnify the miner for such suffering?' Engels was well aware that few workers were totally destitute or starving, but argued that, given the inevitable booms and slumps of the capitalist economy, all were faced with this threat. Indeed, Engels claimed that, 'far more demoralizing than his poverty in its influence upon the English working-man, is the insecurity of his position' since 'he knows that he has something today and that it does not depend upon himself whether he shall have something tomorrow.' The workers had to live, even in times of prosperity, with the knowledge that they would eventually face a slump, short-time working, unemployment and the need for charity, an eventuality against which individual measures, such as thrift and sobriety, offered no remedy (CW 4: 330/1, 335, 382, 413, 431, 534).

Nor is it true to say that Engels' indictment of the bourgeoisie depended on a contrast of nineteenth-century conditions with a mythical pre-industrial Golden Age (Henderson and Chaloner: xiv). It is true that, following Gaskell, Engels did paint a misleadingly optimistic picture of the prosperous yeomen and happy craftsmen of the eighteenth century, but he also added that, even in these conditions, the workers 'vegetated' in an existence 'which, cosily romantic as it was, was nevertheless not worthy of human beings. In truth they were not human beings, they were merely toiling machines ... the industrial revolution has simply carried this out to its logical end.' Engels' condemnation of capitalism rested essentially, not on a contrast with eighteenth-century standards of living, but rather, as we have seen, on a series of claims about man's potential for an authentic human existence, a potential which Engels believed was frustrated by contemporary society (Henderson and Chaloner: xxvi; Gaskell, 1833: 15-21; CW 4: 308-9).

When Engels referred to the 'degradation' of factory life he, like other contemporary observers, had in mind not just a statistical analysis of real wages. Rather, he criticised the effects of industry on family life; of its concentration of population into unhealthy urban environments; of the monotonous work which it entailed; of the arbitrary jurisdiction and fines which the employers could impose on their workers; and the total reliance of the workers on wages, which put them at the mercy of the booms and slumps of the economy. Again and again, he compared wage-labour to slavery and serfdom, concluding that, although the proletarian had the advantage of some real freedom, he also had the disadvantage that, unlike the slave or serf, his master could freely repudiate him, leaving him to starve if it suited the master (Gaskell, 1833: 7, 23, 89-94, 147-9, 240, 327, 341; Gaskell, 1836: 5, 321; Hobsbawm, 1972: 94; CW 4: 375-80, 413, 424, 467-70, 473-4, 488).

In this perspective, the fact that Engels claimed that there were forty thousand prostitutes in London, when his source only allowed him to refer to *between* thirty and forty thousand, (Chaloner and Henderson: xxvi, 144) ceases to be of particular significance for an assessment of the accuracy of his description of the 'social pauperisation' involved in the early industrial revolution. As we shall see, Engels' major weakness was not his description of such pauperisation but rather his predictions about its future course and political consequences.

If we turn to the broader issue of Engels' contribution to the formation of Marxism, *The Condition of the Working Class*, Engels' work can, in its refusal to present history as the saga of man's necessary return to himself, be seen as a crucial break with the anthropogenetic teleology of works such as Marx's 1844 *Manuscripts* and Engels' own earlier writings. In its pragmatological social theory, Engels' book prefigures, to an extent which has rarely been appreciated, the historical materialism which was to be set out in more general terms in *The German Ideology*. Whilst not abandoning his earlier, humanist critique of capitalism, Engels offered the first application of the historical outlook which had been outlined, in very general terms, in *The Holy Family*, an outlook which refused to reduce human history down to a series of categories and principles, or to erect a supra-human 'History' which determined human actions.

As Engels wrote to Marx in November 1844, having just read Stirner's critique of Feuerbach, 'I find all this theoretical twaddle daily more tedious and am irritated by every word that has to be expended on the suject of "man", by every line that has to be read or written against theology and abstraction no less than against crude materialism. But it's quite another matter when, instead of concerning oneself with all these phantasms ... one turns to real, live things, to historical developments and consequences' (CW 38: 13).

Nevertheless, it should not be assumed that, from the time of *The Holy Family*, Marx and Engels totally abandoned their old philosophical outlook, and adopted a new, purely, historical method. On the contrary, as Althusser has pointed out, Marx and Engels continued to use Hegelian language, and to lapse into Hegelian logic, even after they themselves had arrived at an historical outlook which had gone far beyond the Hegelian system (Althusser, 1971: 89-91). In this sense, it is perhaps misleading to refer to Engels' development as simply constituting a 'break' with Hegelian philosophy, and its replacement with historical science.

Certainly, in *The Condition of the Working Class*, traces of Hegelian logic, where history is presented in terms of the necessary development of categories and principles, continued to exist alongside an analysis in which history consisted solely of the effects, intended and unintended, of human actions. For example, Engels wrongly predicted that, with the repeal of the Corn Laws, the principle of free competition would be 'carried to its extreme point; all further development within the present order comes to an end, and the only step farther is a radical transformation of the social order.' Yet, as Engels himself pointed out, competition arose *not* as the expression of some Hegelian 'principle', but from the specific position and interests of the individuals and classes of modern society (CW 4: 375-6, 555). Similarly, Engels also continued, as he had in his earlier writings, to offer social explanations in terms of 'national characters', for instance, of the 'Latin' character of the Irish, with whom feeling and passion predominated (CW 4: 390-1, 559-61).

Perhaps because it is a book about a specific time and place, *The Condition of the Working Class* has rarely been given the credit it deserves for its wider role in the genesis of historical materialism (see, however, Jones, G. S., 1977). Engels himself referred to the book as merely an embryonic stage in the development of Marxism, whilst Draper refers to it as a 'treasury of seedlings' of later Marxism (CWCE: 26; Draper: 183). In fact, *The Condition of the Working Class* was a sturdy sapling rather than a mere seedling. Its claims for the social primacy of the productive forces, its account of the polarisation of modern society into two main classes, its analysis of the booms and slumps of capitalism and their creation of a 'reserve army of workers' (CW 4: 384), its conception of the state as a 'class state', its description of modern political economy as the ideology of the bourgeoisie, and its prediction that capitalist crisis would lead inevitably to socialist revolution, were all to become permanent contributions to Marxist thought. *The Condition of the Working Class* reveals Engels' central role in the formation of the outlook which we now associate with Marx's name, a role which was soon to be emphasised by his collaboration with Marx in the production of *The German Ideology* and the *Communist Manifesto*.

CHAPTER FOUR

Historical materialism

> In the whole conception of history up to the present, [the] real basis of history has either been totally disregarded or else considered as a minor matter' (Marx and Engels, 1845/6. CW 5: 55).

Given the massive amount of analysis which commentators have devoted to Marx's cryptic *Theses on Feuerbach* (1845) and to the condensed version of his social theory set out in his '1859 Preface', it is surprising that more attention has not been paid to the lengthy formulation of historical materialism offered in his and Engels' *The German Ideology*, written between November 1845 and August 1846 (although mainly completed by April 1846) when the two men were in Brussels. Their aim in this work was to criticise contemporary German philosophy (the works of Feuerbach, Bruno Bauer and Max Stirner) and socialism ('True Socialism'), and through this critique to clarify their own ideas (CW 38: 50, 60). It was the social theory set out in *The German Ideology* which Engels was then to apply to the German Reformation, in his *Peasant War in Germany* (1850), a work whose historical analysis Abrams saw as more subtle even than Marx's much admired *Eighteenth Brumaire* (Abrams: 63), and to the Revolution of 1848 in his *Germany: Revolution and Counter-Revolution* (1851/52).

What was Engels' contribution to this work which, for the first time, set out the general theses of historical materialism in an explicit form? In 1847 and 1859, Marx was to refer to *The German Ideology* as a joint work by himself and Engels, but later commentators have differed in their assessments of Engels' role in its production (CW 6: 73, CPE: 22). Some have argued that, unlike *The Holy Family*, to which Marx and Engels contributed separate chapters, *The German Ideology* was 'in every sense a collective product' (Ilyichov *et al.*: 69). Fleischer even went so far as to say that the book's key chapter on Feuerbach, which sets out Marx and Engels' positive claims about history and social theory, was actually drafted by Engels (Fleischer: 33). However, the fact that most of the manuscript of *The German Ideology* is in Engels' handwriting is no guide to its authorship; Marx's own handwriting was notoriously illegible and unsuitable for delivery to the publisher.

On the other hand, writers such as Adams have minimised Engels' role in the production of the text (Adams: 181), whilst Rubel and Manale claim that at this date Engels was merely a disciple of Marx and was hardly capable of formulating the views expressed in *The German Ideology*. Yet, Rubel and Manale's own summary of *The German Ideology* bears a striking resemblance to many of the arguments which Engels had already advanced in *The Condition of the Working Class* (Rubel and Manale: 59-63).

Certainly, in a letter to Harney at the time of the composition of *The German Ideology*, as in his later reminiscences, Engels described himself and Marx composing their work together. In their correspondence of this period, the two men consistently referred to *The German Ideology* as 'our manuscripts' and 'our critique', in contrast to Marx's *The Poverty of Philosophy*, a polemic against Proudhon, which Engels always referred to as 'your book'. Indeed, Engels specifically gave Marx permission to use the material from 'our publication' (i.e. *The German Ideology*) in his attack on Proudhon (CW 38: 38, 75-6, 79, 109, 112, 134, 533, 638). Engels' knowledge of English conditions is certainly evident in *The German Ideology* (CW 5: 71, 401), but, as we shall see, his influence went far beyond providing such factual material.

HEGELIANISM AND FEUERBACH

The philosophical basis of *The German Ideology* was the critique of Hegel which Marx had developed in *The Holy Family*, i.e. that as a form of speculative idealism, Hegelianism inverted reality, presenting the development of human history as a logical succession of principles unfolding towards their teleological end (CW 4: 7, 59-60, 82, 159, 192). Engels himself had adopted this criticism of Hegelianism in the commentary on his translation of Fourier's 'Fragment on Trade', the only volume ever to appear of his and Marx's planned 'Library of the Best Foreign Socialist Writers' (CW 38: 25-7; CW 4: 667). He referred approvingly to Fourier's 'great hatred of philosophy' and criticised Hegel for producing a theory which 'arranges past history according to its liking', forcing historical development into the 'semblance of a trichotomy'. He was even more critical of the Young Hegelians: at least 'Hegel's speculative construction still made sense, even if it is turned upside-down', whereas that of later 'systems manufacturers no longer makes any sense at all' (CW 4: 641-2).

These arguments were developed in *The German Ideology*, which proclaimed its intention to offer a comprehensive criticism of the Hegelian system, rather than simply using one part of Hegel's works against another, as the Young Hegelians did. As in *The Holy Family*, Hegel's self-sufficient philosophy was criticised for presenting human history as the evolution of self-developing concepts, which progressed rationally towards a future which teleologically determined the present. By this means, the Hegelians could present whatever happened in history as an inevitable necessity, as a 'task' of

'History' as it ascended logically through its series of categories. In order to present history in this way, Hegelian philosophy had to begin not with research about 'real, active men' but rather with arbituary constructions which abstracted the ideas of each epoch from the empirical individuals who held them. These ideas were then said to represent the forms of the self-unfolding of the original idea so that history became the work of 'self-consciousness', or, in a slightly more empirical version, the work of the philosophers who came up with such ideas.

As a result of their idealism, the Hegelians could not go beyond reproducing the ideas of each epoch about itself, ideas which they transformed into the sole determining force behind human action: 'whilst in ordinary life every shopkeeper is very well able to distinguish between what somebody professes to be and what he really is, our historiography has not yet won this trivial insight. It takes every epoch at its word and believes that everything it says and imagines about itself is true.' Marx and Engels repeatedly argued that morality, metaphysics, religion and ideology 'have no history, no development' of their own, and could 'no longer retain the semblance of independence': it is 'not consciousness that determines life but life that determines consciousness.' As always, however, Marx and Engels were more generous to Hegel himself than they were to his followers (CW 5: 29, 36-7, 44-5, 55, 57, 59-62, 92, 144-5, 168, 176, 236, 269, 274-5, 282, 419, 434).

Above all, it was Stirner's philosophy of history which provided the main butt of Marx and Engels' critique of Hegelian system-mongering. Following Hegel (Hegel, 1956: 105-9), Stirner based his scheme on the stages of life through which the individual arrived at self-discovery: the 'realism' of childhood; the 'idealism' of youth; and the final negative unity of these two stages in the egoism of manhood. Stirner then transposed this development on to world history so that child, youth and man 'return "in various transformations" and in ever-widening circles until, finally, the entire history of the world of things and the world of the spirit is reduced to "child, youth, man".' Thus history is divided into three phases of development: the Negro, equated with childhood; the Mongol, equated with youth; and the Caucasian, equated with manhood. However, each of these three stages of development is repeated within the category of the Caucasian: the realism of the ancients represents childhood; the spiritualism of Christianity represents youth; and so on. Marx and Engels rejected this 'monotonous formalism', in which Stirners's own speculative idea became 'the driving force of history'. Stirner had thus replaced real historical development with illusory ideas; used empirical history only 'to provide body for these ghosts'; and presented actual historical individuals merely as concepts and categories which unfolded logically towards their goal (CW 5: 128-34, 159-60, 269, 274-5, 282, 287; Stirner: 43-9).

Ironically, in the light of the frequent accusations that Marx and Engels constructed a 'Procrustean bed' of history, an *a priori* construction to which historical facts have to be twisted in order to fit, *The German Ideology*, took as its main target those Hegelians who provided such philosophical schemes to which history had to be 'trimmed'. In particular, Marx and Engels criticised those such as Stirner who ended up writing illusory history because, like Hegel, they want 'everywhere to demonstrate the negation of the negation.' Against such idealist system-mongering and the empiricist 'collection of dead facts', Marx and Engels counterposed the 'study of the actual life-process and the activity of the individuals of each epoch' (CW 5: 37, 305).

The German Ideology attacked not only Hegelian social theory but also the political implications of Hegelian idealism which, despite the professed radicalism of the Young Hegelians, Marx and Engels saw as profoundly conservative. The Young Hegelians continued to see human existence in terms of self-consciousness; they thus reduced the world to categories which they overcame in the realm of thought, whilst leaving objective reality unchanged. The power of criticism, which Engels himself had once triumphantly hailed, was now seen as a substitute for effecting change in the real world. Bauer and the Young Hegelians may have destroyed the church and the state in the realm of thought, but in reality these institutions retained their power. Thus the point was not to fight against the illusions of consciousness, but rather to identify the real social agents who would destroy the material conditions which generated such illusions (CW 5: 24, 28, 54, 94).

In *The Holy Family*, Marx and Engels had praised Feuerbach's materialism as the means by which to escape from the realm of Hegelian speculation into the study of real man (CW 4: 139). Yet, a year later, both Marx and Engels prepared for their writing of *The German Ideology* by producing critiques of Feuerbach. Engels' theses do not rival Marx's in their scope but do reveal the extent to which he now wished to distance himself from Feuerbach whom he criticised for his passive adoration of nature, his sermons on the need to live up to the concept of 'Man', and his philosophical obscurity and banality. Anticipating *The German Ideology*, Engels argued that, despite its professed materialism, Feuerbach's work lapsed into an idealist history of philosophy where thought developed through its own internal needs (CW 5: 11-14)..

Far more significant was the Stirner-based critique of Feuerbach which Engels had offered in his letter to Marx of November 1844 (see pp. 49, 62 above), a letter which forms a crucial stepping stone towards the outlook of *The German Ideology*, in which Engels criticised Feuerbach for arriving at the concept 'Man' deductively, rather than through the empirical study of concrete individuals. This point was repeated by Engels in his theses of 1845, which criticised Feuerbach for claiming that the key task of modern times was the 'humanisation of God' and the 'negation of theology' (CW 38: 12; CW 5: 12).

These arguments were expanded upon in *The German Ideology*, where, in attacking Feuerbach for his inability to produce a genuine materialist history, Marx and Engels offered a critique of their own, earlier anthropogenetic selves. They argued that, rather than studying the forms of social intercourse which men entered into in their productive activity, Feuerbach's analysis of human relations dealt with men only in terms of their emotions, of love and friendship. Feuerbach thus converted the real empirical history of individuals into the unfolding of the category of 'Man', an Hegelian principle which progressed, through a stage of alienation, towards the full realisation of its 'essence', which constituted the consummation and goal of world history. Thus, Marx and Engels rejected both the abstract, ahistorical individuals of Stirner, and the abstract, universal category of 'Man', of Feuerbach, and called instead for a history of 'real living individuals' who, in 'developing their material production and their material intercourse, alter, along with this their actual world, also their thinking and the products of their thinking' (CW 5: 36-7, 39-41, 56-9, 88).

In *The German Ideology*, Marx and Engels employed the term 'materialism' to contrast their own claim, that the real premises of thought are the 'actual relations of the world', with the idealist conception that ideas enjoy an independent self-development. The 'materialistic view of the world' thus arrives at reality through empirical observation, rather than through the speculative constructions of philosophy: 'philosophy and the study of the actual world have the same relation to one another as onanism and sexual love.' In so far as Feuerbach *was* a materialist, he could offer no satisfactory account of human history since his materialism began, not with real, historical man, but rather with external Nature. He thus ignored the fact that the material world confronting humanity is not a given, which man encounters merely through passive contemplation, but is itself the product of previous human activity, of production, industry and commerce. In fact, nature in its pure sense no longer exists: 'the nature that preceded history, is not by any means the nature in which Feuerbach lives.' Thus, 'as far as Feuerbach is a materialist he does not deal with history, and so far as he considers history he is not a materialist' (CW 5: 37, 236, 434, 470, 486).

If a materialist history could not begin with the categories of 'Man' or of 'Nature', then still less did Marx and Engels accept Bauer's accusation that materialism worked from the concept of matter, which 'realised' itself in Nature. Just as *The Holy Family* had rejected the idea that 'Fruit' was a category which enjoyed an existence prior to specific fruits, so *The German Ideology* rejected the presentation of 'Matter' as a creative category which generated reality (CW 5: 105). Marx and Engels argued that their materialism neither deduced reality from the concept of matter, nor accepted Nature as an ahistorical given. Such materialism was thus nothing to do with the primacy of matter or of nature, even though Marx and Engels certainly believed that there had once been a nature which 'preceded human history'. What then did Marx and Engels mean by the historical 'materialism' which they advocated in *The German Ideology*?

HISTORICAL MATERIALISM: THE PRODUCTIVE FORCES AND THE FORMS OF SOCIAL INTERCOURSE

If the 'materialism' of *The German Ideology* functioned merely as a negative critique of Hegelian ontological idealism, and of the passive materialism of the eighteenth century, it would now be of little interest to social scientists. Of more interest are Marx and Engels' positive claims about the 'individuals and world conditions' which they regarded as the 'source' of ideas. The premise of Marx and Engels' historical materialism, and the basis of their materialist philosophy of history, was the conception of man as primarily a producer and of production as the basis of social, political and intellectual life: 'men can be distinguished from animals by consciousness, by religion or anything else you like. They begin to distinguish themselves from animals as soon as they begin to produce their means of subsistence' (CW 5: 31).

The first premise of human history, they claimed, is the production of the means to satisfy the basic needs (food, drink, housing and clothing) which are the preconditions for humans to 'make history'. The second premise is that the satisfaction of one need leads to the creation of new needs and so produces a self-conscious humanity which actively works upon the environment which confronts it. The third premise of human development is the reproduction of the species through the family which is, at first, 'the only social relation' but which later becomes a 'subordinate one'. These premises of human history are not consecutive stages of development, but rather constitute three 'moments' of existence whose influence continues to be felt to the present day. Finally, the production of life and the reproduction of the species involves the relations of man to nature and to other men; it is thus 'social' in the sense that it involves the co-operation of several individuals. 'It follows from this', Marx and Engels claimed, 'that a certain mode of production, or industrial stage, is always combined with a certain mode of co-operation, or social stage, and this mode of co-operation is itself a "productive force"' (CW 5: 31, 37, 41-3, 60).

Marx and Engels seem to have taken the term 'productive force' from Friedrich List's *The National System of Political Economy,* with which they were both familiar by early 1845. In List's work, 'productive forces' has the broad meaning of 'causes of wealth', so that it can include, for example, education, law and order, liberal government and so on (CW 3: 179; CW 4: 258-9, 266, 276-7, 284-6; Henderson, 1983: 177). Marx and Engels used the term in a more specific sense, to refer to the 'historically created' relation of man to nature. The productive forces thus include the raw materials given by nature (such as land and water) and the instruments of production created by civilisation, although, like modern Marxists, Marx and Engels were unsure as to whether the co-operative work relations needed to carry out such production should be included in the productive forces (CW 5: 32, 43, 46; Cohen, 1978: 113; Shaw: 25; McMurtry: 72; Miller, 1984, ch. 5; Sayer: 2-3; 25, Althusser and Balibar: 235).

The German Ideology refers to this 'material production of life' carried out through specific productive forces as society's 'mode of production', and claims that 'connected with and *created by* this mode of production' was a specific 'form of intercourse', i.e 'civil society in its various stages.' Later, however, Marx was also to use the term 'mode of production' to refer not just to society's productive forces, but rather to the combination of such productive forces with specific property relations; it is in this broader sense that modern Marxists usually use the term (CW 5: 53; Mishra).

The German Ideology thus claims that society's 'forms of intercourse', or social relations, 'corresponded to a definite stage of development of the productive forces.' Rents, profit and other forms of private property, for example, are the 'social relations corresponding to a definite stage of production' and could only be replaced by socialism when 'productive forces have been created for which private property becomes a restricting fetter.' Marx and Engels thus distinguished between, on the one hand, work relations, the division of labour within the production process, and, on the other, broader social relations, including class, or property, relations. Later, Marx and Engels were more normally to refer to such property relations as 'relations of production', although this phrase did appear in their work as early as *The German Ideology* (CW 5: 31-2, 40, 53-5, 63, 81-2, 195, 231, 355).

Given their claims for the primacy of the productive forces, it was logical for Marx and Engels to trace the evolution of specific forms of property, from prehistory to their own time, in terms of their correspondence to the growth of society's productive forces. However, whilst Marx and Engels *described* the slow pace and the unplanned nature of the development of society's productive forces, they made no attempt to *explain* this growth. Rather, as Engels had in *The Condition of the Working Class*, they merely assumed an inherent tendency of the productive forces to develop as the premise of their argument (CW 5: 82-3).

The first stage in the development of property was, they claimed, tribal property. This form of property 'corresponds to the undeveloped stage of production', where the division of labour is still very elementary, and social structure, in the form of the tribe, is an extension of the family. As the advance of society's productive forces is manifested, above all, in the growth of society's division of labour, eventually, the opposition of town and country appears. In this second stage of development, property takes the form of the communal property of the city-state (which, like the tribe, can own slaves). Eventually, however, this communal property is replaced by private property, including the citizen's individual ownership of slaves. Feudal property, based on the power of the nobility over the serfs in the countryside and the guild system in the towns, was the next form of property identified by Marx and Engels. It too was linked with the contemporary level of the productive forces, since its existence was 'determined by the restricted conditions of production the scanty and primitive cultivation of the land, and the craft type of industry', and by the correspondingly low development of the division of labour (CW 5: 32-5, 159).

For Marx and Engels, it was was the continued growth of society's productive forces, the intensification of the social division of labour, the appearance of separate classes of merchants and craftsmen, and urban specialisation in particular industries, which led to the development of capitalism. There was a growth of manufacturing outside the guild system, the emergence of movable capital and of a 'big bourgeoise', and the replacement of the guild-relations between master and journeyman, with the capitalist relationship between worker and employer. Finally, beginning in England, but spreading elsewhere, came the growth of large-scale industry which 'created everywhere the same relations between the clases of society'. In particular, as Engels had earlier claimed in *The Condition of the Working Class*, such large-scale industry 'created' the proletariat (CW 5: 64-74).

Marx and Engels' outline of historical development is often seen as a universally applicable account of social change in which society's relations of production are periodically cast aside as they come to fetter the progress of the productive forces (Bertrand: 152, 202). Kitching, however, has rejected this traditional interpretation. He argues that the scheme of historical development outlined in Marx's 'Preface' to *A Contribution to the Critique of Political Economy* (1859), the classic statement of historical materialism which draws heavily on *The German Ideology*, applies, 'at most', to the transition from feudalism to capitalism, and from capitalism to socialism, in western Europe (Kitching: 48-9; CPE: 20-2).

In fact, even in the 'Preface', Marx makes the 'universalist' claim that 'No social order is ever destroyed before all the productive forces for which it is sufficient have been developed' (CPE: 21). *The German Ideology*, is even more explicit in identifying a universalist 'coherence' in history which is based on the development of the productive forces and it the periodic fettering by society's forms of intercourse which thus made necessary a new form of intercourse 'corresponding to the more developed productive forces.' This friction between society's productive forces and its forms of intercourse formed the basis for Marx and Engels' theory of revolution, since such contradictions 'necessarily on each occasion burst out into a revolution' (CW 5: 74, 81-2).

A number of writers have argued that it is the primacy of class and of class struggle, rather than an emphasis on society's productive forces, which constitutes Marx's main contribution to the explanation of historical change (see, for example, Rosenberg: 11-13). Yet, as early as *The German Ideology*, Marx and Engels were quite explicit in their claims that class struggles, like battles of ideas, political conflicts and so on, were merely the '*subsidiary forms*' of the contradiction between society's productive forces and its social relations which have become fetters. 'Thus *all* collisons in history have their origin in the contradiction between the productive forces and the form of intercourse' (CW 5: 74, 81-2).

Similarly, Levine has rejected the claim that historical materialism identifies the basis of human history in its developing 'industrial' stages and argues that Marx emphasised the determining role of society's 'forms of ownership' (Levine, 1987). Yet, in *The German Ideology* at least, Marx and Engels frequently and explicitly claim that each 'form of ownership', or of property, is determined by the organisation of production and corresponds to a specific stage of development of the productive forces. Thus 'forms of ownership' do *not* enjoy an historical primacy but are seen as corresponding to the 'industrial stage' (CW 5: 43) through which man obtains his subsistence.

Nor can the blame for such views simply be laid at the feet of Engels. On the contrary, in 1857, Marx wrote to Engels, having received the latter's article on the 'Army' for the *New American Cyclopaedia*, that 'More graphically than anything else, the history of the army demonstrates the rightness of *our* views as to the connection between the productive forces and social relations' (CW 18: 85-126; CW 40: 186, emphasis added). Indeed, Marx had made this point as early as 1847, when, in illustrating his theory of social change with the analogy of military history, he had claimed that 'With the invention of a new instrument of warfare, firearms, the whole internal organization of the army necessarily changed; the relationships within which individuals can constitute an army and act as an army were transformed and the relations of different armies to one another also changed' (SW I: 89-90). The fact that *we* may prefer historical explanations based on the primacy of class, rather than of the productive forces, should not lead us assume that Marx and Engels must therefore have shared this preference.

BASE AND SUPERSTRUCTURE

The German Ideology did not only claim that the nature of society's forms of intercourse was determined by the level of development of its productive forces.

It also argued that, in turn, the productive forces and forms of intercourse determined the nature of society's political institutions, laws and forms of social consciousness. As a result of this description of society as consisting of a 'political and intellectual superstructure' which was determined by its 'economic base', Cold War critics of historical materialism attempted to portray historical materialism as nothing more than a form of simple economic reductionism (Carew-Hunt: 70, 77). Recent defences of Marxism have, therefore, tended to reject the metaphor of base and superstructure and have even put the responsibility for it on Engels, rather than on Marx (Colletti, 1972: 65; Rader: ch. 2; Sayer, 145).

Yet, in *The German Ideology*, Marx and Engels *did* frequently employ the metaphor of base and superstructure, along with a number of other similar metaphors, in order to convince their readers of their claims for the socio-economic determination of society's political institutions. Society's productive forces and its forms of intercourse, the 'economic conditions of society', are thus described as the 'basis of all history', a 'basis' which has been neglected by previous writers yet which 'in all ages' is 'the real basis of the state and remain so at all the stages at which division of labour and private property are still necessary.' Thus the productive forces and forms of intercourse are 'in no way created by the state power; on the contrary they are the power creating it' (CW 5: 53, 55, 89, 329, 355-6).

Similarly, *The German Ideology* employed the metaphor of base and superstructure to capture the relationship between society's economic conditions and its 'idealistic', or 'ideological', superstructure. Thus, all theoretical products and forms of consciousness, religion, philosophy, morality etc. etc.', are said to 'arise from' the 'basis' of history (i.e. the productive forces and forms of intercourse). All philosophical systems are 'based on the whole of the antecedent development of a nation, on the historical growth of its class relations with their political, moral, philosophical and other consequences' (CW 5: 53, 89, 373).

Marx and Engels also formulated their claims for the social primacy of society's economic conditions over its political institutions and forms of consciousness, through the metaphors of 'expression', 'correspondence' and 'reflection'. Thus property rights are said to be the 'legal and political expression' of society's economic conditions whilst the dominant ideas of an age are 'nothing more than the ideal expression of the dominant material relations' and ideology 'only an expression and symptom' of social relations. Similarly the state and ideas are said to 'correspond' to society's forms of property: the modern liberal state, for instance, corresponds to a 'developed bourgeoisie', whilst Protestantism is the form of consciousness 'corresponding to' the rise of capitalism. Finally, forms of consciousness are said to be the 'ideological reflexes and echoes' of man's material life-process (CW 5: 36, 52, 59, 90, 193, 196, 250, 356, 363, 410, 420, 463).

THE STATE

As early as his writings of 1843-44, Marx had criticised Hegelian social theory for inverting reality and presenting the state as the basis of society when, in fact, it was the family and civil society which were the 'premises of the state'. Bourgeois civil society thus provided the 'natural foundation on which the modern state rests, just as the civil society of slavery was the natural foundation on which the ancient state rested.' Marx thus *anticipated* Engels in the metaphor of property relations as society's 'foundation' as he did in the claim that the state is the 'expression' of social structure (CW 3: 8, 198-9).

Nevertheless, in general, Marx's early writings tend to emphasise the state as an alien power over society, a parasite which, as in the example of Prussia, ruled 'as a self-serving hierarchy of professional administrators' (Hunt I: 125; Callinicos, 1987a: 34; Maguire: 6). As we have seen, Engels' involvement in the English labour movement led to a rather different outlook, in which the state was seen as an 'organized coercive power in the hands of the dominant social class' (Hunt I: 125). Thus, by March 1844, Engels was arguing that, in England, it was property which ruled and that politics were now subservient to social life, an argument which was developed at length in *The Condition of the Working Class* where he claimed, as we have seen, that the English state was the bourgeoisie organised as a party (CW 3: 464, 497; CW 4: 567).

The German Ideology was to fuse both approaches, arguing for the social determination of political institutions, emphasising the extent to which the modern state was dominated by the capitalist class, and yet also specifying the social conditions which allowed the state the autonomy to pursue interests of its own (Hunt I: 127). It was this outlook which Engels was to rehearse in *The Origin of the Family, Private Property and the State* (1884) (Draper: 190). It thus makes little sense to contrast Marx's theory of the state with that of Engels' on the basis of Marx's writings of 1843 since Marx himself was, almost immediately afterwards, to synthesise his approach with that of Engels (Avineri, 1971: 203).

The German Ideology defined the state as an 'illusory community', a substitute for the real community within which the individual could obtain true freedom. Yet, the state is not just an illusion which can be wished away. Rather, it is based on real social ties, particularly those between the social classes, 'one of which dominates the others.' Through the state, the class relations which constitute the conditions of existence for specific productive forces receive their 'practical-idealistic expression'; the state thus expresses, in universal form, the will of the ruling class. It follows, therefore, that 'every revolutionary struggle is directed against the class which till then has been in power.' All political struggles within the state, such as those between democracy, aristocracy and monarchy or the struggle for the franchise, are thus 'merely the *illusory forms* ... in which the real struggles of the different classes are fought out amongst one another.' Each class which is seeking social domination must therefore 'first conquer political power in order to represent its interest ... as the general interest', and to replace the class which continues to retain state power even though its basis in the material production has been undermined (CW 5: 46/7, 52, 78, 83, 329, 348).

Ironically, in the light of the time which modern Marxists have devoted to the study of the 'relative autonomy' of the capitalist state, Marx and Engels' emphasis in *The German Ideology* was on the modern state's *lack* of autonomy and its subordination to the capitalist class. It is true, they argued, that, with the establishment of economic exchange as the basis of modern social relations and the creation of a pure form of private property, free from any vestiges of communal control, the state has become a 'separate entity, alongside and outside civil society.'

Nevertheless, despite this separation of economics and politics, the modern state is 'nothing more than the form which the bourgeois are compelled to adopt, both for internal and external purposes, for the mutual guarantee of their property and interests.' Thus in France, England and America, it is recognised that 'the state only exists for the sake of private property.' Marx and Engels thus explicitly rejected Stirner's claim that the modern state was a separate power, rivalling the socially dominant class. Instead, they saw the modern state as only being allowed as much power as the bourgeois requires for its own safety: 'bourgeois gain is quite independent of politics' but politics is 'entirely dependent on bourgeois gain.' Far from the state being independent of the bourgeoisie, 'the state has to beg from the bourgeoisie and in the end it is actually bought up by the latter' (CW 5: 90, 355/6, 359, 361).

Following the experience of France in the period 1848/52, Marx and Engels were to place more stress on the potential for autonomy enjoyed by the modern state, whilst by 1866 Engels saw such 'Bonapartist semi-dictatorship' as the norm for bourgeois society (SC: 166). However, even in *The German Ideology*, Marx and Engels recognised that their claim that the state is the form in which 'the whole civil society of an epoch is epitomised' need not mean that the state is simply an instrument of the economically dominant class, as they believed was the case under contemporary capitalism. On the contrary, they argued that particular social conditions could lead to a much greater autonomy for the state apparatus than that which they believed was typical in the modern capitalist state.

In particular, their analysis of absolutism stressed the 'abnormal independence' of the state in those societies where the estates were so evenly balanced that 'no section of the population can achieve dominance over the others'. Thus, the extent to which the interests of the state and the ruling class merged was the product of specific historical circumstances. *The German Ideology* did not merely assume that the state would be functional for the ruling class, but explained the varying degrees of this functionality in terms of the constraints imposed by particular social situations (CW 5: 90, 195, 200).

In his study of the 1848 Revolution in Germany, Engels was to apply this analysis to the Prussian and Austrian absolutisms of the nineteenth century. In Prussia, Frederick William IV was in total sympathy with the feudal elements of the state and thus aimed to restore, as completely as possible, the 'predominant social position of the nobility.' Yet, even Frederick, with his dream of creating an hierarchical society of estates headed by the nobility, aimed to balance these estates 'so nicely in power and influence, that a complete independence of action should remain to the king.' Similarly, in Austria, the government provided support for the feudal landowners against the peasantry and was crucial for the financial well-being of the 'stock-jobbing capitalists' and yet, as had always been 'the fundamental principle of absolute monarchies', it also used these two classes to balance each other 'so as to leave full independence of action to the government' (GRCR: 21-2, 33).

The Peasant War in Germany had less to say about the state than it did about ideology, partly because Germany in the time of Luther lacked a really effective centralised power. Engels' analysis thus tended to treat the German princes as a private class interest rather than as a public authority. He did, however, argue that the lack of a centralized political power was crucial for the success of the Swiss peasant rising of the sixteenth century, whereas, in Germany, 'the peasants managed to dispose of their local lords everywhere, but succumbed to the organized armies of the princes', which were lacking in Switzerland (PWG: 30-1, 72-3).

Despite their claim that that the modern state was the means which the bourgeoisie adopted for its 'internal and *external* purposes', Marx and Engels' analysis of the state centred, in practice, upon society's internal class relations. They saw the the state essentially as a guarantor of the property of the ruling class and explained its autonomy in terms of the balance of internal class forces. As a result historical materialism has frequently been criticised for its failure to emphasise the impact of foreign affairs, diplomacy, warfare, etc., on the nature and autonomy of the state (Taylor, 1986: 8; Skocpol: 22, 32; Giddens, 1981: 250).

Interestingly, in *The German Ideology*, Marx and Engels themselves anticipated the argument that their social theory ignores the historical importance of violence, conquest and war. For example, it is the Germanic tribes' conquest of the Roman empire which seems to explain the end of the Ancient world and the creation of a new, feudal organisation of society. Marx and Engels' reply to this argument was that such 'taking' is determined by the level of the productive forces of the conquerors and by the object taken: 'A banker's fortune, consisting of paper, cannot be taken at all without the taker's submitting to the conditions of production and intercourse of the country taken. Similarly the total industrial capital of a modern industrial country. And finally, everywhere there is very soon an end to taking, and where there is nothing more to take, you have to set about producing.' The form of community adopted by the conquerors would then 'correspond to the stage of development of the productive forces they find in existence', or 'it must change according to the productive forces.'

Finally, *The German Ideology* stressed that conquest did not spring from the blue but was itself socially determined. Thus for the barbarians, 'war itself is ... a regular form of intercourse which is the more eagerly exploited as the increase in population' puts pressure on society's existing productive forces and creates the need for new sources of wealth. Thus, for Marx and Engels, both the impetus to conquest and its social consequences were determined by the state of development of the productive forces reached by conquerors and conquered (CW 5: 34, 83-5).

IDEOLOGY

Marxists have tended to use the word 'ideology' either to refer to social consciousness in general or, more specifically, to those forms of social consciousness of which they disapprove and which they contrast with Marxist science (Rigby, 1987: 284). However, the 'ideology' referred to in the title of *The German Ideology* had an even more specific meaning, a meaning made clear when Marx and Engels claimed that 'in all ideology men and their relations appear upside down, as in a *camera obscura*.' 'Ideology' in this context refers not to social consciousness in general, as is often assumed, but specifically to the idealism of Hegel and the Young Hegelians, whose inversion of reality and abstraction of ideas from their connection with man's productive and social activity formed, as we have seen, the main target of Marx and Engels' polemic (CW 5: 30, 36, 61, 107-9, 126; Heath: 2).

However, by 1845-46, Marx and Engels had also developed the theory which is now more usually associated with the term 'ideology', namely that specific forms of social consciousness are associated with specific social groups and, in particular, that the ideas propagated by the ruling class serve to legitimise its rule and to obscure the true nature of society. As one of the most frequently quoted passages in *The German Ideology* put it, 'the ideas of the ruling class are in every epoch the ruling ideas: i.e., the class which is the ruling material force of society is at the same time its ruling intellectual force.' The existence of a specialised class of intellectuals, which is itself the social basis for the idealism of philosophers, does create the potential for a 'certain opposition and hostility' between the ruling class and those thinkers who 'make the formation of the illusions of the class about itself the chief source of their livelihood.' Nevertheless, whenever the ruling class is threatened it closes ranks and the class origin of the ruling ideas becomes apparent once more (CW 5: 59-60).

Marx and Engels argued that the ideology of the ruling class worked by presenting its 'particular interests as universal interests', but this did not mean that those thinkers who produced such ruling class ideology were involved in a conscious deception. For instance, those philosophers (such as Holbach), whose theories expressed the interests of the emerging bourgeoisie, quite sincerely believed that the establishment of the conditions suitable for the growth of capitalism were also those which would be most conducive to 'the full development of individuals'. This illusion was, during the rise of the bourgeoisie, philosophically justified because the victory of this class meant the further growth of society's productive forces and involved the smashing of the feudal fetters to the development of the individual. However, once the rule of the bourgeoisie was established, its social theory, as exemplified by its political economy, became, as Engels had already argued, a 'mere apologia for the existing state of affairs, an attempt to prove that under existing conditions the mutual relations of people today are the most advantageous and generally useful' (CW 5: 44-5, 59-60, 180, 290, 410-14).

The claim that 'the ideas of the ruling class are in every epoch the ruling ideas' can be interpreted in 'stronger' or 'weaker' forms. In its weaker, or descriptive, version, Marx and Engels' claim would simply mean that the ideas of the ruling class are in every epoch the *official* ideas of the age. Such ideas are the ones which dominate in the press, literature, education and so on, since 'the class which has the means of material production at its disposal, consequently also controls the means of mental production' (CW 5: 59).

However, in its stronger, or explanatory, form, Marx and Engels' claim could also be seen to mean that since the ruling class enjoys a monopoly of mental production, so 'the ideas of those who lack the means of mental production are, on the whole, subject to' the ruling class who possess such means of mental production (CW 5: 59). In this century, many Marxists have fallen back on the effects of such a hegemonic, 'dominant ideology', which incorporates the working class into capitalism, as an explanation of the failure of the western proletariat to carry out the revolutionary tasks which *The German Ideology* ascribed to it (Abercrombie, *et al*: ch. 1).

Yet, ironically, in *The German Ideology*, Marx and Engels themselves criticised their opponents for the belief that 'the rule of a certain class is only the rule of certain ideas.' Similarly, Engels, in a letter of October 1846, criticised Feuerbach for the latter's belief that 'it is opinion, the fear of public opinion, of laws and of other ideas which now holds the world together.' For

Marx and Engels, the appearance of revolutionary ideas which can effectively challenge the dominance of the ruling class required the existence of a revolutionary class and such a class could only emerge when society's productive forces came into conflict with its forms of intercourse. Only then, when the ruling class itself is divided, and class conflict becomes particularly intense, is the traditional ideology of the ruling class exposed as false. It is, however, precisely during such periods, when the ruling class is most under attack, that this ideology is more virulently expressed than ever (CW 5: 52, 60/1, 292, 413; CW 38: 78).

Thus, rather than the power of ideology explaining the persistence of the rule of a particular class, Marx and Engels' analysis was intended to show that it was the dominance of a particular class which explained the persistence of ideology. Such class dominance was, in turn, to be explained by its suitability for the development of material production rather than by the power of social consciousness.

It was the account of ideology set out by Marx and Engels in 1845/46 which was to form the basis of Engels' analysis in *The Peasant War in Germany* where his aim was to present the political and religious controversies of the German Reformation 'as a reflection of the contemporary class struggles'. Such ideological struggles were to be seen 'not as causes but as results of the stages of development of agriculture, industry, land and waterways, commerce in commodities and money then obtaining in Germany' (PWG: 7/8, 27). Engels thus criticised 'the German ideology' which could see 'nothing except violent theological bickering in the struggles that ended the middle ages', and so accepted unquestioningly 'all the illusions that an epoch makes about itself, or that ideologists of some epoch make about that epoch.' Such ideologists had no idea that the religious wars of the sixteenth century 'involved positive material interests'. The religious wars were thus 'class wars', just like the revolutions of 1649 in England and of 1789 in France, even if their class conflicts were 'clothed in religious shibboleths' and 'concealed behind a religious screen' (PWG: 41/2; Bak: 89/116).

Yet, despite his explicit claim that he was attempting to present religious beliefs as the 'expressions' or 'reflections' of social interest and that he saw such beliefs as 'effects' rather than as 'causes', Engels could not, in practice, avoid showing that such ideologies also had an historical force and effect of their own. He argued, for instance, that, given the economic and political decentralisation of Germany and the complexity of its social structure, it was 'politicio/religious ideas' which welded the numerous social groups into three main political camps: the reactionary Catholic camp; the reformist Lutheran camp; and the revolutionary camp (PWG: 40/1).

In general, Engels saw the Catholic camp as drawing support from the Imperial authorities, the higher ecclesiastics, some of the lay princes, the richer nobility, the prelates and the city patricians; the Lutheran camp as based on the lesser nobility and burghers; and the revolutionary camp as expressing the demands of the peasants and the urban plebians. Nevertheless, he also laid great emphasis on the complexity of alignments and allegiances so that, in different regions of Germany, a particular estate might find itself in different camps. Furthermore, particular estates might find themselves pulled in opposite directions. The lay princes, for instance, had an interest in order, which drove them into the arms of the Catholic party; yet they would also benefit by the opportunity to seize church property and to assert themselves against the Imperial authorities, which might lead them to join the Lutheran camp.

Engels thus saw Christianity as a very malleable ideological raw material, which each class could put to its own uses. The Bible could be invoked by Luther to justify the obedience of the subject to their prince and the continuation of serfdom; by the revolutionary peasants to legitimise their resistance to the princes, nobility and clergy; and even, by Munzer, to provide a vision of an egalitarian, communist future (PWG: 43/5, 52, 56).

Yet, despite the sophistication of much of Engels' analysis, he did at times lapse into a rather cynical view of the motivations at work in the conflicts of the Reformation. In attempting to demystify ideological illusions and to reveal their social basis, Engels sometimes presented them simply as conscious deceptions practised by those who wished to secure some ulterior social purpose. Thus he referred to Munzer's revolutionary propaganda as having a dual form and effect: 'on the one hand, on the people, whom he addressed in the only language they could comprehend, that of religious prophecy, and on the other hand, on the initiated, to whom he could disclose his ultimate aims.' Munzer was therefore using religious phraseology as a cloak 'behind which the new philosophy had to hide for some time', although he 'obviously took the biblical cloak much less in earnest than many a disciple of Hegel does in modern times' (PWG: 55).

In general, however, Engels managed to avoid such cynicism about the ideological forms in which the people of the sixteenth century fought out their social conflicts, and presented them as genuinely shared by those who expounded them. That social interests were expressed in religious form was, he claimed, 'easily explained by the conditions of the time'. In particular, the church's monopoly of intellectual production and education, which it used to offer a 'general sanction of the existing feudal domination', meant that 'all the generally voiced attacks against feudalism, above all the attacks against the church, and all revolutionary social and political doctrines had mostly and simultaneously to be theological doctrines. The existing social relations had to be stripped of their halo of sanctity before they could be attacked' (PWG: 41/2, 61).

It was thus the church which acted as the 'bearer' of the dominant 'medieval feudal ideology'. After all, the churchmen, or at least the prelates, 'were either imperial princes themselves, or reigned as feudal lords' with extensive lands and tenants of their own whom they exploited as did other feudal landlords. Yet, as *The German Ideology* had noted, the existence of a specialised group of intellectuals within the ruling class also meant that 'a certain opposition and hostility' could develop within this class. Thus, despite the ideological defence of feudal relations offered by the clergy, 'the knight regarded the arrogant clergy of the day as an entirely superfluous Estate and envied them their large possessions and the wealth held secure by their celibacy and the church statutes.' However, when the ruling class is seriously challenged by social unrest from below, such ideologists could be expected to rally to the support of its class. Thus Luther, whose revolutionary ardour had initially helped to set in motion the risings of the peasants and plebians, was appalled by the consequences of his own teaching and moved first to a renunciation of violence and then, as the Peasants' War spread even to Protestant regions, to a call for the violent suppression of the rebels (CW 5: 59-60; PWG: 32-3, 42, 48-52).

CONCLUSION: PRAGMATOLOGICAL HISTORICAL MATERIALISM

Modern interpretations of Marxism have been dominated by the impact of the discovery of Marx's *Paris Manuscripts* with their powerful critique of the alienating effects of capitalist society. The attractiveness of this humanist Marxism, in a century in which totalitarian 'Marxism' has had such nightmarish effects has, however, blinded many readers to the fact that, almost as soon as the *Paris Manuscripts* had been written, their anthropogenetic conception of historical change was subject to a powerful critique by Marx and Engels themselves.

Marx and Engels were to retain their humanist moral ideals throughout their lives. Nevertheless, in *The German Ideology*, they replaced their earlier, Hegelian conception of history as a teleological process of 'humanisation' with a pragmatological historical materialism which, to a large extent, consisted of a synthesis of the critique of Hegelian idealism offered by Marx in *The Holy Family* with the sociological analysis developed by Engels in *The Condition of the Working Class*. It was this pragmatological version of historical materialism which formed the basis for the sketch of capitalist development offered by Marx and Engels in the *Communist Manifesto*, and which provided the foundation of Engels' analysis of the German Revolutions of the sixteenth and the nineteenth centuries.

This conception of history as 'nothing but the activity of man pursuing his aims' (CW 4: 93) did not, however, mean that Engels saw history simply as a product of individual will. On the contrary, his explanation of the 1848 Revolution was dismissive of the 'superstition which attributed revolutions to the ill will of a few agitators. Everyone knows nowadays that wherever there is a revolutionary convulsion, there must be some social want in the background, which is prevented, by outworn institutions from satisfying itself' (GRCR: 9-10; see also PWG: 47, 62). Similarly, in his analysis of Munzer, Engels concluded, in a passage which to the modern reader seems pregnant with the anticipation of future events, that 'The worst thing that can befall a leader of an extreme party is to be compelled to take over a government at a time when society is not yet ripe for the domination of the class he represents' (PWG: 46, 115-17). Thus, in Engels' pragamatological historical writings, events were explained, as in Marx's formulation from *The Eighteenth Brumaire*, in terms of men making their own history 'but under circumstances directly encountered, given and transmitted from the past' (SW I: 247).

Krieger has argued that although *The Eighteenth Brumaire* opens with one of the classic statements of pragamatological historical materialism, this work in fact represents Marx's abandonment of the pragamatological outlook of his *Class Struggles in France* (and of Engels' *Peasant War* and *Revolution and Counter-Revolution*) and his adoption of a new outlook in which historical actors become the puppets of the unfolding of the pre-appointed ends of 'History' (Krieger, 1953: 403). Thus despite its pragamatological opening, *The Eighteenth Brumaire* concludes with a reification of the process of 'Revolution' into a subject which 'does its work methodically', perfecting the parliamentary power 'in order to' be able to overthrow it, then perfecting the executive power, 'in order to' concentrate all its forces of destruction against it (SW I: 332). In fact, similar passages are also to be found in Marx's *The Class Struggles in France* (SW I: 139), where both the pragamatological and the teleological outlooks can be found side by side within the same work.

In this period, Engels too came close to presenting history as a process apart from human agency, the very outlook which he himself had criticised at the moment of birth of historical materialism (CW 4: 93). Thus, in a a letter to Marx of February 1851, written in the period between the composition of *The Peasant War* and *Revolution and Counter-Revolution*, he argued that 'A revolution is a purely natural phenomenon which is subject to physical laws rather than the rules that determine the development of society in ordinary times. Or rather, in a revolution, these rules assume a much more physical character, the material force of necessity makes itself more strongly felt. And as soon as one steps forward as the representative of a party, one is dragged into this whirlpool of irresistible natural necessity' (CW 38: 290).

Nevertheless, in practice, Engels' historical works of the period 1850-52 continued to explain events in pragamatological terms, through the actions of individuals and classes in the context of specific economic, political and superstructural constraints. As we shall see (chapter ten, below), it was only long afterwards that Engels was to expound, at length, the 'nomological' conception of history as a law-bound process, at which he had first hinted in his letter of 1851.

CHAPTER FIVE

Communism: practical materialism

> For the *practical* materialist, i.e. the *communist*, it is a question of revolutionising the existing world, of practically coming to grips with and changing the things found in existence' (Marx and Engels, 1845/46. CW 5: 38/9, original emphasis).

THE PRODUCTIVE FORCES AND PROLETARIAN REVOLUTION

Nowhere in *The German Ideology* do Marx and Engels use the phrase 'scientific socialism', the term which they later used to distinguish their beliefs from the 'Utopian' socialism which, as Marx put it, 'wants to attach the people to new delusions, instead of limiting its science to the knowledge of the social movement made by the people itself' (FIA: 337). Nevertheless, it was only a small step from *The German Ideology*'s claim that communism was not 'an *ideal* to which reality will have to adjust itself' but rather 'the *real* movement which abolishes the present state of things' (CW 5: 49), to Marx's comment, made a year later in *The Poverty of Philosophy*, that 'just as the economists are the scientific representatives of the bourgeois class, so the Socialists and the Communists are the theoreticians of the proletarian class.' With the development of the productive forces and of the class struggle under capitalism, these theoreticians 'have only to take note of what is happening before their eyes and to become its mouthpiece.' Science then ceases to be doctrinaire and becomes revolutionary (CW 6: 177/8).

Thus, while Marx and Engels may not have had the *term* 'scientific socialism' in 1845/46, they certainly had the *concept*. This conception of socialism was nothing to do with the philosophy of dialectical materialism or the 'dialectics of nature' which Marx and Engels were later to develop and with which the phrase 'scientific socialism' is often now associated. Rather, in *The German Ideology*, as in *The Poverty of Philosophy*, they distinguished their communism from the fantasies of the Utopians and the idealism of Hegelian socialism by claiming that it was based on 'real, positive science, the expounding of the practical activity, of the practical process of the development of men' (CW 5: 37/9). They legitimated their political beliefs by presenting them not merely as another philosophical or ethical scheme but rather as an expression of the real historical movement of modern society.

Marx and Engels thus presented their prediction of revolution as the necessary 'conclusion' of their social theory, in particular of their account of the functional relationship between society's productive forces and its forms of intercourse. In this perspective, private property constituted a form of intercourse *necessary* for certain stages of development of the productive forces. It followed, therefore, that private property could not be abolished until the productive forces had been created for which private property was a restrictive fetter. Writing in 1845/46, Marx and Engels believed that capitalism had already arrived at this stage of development. Private property had, they claimed, become 'just as much a fetter as the guild system had been for manufacture.' It was as a result of this belief that they argued that 'at the present time individuals *must* abolish private property' (CW 5: 52/3, 73, 355, 439).

It was the growth of the productive forces which had pride of place in Marx and Engels' prediction of revolution since, they argued, the extent to which people can win their freedom is 'dictated and permitted not by their ideal of man but by their existing productive forces.' It was not merely the 'will' of the oppressed and exploited classes which would bring about communism. So long as society's productive forces had not developed to the point where capitalist competition had become superfluous, 'the classes which are ruled would be wanting the impossible if they had the "will" to abolish' it. Until such material conditions were brought into being, the *idea* of revolution was irrelevant: the proletariat could only abolish modern society 'on the basis of the existing productive forces.' This development of the productive forces was not only essential for the immediate possibility of communist revolution, but also for the longer term success of the new society since, without this 'absolutely necessary practical premise of communism', 'want is merely made general, and with want the struggle for necessitites would begin again and all the old filthy business would necessarily be restored' (CW 5: 4, 49, 54, 211, 329/30, 431).

This emphasis on the material preconditions necessary for revolution did not, however, mean that *The German Ideology* discounted the role of class conflict and of revolutionary consciousness in the transition to communism. On the contrary, Marx and Engels argued that, as society's productive forces clash with its forms of intercourse and the contradictions between the social classes reach their extreme limit, there emerges 'the consciousness of the necessity of a fundamental revolution.' As in *The Condition of the Working Class*, it was the concept of class/interests and needs which provided the connecting link between the objective, material preconditions for revolution and the consciousness and human agency needed to bring the revolution about. Marx and Engels assumed that the proletariat would arrive at such a consciousness in a relatively straightforward way as the product of its struggles against the bourgeoisie. They argued that the Welsh Chartist rising of 1839 and the English rising of 1842 showed that the experience of strikes would lead the workers to act in a revolutionary way. Political agitation would also help to encourage the emergence of a revolutionary consciousness amongst the proletariat. An appeal to the workers' 'rights', for instance, would play a part in the 'long process of development' through which the proletariat 'take shape as "they", as a revolutionary, united mass' (CW 5: 52, 204-5, 323, 378, 439).

Members of other classes, such as the intelligentsia, could arrive at a revolutionary consciousness through the contemplation of the position of the proletariat in modern society. Nevertheless, Marx and Engels were rather scathing about the need for the proletariat to turn to intellectuals for advice about the meaning of their own movement or about what should be done in their war against the bourgeoisie (CW 5: 52, 204-5).

However, whilst Marx and Engels emphasised that the formation of a revolutionary mass was a necessary condition of successful revolution, they also argued, in turn, that this revolutionary mass would itself be the product of the the growth of large-scale industry. *The German Ideology* thus repeated Engels' claims in *The Condition of the Working Class* that, even though the workers excluded from modern industry experienced the worst living standards, it was those workers in the most industrialised branches of capitalist production who provided the leadership of the proletarian movement and of communist uprisings (CW 4: 324, 433, 498; CW 5: 74 543, 73-4, 220). Thus both the existence of a revolutionary class and the possibility of its success were, for Marx and Engels, dependent upon the stage of development reached by the productive forces. This perspective, along with Engels' warnings about the dangers of premature revolution set out in *The Peasant War*, thus provided the basis for Kautsky's attacks on the Bolsheviks' seizure of power in Russia in 1917, which he saw as an act of revolutionary will which ignored the stage of development of the productive forces needed to build socialism (Geary: 80-3).

Finally, in arguing that the success of communism required a certain level of development of society's productive forces, *The German Ideology* rejected the possibility of the achievement of 'socialism in one country.' Marx and Engels argued, in 1845-46, that communism was 'only possible as the act of the dominant peoples "all at once" and simultaneously.' They were optimistic, however, that the spread of capitalism, the development of the productive forces and the growth of a world market were creating the conditions which would make such a revolution possible and thus allow the proletariat to realise its 'world-historic' existence. Nevertheless, this did not mean that a uniform level of development of the productive forces was necessary in all countries in order for such an international revolution to occur. On the contrary, competition on the world market could produce economic crisis, and thus the conditions needed for proletarian revolution, even in those countries such as Germany which lagged behind England in their industrial development (CW 5: 49, 74-5).

THE CRITIQUE OF CAPITALISM

It would, in theory be possible to be persuaded by Marx and Engels' arguments for the inevitability of communism even if one were opposed to a communist society and wished to delay its advent for as long as possible. In practice, of course, only those already convinced of the desirability of communism are likely to believe in its inevitability. But why, if communism represented the class standpoint of the proletariat, should intellectuals find communism desirable and thus agitate amongst the proletariat as Marx and Engels were doing at the same time as they were writing *The German Ideology*? Why, if communism was not a matter of preaching morality but of class interest, did Engels, in works from *The Condition of the Working Class* (1845) to *The Housing Question* (1872) and beyond, so forcefully express his indignation at the injustice, oppression and suffering produced by capitalist society (SW II: 608-10)?

The answer to such questions is, of course, that, even after 1845-46, Marx and Engels did not see communism as merely representing the standpoint of a particular class. Rather, they continued to offer a broader critique of capitalism in terms of its anti-human effects and saw communism as the only means of overcoming such effects. Thus, although *The Condition of the Working Class*, *The Holy Family* and *The German Ideology* mark a break in the development of Marx and Engels' social theory and their abandonment of Hegelian teleological explanation in history, the two men remained committed to a moral critique of modern society. In practice, they continued to argue, as they had in their explicitly Hegelian works, that under capitalism, Man's own products confront him as alien powers and that such powers could only be restored to Man's conscious control through the creation of an alternative, communist society.

In *The German Ideology*, Marx and Engels' critique of capitalism laid particular emphasis on the alienating effects of the division of labour of modern society which, they claimed, enslaved the individual within a specialised sphere of activity, a sphere which becomes 'a material power above us.' Under such conditions even our own passions confront us as 'an alien power' since 'if the circumstances in which the individual lives allow him only the one-sided development of one quality at the expense of all the rest ... then this individual achieves only a one-sided, crippled development' (CW 5: 262).

In communist society, by contrast, 'where nobody has one exclusive sphere of activity but each can become accomplished in any branch he wishes, it is possible for me to do one thing today and another tomorrow.' Communism thus does away with 'labour', the negative, stunting form of human activity, and replaces it with 'free activity', 'the creative manifestation of life arising from the free development of all abilities' of the individual. 'This free development was not merely the attainment of a negative 'freedom *from*' but rather the realisation of a positive 'freedom *to*', a freedom whose extent was, as in all historical eras, 'dictated and permitted ... by the existing productive forces.' As in Hegel's vision of a future realm of freedom, Marx and Engels' vision of a communist society which 'stimulates the real development of the abilities of the individual' is one which is 'under the control of the individuals themselves.' As a result, the clash between the particular interest and the general interest, where the general interest confronts individuals 'as an interest "alien" to them', would also be overcome (CW 5: 47, 52, 87, 225, 262, 292, 305-8, 431).

Marx and Engels thus retained many of the moral criticisms of capitalism which they had offered in their earlier writings, criticisms which, as before, grounded themselves in the concept of an authentic human existence whose realisation was frustrated by modern society. Indeed, *The German Ideology* specifically repeated Engels' previous criticism of Feuerbach that the latter, by claiming that 'what my essence is, is my being', offered a conservative defence of the existing state of things: millions of proletarians 'think quite differently and will prove this in time when they bring their "being" into harmony with their "essence" by means of a revolution.' The essence of, say, a fish 'is its "being", water ... but the latter ceases to be the "essence" of the fish and is no longer a suitable medium of existence as soon as the river is made to serve industry, as soon as it is polluted with dyes and other waste products.' Similarly the 'being' of a seven year old as a door-keeper in a coal-mine for fourteen hours a day does not necessarily correspond with his 'essence' (CW 5: 13, 58, 262).

However, Marx and Engels also emphasised that whilst material circumstances had not developed to the point which made communist society possible, then 'no moral preaching avails.' What has misled some commentators is that, as Fleischer has pointed out, Marx and Engels' rejection of moralising becomes, at times, a rejection of morality itself, resulting in an 'anti-normative misrepresentation of the self' (Fleischer: 24). In practice, however, Marx and Engels remained committed to a moral critique of capitalism, and to the vision of an ethically superior future; what they rejected was the belief that moral exhortation and outrage were, in themselves, enough to bring this future into being.

That communism, however morally superior it was, would be achieved only through the class-struggle of the proletariat, was the essence of the critique of contemporary German 'True Socialism' offered in *The German Ideology* and, in particular, in an addendum to this text written by Engels. This critique repeated the scathing comments about Hegelian socialism which Engels had made in his commentary on Fourier's 'Fragment on Trade', where he had argued that German socialism had taken over the worst aspects of English and French socialism, its 'schematic plans for future society', whilst ignoring its best aspect, 'the criticism of existing society' and the 'investigation of social questions' (CW 4: 614). The True Socialists thus detached the communist systems of the French and English which 'spring from the practical needs, the conditions of life in their entirety of a particular class in a particular country', and forced them into an arbitrary connection with German philosophy. They replaced concern for 'real human beings' with the abstraction of 'Man', and so substituted revolutionary enthusiasm with 'the universal love of mankind' (CW 5: 455-7, 574; CW 38: 109-10).

Thus when Marx and Engels criticised Grün and the True Socialists for presenting '"man", "pure genuine man", as the ultimate purpose of world history' and the human essence as the 'measure of all things', their real target was not the concept of an authentic human essence, since, in practice, they themselves retained this concept. Rather, their target was True Socialism's idealistic teleology, its failure to identify the agency which would bring about socialism, and its replacement of the analysis of 'the real development of society' with metaphysical abstractions (CW 5: 470, 476, 486). Marx and Engels thus offered a powerful critique of the inadequacies of Utopian moralising and rightly insisted that *if* communism was to be established, it had to have a material basis in social reality. The problem with this argument was not its internal coherence, but rather that reality itself was to fail to create this basis, without which Marx and Engels' socialism was just as 'Utopian' as any other. We shall return to this problem in chapter nine, below.

ENGELS AND THE MAKING OF *THE COMMUNIST MANIFESTO*

Although it had no impact on its first appearance, *The Communist Manifesto* (1848) has since become the most famous and accessible statement of Marxism. What was Engels' contribution to this classic work which was published, at least after its anonymous first edition, under both of their names? Although Marx and Engels themselves referred to the *Manifesto* as their joint production, Engels, as usual, gave Marx the credit for its central ideas (CM: 54, 62). Inevitably, however, later writers have differed in their assessments of the relative contributions of the two men. Struik's emphasis is on the extent to which the 'Principles of Communism', Engels' draft version of the *Manifesto*, anticipated many of the leading ideas of the *Manifesto* itself (Struik: 60). Yet, as early as 1901, Andler argued that Marx and Engels' differences on issues such as the effects of mechanisation and the nature of the coming revolution helped to explain the incoherence of parts of the *Manifesto* (Jacoby: 55; Andler: 104-14, 129-39).

More recently, Lichtheim and McLellan have claimed that the outlook Engels expressed in works such as *Anti-Dühring* (1878) was in evidence as early as the 'Principles of Communism' and that, even at this early date, his perspective was 'significantly different' from that of Marx. They counterpose Engels' determinism, emphasis on technology, Enlightenment optimism and conception of communism as the liberation of the productive forces against Marx's stress on subjective agency, emphasis on class, awareness of the catastrophic nature of progress, and his vision of communism as a transformation of human and social nature (Lichtheim, 1971a: 58-61; McLellan, 1976: 180). How, then, was the *Manifesto* written? What was Engels' contribution to its production? Did the views Engels expressed in his 'Principles of Communism' differ significantly from those of the *Manifesto*?

In 1847, Marx and Engels joined the League of the Just, an association of German workers, with branches or contacts in France, England, Germany, Switzerland, Sweden and America. At its congress in London, in June 1847, the League changed its name to the Communist League and discussed the publication of a 'Communist Credo'. A draft of this Credo, consisting of twenty-two questions and answers (the 'Draft of a Communist Confession of Faith'), was drawn up by Engels, who, unlike Marx, was present at the congress, although it is not clear exactly how and when this 'Draft' was written (CW 6: 96-103, 585, 589-600, 607-13; SW 2: 315; McLellan, 1976: 179).

The 'Draft' was then circulated to the local 'communities' of the League, for comments. Moses Hess compiled his own 'delightfully amended' (as Engels sarcastically put it) 'Credo', which was discussed by the Paris communists. In the light of the criticisms which Engels made of Hess's 'Credo', the Parisian communists then requested him to draw up his own version. This document, the 'Principles of Communism', which was over three times the length of the original 'Draft' (much of which it incorporated), was written in October 1847. It was then taken by Engels for discussion at the second congress of the League, which was held in London from 29 November 1847 (CW 38: 138, 178; CW 6: 341-57).

However, even before the second congress met, Engels seems to have assumed that Marx himself would help prepare a further improved draft of the 'Credo' since he wrote to Marx saying 'Give a little thought to the Confession of Faith.' He suggested that they abandon the catechismal form of the first two drafts and that they should 'call the thing Communist *Manifesto*.' Both Marx and Engels attended the second congress where they were commissioned to draw up a manifesto for the League. The two men then returned to Brussels in mid-December 1847, where Engels remained until the end of the month. However, Engels then returned to Paris, whilst Marx continued to work on the *Manifesto* until the end of January 1848 when it was sent to the publishers (CW 38: 149; SW 2: 315; CW 6: 477-519; Ilyichov et al: 108).

The degree to which Engels himself composed the original 'Draft of a Communist Confession of Faith' is, as we have seen, unclear. Certainly, the 'Draft' contains a number of concessions to the Utopian socialist sensibilities of many members of the League. For instance, it argued that communism did not only arise from the development of the productive forces generated by capitalism, but also from 'certain irrefutable basic principles' whch exist 'in the consciousness or feeling of every individual'. Such principles, which were said to 'require no proof', included the fact that 'every individual strives to be happy' and that 'the happiness of the individual is inseparable from the happiness of all.' This perspective was rather different from that of the 'Principles', where Engels abandoned many of his earlier concessions to Utopianism and presented communism as 'the doctrine of the conditions for the emancipation of the proletariat' (CW 6: 96, 341, 597-8, 641, 684). What then was the relationship between Engels' 'Principles' and the *Manifesto*?

Certainly, in its plan, the *Manifesto* owes much to the 'Principles', although these similarities are often obscured by the question and answer format of Engels' text. The *Manifesto* is divided into four sections which follow the same order as that of Engels' 'Principles'. The first section, corresponding to questions one to fifteen of the 'Principles', gives an account of the rise of capitalism, and prophesies the forthcoming victory of the proletariat over the bourgeoisie. The second section of the *Manifesto* (questions sixteen to twenty-three of the 'Principles') defines the position of the communists in relation to the proletariat, deals with various bourgeois objections to communism (such as the claim that the communists wish to abolish the family and nationality), and sets out a series of measures which a proletarian government would be obliged to undertake to wrest power from the bourgeoisie. The third section (question twenty-four of the 'Principles') analyses contemporary socialism, which it divides into reactionary, conservative and Utopian forms. The final section (question twenty-five of the 'Principles') defines the position of the communists in relation to the existing parties of the working class (CW 6: 341-57; 477-519).

Do the *Manifesto* and the 'Principles' differ in their content? As Lichtheim and McLellan point out, Engels' text certainly exhibited an Enlightenment belief in progress, praising the rise of the world-market for bringing the 'semi-barbarian' Orient, which had stood 'outside historical development', into the flow of world history. Yet, the *Manifesto* too is famous for its eulogy of the progress achieved by the bourgeoisie, referring to its success in overcoming 'rural idiocy' and in drawing all nations, 'even the most barbarian', into civilisation (CW 6: 345, 488). On the other hand, despite his emphasis on progress in the 'Principles', Engels had already, in *The Condition of the Working Class in England*, shown his awareness of the catastrophic effects entailed by industrialisation, an awareness apparent too in the 'Principles' whose description of the social ills of capitalism anticipate those of the *Manifesto* (CW 6: 346/8, 489/90).

It is also true that, as Lichtheim argues, Engels places great emphasis on technology and its impact on social relations. Thus the 'Principles' repeated the claim made in *The Condition of the Working Class* that it was the massive growth of society's productive forces since the Industrial Revolution which had created regularly recurring crises of over/production and encouraged the polarisation of society into bourgeoisie and proletariat. However, as Engels optimistically concluded, this expansion of society's productive capacity had also brought into being the conditions which had made possible the abolition of private property and the creation of a new social order based on the social planning of production for the general good (CW 6: 341/8).

Yet, it is also true that Marx's *Manifesto* itself places great emphasis on the impact of machinery, chemistry, steam/navigation, railways, electric tel/ egraphs, canals and so on. Indeed, in both the 'Principles' and the *Manifesto*, it is the creation of new productive forces which is seen as the basis of 'every revolution in property relations', and, in both works, the productive forces of capitalism were said to have reached the point which provided the practical material basis for communism. Nor did Engels' 'Principles' ignore the subjective agency required for communism; like Marx, he simply rooted this agency in the 'industrial revoluion' which had created both the growing discontent of the proletariat and its growing power which were needed to effect social revolution (CW 6: 346, 348/9, 489/90, 492/3).

Politically, it is difficult to see significant differences between Marx and Engels at this date. The account of the evolution of the working/class movement offered in the *Manifesto* is based on that of Engels' *The Condition of the Working Class*, whilst the list of measures to be taken by a proletarian government, offered by Engels in the 'Principles', is largely reproduced, often verbatim, by the *Manifesto*. In the 'Principles', Engels presents a vision of communism as a society which allowed each individual to 'develop and exercise all his powers and abilities in perfect freedom', with the 'unlimited expansion of production' made possible by large/scale industry. Similarly, the *Manifesto* described communism as 'the product of the growth of modern industry', which would produce 'an association in which the free development of each is the condition for the free development of all' (CW 5: 47; CW 6: 347, 350/1, 496, 505/6; Carver, 1988).

The criticisms made by Engels' 'Principles' of other contemporary brands of socialism also largely anticipate those of the *Manifesto*. In both works the anti/bourgeois, 'reactionary' socialists are criticised for wanting an impossible return to feudalism and for being, in practice, supporters of coercive measures against the working class. Similarly, both works criticise reformist socialists for wishing to abolish the evils of modern society but not the social relations which, Marx and Engels believed, brought such evils about. Finally, the definition of the attitude of the communists to other working-class parties offered in the 'Principles', which stressed the importance of the peculiarities of national conditions and the need for the communists to adapt to such peculiarities, provided the model for section four of the Manifesto (CW 6: 355-7, 507-19).

Anyway, even *if* we agreed that Engels' emphasis on technology in the 'Principles' provided a contrast with Marx's concentration on class struggle in the *Manifesto*, we would also need to bear in mind the emphasis on technology in Marx's *The Poverty of Philosophy* (1847) and his letter to Annenkov of December 1846, and to note Engels' stress on class consciousness and class struggle in *The Condition of the Working Class* (CW 4: 501-29, 562-83; CW 6: 165-6, 170, 175; CW 38: 96, 103). Nothing is easier than to *begin* with the assumption that significant differences must have existed between Marx and Engels, and then to *illustrate* such differences by counterposing *particular* passages from their works. In fact, it is the similarities between the 'Principles' and the *Manifesto* which are most striking.

This is not, of course, to claim that Engels was somehow responsible for the content of the *Manifesto*. On the contrary, the similarities between the 'Principles' and the *Manifesto* were the product of Marx and Engels' attempts to express in a popular and concrete form the outlook which they had defended in *The German Ideology*. Where the two texts do differ is that, as Struik rightly says, the 'Principles' lack the 'superb style and grand design of the *Manifesto*', a criticism anticipated by Engels himself who described the 'Principles' as 'wretchedly worded', excusing himself by noting the limitations of the catechismal form and its being written in a 'tearing hurry' (Struik: 60; CW 38: 149).

CONCLUSION: ENGELS AND THE GENESIS OF MARXISM

What then was Engels' contribution to Marxism in the formative years before 1848? Adams, basing himself on Engels' own modest memoirs, has argued that it was Marx who 'unfolded to him [i.e. Engels] the completed materialist theory of history in the spring of 1845' when the two men met in Brussels. The views expressed in *The German Ideology* were thus largely those of Marx (Adams: 182; SW 2: 312; CM: 57, 63). In fact, Marx's own generous testimony of 1859 may have been nearer the truth when he said that Engels had 'arrived by another route at the same result as I', citing as evidence Engels' *The Condition of the Working Class*. Certainly, as we have seen, many of the central ideas of *The German Ideology* were anticipated by *The Condition of the Working Class*, a work which Engels was writing by November 1844, had almost completed by January 1845 and which had been sent to Engels' publishers by 17 March 1845, i.e. *before* his move to Brussels (CPE: 22; CW 38: 10-11, 17, 26).

Indeed, as Engels himself reported, his intellectual co-operation with Marx had begun at least as early as the summer of 1844, when he had visited Marx in Paris (SW 2: 311). Marx dated their co-operation even earlier, claiming that he had corresponded with Engels since the publication of the latter's 'Outlines of a Critique of Political Economy' in the *Deutsch-Französische Jahrbücher* of February 1844 (although Marx, as one of the editors of this journal, must have read it even earlier than this date) (Ilyichov *et al*: 41; CPE: 22). Unfortunately, the first surviving letter between Marx and Engels dates only from October 1844 (CW 38: 3-6) whilst, naturally, the two men had no need to correspond while they were both in Brussels, jointly writing *The German Ideology*. It is thus virtually impossible to specify the precise extent of each of the two men's contributions to the formation of 'Marxism' during this key period from late 1843 to mid-1846, a period when, through a critique of their contemporaries, the two were developing their views with a bewildering rapidity.

However, the *Manifesto*, a text drafted by Engels but written by Marx, which was seen by the two men as a joint production, and which summarised their own previous intellectual co-operation on *The German Ideology*, may be taken to summarise the degree to which the formation of Marxism was a collaborative effort. In its formative years at least, the 'Marxist' paradigm was the product of the collaboration of Marx and Engels. In this period, even those of their texts which bear the name of one individual cannot be seen as purely the work of one of them (Krieger, 1967: xliii; Gouldner: 280-1).

By 1848, Marx and Engels had jointly created the historical, sociological and political outlook characteristic of Marxism, even though Marx's studies of the political economy of capitalism had hardly begun. Marx and Engels' later reissues of the *Manifesto*, and their 1872 claim that its 'general principles' were 'on the whole, as correct today as ever', emphasise the degree to which Marx and Engels perceived themselves as remaining loyal to the outlook of the period 1845-48 (CM: 53-4, 62). But how accurate was this self-perception? Did Engels' later writing depart from the perspective which he and Marx had adopted by 1848? Did Marx himself share Engels' intellectual development in the years after 1848? It is to these questions that we must now turn.

PART TWO

*The return to Hegel:
Engels and dialectical materialism*

CHAPTER SIX

Dialectical materialism

> This morning while I lay in bed, the following dialectical points about the natural sciences occurred to me ... (Engels to Marx, 1873. SC: 264).

In *The German Ideology*, Marx and Engels outlined an historical materialism which, like any other sociological or historical paradigm, could be assessed in terms of its logical coherence and empirical validity. Yet, it is often claimed that historical materialism is something more than just another variety of social theory; it is the application to human history of a broader philosophical outlook or world-view: dialectical materialism (Stalin: 5; Cornforth: 126; Meikle, 1985: 1). Neither Marx nor Engels themselves ever used the phrase 'dialectical materialism'. Both men did, however, argue for an outlook which was 'dialectical and at the same time materialist' (AD: 11; SC: 187), although it is with the later works of Engels, such as *The Dialectics of Nature* (1873-86), *Anti-Dühring* (1876-78) and *Ludwig Feuerbach and the End of Classical German Philosophy* (1888), that this outlook is usually associated.

It was *Anti-Dühring* and *Ludwig Feuerbach* which formed the basis for the official philosophy of the Second International and of the world communist movement for much of the twentieth century, a philosophy expounded by writers such as Plekhanov, Stalin, Trotsky and Mao (Plekhanov: 43-8; Stalin; Pomper: 37-48; Schram: ch. 2; Lewis) and which has thus been a regular target of attack for Marxism's critics (Hook, 1950; Leff; Kolakowski III: 63-72, 91-153; Carew-Hunt: ch. 4; Popper, 1940). One response to such attacks, ever since Engels' own defence of Marx against Dühring, has been to attempt a justification of the dialectical outlook (Cornforth; Somerville; Lewis; Norman and Sayers: ch. 1, 4; Marquitt).

However, given the persuasiveness of the attacks made upon dialectical materialism, many Marxists, including Gramsci, Adorno, Lukács, Marcuse, Della Volpe and Sartre, have opted to abandon this outlook, preferring to see it as the work of Engels rather than of Marx himself (Carver, 1980, 1981, 1983, 1984b; Levine, 1975, 1984; Colletti, 1973: ch. 3; Schmidt, 1971: ch. 1 and appendix; Fetscher; Gunn; Howard and Klare: 99, 331, 339, Kolakowski III: 249; Jacoby: 118; Norman and Sayers: 95: Callinicos, 1987a: 55). In other words, Engels, at the end of his life, forgot the advances which he and Marx had accomplished in their critique of contemporary idealism and materialism in the 1840s (Lichtheim, 1971a: 253; Avineri,

1971: 66: Carver, 1983: 116, 154-8).

Here we will offer an account of the dialectical ontology and epistemology contained in Engels' later works (chapter six); assess the utility of this outlook (chapter seven); examine the degree to which Marx himself shared Engels' dialectical materialism (chapter eight); and explore the implications of Engels' philosophical outlook for his historical materialism (chapter nine) and his theory of revolution (chapter ten).

THE RETURN TO HEGEL AND THE TURN
TO THE NATURAL SCIENCES

The critique of Hegelianism which Marx and Engels had arrived at in the mid-1840s culminated in Marx's onslaught against Proudhon (1846-47), whom he attacked for producing a 'dialectical phantasmagoria', 'Hegelian trash' in which real history was replaced with the rational unfolding of concepts, a 'sacred history' based on the 'ritual formula' of Hegelianism: 'affirmation, negation and negation of the negation' (CW 6: 162-3; CW 38: 97). For the next decade, Marx and Engels hardly ever referred to Hegel, except as the source for aphorisms such as Engels' remark in 1851 that 'it really seems as though old Hegel, in the guise of the World Spirit, were directing history from the grave, and with the greatest conscientiousness, causing everything to be re-enacted twice over, once as grand tragedy, the second time as rotten farce', a comment repeated by Marx in the famous opening passage of *The Eighteenth Brumaire* (CW 38: 505; CW 11: 102; see also CW 3: 179).

Yet, from the late 1850s, both Marx and Engels began to take a new interest in Hegel and to temper their criticisms of him. Naturally, they continued to reject his idealist ontology but they now sought, as Marx put it, in the 'Postface' to the second edition of *Capital*, to 'invert' Hegel in order to 'discover the rational kernel within the mystical shell' of his philosophy (I: 103; SC: 187). Such metaphors had been anticipated by Engels as early as 1859 when, in his review of Marx's *A Contribution to the Critique of Political Economy*, he argued that in Hegel's philosophy reality had been 'stood ... on its head' but that Marx had succeeded in extracting the 'nucleus' of the rational method from Hegel's philosophy which Hegel himself had obscured by 'idealist wrappings' (CPE: 224-5). When did this change in Marx and Engels' attitude to Hegel come about and what exactly did it involve?

Perhaps the first hint of this change in attitude to Hegel came in January 1858 when Marx wrote to Engels that he had looked at Hegel's *Logic*, 'by mere accident', and had found it to be 'of great use as regards *method* of treatment' (Marx's emphasis) in his critique of previous theories of profit in the work since published as the *Grundrisse*. He concluded: 'I should very much like to write two or three sheets, making accessible to the common reader the rational aspect of the method which Hegel not only discovered but mystified', although, unfortunately for the modern student of Marx, he never actually completed this task (CW 40: 249). Despite his criticisms of Lassalle's dialectics, the influence of Hegel can clearly be seen in the abstract of *A Contribution to the Critique of Political Economy*, which Marx sent to Engels in April 1858. Here Marx refers to share-capital as the 'most perfected form' of capital 'turning into communism' which he intended to present 'together with all its contradictions', and to the 'dialectical transition' of landed property to wage labour. Here, as in the *Grundrisse*, Marx's abstract even seems to lapse into the speculative, Hegelian unfolding of concepts through their inner logic which had been the nub of Marx's own earlier critique of Proudhon's political economy (Mepham). He claimed, for instance, that the category of money was the product of the 'contradiction between the general characteristics of value and its material existence as a particular commodity.' Engels' reply was distinctly unHegelian: 'it is a very abstract abstract indeed ... and I often had to search hard for the dialectical transitions, particularly since all abstract reasoning is now completely foreign to me ... The abstract, dialectical tone of your synopsis will, of course, disappear in the development' of the final version (CW 40: 298-301, 304).

This emphasis on dialectics as a method for the exposition of political economy was repeated in Engels' review, written at Marx's own request, of Marx's *A Contribution to the Critique of Political Economy*, published in *Das Volk* in August 1859. Part I of the review, which Engels told Marx to tear up if it did not prove suitable, concentrated on the materialist conception of history set out in the 'Preface' to Marx's work (CW 40: 471, 478, 487; CPE: 218-22). In the absence of surviving letters, it is impossible to know for sure whether Marx saw part II of Engels' review before publication but, as Marx was at this time virtually the editor and manager of *Das Volk* (CW 40: 730), it seems likely that he did. It was in this second part of his review that Engels linked Marx's work with Hegel's. As always, Engels criticised the speculative, idealist elements of Hegelian thought, but he also praised Hegel's emphasis on the inner coherence of historical evolution and applauded Marx's critical adaptation of his 'dialectical method' as the 'only correct mode of conceptual evolution'. For this reason he welcomed Marx's decision to present his critique of economic categories logically, rather than in the order of their actual historical evolution (CPE: 222-7).

However, by the time of this review, Engels had already embarked upon a much broader interpretation of dialectics, an interpretation which was, eventually to lead to his *Dialectics of Nature*. It first appears, without any prior warning, in a letter to Marx of 14 July 1858 in which he asked Marx to send him Hegel's *Philosophy of Nature* 'as proposed'. Engels mentioned that he was studying physiology, which he intended to combine with some comparative anatomy, and that he was exceedingly curious to see whether Hegel may not have had 'some inkling' of the recent developments in these fields. In particular he stressed the discovery of the cell in plants and animals: 'Everything consists of cells. The cell is the Hegelian "being in itself" and its development follows the Hegelian process step by step right up to the emergence of the "idea" – i.e. each completed organism.' Similarly, the discovery that mechanical motion, heat, light, chemical affinity, electricity and magnetism are all mutually convertible had provided a 'spendid proof of how the reflex categories dissolve into one another.' Finally, Engels stressed how much the physiological structure of man 'corresponds to that of the other animals', not only the other mammals but even ', if less distinctly , with insects, crustaceans and tape worms, etc.' although, he added, 'Hegel's stuff about the qualitative leap in the quantitative sequence fits in very nicely' here (CW 40: 326/7).

Engels' interest in the natural sciences is evident from his reading of Darwin's *On the Origin of Species* shortly after its publication (1859). He wrote to Marx that Darwin's work was 'absolutely splendid' and that it had demolished all remaining teleology in its demonstration of 'historical evolution in nature', even though, 'one does, of course, have to put up with the crude English method.' Marx passed on these comments, virtually verbatim, to Lassalle in 1861 (CW 40: 551; CW 41: 246/7).

As Marx's reading of Darwin showed, he too was becoming interested in the natural sciences. In July 1864, he was reading about physiology, the anatomy of the brain and of the nervous system, and 'on the cells business'. As he said to Engels: '1. I'm always late off the mark with everything and 2. I invariably follow in your footsteps. So it's probable that I shall now devote much of my spare time to anatomy and physiology and, in addition, attend lectures' (CW 41: 546/7). In the following month, Marx was reading Grove's *Correlation of Physical Forces*, a work he praised for showing that heat, light, and electricity were all 'simply modifications of the same force' and which had put an end to concepts such as 'latent heat' , exactly the points which Engels had made to Marx in his letter of July 1858 (CW 40: 327; CW 41: 551; CW 42: 138). Marx's letters thus began to discuss matters such as Darwin, nitrogen and plant nutrition, microscopic physiology, the influence of soil and rock types on the evolution of the species and the views of Hofmann (whose lectures Marx had attended) on molecular structure (CW 41: 381; CW 42: 231/2, 283/4, 304/5, 322, 385).

Marx had previously ridiculed Lassalle's attempt to produce a new Hegelian philosophy (CW 40: 259/61, 316; CW 41: 281, 333). Yet, when asked to assess Proudon in 1865 he not only repeated his polemic of the 1840s which had criticised Proudhon for his speculative idealism, but, significantly, added the point that Proudhon had failed to penetrate 'the secret of scientific dialectics' (SC: 144, 148, 187; Cap. I: 744; Thomas: 3). As in the late 1850s, Marx and Engels continued to refer to dialectics in terms of a method of arriving at and presenting theoretical results (CW 42: 173, 381-2, 390, 464, 513).

Yet, despite his attempt to apply the dialectical method in his political economy, Marx told Kugelmann that 'my method of exposition is *not* Hegelian, since I am a materialist, and Hegel an idealist. Hegel's dialectic is the basic form of all dialectic but only *after* being stripped of its mystical form, and it is precisely this which distinguishes my *method*' (CW 42: 544, original emphasis). In 1870, Marx defended the use he and Engels had made of Hegel against the criticisms of Lange whom, he claimed, had misunderstood his 'critical manner' of applying Hegel's 'dialectical method' (SC: 225). Similarly, in Marx's 1873 'Postface' to *Capital*, he argued that his 'dialectical method' was the 'opposite' of Hegel's, but that, nevertheless, Hegel's philosophy did have a useful 'rational kernel'. It was because Hegel was regarded with contempt in contemporary Germany that he had 'openly avowed' himself as 'the pupil of that mighty thinker' (Cap. I: 102-3).

The change of emphasis in Marx and Engels' attitude to Hegel is apparent in the contrast between *The Holy Family* (1844), where they hailed Feuerbach's achievement in putting an end to Hegelian idealism, and Marx's letter to Kugelmann of 1868, which blamed Feuerbach for the low esteem in which Hegel's dialectics were held in contemporary Germany (CW 4: 93; CW 42: 520). According to Carver, it was Engels' 1859 review of Marx's *Critique of Politcal Economy* which marked the genesis of the misunderstanding of Marxism as a unified method based on Hegelian dialectics, a view which, for Carver, represents a misunderstanding of Marx's work (Carver, 1983: ch. 4). This may well be the case, but if so, it was, by the time of his 1873 'Postface', a misunderstanding which Marx himself evidently shared.

For Engels at least (for Marx's views see chapter eight, below), Hegel's philosophy offered far more than simply a method for presenting economic categories: it also, despite its idealism, offered genuine ontological truths. Thus, in 1865, Engels wrote to Lange that although the detail of Hegel's philosophy of nature was 'full of nonsense', nevertheless, 'his *real* philosophy of nature', and the core of his doctrine, was to be found in the theory of essence expounded in the second part of his *Logic*. Hegel was not to be rejected out of hand since the modern scientific theory of the interaction of natural forces was 'only another expression or rather the positive proof of Hegel's argument about cause, effect, interaction, force etc. I am no longer an Hegelian, of course, but I still retain a deep feeling of piety and devotion for the titanic old fellow' (CW 42: 138).

Engels' dialectical view of nature was expounded further in a letter to Marx of May 1873, which was based on the definition of the natural sciences as the study of matter in motion. Bodies cannot be separated from motion, thus to understand the different forms of motion is equivalent to understanding such bodies. The simplest form of motion is change of place (mechanical motion) which can, however, be transformed into heat, light, electricity, magnetism, etc. Physics thus shows that under certain conditions all of these forms of motion pass into each other and that ultimately all of them produce changes in the internal structure of bodies, effects which transcend physics, i.e. chemical effects. Chemistry then provides the transition to the sciences concerned with organic life but, of organisms themselves, Engels concluded 'here I will not embark on any dialectics for the time being' (SC: 264/5). As we shall see (chapter eight, below), Marx's response to this letter is crucial for the debate about whether he shared Engels' views on the dialectics of nature.

The ideas contained in Engels' letter of May 1873 were developed in his *Dialectics of Nature* which similarly defined the natural sciences as being the study of matter in motion, each science analysing a single form of motion which, however, is able to pass into the others despite the qualitative differences between them (DN: 251/2). In fact, Engels seems to have been planning a work on the philosophy of the natural sciences even before his letter to Marx as in February 1873 Liebknecht wrote to Engels: 'As for Buchner, go ahead', a reference, apparently, to Engels' intention to write a polemic against Buchner's materialism (DN: 336).

Engels' notes on Buchner, Vogt and Moleschott form the earliest part of his *Dialectics of Nature*, his chief criticism of these writers being their 'abuse against philosophy' and their 'presumption of applying the theories about nature to society' (DN: 205). The works of Vogt, Moleschott and Buchner enjoyed a massive influence in mid-nineteenth century Germany, attacking religion and spreading knowledge of new scientific discoveries. Their philosophy offered a critique of speculative idealism, advocated a materialist monism in which there was no room for vitalism, and presented thought as merely another property of matter. They were all accused by their critics of explaining the world solely in terms of the motions of molecules of matter, although it was only Buchner who explicitly made this claim. They did, however, see mechanical physics as the paradigm of knowledge about the world and defended a reductionism in which physiology, for example, could ultimately be explained in terms of molecular mechanics. These writers also attempted to use science to justify their political opinions. Vogt, for instance, saw science as a radical force against the authority of church and state, whilst Buchner invoked biology to argue that social inequality was a natural phenonenon (Gregory).

The aim of Engels' critique of these writers was to show the superiority of the 'dialectical', over the 'metaphysical', conception of nature, and to obtain a recognition that 'dialectics divested of mysticism becomes an absolute necessity for natural science' (DN: 17, 31, 206/8). The work published in 1925 as the *Dialectics of Nature* actually consisted of a number of studies written in the period 1873 to 1886, although the main chapters of it were written in the period 1878/82 (CW 25: xix). Engels' intention in these works was to criticise speculative idealism and contemporary spiritualism by means of a philosophical materialism whilst, at the same time, opposing what he saw as the shortcomings of contemporary 'mechanical', or 'vulgar', materialism by invoking Hegelian dialectics.

Engels largely abandoned work on *The Dialectics of Nature* after Marx's death in 1883, when he began to devote himself to the massive task of preparing *Capital* volumes II and III for publication. However, many of its arguments were to appear in *Anti-Dühring*, a work which Engels was obliged to interrupt his studies on the philosophy of nature to write (DN: 7; CW 25: xix). Eugen Dühring was a lecturer at the University of Berlin whose work on political economy and attack on Hegelian dialectics had, according to Marx, been 'buried' by the appearance of *Capital* (SC 186/7, 225). According to Engels, Dühring became a socialist in 1875 and it was his works of the mid-1870s, *A Course of Philosophy* (1875), *A Course of Political and Social Economy* (1876) and *A Critical History of Political Economy and Socialism* (1875), which Engels was to attack in *Anti-Dühring*.

Dühring's conversion to socialism coincided with the foundation of the Socialist Workers' Party of Germany from the merger of the Marxist-influenced Social-Democratic Workers' Party, led by Liebknecht and Bebel, and the Lassallean-inspired General Association of German Workers. Marx and Engels had been extremely critical of the concessions to Lassalleanism made in the founding programme of the new party and were disturbed by the influence of, in Marx's words, 'super-wise Doctors of Philosophy' who wanted to replace socialism's 'materialistic basis' with the 'goddesses of Justice, Liberty, Equality and Fraternity.' Dühring, in particular, was attracting support even from Bebel and Bernstein and, in response to Liebknecht's promptings, Engels finally felt obliged to 'tackle the boring Dühring' head-on. Engels started work on *Anti-Dühring* in May 1876, it was published in three parts in *Vorwärts*, then as two pamphlets and was finally issued in book form in 1878. Further editions were published in 1884 and 1894 on the grounds that, even though the target of Engels' attack was by then 'practically forgotten', it offered not only a polemic against Dühring but also provided 'a more or less connected exposition of the communist world outlook' (SC: 272/81, 290; SW II: 13/34; AD: 3/4, 7/8, 454, 457; Henderson, 1976 II: 581/2, 587/8)

As we have seen, Marx never actually completed his intention to elucidate what was rational in the philosophy of Hegel for the benefit of the 'common reader'. However, in 1886, the editors of *Neue Zeit* invited Engels to write a review of K. N. Starcke's *Ludwig Feuerbach*, an invitation which Engels used as an opportunity to offer 'a short coherent account of our relation to the Hegelian philosophy, of how we proceeded, as well as of how we separated from it', and to fulfill his and Marx's 'undischarged debt of honour' to Feuerbach himself (SW II: 324⁄5). Engels' review was published in book form in 1888 as *Ludwig Feuerbach and the End of Classical German Philosophy*. It attempted to set out the 'rational kernel' of Hegel's philosophy and to show how, in Engels' opinion, his and Marx's materialist dialectic differed from that of Hegel. What, then, was the exact nature of the dialectical materialist ontology and epistemology expounded by Engels in these works? How different was it from the outlook which he and Marx had developed in the 1840s? To what extent had Marx's thought evolved in a similar direction to that of Engels?

ENGELS' ONTOLOGY

Philosophical materialism
In 1885, Engels claimed that he and Marx were 'pretty well the only people to rescue conscious dialectics from German idealist philosophy and apply it in the materialist conception of nature and history' (AD: 11). What did Engels mean by this 'materialist conception of nature and history'? In *The Dialectics of Nature*, Engels defined the materialist outlook on nature as seeing it 'just as it is, without alien addition' (DN: 202). However, as Kolakowski has pointed out, it would be possible for those who believed in the existence of God and the archangels to claim that they too saw nature 'just as it really is, without alien addition'; a belief in an external, knowable reality, need not imply a commitment to materialism (Kolakowski III: 153; Timpanaro: 80). Engels himself saw this when he argued, against Dühring, that the unity of the world did not merely consist in its being, but that 'the real unity of the world consists of its materiality' so that *if*, for example, ether particles existed they had to be of a material nature (AD: 54; DN: 247). This does not, however, bring us any nearer to an understanding of what this materiality actually consists of.

By materialism, Engels certainly did not mean the claim that the universe was made up of identical smallest particles, a theory which he regarded as impossible either to refute or to prove. Matter, for Engels, was not a 'thing', but a concept. It was a 'pure creation of thought', which we use as an abbreviated means of referring to the totality of material things. Matter is an abstraction and can only be known through the study of the concrete material things (and their inherent forms of motion) which make it up. Recalling Marx's comments in *The Holy Family*, Engels described the concept of matter as similar to that of 'fruit': we cannot eat 'fruit' as such but only cherries, plums and so on (DN: 239-40, 256-8). To what aspects of reality does the concept of matter refer in Engels' philosophy?

Engels' materialism can only be understood in terms of what he saw as its opposite: idealism. It functioned chiefly as a rejection of idealism's 'alien additions' to reality, and of its 'preconceived crotchets', which had dominated philosophy for the previous two thousand years (SW II: 349-50; AD: 176-7). For Engels, the classic instance of such idealism was the philosophy of Hegel which, in contrast to the interpretation of Hegel which he had offered in 1842, he interpreted as involving the claim that there is an 'absolute concept,' which pre-exists the material world, and which alienates itself in the form of nature, only to return to itself via human self-consciousness (CW 2: 216; SW II: 350).

Engels' materialism did not, however, only function as a denial of Hegel's *supernatural* idealism. He also rejected the Hegelian claim that mind pre-exists matter and that reality consists of the rational unfolding of concepts, a belief which Engels also ascribed to Dühring, for all of the latter's professed materialism. In the metaphor familiar from *The German Ideology*, he thus accused Hegel of inverting reality, of standing the world on its head. Indeed, as in 1845-46, Engels referred to this abstraction of concepts from reality, and their inversion into the basis of reality, as the essence of 'ideology' (AD: 43-5, 56-7, 111; SW II: 350).

Thus, whilst thinkers such as Descartes and Hegel separated the concepts of mind and of matter (Descartes: 156, 164; Hegel, 1956: 17), Engels argued that it is 'impossible to separate thought from matter that thinks.' Mind, whether in the form of God, gods, the Hegelian Idea or human consciousness, does not pre-exist nature. 'No spiritual world exists separately besides the material world.' Rather, thought and consciousness are 'products of the human brain' and thus 'products of Nature'. Whilst Hegel presented material reality as the 'images made real of the "Idea" existing somewhere or other already before the world existed', Engels saw our thoughts as the 'more or less abstract images of real things.' As he wrote to Schmidt in 1891, 'the dialectics in our heads is merely the reflection of the actual development going on in the world of nature and of human history' (for Engels' epistemology, see pp. 117-21 below). He rejected any dualism of mind and matter, of man and nature, or of soul and body, preferring instead a conception of the unity of nature based on its materiality (AD: 31, 44, 429; CW 25: 598; SC: 415; DN: 183).

Engels' materialism has frequently been criticised as a form of 'positivism' which, unlike Marx's historical materialism, fails to see that a different form of causation is involved in society from that found in nature since human activity involves will and consciousness. Engels thus remained trapped within the eighteenth-century materialism which Marx had criticised in 1845 in his *Theses on Feuerbach* (CW 5: 3-8) (a text which, ironically, Engels himself was responsible for publishing in 1888). Engels' materialist philosophy ignored the dialectic between subject and object and presented Man as a passive reflection of the process of natural evolution (Levine, 1984: 12, 66-7, 81, 106, 120; Avineri, 1971: 6, 66; Carver, 1980: 353, Fetscher: 151, 168; Kolakowski I: 181, 317; Schmidt, 1971: 55-9; Rex: 73-4).

Did Engels' belief in the material basis of mind and his rejection of mind's independent existence, commit him to a denial of mind's specific characteristsics and to a 'reduction' of mind to the motion of atoms? Was he a 'positivist', who subsumed philosophy into natural science and who overlooked the difference between change in nature and human activity? Or, as Jones, Weiss and Timpanaro have argued, was Engels an anti-positivist who advocated an explicitly anti-reductionist position (Jones, 1977: 84; Jones, 1982: 301; Weiss: 19; Timpanaro: 16, 84)?

The materialist monism defended by Engels would, at first sight, certainly seem to suggest that he can accurately be described as simply a 'positivist' or 'reductionist'. He claimed, for instance, that 'the same dialectical laws of motion apply in the development of nature, history and thought.' The law of the negation of the negation thus 'holds good in the animal and vegetable kingdoms, in geology, in mathematics, in history and in philosophy.' Similarly, 'in biology, as in the history of human society' the law of the transformation of quantity into quality 'holds good at every step' (AD: 12, 179; DN: 69, 228).

Yet, whilst claiming that dialectics was the 'science of the *general* laws of motion and development of nature, human society and thought' (AD: 180), Engels quite explicitly rejected a reductionist materialism. Instead he committed himself to the 'emergent evolutionist' proposition that the specific character of the particular forms of the motion of matter should *not* be obliterated by their reduction to forms of mechanical motion (Jordan: 164-5). His argument was based on the Hegelian belief that a whole is greater than the sum of its parts. Hegel had argued that a substance such as granite was made up of constituent elements, each of which could exist independently outside their combination. However, whilst 'an animal may be said to consist of bones, muscles, nerves, etc.', this is to use 'the term "consist" in a very different sense from its use when we spoke of the piece of granite' since, unlike the components of granite the different parts and members of an organic body 'subsist only in their union: they cease to exist as such, when they are separated from each other' (Hegel, 1987: 183).

Engels applied Hegel's anti-reductionist holism to the classification of the sciences when he argued *against* the reduction of chemical processes to mechanical ones. To refer to chemistry as the physics of atoms, and to biology as the chemistry of proteins, did draw attention to the 'the passing of each of these sciences into another'; nevertheless, he continued, we need to be aware not only of their connection and continuity but also their 'distinction and discrete separation.' To go further and to define chemistry as ... a kind of mechanics seems to me inadmissible.' He extended this argument to animal life when he said that 'an animal is expressed neither by its mechanical composition from bones, blood, gristle, muscle, tissues, etc., nor by its chemical composition from the elements.' Rather, an organism is a 'higher unity which within itself united mechanics, physics and chemistry into a whole where the trinity can no longer be separated' (DN: 217, 253).

Similarly, Engels drew attention to the qualitatively specific forms of the motions of matter which constituted the human mind, and went out of his way to separate human history from the history of nature. As he said in *Dialectics of Nature*, 'One day we shall certainly "reduce" thought experimentally to molecular and chemical motions of the brain, but does that exhaust the essence of thought?' He criticised eighteenth-century materialism for reducing man to a machine ruled merely by mechanical laws. Such laws are certainly valid in organic nature but, nevertheless, 'they are pushed into the background by other, higher laws.' Engels not only distinguished the human mind from other forms of matter but even from the consciousness of other animals who, although sharing certain modes of thought with humanity, are incapable of the self-conscious investigation of thought itself which characterises humanity (DN: 22-3, 228, 251; SW II: 338).

Thus Engels himself repeatedly drew a distinction between the the natural and the human sciences of the type which his critics accuse him of overlooking. In *Anti-Dühring* he praised Hegel, despite the latter's idealism, for realising that the history of mankind was not just a whirl of senseless deeds but was 'the process of the evolution of humanity itself', an evolution which involved Man's *separation* from the animal kingdom and his entry into the realm of freedom. In his *Dialectics of Nature*, he argued that although both humanity and the animals exerted a lasting influence on their environment, nevertheless, the two were very different since the further removed men are from the animals 'the more their effect on nature assumes the character of premeditated, planned action directed towards definite pre-conceived ends.' There was thus an 'unbridgeable gulf' even between humanity and the apes, since although animals undergo an historical evolution, this is a process which takes place 'without their knowledge and desire whereas humans make their history consciously.' Thus the key distinction between Man and the animals is that 'the most that the animal can achieve is to collect' whereas 'man produces, he prepares the means of life ... which without him nature would not have produced.' (AD: 29, 144; DN: 34⁄5, 180⁄1, 240, 313).

We might now reject the Lamarckianism of some of Engels' views on 'the part played by labour in the transition from man to ape'. Nevertheless, Engels' central point, that through the productive praxis involved in the dialectic between Man and his environment, Man achieves his full humanity and realises his own nature, is precisely the one which he is usually accused of forgetting and for which Marx is so often praised for emphasising. Engels himself criticised natural scientists for their 'one-sided' belief that 'nature exclusively reacts on man and natural conditions everywhere exclusively determined his development.' They forgot that 'man also reacts on nature, changing it and creating new conditions of existence for himself. There is devilishly little left of "nature" as it was in Germany when the Germanic peoples immigrated into it. The earth's surface, climate, vegetation, fauna and the human beings themselves have infinitely changed and all this owing to human activity while the changes which have occurred in this period of time without human interference are incalculably small' (CW 5: 6; DN: 172⁄86, 234⁄5; Woolfson: ch. 1).

Avineri describes *The Dialectics of Nature* as 'a vulgarized version of Darwin and biology with the Hegelian terminology serving only as an external and rather shallow veneer' (Avineri, 1971: 70). Yet, far from being a mere veneer, it was an Hegelian holism which provided the basis for Engels' anti-reductionist monism and which allowed him to reject explicitly the simple fusion of human and natural history favoured by the social Darwinists (Norman and Sayers: 156⁄9; Jones, 1977: 83; Benton, 1979: 117; Timpanaro: 86). It was the qualitative difference between man and the animals which, said Engels, 'makes impossible any unqualified transference of the laws of life in animal society to human society' (AD: 313).

This argument was developed, at length, in Engels' letter to Lavrov of 1875 which concluded that the laws of animal societies could not be simply transferred to human society. Thus the procedure of 'reducing the whole of historical development with all its wealth and variety' down to the one-sided and meagre Darwinian phrase 'struggle for existence', 'really contains its own condemnation' (SC: 283⁄5). Such quotations throw into doubt Walton and Gamble's claim that, for Engels, Darwin served to show that the 'same dialectical laws' were at work in human society as in other forms of life (Walton and Gamble: 72). In fact, as we shall see (in chapter eight below), far more 'social Darwinist' formulations were to appear in Marx's works, than in Engels'.

Thus, in practice, Engels' materialism was primarily negative. It functioned chiefly as a refutation of a belief in the existence of mind independently of, or prior to, the existence of matter and as a critique of the 'senseless and unnatural' idealist concept of 'a contrast between mind and matter, man and nature, soul and body.' Above all, his materialism was a denial of the existence of God (Kolakowski III: 153). This is particularly evident in the 'Introduction' to the 1892 edition of his *Socialism: Utopian and Scientific*, where Engels opposed 'materialism' to religious belief and also to agnosticism, which he labelled 'shamefaced materialism'. Similarly, in *The Dialectics of Nature*, he contrasted his materialist rejection of the immortality of the soul with the credulity those scientists, including some even of the stature of Alfred Wallace, who were willing to believe in the possibility of spiritualist communication with the dead (DN: 51/62, 183, 300; AD: 427/35).

It is in this context that we need to see Engels' famous claim, in *Ludwig Feuerbach*, that the basic question of all philosophy was 'the relation of thinking and being' and that, in their answers to this question, philosophers were split into 'two great camps': idealists and materialists. Since Engels clearly favoured the materialist side of this debate, it is easy to see him as advocating a one-sided materialism and thus neglecting Marx's achievement which was to synthesise the two traditions (Avineri, 1971: 66/9; Fromm: 9).

Yet, when Engels rejected idealist philosophy, it was specifically because of its supernaturalist ontology and for its deduction of the nature of reality from *a priori* abstractions (SW II: 334/5; SC: 393; CPE: 222/3; AD: 31, 45). Engels certainly regarded 'nature as primary', the brain and thought as a product of nature, and the mind as the 'highest form of matter' but, nevertheless, his opposition to Hegelian idealism did not lead him to advocate a return to eighteenth-century 'mechanical materialism'. On the contrary, Engels, as we have seen, repeatedly criticised mechanical materialism, a form of materialism which he saw as still dominant amongst the 'vulgar' materialists of mid-nineteenth century Germany, for its static view of nature and its reductionist concept of humanity. He believed that his own materialism was not simply the opposite of Hegelian idealism but rather that it had sublated the achivements of idealist philosophy and achieved the synthesis of two advocated by Marx in the *Theses on Feuerbach* (SW II: 333, 337/9).

The universe as an evolutionary process
Although Engels' materialism was of the 'minimalist' variety, it did involve rather more than an affirmation of the existence of material reality and a denial of the existence of God. In particular, his materialism involved the claim that motion is an inherent characteristic of reality: 'motion is the mode of existence of matter', whether in the form of motion in space, the vibration of molecules, the growth and decay of organic life, or of thought itself. Matter without motion is thus as 'inconceivable as motion without matter. Motion is therefore as uncreatable and indestructible as matter itself.' But this motion is not merely the 'incessant repetition of the same processes'. Rather, nature undergoes an historical evolution of its own. The world does not consist of a collection of

immutable things but is a complex of processes involving transformation and development (AD: 28/9, 70, 74; DN: 27/31, 70/1; SW II: 349/52).

The conception of nature as 'immutable' was, for Engels, one of the defining characteristics of the 'metaphysical world-view'. It was this outlook which, he claimed, had characterised Newtonian science and eighteenth-century materialism but which had since been undermined by Kant's philosophy, which had replaced Newton's stable and eternal solar system with the conception of the universe as the product of an historical process, and by developments in geology and palaeontology. Above all, it was Darwin who dealt the metaphysical conception of nature its heaviest blow, with his proof that the organic world had undergone a process of evolution which has lasted for millions of years (DN: 26/9; AD: 28).

He distinguished such 'metaphysics' from his own 'dialectical' outlook, which conceived of natural change not as 'an eternally uniform and perpetually recurring circle', but as 'a genuine historical evolution.' Dialectics is the 'science of the most general laws of all motion', whether in nature, human society or thought. Since 'our subjective laws and the objective world are subject to the same laws', Engels' dialectical philosophy claimed to function both as an ontology and as an epistemology (DN: 270/1; AD: 28, 180).

Engels had adopted the term 'metaphysical' from Hegel as a way of referring to those thinkers who investigated 'things as given, as fixed and stable.' Yet, even Hegel had, in his natural philosophy, expressed natural change as simply a 'perpetually self-repeating cycle', reserving real progress for the realm of human spirit (Hegel, 1956: 54; DN: 24, 241, 253; SW II: 328/9; 351/2). For Engels, nature, as well as human history, was characterised by evolutionary development. At times, Engels refers to such development as an 'infinite *progress*' consisting of an 'endless ascendancy from lower to higher.' However, the thrust of his argument was mainly directed against the conception that change in nature is simply an 'eternal *repetition* of the same thing.' If natural change was a 'development' it could, in fact, consist of 'an advance *or a regression.*' The earth, for instance, had evolved through ever more complex forms of matter yet, eventually, it could be totally destroyed (DN: 240/1; SW II: 328/9).

Nevertheless, Engels claimed that even if the earth were destroyed and life exterminated, matter would, with an 'iron necessity', eventually evolve into the thinking mind, in however distant a time or place. 'It is in the nature of matter to advance to the evolution of thinking beings, hence this always occurs wherever the conditions for it ... are present.' Engels thus characterised the theory of evolution as involving the belief that organic life, once given, 'must evolve by the development of the generations to a genus of thinking beings' (DN: 38/40, 212, 214). Engels' conception is, in effect, the same as the Aristotelian doctrine of essential nature, i.e. that something has an inner nature which is expressed through its normal cycle of development (Hook, 1950:

213; Meikle, 1985). However, whilst the same general laws of motion apply to all matter, Engels argued that these laws differ in their expression in the realms of nature and of thought since 'the human mind can apply them consciously', whereas in nature they are an external necessity. For this reason, it is human history which marks the transition from the realm of unfreedom of the animal kingdom (SW II: 350; AD: 144).

Quantity and quality
If dialectics is the science of the most general laws of motion of matter, then what laws of motion did Engels suppose that it had established? In the *Dialectics of Nature*, Engels defines three such laws: i) the law of the transformation of quantity into quality; ii) the law of the negation of the negation; iii) the law of the interpenetration of opposites (DN: 17, 63). What claims do these laws entail about the development of nature and of human society?

By the 'law of the transformation of quantity into quality and vice versa', Engels meant the claim that 'in nature, in a manner exactly fixed for each individual case, qualitative changes can only occur by the quantitative addition or quantitative subtraction of matter or motion' (DN: 64). As in the case of water which, as it is gradually heated or cooled, changes into ice or steam at the the nodal points of freezing and boiling, 'the transition from one form of motion to another always remains a leap, a decisive change' through which 'quantity changes into quality' (AD: 56, 82).

For Engels, the area where this law celebrated its most important triumphs was that of molecular structure. Here, variations in the quantitative proportions in which, say, oxygen, nitrogen and sulphur are combined produce qualitatively different substances. However, he also believed that the law of the transformation of quantity into quality was applicable in biology and in human history. As historical examples of the transition of quantitative into qualitative change, he cited the minimum amount of exchange-value which was necessary for it to be transformed into capital and the definite number of cavalry needed to permit the force of discipline to overcome greater numbers of irregular cavalry. He concluded that this 'allegedly confused and foggy Hegelian notion' was really quite rational and 'even rather obvious.' He denied however, that this principle could be dismissed as self-evident, trivial or commonplace. On the contrary, 'to have formulated for the first time in its universally valid form a general law of development of nature, society and thought, will always remain an act of historic importance' (DN: 56, 64, 69, 237, 256; AD: 82, 163).

The negation of the negation
The second dialectical law of motion of 'nature, history and thought' is that

of the negation of the negation. In this process, the internal contradictions of a thing lead, by an 'inner and inexorable dialectic', to its transformation into its opposite, an opposite which is, in its turn, also negated (AD: 179, 207). This idea had its roots in Hegel's claim that the progressive unfolding of philosophical truth can be compared with the growth of a plant through the stages of bud, flower and fruit: 'one might say that the former (the bud) is *refuted* by the latter (the flower); similarly when the fruit appears, the blossom is shown up in its turn as a false manifestation of the plant and the fruit now emerges as the truth of it instead' (Hegel, 1971: 68). Each of these stages is mutually incompatible with the former, yet each is a necessary stage within a development which constitutes an organic unity (DN: 225; AD: 180).

Engels himself gives a similar example, the germination of a grain of barley through which there appears, in the place of the seed, 'the plant which has arisen from it, the negation of the grain.' This plant then grows, flowers, produces grain and dies: the plant 'is in its turn negated.' But 'as a result of this negation of the negation we have the original grain of barley again but not as a single unit, but ten-, twenty-, thirty-fold' (AD: 172-3).

The negation of the negation may also be found at work in human history as in the evolution of society from an initial communal property, which is then negated by private property which is, in turn, negated by a new form of communism. However, this final negation of the negation does not simply mean a return to primitive communism. Rather, it involves the creation of a 'much higher and more developed form' of communism which is compatible with the growth of society's productive forces (AD: 176). Similarly, in philosophy, Engels believed that the natural materialism of Antiquity had been negated by idealism but that, in turn, this idealism had been negated by the re-establishment of materialism. But, as in the case of communism, the negation of the negation did not simply mean a pendular swing back to the original state, but rather involved an evolution to a higher stage of thought which took account of and subsumed the previous two thousand years of intellectual development (AD 176-9).

Engels use of the world 'negation', in this context, should not be taken to mean that some previous condition is nullified, or some statement disproved. Engels' examples make it clear that, by 'negation', he does not simply mean the destruction of an original state, as would be the case if a barley grain were to be milled and consumed. Rather, negation refers to a transformation by which a second act of negation becomes possible. 'If I grind the barley ... it is true that I have carried out the first act, but have made the second act impossible.' He thus concluded with the general claim that: 'every kind of thing has its characteristic way of being negated in such a way that it gives rise to a development' (AD: 172, 180-1).

The return to Hegel: Engels and dialectical materialism

The interpenetration of opposites

In a letter of 1891, Engels recommended to Schmidt that he should read Hegel's *Logic*, and claimed that, although Hegel's section on Quantity and Quality was 'much finer' than that on Being and Nothing, the 'main section' was that on Essence, where Hegel set out the notion of the interpenetration of opposites (SC: 414). Indeed, as Norman has pointed out, the transformation of quantity into quality is, in one sense, merely an instance of the law of the interpenetration of opposites (Norman and Sayers: 159). What did Engels mean by this law?

In Hegel's *Logic*, metaphysical thought is defined not only in terms of its denial of historical evolution and its employment of fixed categories, but also by its seeing things 'cut off from their connection' with each other, so that each thing is 'believed valid by itself' (Hegel, 1987: 48/9). Engels followed Hegel in arguing that, for the metaphysician, 'a thing either exists or it does not exist; a thing cannot at the same time be itself and something else. Positive and negative absolutely exclude one another; cause and effect stand in a rigid antithesis one to the other.' Yet, although this common sense attitude has its place, Engels believed that it could not deal with the reality of process and change in a world where, for example, 'every organic being is at every moment the same and not the same', since at 'every moment it assimilates matter supplied from without and gets rid of other matter; every moment some cells of its body die and other build themselves anew' (AD: 26/7).

Similarly, dialectics claims that the two poles of an antithesis, such as positive and negative, 'are as inseparable as they are opposed and that despite all their opposition, they interpenetrate. In like manner we find that cause and effect are conceptions which only hold good in their application to the individual case as such; but as soon as we consider the individual case with its connection with the universe as a whole, they merge, they dissolve in the concept of universal action and reaction in which causes and effects are constantly changing places, so that what is effect here and now will be cause there and then and vice versa' (AD: 27).

Thus, only dialectical thought, 'which grasps things and their conceptual images essentially in their interconnection, in their concatenation, their motion, their coming into being and passing out of existence', can grasp the true nature of reality. Dialectical thought replaces the fixed categories of metaphysics with fluid categories which break down the simple oppositions between 'basis and conequence, cause and effect, identity and difference, appearance and essence', since in each of these oppositions 'one pole (is) already present in the other *in nuce*' and, at a definite point, 'becomes transformed into the other' (AD: 27; DN: 208).

For Engels, the scientific advances of the sixteenth and seventeenth centuries had, for all of their massive achievements, observed natural objects and processes 'in isolation, detached from the general context, an outlook which represented the negation of the holism characteristic of the scientific outlook of the ancient Greeks. In turn, however, this negation had been negated and the scientific advances of the nineteenth century had begun to prove the truth of the dialectical conception through their insistence on the 'identity of the forces of nature and their mutual convertibility.' In physics, Joule and Mayer had 'demonstrated the transformation of heat into mechanical force and of mechanical force into heat', whilst Grove showed that 'all so-called physical forces, mechanic force, heat, light, electricity, magnetism, indeed even so-called chemical force, become transformed into one another under definite conditions without any loss of force occurring.' The whole motion of nature is thus reduced in this conception to the 'incessant process of transformation from one form [of energy] into another' (SW II: 352-3; AD: 24-6; DN: 29, 197, 206-8, 235).

Similarly, advances in chemistry and biology were also revealing the interconnectedness of nature. Darwin's theory of evolution, for example, rejected the drawing of hard and fast lines between the species. The differences between the species were increasingly being blurred by the discovery of intermediate stages of evolution, so that the borderlines between vertebrates and invertebrates, fishes and amphibians, birds and reptiles, dwindle more and more everyday (SW II: 352; DN: 29, 215-16).

With his Hegelian emphasis on the whole as the truth (Hegel, 1971: 81), Engels saw dialectics as dealing with 'the inadequacy of all polar opposites.' Since all poles are present in, and change into, their opposites, it follows that all one-sided thinking must be inadequate and incorrect. Boyle's Law, for instance, had been shown to be not universally true but this did not mean that it was absolutely untrue. Rather, the law holds good in certain limits, limits which might well, in the future, prove to be even more restricted than we presently imagine. Thought progresses via oppositions, which means that it would be quite wrong to see one side of such oppositions as representing the whole truth (AD: 114-15; DN: 206, 216).

Contradiction
Lenin described dialectics as 'the study of contradiction' (Collier: 35; Norman and Sayers: 1). Certainly, Engels' adoption of law of the negation of the negation, and of the interpenetration of opposites, committed him to what is the most controversial aspect of dialectical thought: a belief in the existence of contradictions in reality. He referred, for instance, to his law of the negation of the negation as 'development though contradiction' and argued that the law of the interpenetration of opposites meant the rejection of the metaphysical claims that positive and negative necessarily exclude each other and that something cannot at the same time be itself and something else (DN: 17; AD:

26). In other words, both Engels' adoption of Hegel's temporal or diachronic dialectic (the negation of the negation) and of his structural or synchronic dialectic (the concrete as a unity of opposites) involved a belief in the existence of contradictions.

A belief in the real existence of contradictions clashes with the fundamental principle of formal logic: the exclusion of contradiction. According to such formal logic, 'the contradictory is a category which can only appertain to a combination of thoughts, but not to reality. There is no contradiction in things.' Contradiction is thus 'contra-sense and cannot occur in the real world' (AD: 77, 150-1). For formal logic, the exclusion of contradiction is thus the precondition of all logic: if two contradictory statements about reality are admitted, then all statements are admitted and logical deduction becomes impossible. Yet, the existence of contradictions in reality is a fundamental tenet of dialectical thought. Did Engels deny this fundamental principle of formal logic and what did he mean by the real existence of contradictions?

In *The Science of Logic*, Hegel rejected the law of the excluded middle, fundamental to formal logic, where 'A' is either 'A' or not 'A', everything is either positive or negative, and there is no middle alternative. As an alternative to this law, he offered the law of contradiction: 'everything is inherently contradictory.' Formal logic, like metaphysical thought, is only able to see objects in terms of their self-identity, and as fixed and isolated. Dialectical thought, with its acknowledgement of the existence of contradictions, allows us to see more profoundly into reality since contradiction is the 'root of all movement and vitality'. Thus contradiction should not be seen as a 'sickness', or a blemish, since there are a host of contradictory things in reality, even motion itself is contradictory (Hegel, 1969: 438-42).

As an example of a contradictory interpenetration of opposites which generates change, we may cite Hegel's characterisation of World History as 'advancing from the imperfect to the more perfect.' This development has not happened merely by chance. Rather, the goal of history was always immanent within it as an internal principle which develops from its potentiality to its actuality. Thus the imperfection with which World History begins 'must not be understood abstractly as *only* the imperfect but as something which involves the very opposite of itself – the so-called perfect – as a germ or impulse', a possibility, destined to become actual. The Imperfect thus involves its own opposite, a contradiction which has an existence in reality and through which History is driven forward towards the realisation of its own inner nature (Hegel, 1956: 55, 57).

A similar conception of development is outlined in Engels' *Anti-Dühring* and *The Dialectics of Nature*, where dialectical logic is said to have broken through the 'narrow horizons of formal logic' and allowed us to to see things in their transitions and interconnections. 'So long as we consider things at rest and lifeless, each one by itself, side by side and in succession, we do not run up against any contradictions in them' and we can 'get along on the basis of the usual metaphysical mode of thought.' Things are quite different, however, 'as soon as we consider things in their motion, their change, their life, their reciprocal influence. Then we immediately become involved in contradictions.' The Hegelian source of Engels' argument was made explicit when he concluded that 'motion itself is contradictory' (AD: 152, 171; DN: 44, 227).

Engels thus explicitly rejected the law of identity or of non-contradiction, claiming, for instance, that the conception of abstract identity, where 'A' cannot be simultaneously equal and unequal to 'A', was inapplicable in the study of organic and inorganic nature. The law of identity, 'like all metaphysical categories, suffices for everyday use', where science deals with small dimensions or brief periods of time, but was inadequate for natural science 'in its comprehensive role' (DN: 217-19).

Yet, as Norman has argued, this rejection of the law of non-contradiction was *not* really necessary for Engels' defence of the dialectic (Norman and Sayers: 47-8). After all, Engels himself frequently criticised those thinkers whose thought was contradictory. He referred to Dühring's self-contradictions, for example, as 'absurd' and 'impossible' and praised those theories which were logically consistent. He did not resign himself to the existence of contradictions in thought on the grounds that reality itself was inherently contradictory. Rather, he anticipated Popper in arguing that such inconsistencies (and those of other theorists) had to be resolved by the development of a superior theory (AD: 63, 65, 80, 376; DN: 93, 140; Popper, 1940: 407, 410).

Perhaps the best way to understand the meaning of 'contradiction' in Engels' thought is to look at the wide variety of examples of contradictory phenomena which he gave in *Anti-Dühring* and *The Dialectics of Nature*. As we have seen, Engels shared Hegel's belief that motion was contradictory since it comes about 'through a body being both in one place and in another place at one and the same moment of time, being in one and the same place and also not in it.' Similarly, it is also a contradiction that 'motion should find its measure in its opposite, in rest.' Life, 'the mode of existence of protein', is also contradictory as the body, through its uninterrupted metamorphosis of its constituents through excretion and nutrition, is thus 'itself and at the same time something else.' In mathematics, under certain circumstances, 'straight lines and curves may be identical'; whilst the concept of infinity is a contradiction since 'it is composed of purely finite terms' (AD: 27, 63, 77, 103, 152-4; DN: 217-18).

Engels also regarded human history as involving real contradictions. Capitalism, for example, is riven by its own inherent contradictions, above all by the contradiction between its ever more social organisation of production and its private appropriation of the social product. From this fundamental contradiction flowed a whole number of other contradictions: i) the antagonism of the proletariat and bourgeoisie; ii) the contradiction between social organisation in the individual unit of production and social anarchy in production as a whole; iii) the contradiction between the mode of production of capitalism and its mode of exchange, embodied in its inability to use its massive expansion of production for the general social-good; iv) the fact that capitalism itself rendered the capitalist class superfluous, as the salaried employees of joint-stock companies performed the functions once carried out by individual capitalists (AD: 368-9).

Dialectical thought emphasises that 'nothing is final, absolute, sacred' and that 'progress makes its appearance as the negation of the existing state of things.' Thus, for Engels, a recognition of the contradictory nature of capitalism allows us to predict its passing away. Just as capitalism had negated the small-scale personal property of the Middle Ages, so capitalism would, in turn, be negated by the establishment of socialist forms of property through proletarian revolution. It is socialism which, by bringing the ownership of the means of production into line with the increasingly socialised organisation of production, permits the 'solution of the contradictions' of capitalism . Thus 'just as formerly petty industry by its very development necessarily created the conditions for its own annihilation, i.e. for the expropriation of the small proprietors, so now the capitalist mode of production has itself created the material conditions which will necessarily make it perish' (SW II: 328; DN: 214; AD: 168-70, 367-9).

Historical materialism
So far we have studied Engels' materialist philosophy as a form of philosophical anti-supernaturalism and anti-idealism which denies the existence of anything in the universe except matter in motion. However, Engels believed that, since the publication of *The Holy Family*, he and Marx had created a 'materialist conception' of both nature *and* history. In *Ludwig Feuerbach*, he argued that the science of human society had to be brought into harmony with its 'natural-scientific' and 'materialist foundation'. Yet, as we have seen, Engels' philosophical monism did not necessarily involve a mechanical materialist reductionism, or a rejection of the specific qualities which characterised human history (AD: 11; CW 25: 596; SW II: 340, 348). What, then, was the connection between Engels' philosophical materialism and his 'materialist' conception of society?

It may seem that those writers such as Engels who use the word 'material' to refer both to nature in general and to the realm of production are committed to the claim that philosphical materialism (the belief that matter is primary and thought secondary) entails, by analogy, the belief that, in society, material production is primary whilst ideas and political institutions are secondary (SW II: 359; Stalin: 24; Avineri, 1971: 76). Certainly, in his 1892 'Introduction' to *Socialism: Utopian and Scientific*, Engels does attempt to defend the term '*historical* materialism' to his English audience by showing that England itself had a long history of *philosophical* materialism (AD: 427-30).

Yet, in practice, Engels did not employ the term 'historical materialism' to embrace any particular philosophical or metaphysical views. Rather, he explicitly used it to designate the view of history 'which seeks the ultimate cause and the great moving power of all important historic events in the economic development of society, in the changes in the modes of production and exchange, in the consequent division of society into distinct classes, and in the struggles of these classes against one another.' He claimed that this approach had revealed the inadequacy of idealist philosophy, which saw history only in terms of the 'history of civilization'. Instead, historical 'materialism' emphasised the role of class struggles, material interests, production and economic relations in human history (AD: 32, 435).

In other words, despite having developed a philosophical materialism, Engels continued to define historical materialism in terms of the outlook which he and Marx had originally set out in *The German Ideology*. As we shall see, historical materialism is certainly not a logical consequence of philosophical materialism, nor does historical materialism require philosophical materialsm as its metaphysical foundation. As a result, historical materialism must be assessed as a theory in its own right rather than as an appendage of dialectical materialism (chapters seven and nine, below).

ENGELS' EPISTEMOLOGY

That it is we, as readers, who constitute an author's meaning through our interaction with his or her texts, is nowhere more apparent than in the attempts of commentators to establish the nature of Engels' epistemology. Here, many writers have seen Engels as an 'empiricist' and, unlike Marx, as the exponent of a 'reflection' theory of knowledge which entails the belief that the mind is essentially passive in the production of knowledge (Benton, 1977: 21; Miller, 1979: 107, 109; Leff: 28, 67; Hook, 1934: 38; Edgley: 250, 267; Kolakowski I: 263; Lichtheim, 1971b: 70 Lichtheim, 1978: 299).

Other writers, however, emphasise that both Marx and Engels referred to thought as a 'reflection' of reality although, inevitably, there is disagreement as to whether this meant the same thing to both of them (Wood, A. W., 1981: 180, 185-6; Maguire: 106; Kain: 84). According to Levine, Marx, with his Hegelian emphasis on the interaction between the subject and object of knowledge, did not possess a correspondence theory of truth, although he did

The return to Hegel: Engels and dialectical materialism

according to Colletti and to Wood (Levine, 1984: 9-10, 67, 158-9; Colletti, 1975: 14; Wood, 1981: 180-6). Here we will examine the nature of Engels' epistemology before going on to assess its utility (chapter seven) and the extent to which it differed from the theory of knowledge advocated by Marx (chapter eight).

It is in *Ludwig Feuerbach* that Engels did come nearest to a passive, 'reflectionist' theory of knowledge when he argued that 'the influences of the external world upon man express themselves in his brain, are reflected therein as feelings, thoughts, impulses, volitions – in short as "ideal tendencies" and in this form become "ideal powers".' Thus dialectical philosophy is itself 'nothing more than the mere reflection' of the dialectical process at work in the real world. The dialectics of concepts is thus 'merely the conscious reflex of the dialectical motion of the real world', i.e. of nature or society (SW II: 328, 340-1, 350; AD: 28; CW 25: 596; Levine, 1984: 277).

Such 'reflectionist' passages need to be seen, however, in their context, which was that of Engels' polemic against ontological idealism in which he had to insist that human thoughts were the 'more or less abstract images of actual things and processes' (AD: 30). The metaphor of 'reflection' did not, however, commit Engels to a belief in the passivity of mind. After all, if the claim that thought is the 'reflection' of reality meant that the mind were passive in the production of knowledge, the production of accurate knowledge of the world would be an automatic process and it would be difficult to explain how intellectual error could ever come about.

In fact, even in *Ludwig Feuerbach*, Engels laid great emphasis on the fact that the mind did not simply passively receive knowledge from the outside world. Far from seeing the mind as passive, Engels argued that dialectical philosophy had shown that truth lay 'in the process of cognition itself, in the long historical development of science, which mounts from lower to ever higher levels of knowledge without ever reaching, by discovering so-called absolute truth, a point at which it can proceeed no further.' In dialectical thought, 'the demand for final solutions and eternal truths ceases once and for all; one is always conscious of the necessary limitation of all acquired knowledge, of the fact that it is conditioned by the circumstances in which it was acquired' (LF: 328, 351).

Thus 'an exact mental image of the world system in which we live remains impossible for us as it does for all times' since such images are 'limited objectively by the historical situation and subjectively by its author's physical and mental constitution.' Knowledge progresses through a 'series of relative errors', so that ultimate truths are 'remarkably rare', even in the realm of mathematics, let alone in the other sciences, and least of all in the historical sciences, even though 'it is precisely in this sphere that we most frequently encounter truths which claim to be eternal, final and ultimate' (AD: 45-6, 108-12).

In his *Dialectics of Nature*, Engels defined more precisely the constraints which make the full knowledge of the world into an impossibility. He stressed, again and again, that empiricist philosophy misrepresents the real nature of scientific progress for, while it imagines that it 'operates only with undeniable facts', in reality, it 'operates predominantly with traditional notions, with the largely obsolete products of thought of its predecessors.' The empiricist 'believes that he is still in the field of sensuous experience when he is operating with abstractions.' The facts which empiricism imagines that it deals with do not, and cannot, enjoy an objective, theory-free existence. On the contrary, 'even the experimentally established facts become inseparable from their traditional interpretations', so that empiricist accounts of electricity 'cannot any longer describe the facts correctly, because the traditional interpretation is woven into' their description. Experiment and theory are thus intertwined so that, as knowledge develops, previous experiments, 'made from an obsolete scientific standpoint', have themselves to be revised. It was this critique of empiricism, and his insistence on the role of theory, which led Engels into his sometimes excessive praise of the advances made by 'philosophy' in the natural sciences (DN: 139-40, 171, 208, 239).

Science is thus the work of minds which, inevitably, are 'committing practical and theoretical blunders, setting out from erroneous, one-sided, and false premises, pursuing false, tortuous and uncertain paths and often not even finding what is right when they run their noses against it.' Nevertheless, Engels believed that, unlike the spiritualists, scientists were, to some extent, capable of breaking free from the fetters of a particular paradigm and, as an example cited the abandonment of the 'phlogiston' theory of combustion (DN: 238).

Basing his account on Roscoe and Schorlemmer's *A Treatise on Chemistry*, Engels showed that, prior to Priestley, chemists had conceived of combustion in terms of 'phlogiston', a hypothetical substance which supposedly detached itself from burning bodies. In 1774, Priestley discovered 'phlogiston-free' air and, soon afterwards, Scheele demonstrated its presence in the atmosphere. Nevertheless, 'both men remained captives of the phlogistic categories they had inherited.' It was Lavoisier who showed that this so-called de-phlogisticated air was actually a new chemical element: oxygen. He demonstrated that, in combustion, phlogiston did not escape from the burning body but rather that oxygen combined with it. It was Lavoisier who discovered oxygen and who realised its significance whereas Priestley and Scheele had 'merely produced it, without having the slightest inkling of what they had produced.' Similarly, Engels argued that although Marx was not the first political economist to use the concept of surplus-value, it was he who had realised that this concept was the key to understanding the capitalist mode of production, and that it was the basis from which to investigate all the other categories of economics (Roscoe and Schorlemmer: 13-16; Cap. II: 97-8).

The return to Hegel: Engels and dialectical materialism

Engels argued that, as in cases such as Priestley's, 'it was not the lack of factual data' that prevented scientists from arriving at the truth, 'but solely a preconceived *false theory*.' Induction is thus not an infallible method; on the contrary, its supposed findings (such as light corpuscles and caloric) 'are every day overthrown by new discoveries.' The significance of 'correct facts' was thus not realised because they were understood within the framework of 'incorrect notions'. The limits of induction and the importance of theory were further emphasised by the example of atoms and molecules which 'cannot be observed under the microscope, but only by the process of thought' (DN: 113-14, 162, 208, 232).

Yet, whilst Engels believed that concepts played an essential part in our exploration of reality, he also emphasised that they referred to, or to some extent corresponded with, that reality. Scientific experiments thus allow us to test the predictions which we have made on the basis of deduction from our previous sense-perceptions. Concepts and reality are 'always approaching each other yet never meeting. This difference between the two is the very difference which prevents the concept from being directly and immediately reality, and reality from being immediately its own concept.' Concepts do not directly coincide with reality but, nevertheless, they are more than convenient fictions, they are 'abstracted from reality' and allow us to grasp, at least partially, some aspect of reality. Thus Engels claimed that even infinitesimal calculus, apparently 'a pure and exclusive feat of human intelligence' does in fact have a corrsponding reality in the objective world: 'Nature offers prototypes for these imaginary creations' (AD: 271-2, 432; SC: 457).

The fact that science develops through a series of hypotheses, which are thrown into doubt by the production of awkward facts, means that even natural scientists are tempted to believe that we can never know the 'essence' of things. But for Engels, this assertion, even when made by Kant (Kant: 59-60), was a 'fantasy'. Such a concept 'does not add a word to our scientific knowledge, for if we cannot occupy ourselves with things, they do not exist for us.' The Kantian thing-in-itself was thus a mere phrase, incapable of application: 'What would one think of a zoologist who said: "A dog *seems* to have four legs, but we do not know whether in reality it has four million legs or none at all"?' Thus the only meaning of the thing-in-itself was that 'we can only know under the conditions of our epoch and *as far as these allow*' (original emphases) (DN: 244-5).

Related to the belief that Engels was an empiricist and positivist is the claim that Engels, unlike Marx, failed to see the social origins of scientific theories (Fetscher: 163). Yet, in fact, Engels repeatedly asserted that all ideas were socially and historically determined. He thus criticised idealist philosophers, who saw human history in terms of the logical progression of ideas, and scientists, who concentrated merely on the influence of nature on man. Both 'neglected the influence of men's activity on their thought ... it is precisely the alteration of nature by men, and not solely nature as such, which is the most essential and immediate basis of human thought' (DN: 234; SC: 441).

As an example of Engels' failure to see the social origin of ideas, Fetscher cites the close link which Marx perceived, but which Engels allegedly ignored, between the science of Darwin and the political economy of Malthus (Fetscher: 163; see CW 41: 381; AD: 86). Yet, Engels himself argued that 'the whole Darwinian theory of the struggle for existence is simply the transference to organic nature of Hobbes' theory of the *bellum omnium contra omnes* and of the bourgeois theory of competition, as well as the Malthusian theory of population' (DN: 313). In itself, of course, Fetscher's error is of minor importance. Its significance lies, rather, in its illustration of the now-habitual method of reading Marx and Engels' works as part of a compulsive quest to prove that Marx's thought was fundamentally different from, and superior to, that of Engels. Certainly, given Engels' repeated emphasis on the active role of mind in the creation of knowledge, the criticisms of him as *simply* an empiricist or an advocate of a passive, 'reflectionist' theory of knowledge become virtually incomprehensible except as the result of a mania to see Marx and Engels in terms of a binary opposition constructed by means of selective quotation.

CHAPTER SEVEN

Dialectical materialism: an assessment

> The more general the generalization, the more successful it is in incorporating a range of occurrences which may be subsumed under it ... the less it tells us about the specific event or phenomenon in question (Giddens, 1974: 7).

ENGELS' ONTOLOGY

Philosophical materialism

How valid is the dialectical and materialist ontology which Engels defended in his later works? Is his philosophical outlook in contradiction with the historical materialism which he and Marx had arrived at in the 1840s? In order to assess Engels' dialectical materialism, we need to distinguish betweeen his broad philosophical outlook and his more specific claims about the dialectical nature of reality. As we shall see, the former is sometimes useful, but often extremely vague; the latter are inconsistent, and internally incoherent.

Jordan has usefully distinguished between a 'minimalist' and a 'maximalist' version of dialectical materialism. The former involves broad metaphysical claims (such as the non-existence of God) but, unlike the maximalist interpretation, does not allow us to choose between conflicting scientific theories about the nature of reality (Jordan: 394-5). Engels' claim that only matter in motion exists was, as we have seen, primarily negative in its content; it consisted chiefly of the denial of the existence of God or of mind independent of matter. Rather than being a dogmatic ontology, his materialism involved little more than the vague claim that nothing but nature exists. As Engels himself stressed, with each epoch-making discovery of natural science, materialism has to change its form (SW II: 338).

Thus, Engels' materialism did not commit him to any particular scientific theories, such as the existence of ether as the medium through which wave phenomena were propagated, and is quite compatible with, say, Planck and Einstein's view of matter as the manifestation of energy (DN: 111, 247; Levine, 1984: 95, 273). It would, therefore, be perfectly possible to convert the advances of twentieth-century science into the language of dialectical materialism, and to see Rutherford's demonstration that nitrogen could be converted into oxygen as an example of the interpenetration of opposites, or the quantum theory as a demonstration of the transformation of quantity into quality.

Dialectical materialists should not, however, rejoice at the ease with which twentieth century science can be seen to prove, yet again, the truth of dialectical materialism. On the contrary, a crucial weakness of the minimalist reading of Engels' materialism is that it is compatible with virtually any phenomena, except the existence of God, archangels and Hegel's Idea, whereas, as Popper put it, a good scientific theory is one which 'forbids certain things to happen. The more a theory forbids the better it is ... A theory which is not refutable by any conceivable event is non-scientific' (Burke: 51). In its minimalist version, materialism does not put itself at risk in this way; it is thus not so much wrong, as redundant.

Engels' materialism can, however, also be given a maximalist reading, a reading which was to triumph in Stalin's Russia. Here, dialectical materialism is seen as a strict ontology, a precise scientific paradigm, whose principles would allow us to choose between rival explanations of natural phenomena. Thus, just as in the seventeenth century Galileo's opponents were able to deduce that the moon did not contain craters or mountains on the basis of the Aristotelian principle that all the celestial bodies are perfect spheres, so dialectical materialism was used to show that Einsteinian physics was idealist (and thus incorrect) or as the basis from which to deduce that genes could not exist (Kolakowski III: 131-8; Chalmers: 52).

Engels himself had repeatedly criticised the idea that materialism constituted a 'philosophy standing above the other sciences' and that that reality could be deduced from first principles. Indeed, one of his main criticisms of Hegelianism was that it required reality to conform to its abstractions, using its own *a priori* principles as levers for constructing reality. For Engels, such principles were not the starting point of investigation, but rather its final result; they are not applied to nature and to human history but abstracted from them (AD: 31, 43, 54; SC: 395).

However, in a sense, even the minimalist version of Engels' materialism does involve certain *a priori* principles. For instance, on the basis of the certainty that matter exists, Engels denied the existence of God and rejected the validity of spiritualism (CW 25: 598; DN: 51-62; AD: 431). Yet, although it is easy to feel sympathy with his impatience with those scientists taken in by the claims of spiritualist frauds, Engels was wrong to argue that spiritualism could be refuted on *a priori* grounds and its truth denied by a deduction from the principles of philosophical materialism (DN: 51-62). If spiritualism is to be rejected, it must either be on the basis that its claims are empirically untestable or, alternatively, that the empirical evidence for it is unreliable or is open to some alternative explanation. Otherwise our materialism becomes an *a priori* principle, from which we can deduce the nature of the universe, of exactly the type which Engels himself criticised.

Similarly, although Engels argued for atheism in preference to agnosticism, both the existence and the non-existence of God are scientifically unfalsifiable propositions. In fact, Laplace's agnostic comment that he 'had no need of the hypothesis of God' is quite adequate to allow the natural and social sciences to go about their business. Certainly, as Engels pointed out, those who wish to retain the concept of divine intervention in earthly affairs have increasingly reserved it for those events for which, as yet, we have no other explanation, a strategy which Engels opposed by quoting Spinoza: 'Ignorance is no argument.' As scientifc knowledge ever increases and our ignorance decreases, so the role of God becomes ever smaller. God is thus evacuated from one sphere after another until He is reduced to nothing but a 'first impulse' of the universe who is then shut out from the existing world: 'What a distance from the old God – the Creator of heaven and earth, the maintainer of all things – without whom not a hair can fall from the head!' (AD: 431/5; DN: 203/4; Carr: 74/5). In practice, Engels' 'materialist' assumption that God does not exist *is* the basis of any 'rational' (i.e. testable) exploration of the world. An 'irrational' assumption that God does not exist is the precondition of any rational investigation of nature or of human history.

The universe as an evolutionary process
Engels' attacks on 'metaphysical' science and his alternative emphasis on the fact of evolution in both the natural world and human society, a belief which he shared with many of his contemporaries, is perhaps the least controversial aspect of his dialectical materialism. Indeed, Leff, who launches an onslaught on to most of Engels' philosophy, refers to the latter's claim that 'the world is not to be comprehended as a complex of ready-made things, but as a complex of processes' as 'the essence of a proper understanding of existence. It constitutes the foundation of virtually all branches of knowledge and the sciences ... For that reason it must be acknowledged that the dialectical view of existence harmonises with the modern scientific outlook and in this case it can claim to be pertinent' (Leff: 60/1; Shanin, 1981: 4).

Nevertheless, whilst the assumption of the inevitability of development and interconnection may provide the broad basis for modern scientific knowledge it does not advance that knowledge very far. In biology, for instance, an awareness of the general fact of the evolution of species does not tell us anything about the evolution of any particular species: whether it survives or becomes extinct; whether it undergoes rapid evolution or remains unchanged for millions of years.

Similarly, in human history we cannot deduce a knowledge of any actual historical change from a general awareness that historical change has taken place. When, for instance, Alan Macfarlane argues that 'England was as "capitalist" in 1250 as it was in 1550 or 1750' (Macfarlane: 195), Marxists (and many others) are likely to disagree with his claim not because it contradicts an *a priori* ontological assumption about the universality of change, but rather because of empirical evidence that the English economy was, in fact, transformed between these dates (Brenner: 1976). Thus, Engels' general emphasis on evolution and development, whilst valuable and widely accepted, tell us very little about any specific natural or historical change. His attempts to be more precise about the characteristic forms of such change have, as we shall see below, proved rather more controversial.

A second, although less significant, problem with Engels' critique of 'metaphysical' science, is that it has been questioned whether it is true that supposedly metaphysical thinkers such as Kepler, Galileo and Newton did see the universe in static and fragmented terms (Levine, 1984: 24; Colletti, 1973: 42-3). However, Engels certainly realised that the scientists and philosophers of the previous three centuries did not see the world as at rest. His central criticism of the Newtonian, and even of the Hegelian, view of Nature, was rather that whilst such thinkers were aware of motion in nature, they saw it in terms of 'an eternally uniform and perpetually recurring circle', rather than a genuine historical evolution and development (AD: 12-13, 28; DN: 197). Here Engels' interpretation of the history of science does seem to have much to recommend it since, as he argued, the theory of the evolution of the solar system did have its origins in the work of Kant and Laplace whilst the theory of biological evolution was, of course, largely the work of the nineteenth century (Whitehead: 95).

A far more significant criticism of Engels' critique of 'metaphysical' science is that his target of attack is not entirely clear, since he himself admitted that in the 'everyday use' of the 'small change of science', 'the metaphysical categories retain their validity' (DN: 216). The problem here is that it is difficult to imagine what an alternative 'non-everyday' science would look like. In practice, Engels' critique of 'metaphysical' thought seems to shift away from actual scientific practice to those thinkers, such as Bacon and Locke, who attempted to express this practice in philosophical terms through a now outmoded empiricism and inductivism (DN: 47, 196, 208).

Quantity and quality
One possible objection to Engels' theory of the transformation of quantitative into qualitative change is the claim, made by writers from Descartes, Hobbes and Locke onwards, that qualitative differences do not exist in objective reality, but are rather the product of human classification. The perception of qualities depends upon the perspective of the observer: it is only within a specific perspective that we perceive the boiling point of water as the nodal point of qualitative change. If we were interested in some other issue, such as heating radiators or whether water is hot enough to scorch human flesh, then we would perceive a different temperature as the nodal point of change (DN: 237; Kolakowski I: 389; Hook, 1950: 216; Hook, 1955: ch. 3; Leff: 58).

However, the fact that specific observers are interested in particular qualitative changes, does not mean that such changes do not objectively exist. For example, whether water is a gas, a liquid or a solid does represent some real, qualitatively specific state: gases expand to fill their containers; liquids adjust to their containers; solids do neither. These qualitatively different states all exist in reality even if, for the moment, we happened to be interested in other qualities of water. Indeed, such qualitatively different states would exist even if there were no observers to perceive them. As Engels said, things have 'infinitely many qualities' (DN: 236), there is no reason why the nodal points of change for one quality should be the same as that for another.

It would also be wrong to criticise Engels on the grounds that the law of the transformation of quantity into quality does not apply to abstract qualities, such as weight or learnedness (Hook, 1950: 219-20). Engels himself anticipated such criticism when he argued that 'qualities do not exist, but only things *with* qualities' and it is these things which change (DN: 236). Thus if we add more stones to a a heap of stones, it is true that the the quality of 'weight' does not eventually disappear but, nevertheless, at particular points the real nature of the pile will alter; eventually, for instance, the weight of the stones will fuse them into cohesive strata (Hook, 1955: ch. 3).

However, not all change can be characterised in this way. At what point, for instance, did capitalism replace feudalism in England? It would certainly be difficult to say that English society was feudal in one year (or even decade) and capitalist in the next. One answer might be that the English Civil War, as a bourgeois revolution, represented this nodal point of change. The problem here is that even if we accepted this characterisation of the Civil War, it would not, even in terms of Marxist theory, represent such a distinct point of transition. Whether we see bourgeois revolution as the product of a society which is not yet capitalist (and so requires the revolution to clear the way for *future* capitalist development) or as the result of the fact that society is *already* capitalist (and so requires a political revolution to bring its superstructure into line with its economic base), in neither case does bourgeois revolution mark the nodal point of qualitative change where society becomes capitalist (Hill, 1940: 25, 29-30; Brenner, 1978). The major objection to Engels' first law of the dialectic is thus that even if *certain* changes can be characterised as qualitative leaps arising out of prior quantitative change, this is not a universal form of development.

Ironically, in order to defend the law of the interpenetration of opposites, Engels himself provided a number of examples of development which did *not* take the form of 'a leap, a decisive change' of quality (AD: 82). For example, in his critique of metaphysical philosophy's fixed categories, he argued that 'hard and fast lines are incompatible with the theory of evolution. Even the borderline between vertebrates and invertebrates is no longer rigid, just as little as is that between fishes and amphibians, whilst that between birds and reptiles dwindles more and more every day.' Thus 'all differences become merged in intermediate steps' and a dialectical concept of evolution which 'knows no hard and fast lines' emerges (DN: 205/6, 215/16). Engels also gave the example of death where 'it is ... impossible to determine the moment of death, for physiology proves that death is not a sudden instantaneous phenomenon but a very protracted process.' Thus, in modern science, 'the old rigid antagonisms, the sharp, impassable dividing lines are disappearing more and more', a claim which would seem to be incompatible with Engels' own emphasis, on the universality of dialectical leaps of quality (AD: 14, 26/7).

Thus, we can, if we so wish, retain the interpenetration of opposites and its critique of hard and fast categories *or* we can retain Engels' insistence on the existence of qualitative differences in reality, but we cannot retain both as *universal* laws of the dialectic (Leff: 46/7). We have proceeded so far on the assumption that it is our duty to construct the strongest version of Engels' thought, on the principle that intellectual enquiry 'must much more highly prize a good foe than a poor ally' (Bennett, 1981: 28). Nevertheless, at this point, it must be said that it is almost impossible to comprehend why Engels could not see this fundamental flaw in his own thought.

A final criticism of the law of the transformation of quantity into quality is that while we tend to think of scientific laws as specific and predictive, the law of the transformation of quantity into quality is vague and descriptive. Boyle's Law, for instance, says that the volume of a gas varies inversely with the pressure to which it is subjected so long as the temperature remains constant. As Engels himself argued, such laws tend to become *more* specific in their application as time goes by: Boyle's Law, it is now realised, holds good only for certain gases, at certain temperatures and at certain pressures (AD: 114/15). The law of the transformation of quantity into quality is far less precise in its meaning. It does not seem to mean that all quantitative change is qualitative, although Acton has argued that, in reality, this is the case (Acton: 92). (Presumably, Engels could allow this argument as an instance of the interpenetration of opposites.) Nor, given Engels' own examples of changes which do not involve clear nodal points of qualitative change, is the transformation of quantity into quality a universal phenomenon.

What the law of the transformation of quantity into quality asserts is, therefore, rather banal: some things change instantaneously whilst others do not. As Engels himself admitted, such a general law cannot specify the amount of quantitative change needed to bring about a specific qualitative change nor can it predict which specific qualitative change will come about. Thus, in practice, the transformation of quantity into quality is a *post facto* label which we attach to a process which we have already explained and described in more precise terms: it is a wheel which turns nothing.

The return to Hegel: Engels and dialectical materialism

Negation of the negation

If the law of the transformation of quantity into quality is non-predictive, perhaps it is the law of the negation of the negation which reveals the direction and nature of such qualitative change? Certainly, it is the negation of the negation, with its concept of movement through opposition and internal contradiction, which constitutes the heart of Engels' dialectic (Leff: 49; Hook, 1955: ch. 2). More than any other, it is this law which marks the degree to which Engels had 'returned' to Hegelianism since it contrasts markedly with the contempt which *The German Ideology* had evinced for Hegel's desire 'everywhere to demonstrate the negation of the negation' (CW 5: 305).

An initial problem with the negation of the negation appears to be one of terminology since there is no reason why, in Engels' example of the growth of the barley seed, we should see the plant as the opposite or the 'negation' of the plant. One could just as appropriately refer to the plant as the 'affirmation' of the seed. This is not, however, simply a semantic objection. The point is that Engels' dialectical conception of growth via the conflict of opposites is simply a product of the metaphors he has used to describe the process, rather than of the inherent qualities of the process itself (Leff: 60).

Engels' reply to this argument might be that the plant is the negation of the plant because it is qualitatively different from the seed, we have the growth from A to non-A, the second stage constituting the negation or opposite of the first. The problem with this reply is that *whatever* the nature of the second stage of development we could still claim that it consisted of the 'negation' of the first: *whatever* happened would, after the event, prove the theory to be true. Once more, the apparent development via opposition and internal contradiction, which Engels identified as characteristic of the dialectical process is merely the result of the vocabulary or metaphors with which we have chosen to describe it, rather than the real content of the process itself.

Engels himself seemed to realise this problem when he admitted that 'It is self-evident that I am not saying anything concerning the *particular* process of development of, for example, a grain of barley from germination to the death of the fruit-bearing plant, if I say that it is a negation of the negation' (Engels' emphasis). As he himself pointed out, the integral calculus and socialism are both examples of the negation of the negation, yet they have nothing of substance in common. Thus to bring all of these processes under one dialectical law of motion involves 'leaving out of account the specific peculiarities of each individual process' (AD: 180).

The law of the negation of the negation can thus be interpreted in a minimalist and a maximalist sense. In the minimalist sense, the label of 'negation' is simply tagged on to whatever qualitative changes occur in the particular process we happen to be studying. Like the transformation of quantity into quality, this dialectical law ceases to be a genuine predictive law and becomes a vague, *post facto* description for processes which we have already described and accounted for perfectly adequately. The maximalist interpretation of the negation of the negation would involve the claim to be able to predict the nature of the negation which will occur. Examples of where such prediction had proved successful would be the test of this interpretation of the law, although Engels himself offered no such examples.

Strangely, Engels himself seemed to have recognised that the negation of the negation is not necessarily a universal process. After all, not every barley seed will germinate and become a fruit-bearing plant. Some seeds may be crowded out, fall on unsuitable soil, be eaten by birds or, as Engels himself pointed out, be crushed underfoot. Engels' reply to this point was that by 'negation' he did not mean destruction, but rather a negation which makes a further negation possible: 'I must therefore set up the first negation in such a way that the second remains or becomes possible' (AD: 180-1). Yet his own admission that not every seed will develop in this way meant that the negation of the negation ceases to be a universal law of development and becomes, for any individual barley seed, merely a possibility.

A further problem, is that a barley seed must either grow into a barley-plant or cease to develop at all, through being crushed or otherwise destroyed. However, this regularity of organic development is *not* a useful analogy for the development of human society which, if it does not become x must become y or z. Thus, in social development, we are faced with alternative and divergent paths of development (as Engels' own emphasis on national specificities in the transition to capitalism acknowledged (AD: 209)) which do not have parallels in the regularities which characterise organic growth. Despite Meikle's attempts to salvage such 'essentialism', it is misleading to present organic and social development in terms of the same universal laws (Meikle, 1983: 161-6).

Monod has extended this 'anti-organicist' critique of dialectical materialism to the process of natural development itself. As we have seen, Engels claimed that even if the earth were to be destroyed, matter would, with an 'iron necessity', evolve eventually into the thinking mind since 'it is in the nature of matter to advance towards thinking beings' (DN: 38-40, 212-14). For Monod, however, the biosphere is not, as Engels thought, deducible or predictable on the basis of first principles or from the inherent qualities of matter. We cannot predict the recurrence of the thinking mind because 'the biosphere does not contain a predictable class of objects or of events but is a particular event, certainly compatible indeed with first principles but not *deducible* from those principles and therefore essentially unpredictable.' The biosphere, including the thinking mind, is no more predictable from first principles than is the specific configuration of atoms which constitutes a particular pebble, or a particular car accident, even though such structures or accidents may, *post facto*, be explained from such first principles (Monod: 48-9).

The return to Hegel: Engels and dialectical materialism

All of the weaknesses of Engels' argument are apparent in his defence of Marx's description, in *Capital* volume I, of communism as the negation of the negation. Marx had argued that the process of primitive accumulation, which had created capitalism by divorcing the peasant and the artisan from the means of production and replacing them with wage-labour, constituted 'the first negation of individual private property'. However, capitalist production then 'begets, with the inexorability of a natural process, its own negation. This is the negation of the negation' through which private property is replaced by the 'possession in common of the land and the means of production produced by labour itself' (Cap. I: 874, 929).

Dühring, like many writers since, found Marx's section on primitive accumulation to be the most succesful part of *Capital*. He argued, however, that it would have been even better 'if it had not supported itself with the dialectical crutch', which Marx had used as 'the midwife to deliver the future from the womb of the past' by presenting socialism as 'the automatic result' of an Hegelian process. As Engels summarised Dühring's criticisms: 'as an alleged Hegelian, Marx is obliged to produce a true higher unity as the outcome of the negation of the negation' (AD: 164, 167).

Engels' defence of Marx against Dühring's criticisms was profoundly contradictory. He argued that Marx had not forced his account of primitive accumulation into an *a priori* dialectical schema. Rather, it was only *after* Marx had completed his historico-economic proof that he proceeded to refer to capitalism as the negation of petty industry and to socialism as the negation of the negation. But if Marx's account of primitive accumulation and his prediction of the demise of capitalism stood independently of the law of the negation of the negation, then why should Engels object to Dühring's argument that Marx's account has no need of any 'dialectical crutch' (AD: 170-1)?

In fact, given the failure of communism to appear in the century and a quarter since *Capital*, it is by no means clear that Marx *had* shown that the restoration of common ownership of the means of production must occur in the future with the 'inexorability of a natural process' (Cap. I: 929). It is at this point that the rhetorical function of Marx's dialectical language becomes clear, for, by invoking the negation of the negation, and by showing that the first stage of this process had already occurred, Marx was, despite Engels' protestations to the contrary, attempting to give a greater credence to his predictions of the second negation which was to come.

Dühring was thus quite right to accuse Marx of using the negation of the negation as 'as a midwife to deliver the future from the womb of the past.' Engels himself implicitly admitted as much with his reference to the emergence of socialism as a process which 'must occur in the future ... in accordance with a definite dialectical law' (AD: 170-1). Again, the law either has some pay-off in predictive terms (which Engels seems both to affirm and deny) or it is a *post facto* gloss on what we already know, in effect a tautology, another wheel which turns nothing.

A second problem is that it is not clear that capitalism was the 'negation' of the society which preceded it. After all, for Marx and Engels, both capitalist and pre-capitalist society are class societies characterised by the existence of private property, surplus labour, a class state, ruling class ideology and so on (AD: 176). Thus, whether we perceive something, such as capitalism, as the 'negation' or 'opposite' of something else is a matter of our perspective rather than a trait inherent in reality.

A third problem is that even if we believed in the inevitability of the negation of the negation in general, it is by no means clear that this would allow us to predict the inevitability of socialism *in particular*. After all, the final outcome of the dialectical triplicity of social development could take the form of a synthesis of the common property of stage one, with the ruling class and state of stage two, to produce not communism (in Marx and Engels' sense) but rather a form of 'state capitalism'. The vagueness of the concepts of negation and of opposition mean that the law of the negation of the negation has no specific predictive power and we would only be able to perceive what constituted the negation of the negation *after* this process had occurred (Hegel, 1979: 13). The dialectical negation of the negation becomes rather like the workings of Providence: impossible to predict beforehand, but recognisable everywhere after the event.

Engels himself did see the law of the negation of the negation as something more than a dialectical redescription of a process which we have already comprehended when he defended Marx's use of the dialectical method as 'a means of discvovering new results' (AD: 171). But in this case, if dialectics allows us to arrive at 'new results' then it becomes a 'philosophy standing above the other sciences' which deduces reality from *a priori* principles of exactly the type which Engels himself had rejected.

This ambivalence in Engels' thought about the role of philosophical speculation was epitomised by his, on the one hand, welcoming the end of philosophy and its replacement by 'positive science', whilst, on the other, also hailing the achievements of philosophers such as Descartes, whose principle that the universe always contains the same quantity of motion was only 'confirmed by the natural scientist after 200 years' (AD: 31, 45; DN: 41-2, 45, 71, 121, 208, 248-9).

Yet, the fact that philosophical speculation may produce results which are accepted by science is no justification for the method of philosophical speculation *per se* since, as Engels himself was aware, philosophical speculation could, as in the example of Hegel's cyclical view of nature, also produce unacceptable results. The real difference between science and philosophical schematism is thus not the nature of the hypotheses about reality which they arrive at, or even the means they use to arrive at them, but rather the means whereby they test and assess the hypotheses they have produced.

To conclude: the negation of the negation can, like dialectical materialism in general, be interpreted in weaker or stronger forms. In its weaker form, it does not allow us to make predictions about future developments; it is merely a label which can be affixed to any event after it has taken place, provided that we leave out of account 'the specific peculiarities of each individual process' (AD: 180). Interpreted in its stronger form, the law of the negation of the negation should allow us to arrive at new scientific results through the prediction of law-bound development. In practice, however, it is difficult to think of *any* examples of such successful prediction of the negation of the negation. The most famous example, Marx's 1867 prediction of proletarian revolution on the basis that this process was already 'palpably evident', certainly does not inspire confidence (Cap. I: 91).

The interpenetration of opposites

A central problem in attempting to assess the law of the interpenetration of opposites is simply establishing its precise meaning. Engels' claim that the polar opposites, for instance the negative and positive poles of a magnet, are, in a sense, inseparable is certainly true: each is only defined in relation to the other. But this certainly does *not* mean that the two 'interpenetrate', i.e. that one is present in the other (AD: 27; DN: 206-8). Nor does the fact that physical forces, such as light, heat, electricity are 'mutually convertible' mean that the differences between them are not real ones (DN: 235).

The concepts of cause and effect are also poor examples of the interpenetration of opposites. Engels argued that these concepts hold good in individual cases, but that when we consider an individual case 'with its connection with the universe as a whole', the distinction breaks down (AD: 27). The first problem with this argument is that neither in our daily lives, nor in the natural or social sciences, do we consider things in their connections with 'the universe as a whole.' Indeed, the precondition of knowledge is that we discuss things in the specific connections which are relevant for particular purposes. Anyway, as Engels himself pointed out, we will never obtain knowledge of the universe as a whole, since our knowledge is always necessarily partial (CW 25: 597).

Secondly, we do not have to consider things in connection with the universe as a whole in order to see that they can be both cause and effect. One could say, for example, that a car accident was an *effect* of drunken driving but that, in turn, the accident was the *cause* of a broken neck. However, this does not mean that car accidents are a proof of the interpenetration of opposites or of the contradictory nature of reality. This 'proof' only has any credence through a play on words, which ignores the fact that nothing is a 'cause' or an 'effect' in the abstract, but that we can only refer to x as the cause of y or the effect of z.

Engels' classic example of the interpenetration of opposites was that of an organic being which assimilates and excretes external matter, and so is 'at every moment the same and not the same.' Yet, this example is also based on a play on words, involving, an arbitrary definition of what an organic being-in-itself would consist of (i.e. not in interaction with its environment). Yet, Engels' own definition of living beings rightly involves just such an interaction. In other words, one could just as validly say that through its interaction with its environment, an organism is simply being itself since such metabolic change is one of the defining features of an organic being. Thus, the fact that things change and interact does not mean that we must challenge the 'metaphysical' assumption that they either 'exist or do not exist' (AD: 26-7).

Engels seems, at first, to be on safer ground when he uses the law of the interpenetration of opposites to criticise all 'one-sided' thought (AD: 114-15, DN: 119, 216). Even here, however, there are problems since we cannot know *in advance* which thought is 'one-sided'. In his *Dialectics of Nature*, for example, Engels favoured the view of electricity as the motion of particles of the luminiferous ether partly on the grounds that 'this conception reconciles the two earlier ones'. Yet, Engels also admitted that the ether theory too could be 'supplanted by an entirely new one' as was, of course, to happen (AD: 121-2; see also DN: 271). But if this is the case, the mere fact that the ether theory reconciled earlier, one-sided theories did not guarantee its truth. The recommendation to oppose one-sided thinking is a recommendation to be against sin, because it is only *after* a theory has been shown to be inadequate that we can see that it is 'one-sided' in the first place. We do not reject theories because they are one-sided, but tend to see them as one-sided because we have rejected them. Anyway, it is not clear, even on Engels' own account, that 'one-sided' thinking *is* always to be avoided. He himself argued quite 'one-sidedly', that modern science had no room for the existence of a Creator and refused to adopt less one-sided positions such as that God may both 'exist and not exist' at the same time (AD: 432).

Finally, we should re-emphasise the fact that although, in one sense, the law of the transformation of quantity into quality is an instance of the interpenetration of opposites, the two are, from another perspective, in direct contradiction since the former stresses the existence of real qualitative differences whilst the latter emphasises the extent to which all categories merge and lose their fixity (AD: 27, 56, 82; DN: 67, 205, 215-16). Indeed, from the perspective of the interpenetration of opposites, Engels' insistence on the existence of such qualitative differences would seem to be a classic instance of 'metaphysical' thought. As we have argued above for the existence of certain qualitative differences in reality, it follows that the interpenetration of opposites must be abandoned as a universally valid law.

Contradiction

As we have seen, the existence of contradictions in reality is a central tenet of dialectical materialism. Yet, once we admit the existence of contradictions in reality, we put a halt to all possibility of knowledge. It cannot, for instance, logically be true that Engels both did and did not write *Anti-Dühring*, or that Marx both did and did not read Engels' book. In both cases, knowledge of reality involves the removal of contradiction rather than its recognition. If x is both true and not true at the same time then this means the end to all truth (Popper, 1940: 408-10; Norman and Sayers: 49).

It is not surprising, therefore, that of all Engels' dialectical claims, it is his arguments for the existence of contradictions which have provoked the most far-reaching criticism. It is Gunn who summarises such criticisms most clearly when he describes Engels' dialectics of nature as 'an "animist projection" of human (purposive, teleological) structures onto natural processes.' In other words, when Engels describes natural developments in terms of negations and contradictions, he is being anthropomorphic, describing natural processes in terms of categories applicable only to human understanding. Such criticisms have become well known through the work of Colletti, although his arguments had, in fact, been anticipated by writers such as Kautsky, Eastman and Hook (Pomper: 42-3; Hook, 1955; Sartre: 31-3; Leff: 34-52; Colletti, 1973, 1975; Lichtheim, 1971a: 254; Avineri, 1971: 65, 70; Gunn: 52; Monod: 46; Kolakowski II: 52).

To use the concepts appropriate for the human mind to understand natural processes implies, of course, that the universe itself is a rational, ideal structure. Thus, despite Engels' explicit materialist monism, the claim that reality involves negations and contradictions means, implicitly, an acceptance of the most extreme form of idealism. For Hegel, who believed in the identity of thought and being, and who regarded the universe as the unfolding of a rational structure through logically necessary stages, the dialectic of things was neccessarily a part of the dialectic of ideas. Thus, he could, quite logically, refer to a flower as a refutation of a bud, and to the Greek world as the 'solution' to the 'contradictory principles', or to the 'riddle', of the preceding stages of historical evolution (Hegel, 1971: 68; Hegel, 1956: 115). This option was not, however, open to Engels who had, supposedly, rejected Hegel's idealist ontology. If the dialectic requires a consciousness to generate it (such as Hegel's divine Creator), then no dialectic of nature is possible for a materialist monist. The dialectic is inherently idealist and so cannot be inverted into a materialist form (Hook, 1936: 75; Avineri, 1971: 65, 70; Levine, 1984: 8; Colletti, 1973: 14, 21, 46, 49, 61, 121, 127; Colletti, 1975:

12; Timpanaro: 75; Jones, 1973: 27).

For Colletti, movement in reality is not the product of logical contradictions but rather of real oppositions of positive forces, i.e. not of contradiction, but of 'contrariety', as in the Newtonian concepts of attraction and repulsion. If this is the case, then we have no need of any special dialectical logic where contradictions exist, since what dialecticians refer to as contradictions are in fact real and positive oppositions. Negations thus only exist in reality in the sense that x can cancel the effect of y (Colletti, 1975: 6-9, 14, 16, 18).

An immediate problem with such criticisms is whether they accurately represent the thought of Engels or of Hegel. Colletti's criticism of Engels assumes that, for both Hegel and Engels, the contradictions which are said to exist in reality are logical contradictions, rather than real oppositions. Yet, other writers have argued that, despite the problems which he created for himself by adopting Hegelian terminology, Engels was referring to something different from Hegel. Kolakowski, for instance, sees Engels as confused on the issue of the existence of contradictions but, like Norman, believes that Engels' comments could be translated into a form compatible with both materialism and formal logic (Kolakowski I: 407; Norman and Sayers: 34, 47-8; see also Hillel Ruben, 1979: 41; Benton, 1979: 119). In fact, it has been argued that even for Hegel, contradictions were not simply logical contradictions but were rather real oppositions (Lawler: 11-44). We are thus faced with the choice between accepting that both Hegel and Engels were dealing in logical contradictions; that Hegel was concerned with logical contradictions but Engels was not; or, finally, that neither Hegel nor Engels was discussing logical contradictions. As far as can be ascertained, no one is yet to argue that Hegel was dealing in real oppositions but that Engels was not.

If, with Colletti, we accept that Engels' references to contradictions can *only* be understood in Hegelian terms, then his philosophy must, necessarily, be rejected (except, of course by those committed to ontological idealism). But even if we assume that, by 'contradiction', Engels did mean something other than Hegelian contradiction, problems remain. In particular, it is not clear why his so-called contradictory phenomena should in *any* sense be seen as contradictory. Most of them seem to be rather bland paradoxes, such as the fact that the concept of infinity is made up of finite terms, or that under certain cirumstances curved lines may appear to be straight. Some of Engels' examples, such as that of the allegedly contradictory nature of living beings which we have already discussed, are not even paradoxical. Their apparent internal contradictions are simply the result of arbitrary definition. Nor, as we have seen, does the recognition of movement and process require an acknowledgement of the presence of contradiction: the growth of a barley plant can, depending upon our perspective, be seen as much as the affirmation of the seed as its negation or contradiction.

The return to Hegel: Engels and dialectical materialism

Rather than using the term 'contradiction' as a general label for all opposition, it would be best to reserve it for specific forms of social tension. Engels, for instance, refers to the antagonism of proletariat and bourgeoisie as one of the 'contradictions' of capitalism (AD: 36). Yet, this so-called 'contradiction', which is best seen as an example of 'opposition', is rather different in nature from the contradiction, inherent in the process of capitalist accumulation, that capitalism can only develop by producing more and more of the class which will bring about its own destruction, i.e. that the bourgeoisie 'cuts from under its feet the very foundations' on which it produces (CW 6: 496). Marx and Engels identified a similar contradiction in the fact that, in their search for increased profits, the capitalists are obliged to innovate and mechanise, a process which, ironically, results in a *fall* in the general rate of profit going to the capitalist class (Cap. III: ch. 13).

Such instances of 'counterfinality' can (even if we do not accept the validity of these particular examples) appropriately be referred to as 'contradictions'. But this does not mean that such contradictions are inherent in all oppositions, nor that they constitute cause of all movement, nor that the recognition of their existence requires rejection of formal logic. Nor, as we have seen, does a belief that capitalism possesses such inherent 'contradictions' commit us to the belief that socialism will necessarily emerge as the 'solution' to such contradictions (AD: 369).

Yet, despite the fundamental nature of such criticisms of Engels' philosophy, it should also be noted that, just as the dialectical emphasis on the universe as constant process forms one of the foundations of the modern scientific outlook, so the dialectical emphasis on inherent conflict, opposition and contradiction is a vital contribution to modern social theory. If, at first sight, Engels' emphasis on change and conflict seems rather banal, this impression is soon dispelled upon reading alternative accounts of social structure, such as that of Parsonian sociology or the Toronto School's description of medieval society, with their stress on social functionality, equilibrium, stasis and harmony (Hobsbawm, 1973: 277, 280; Razi, 1979: 152-7; Razi, 1983). Nevertheless, just as a general assumption of movement tells us nothing about the rate or extent of any actual movement, so an expectation of inherent social conflicts tells us nothing about the nature, or the degree, of the conflicts of any particular society. The existence and nature of such dysfunctions cannot be deduced from *a priori* principles but must, like any other scientific or social phenomenon, be demonstrated empirically.

Historical materialism
An assessment of Engels' historical materialism is offered, at length, in chapter nine, below. Here, we need only to examine the connection between Engels' philosophical materialism and his historical materialism. It is often argued that

Dialectical materialism: an assessment

the materialism of Engels is in conflict with that propounded by Marx, since Engels' materialism was concerned with nature and Marx's with society (Leff: 24, 26; Levine, 1984: 7, 66, 105-6). Yet, so long as we adopt the non-reductionist reading of Engels' ontological materialism, his philosophical outlook is quite compatible with the claims of historical materialism. The key issue is thus not whether Engels' philosophical materialism is in opposition to historical materialism, but rather whether historical materialism presupposes philosophical materialism as its foundation.

In practice, there is no reason to assume any *necessary* connection between the two. It would, for instance, be perfectly possible to accept Engels' philosophical anti-supernaturalism and his claim that thought is the product of matter that thinks, and yet to *reject* his historical materialism. As thought, according to the philosophical materialist conception, is itself a material phenomenon, no contradiction would be involved in claiming that its role in history was equal, or even superior, to that of other material phenomena such as production and exchange. Conversely, one could reject Engels' ontology, insist on divine agency as the prime mover in the creation of the universe and yet, so long as one rejected the possibility of direct divine intervention in human affairs, accept historical materialism's claims for the primacy of economic conditions in human history.

Thus whilst Engels attempted to defend both a philosophical and an historical, materialism, there was no reason why one belief should automatically entail the other. The dialectical materialism defended in *Anti-Dühring* and *Dialectics of Nature* was thus neither chronologically nor logically prior to the historical materialism which Engels had helped develop in the the 1840s. As Croce long ago pointed out, historical 'materialism' has turned out to be a rather misleading label term for the social theory of Marx and Engels (Leff: 92-3; Miller, 1979: 106; Lichtheim, 1978: 300; Croce: 7-9).

ENGELS' EPISTEMOLOGY

We can distinguish three major competing forms of epistemology: empiricism; conventionalism; and realism. For empiricism, the acquisition of knowledge proceeds through sense-experience and induction; in the interaction between the object and subject of knowledge, it is the object of knowledge which is stressed whilst the role of the subject is down-played. Conventionalism, on the other hand, stresses the role of the subject of knowledge by arguing that the apparently neutral language of observation and sense-experience privileged by empiricism is, in fact, theory-dependent. 'Knowledge cannot be validated by an appeal to experience because the very terms of our experience presuppose certain knowledge-claims and beg the questions which they are supposed to resolve.' Such knowledge-claims are not merely the result of individual prejudice, but are rather the shared frameworks, or paradigms, of particular communities of scientists. Such paradigms are mutually 'incommensurable', so that, according to Kuhn, people who employ different paradigms, in effect, inhabit different worlds; a point taken to its relativist conclusion by writers such as Winch. Realism, as we shall see below, retains the insistence on an independent, knowable world of empiricism, whilst, like conventionalism, emphasising the role of theory and of our conceptual paradigms in the production of knowledge (Benton, 1977; Kuhn: 117-24, 131; Winch: 48, 102-3; Lovell: 15-22).

As we have seen, it is often argued that Engels' metaphor of 'reflection' implies an empiricist passivity of mind in the production of knowledge; yet there is no reason why this should necessarily be the case. After all, the image of an object reflected in a mirror is not solely dependent upon the properties of the object reflected, but also upon the surface of the mirror: the reflection is the product of the interaction of the two. As Engels said in his draft version of *Anti-Dühring*, 'All ideas are taken from experience, are reflections - *true or distorted* - of reality' (CW 25: 596, emphasis added). Thus, Engels referred to religious thought as a 'fantastic reflection' of reality, a point he had made as early as *The German Ideology* (AD: 410; DN: 180; CW 5: 36).

As Wood has argued, Marx and Engels' 'reflectionism' meant, in practice, no more than the traditional theory of truth, 'the familiar tenets of common sense realism', which assumes, as Thompson puts it, that 'there can be no means of deciding the "adequacy or inadequacy" of knowledge ... unless one presupposes procedures ... devised to establish the correspondence of this knowledge to properties "inscribed in" that real' (Wood, 1981: 182, 186; Thompson, 1978: 209, 236). Engels' epistemology was based on a correspondence theory of truth in which our theories are seen as allowing us at least some partial grasp of the qualities of the object of knowledge. Both realism and empiricism are compatible with a correspondence theory of the truth. Engels, however, rejected the possibility of pure empirical knowledge, stressed the limits of inductive thought and insisted upon the centrality of theory in the production of knowledge.

The critique of empiricism contained in Engels' later works presents a contrast with the empiricist rhetoric of *The German Ideology* (Callinicos, 1987a: 48). In this anti-Heglian work, Marx and Engels had associated an emphasis on the role of concepts in the formation of knowledge with that of the deductive speculation from *a priori* premises characteristic of idealism. They thus claimed that, in place of speculation, their method involved the description of reality in which abstractions served, at best, merely to sum up general results which are 'derived from the observation of the historical development of men. These abstractions in themselves, divorced from real history, have no value whatsoever. They can only serve to facilitate the arrangement of historical material' (CW 5: 37). Engels repeated this attack on philosophical speculation in *Anti-Dühring*, where he argued that we should not deduce the nature of the world *from* our mind but only *through* it: 'if we deduce the basic principles of being from what is, we need no philosophy for this purpose but positive knowledge of the world and of what happens in it; but what this yields is not philosophy either, but positive science' (AD: 45, original emphasis).

Yet, in practice, *The German Ideology* itself proved that the rejection of *a priori* philosophical speculation does not mean that social reality can be directly apprehended, or that abstractions merely 'sum up' empirical observations. Marx and Engels' own analysis showed that we can only understand social relations through the employment of concepts such as 'mode of production', 'forms of intercourse', the 'state', 'ideology' and so forth (CW 5: 53). As we have seen, the indispensability of concepts and theories was to constitute the basis of Engels' critique of empiricism in his writings on the natural sciences.

Engels' emphasis on the importance of theory in his later writings did not, however, tempt him into the conventionalism advocated by recent post-Althusserian writers such as Hindess and Hirst, for whom theories cannot be judged in terms of their correspondence to 'reality' but only in terms of their internal coherence (Hindess and Hirst, 1977: ch. 1; Lovell: 36-7). On the contrary, Engels laid great emphasis on the need to test hypotheses with empirical evidence and experiment. Engels did not accept the conventionalist argument that the adherents of different paradigms, such as the supporters or opponents of the phlogiston theory, live, in effect, in different worlds. Rather, as Sayers puts it, 'Priestley and Lavoisier both inhabited one and the same world, which contains oxygen, and which does not, and never has, contained phlogiston' (Kuhn: 117; Sayers, 1985: 123).

For Engels, as for Kuhn, science advances through anomalies which require new forms of explanation of experimental evidence (DN: 244). Engels believed, however, that reference to anomalies which are capable of throwing paradigms into doubt, assumes a correspondence theory of truth in which our theories give us partial access to external reality. Thus, Engels' insistence on the need for empirical procedures and controls was, despite Althusser's claims to the contrary, not 'an empiricist ideology of knowledge.' Engels' theory was empirical, not empiricist; unless, of course, by empiricist we mean all correspondence theories of truth (Althusser and Balibar: 115; Thompson, 1978: 202, 224).

Engels' critique of pure empiricism and inductionism; his rejection of absolute truth, and his insistence that science develops through a series of hypotheses which are progressively falsified; his emphasis on the interaction of theory and of empirical testing in the production of knowledge; and his correspondence theory of truth, may seem to bring him very close to a Popperian realism (Miller, 1983: ch. 17). He even rejected spiritualism on the grounds that it had put itself beyond the possibility of falsification, which is, of course, Popper's requirement for a theory to qualify for scientific status (DN: 62).

Yet, unlike Popper, Engels *did* claim that it was possible to 'prove' scientific theories. In 1878, for example, Engels referred to the Copernican world system as 'still only a hypothesis.' A decade later, however, he argued that this system, which for three hundred years had been a hypothesis, even if one 'with a hundred, a thousand or ten thousand chances to one in its favour', was now, with the confirmation of the existence of the planet Neptune, which had been predicted on the basis of this system, finally 'proved'. Similarly, opposition to Kant's theory of the origin of the celestial bodies from rotating nebular masses had been silenced by the 'irrefutable spectroscopic proof' of the existence of such masses (AD: 70-1; SW II: 336).

For Engels, the test of a theory lies in human practice, a claim which can, of course, be traced back to Marx's *Theses on Feuerbach*. Engels argued that the truth of our theories and perceptions of objects could be tested by turning things to our use: 'if we succeed in accomplishing our aim, if we find that the object does agree with our idea of it, and does answer the purpose we intended it for, then that is positive proof that our perceptions of it and its qualities, so far, agree with reality outside ourselves' (AD: 108, 432; CW 5: 5, 8).

This emphasis on experience in the production of knowledge has recently been reasserted and celebrated by E. P Thompson ('the farmer "knows" his seasons, the sailor "knows" his seas'), yet it involves a number of problems (Thompson, 1978: 199). As Hirst points out, sailors may know their seas, 'but they also know where not to go in order to avoid the sea monsters' whilst 'witch hunters "know" their witches, they can smell them a mile off and can search out their palpable marks with unerring accuracy' (Hirst: 73; see also Anderson, 1980: 27). Similarly, it has been argued that 'experience' did not, at first, refute the Ptolemaic system of astronomy, in which the sun and the planets orbited the Earth. On the contrary, this system 'was compatible with observations of planetary positions and capable of predicting future planetary positions', and could thus be used as the basis of successful navigation (Chalmers: 68). The apparently successful application of a theory does corroborate it but it cannot guarantee the theory against eventual falsification.

The problems involved in Engels' invocation of 'experience' as a test of our theories are emphasised in the work of recent realist writers, who have argued that the reality which our theories attempt to grasp should not be confused with external appearances. They argue that experience has to be interpreted, in terms of our theories and concepts, in order to gain access to the 'deeper' structures which actually determines appearances (Lovell: 19).

Engels himself anticipated this line of argument when he emphasised that although atoms and molecules are not directly observable under the microscope, they are not merely useful fictions for ordering our empirical material, but rather refer to actual properties of material reality (AD: 433; DN: 208). Similarly, in political economy, Engels believed that Marx's theory of surplus-value had revealed the 'inner reality' of modern society. It had allowed Marx to 'lay bare its essential character' which had previously been hidden, and so 'revealed the core around which the whole existing social order has crystallized' (AD: 34, 262-3, 273-4). Thus, in his emphasis on both the centrality of theory and of empirical evidence in the production of knowledge, and in his stress on the deep structures (atoms, molecules, surplus-value), which determine surface appearances, Engels has much in common with modern realist philosophy.

Having, in our assessment of Engels' ontology, avoided making a judgement about the existence of God, it will be hoped that readers will forgive our failure to reach a definitive conclusion about whether we can have access to knowledge about reality in our assessment of Engels' epistemology. Here we will simply note three arguments which may lend some credence to Engels' non-empiricist correspondence theory of truth, although they are unlikely to persuade those who are already convinced sceptics.

We have already accepted the critique of empiricism put forward by both realism and conventionalism, on the grounds that 'all observations are theory impregenated' (Popper, quoted in Giddens, 1974: 18). The choice facing us is thus between realism and conventionalism. Our case against conventionalism rests on three main arguments. The first is that the fact that all observations are theory impregnated does *not* necessarily involve a circular logic, in which our conclusions are implicit in the premises of our paradigm. Lovell cites the example of the theory of planetary motion, which requires the use of the telescope for its empirical observation: 'The telescope is not a theory-neutral instrument of observation, but it may be treated as such for this purpose, since the theory on which it depends - the theory of optics - is not the same as the theory which it is being used to test' (Lovell: 20-1). This argument does not, however, deal with the objection that any one theory is thus, inevitably, based on an infinite regression of other theories.

A second objection to relativist conventionalism is that it is difficult to imagine how this theory could, on its own premises, ever be shown to be true. For, if we claim that all descriptions of reality are merely the product of self-contained and incommensurable paradigms, we are, ironically, making a claim about the real world, whilst at the same time denying ourselves any authority to make such claims: 'Notoriously there is no room for the assertion of relativism itself in a world in which relativism is true' (Gellner, 1986: 85). Relativism thus faces the paradox that if it is covered by its own generalisation, 'it undermines it own truth' whilst, if it is *not* covered by it, 'it falsifies itself, by being itself a truth' (Geras, 1990b: 19-20).

The final reason for preferring realism to conventionalism is that, as we have seen, writers such as Kuhn themselves accept the existence of 'anomalies', which throw paradigms into doubt and cause the rise of new paradigms. Yet, the possibility of such anomalies testifies 'to the existence of a real world which is independent of theory but which theory explains, more or less adequately.' 'The notion of putting theory to the test makes no sense on the conventionalist interpretation of knowledge construction.' If it is impossible to distinguish between theories in term of their reality-claims, then scientific experiments or appeals to historical evidence would have to be seen as 'ritual games' which scientists and historians play, perhaps as a result of their philosophical naiveté or, more sinisterly, as a means of legitimating their authority to make pronouncements about the world (Lovell 19-21; Sayers, 1985: 123). Conventionalism thus teeters between two contradictory positions: lapsing back, on occasion, into the correspondence theory of truth; or, conversely, advancing logically to a full-blown relativism.

Engels' epistemology was based on the assumption that, although we cannot have direct, theory-free knowledge of the world, we could know something about it; our knowledge progresses as hypotheses survive, or fail, the test of experiment and research. Just as, in our discussion of Engels' ontology, we argued for a *de facto* atheism on the pragmatic grounds that only by bracketing the existence of God could we get on with the task of analysing the natural universe and human history, so we have argued in favour of Engels' correspondence theory of truth, on the grounds that it is this theory which, for the moment at least, functions as the working basis of the natural and social sciences.

CONCLUSION

So far we have emphasised the shortcomings of Engels' dialectical materialist ontology: i) the law of the transformation of quantity into quality, whilst accurately describing certain forms of change, is neither predictive nor universal in its application and is in direct contradiction with the claims of the law of the interpenetration of opposites; ii) the law of the negation of the negation is similarly non-universal in its application, depends upon an analogy of organic growth which is not an appropriate way to characterise social development and is based on an arbitrary definition of what constitutes a 'negation'; iii) the interpenetration of opposites must also be rejected as a universal law on the grounds that it is in contradiction with the partially-valid law of the transformation of quantity into quality; iv) the acceptance of the existence of contradictions in reality puts an end to any possibility of knowledge of the world; the term 'contradiction', should, if it is to be used at all, be reserved to describe specific forms of social dysfunction.

Yet, ultimately, for all the ambitiousness of its universal laws of development of material and social reality and the massive shortcomings which they involve, what is most striking about Engels' philosophy is not so much its erroneousness, as its vacuity. In its minimalist version at least, dialectical materialism's main weakness is not that it is wrong, but that it is redundant. In this reading, dialectical materialism becomes merely a *post facto* descriptive gloss which we give to scientific advances which have been arrived at by other means, as in Fock's claim that Einstein's theory of relativity was yet another proof of the truth of dialectics. Dialectical materialism can thus be invoked, *after* the event, to validate virtually any opinion, whilst, in turn, virtually any scientific advance can be invoked to validate dialectics. As a result, Engels' philosophy becomes a scientifically irrelevant banality. As Colletti has pointed out, and as Engels himself was aware, we may, if we so wish, refer to the growth of a tadpole into a frog, and the transition from capitalism to socialism, as examples of the negation of the negation, but this tells us absolutely nothing about these processes which we did not know already (AD: 180; Hook, 1950: 220, 262; Hook, 1955: 24; Leff 19-20; Colletti, 1972: 27).

The banality of dialectical materialism is, ironically, nowhere more apparent than in the works of those writers who have attempted to *defend* it. Somerville, for example, claims that the laws of the dialectic represent universal patterns of change, yet concedes that these laws cannot be used to predict any *specific* change. He nevertheless argues that a knowledge of dialectics is useful since it reminds us that, in dealing with any subject matter, we should seek to establish where it came from; where it is going; and the content and rate of its change (Somerville: 67-70; see also Lewis: 133).

However, in its maximalist version, where it functions as a philosophical thought-police, dialectical materialism necessarily becomes an obstacle to scientifc progress, as for instance, in Maskimov's claim to be able to *deduce* that Einstein's theory of relativity was wrong, on the *a priori* grounds that it was counter to the truth of dialectics (Kolakowski III: 131-2). Engels explicitly warned of the dangers of such philosophical schemata, whilst not avoiding their pitfalls himself.

However, if the major weakness of Engels' dialectical materialism is its vacuity, then its Marxist opponents may be wrong to criticise it on the grounds that it is incompatible with historical materialism. In fact, its real weakness is that it is not incompatible with *anything*, and thus puts itself beyond the possibility of being tested. However, before we examine the relationship between historical and dialectical materialism, we need first to establish the degree to which Marx himself shared Engels' dialectical materialist outlook.

CHAPTER EIGHT

Was Marx an 'Engelsist'?

> The laws of appropriation or of private property, laws based on the production and circulation of commodities, become changed into their direct opposite through their own internal and inexorable dialectic (Cap. I: 729).

Engels himself saw works such as *Anti-Dühring* and *Ludwig Feuerbach* as an attempt to make explicit the outlook which had underlain his and Marx's views since *The Holy Family*, *The Poverty of Philosophy* and the *Communist Manifesto*, views for which he consistently gave Marx most of the credit (AD: 8-9, 423-4; SW II: 348-9). For Draper, *Anti-Dühring* is the only systematic statement of Marxism ever made by Marx or Engels (Draper: 24). Yet, for many others, Engels' dialectical materialism contrasted sharply with Marx's outlook. Indeed, this view has now become so taken for granted that it constitutes the orthodoxy of sociology primers (Rex: 73-4). To what extent did Engels' views of of the 1870s and 1880s depart from those of the 1840s, and how far was Engels' intellectual development shared by Marx?

In order to answer these questions we will, unfortunately, have to enter some rather arcane debates about 'what Marx really said'. It should be stressed, however, that our aim here is not to embark upon the impossible quest for Marx or Engels' 'real meaning', in the sense of some single, coherent, consciously intended message. Rather, our aim is to identify the contradictory discourses present in their texts; discourses which explain the incredible variety of ways in which these texts are received and their 'meaning' constituted.

PHILOSOPHICAL MATERIALISM

Jordan usefully distinguishes 'absolute materialism' (the belief that only matter is real and nothing else exists in the universe) from 'genetic materialism' (the belief that mind is derived from matter). He argues that Engels was an absolute materialist (and thus also a genetic materialist) and contrasts his views with those of Marx: for Engels, only matter was real; for Marx, only nature was real (Jordan: 152-3). Similarly, Avineri denies that Marx shared

Engels' brand of 'mechanistic' materialism, Schmidt claims that Marx, unlike Engels, was not an ontological materialist, whilst Fetscher has argued that Marx and Engels had different conceptions of nature since 'for the young Marx' (sic) extra-human nature was irrelevant for philosophical and political purposes (Avineri, 1971: 65; Schmidt, 1971: 56-9; Fetscher: 162-72).

Yet, for Engels, matter was not a thing, but a concept which he employed as a synonym for 'nature as it really is', without any supernatural addition (DN: 202, 239). It is thus difficult to see any difference between Engels' materialism and Marx's alleged 'naturalism', i.e. the belief that consciousness does not exist prior to matter but is rather its highest form (Hook, 1936: 71). Indeed, even Schmidt, who emphasises the differences between Marx and Engels' world-views, accepts that for Marx the universe consisted of matter in motion (Schmidt, 1971: 77; Cap. I: 133). If, as we have argued, at length, Engels' materialist monism was not inherently mechanistic or reductionist, there is no reason to oppose Engels to the 'anti-positivist' philosophical materialism ascribed to Marx by many writers. Thus, when Marx described himself as a materialist he was, like Engels, defining his views in opposition to ontological idealism which transforms the process of thinking into an independent subject, the Hegelian Idea; for Marx, 'the reverse is true: the ideal is nothing but the material world reflected in the mind of man and translated into forms of thought' (Cap. I: 102: SC: 187).

This is not to say, however, that both Marx and Engels simply shared a non-positivist materialism. On the contrary, the two men not only contradicted each other, but also contradicted themselves on this issue. Thus, as we have seen, Engels both denied and asserted the differences between the natural and the social sciences. Similarly, Marx, who from 1864 was immersing himself in the natural sciences (Gerratana: 76; Rubel and Manale: 197, 210, 243, 308, 328), produced a number of vulgar materialist and positivist claims of the type for which Engels is so frequently criticised, and which are quite incompatible with the anti-positivist 'Marx' with whom we have become so familiar.

The classic instance of such claims is Marx's reception of Darwin. According to Walton and Gamble, it was Engels who saw Darwin as a proof that the same natural laws were valid for human society as for all life, whereas, for Marx, the importance of Darwin was that he had put an end to all teleology outside of human purpose (Walton and Gamble: 72). In fact, as we have seen, it was Engels who first praised Darwin's rejection of teleology (CW 40: 551; CW 41: 246-7). More importantly, however, it was Marx, not Engels, who welcomed *On the Origin of the Species* as 'the book which, in the field of natural history, provides the basis for our views' (CW 41: 232). That, by this formulation, Marx meant that Darwin's views on *biological* evolution were the basis for his and Engels' views on *social* development, was emphasised by Marx's letter to Lassalle, of 1861, in which he claimed that 'Darwin's work is most important and suits my purpose in that it provides a basis in natural science for the historical class struggle' (CW 41: 246-7).

As is well known, Engels did, in his eulogy at Marx's graveside, compare Marx's achievement to Darwin's, in the sense that, just as Darwin had 'discovered the law of development of organic nature, so Marx discovered the law of development of human history' (SW II: 153). Engels did not, however, claim that Marx's discovery was the *same* as Darwin's, although this step had already been taken by Kautsky, who had claimed that, like Marxism, Darwinism showed that 'the transition from an old to a new conception of the world occurs irresistibly' (Salvadori: 23-4). Kautsky's Darwinism is often criticised as a distortion of Marxism, yet it was Marx himself who suggested to Engels that, in reviewing *Capital* in Karl Mayer's *Der Beobachter*, he should argue that, in showing that 'present society, economically considered, is pregnant with a new, higher form', Marx was 'only showing in the social context the same gradual process of evolution that Darwin had demonstrated in natural history' (CW 42: 493-4).

Marx made very similar comments in the 'Preface' to the first edition of *Capital*, where he justified his study of England to his German audience by claiming that just as 'the physicist either observes natural processes where they occur in their most significant form', or sets up experiments to observe such processes in their pure state, so he had studied England as the *locus classicus* of capitalism. Countries such as England, only showed less industrialised countries, such as Germany, the image of its own future, since the tendencies of the 'natural laws of capitalist production' were in the process of 'working themselves out with iron necessity.' A knowledge of such 'natural laws' of social movement did not mean that society could 'leap over the natural phases of its development', but it did mean that the 'birth-pangs' of the new society could be lessened. Thus the present society is 'no solid crystal, but an organism capable of change.' Elsewhere in *Capital*, Marx described the abolition of capitalist private property as a process which occurred with the 'inexorability of a natural process' (Cap. I: 90-3, 929).

In his 'Postface' to the second edition of *Capital*, a copy of which he sent to Darwin (Rubel and Manale: 291), Marx approvingly quoted, at length, the Russian reviewer of the first edition who had seen Marx as treating 'the social movement as a process of natural history, governed by laws not only independent of human will, but rather, on the contrary, determining that will ... As soon as [economic - S.R.] life has passed through a given period of development, and is passing over from one given stage to another, it begins to be subject also to other laws. In short, economic life offers a phenomenon analogous to the history of evolution in other branches of biology.' Thus the historically specific laws of economic life were more like the laws of biology, in which plants and animals differed fundamentally from each other, than those of physics or chemistry. Marx's book had thus illuminated the 'laws that regulate the origin, existence, development and death of a given social organism and its replacement by another, higher one.' It is unfortunate that Marx did not describe his method at such length in his own words, but, nevertheless, after summarising the comments of this reviewer, Marx added, 'what else is he depicting but the dialectical method?' (Cap I: 101-2).

It is difficult, after reading such passages, to see how they differ from the emphasis on the predictability and necessity of social evolution which are so often seen as characteristic of Engels' and the Second International's positivist 'distortion' of Marx (Levine, 1984: 39). It is also difficult to see how their view of social development as that of law-bound organic process through necessary stages differs from that of early positivists such as Comte and Saint-Simon or why the search for a natural scientific methodology suitable for the study of the human world should be blamed solely on Engels rather than on Marx (Benton, 1977: 27-8; Avineri, 1971: 72). To avoid inevitable misunderstandings, it should be emphasised that such comments are *not* made as the result of any desire to rehabilitate Engels' positivist lapses, but rather to show that Marx cannot be defended simply by using Engels as a scapegoat for the views which Marx himself quite explicitly formulated.

Nor can Marx be rescued by the argument that, whereas Engels saw the *same* dialectical laws applying in nature and society, Marx merely saw social laws as *analogous* to natural laws (Levine, 1984: 170). On the contrary, in the passages cited above, Marx ignores the role of consciousness in distinguishing historical from natural development, thus forgetting his own achievement of the 1840s (Jordan: 299, 308). He assumes that, as in the natural sciences, the results of social science can be formulated as law-like generalisations, a central claim, of course, of positivist social science (Giddens, 1974: 4).

It is equally difficult, after reading such passages, to understand those writers who seek to deny that Marx was capable of being 'scientistic' and who reject Lichtheim and McLellan's claim that Marx became more 'positivist' in his writings of the 1860s and 1870s, than he had been in the 1840s. Such passages also throw doubt on their claim that Marx always insisted on the role of human volition in social processes (Thomas: 4, 9, 17; Carver, 1980; Lichtheim, 1971a: 236, 243; McLellan, 1976: 423; see also Timpanaro: 91). Miller is thus certainly correct to say that Marx's views on social causality were liable to what Miller sees as a 'mistaken' positivist reading since they were, in fact, read in this way by some of Marx's earliest readers and even, at times, by Marx himself (Miller, 1979: 86). It seems nowadays that those writers who wish to defend Marx have rejected the traditional Marxist assumption that if Marx said something, it must necessarily be correct, only to replace it with the assumption that if something is incorrect, then Marx could not have said it.

The return to Hegel: Engels and dialectical materialism

Whilst Lichtheim sees Marx as becoming more positivist in his later years, he argues that Marx never completely succumbed to 'vulgar materialism' in the way that Engels did (Lichtheim, 1971a: 243, 258). Yet, that Marx was capable of lapsing into a form of vulgar materialism seems evident from his reception of Pierre Trémaux's *Origine et Transformation de l'Homme et des autres Etres*, an episode which tends to be ignored by those who favour an anti-positivist reading of Marx (Timpanaro: 93).

Trémaux's book, which was published in 1865, argued for an extreme, environmental determinist theory of evolution, in which the nature of regional soil types determined racial differences, and even the psychological characteristics of their inhabitants. That the Bretons were conservative, whilst the Parisians were democractic, was thus the product of their local soil types. Such influences could, however, be affected and distorted by the impact of diet and interbreeding (Paul: 122). Trémaux's book, which is now forgotten (except for Marx's comments on it), was described by Marx, in a letter to Engels of 7 August 1866, as 'a very important work' which, 'despite its many shortcomings' represented, 'a *very significant* advance over Darwin' (Marx's emphasis). Marx welcomed Trémaux's argument that the physical features of the earth were responsible for the evolutionary differentation of the species, as it allowed Trémaux to see evolutionary progress, 'which Darwin regards as purely accidental', as essential 'on the basis of the stage of the earth's development' (CW 42: 304-5).

More importantly, for our purposes, Marx went on to conclude that Trémaux's work was, 'in its historical and political applications, far more significant and pregnant than Darwin. For certain questions, such as nationality etc., *only here has a basis in nature been found.*' As an example, he cited Trémaux's argument that the Russians had been 'tartarised and mongolised' because of the surface-formation predominant in Russia. Marx ended his letter with a long quotation from Trémaux, which warned that all attempts by humanity to ignore the 'great laws of nature' could only lead to calamity, 'witness the efforts of the Czars to make Muscovites of the Polish people ... The same soil will give rise to the same character and the same qualities' (CW 42: 304-5, emphasis added; Elster, 1985: 60-1).

Engels gave his opinion of Trémaux's book in a letter to Marx of 2 October 1866 where he claimed that although he had 'not quite finished' reading it, it was 'utterly worthless, pure theorising in defiance of all the facts' and that Trémaux was 'incapable of even the most common-or-garden literary-historical critique.' Engels did not, as Paul claims, only criticise the factual accuracy and consistency of the geological basis of Trémaux's theories. He also ridiculed Trémaux's ethnographic claims that the differences between the Basques, the French, the Bretons and the Alsatians were the result of 'surface-structure, which is, of course, also to blame for the people speaking four different languages.' Marx replied the following day by defending Trémaux against Engels' criticisms. He emphasised that his 'basic idea about the influence of the soil' was correct, even though Trémaux had ignored man's historical modifications of the influence of soil type through agriculture and so on (CW 42: 306, 309, 320, 322; Paul).

In turn, Engels replied to Marx that, when he had written his first letter he had, in fact, only read the first, and poorest, third of the book. Engels now accepted that Trémaux was correct to emphasise 'the effect of the "soil" on the evolution of races and logically of species as well', although he still criticised the detail of the latter's argument. However, Engels continued, even if Trémaux's emphasis on soil types on evolution were correct, 'all the further conclusions he draws are either totally mistaken or incredibly one-sided and exaggerated.' His *ethnological* examples, 'in particular, the ones that concern countries and peoples which are generally known, are almost without exception erroneous either in their geological premises or in the conclusions drawn from them' (CW 42: 323-4).

The issue was then dropped in the correspondence between the two men. Marx did, however, recommend Trémaux's book to Kugelmann in a letter of 9 October 1866, in which he repeated many of Engels' criticisms but still claimed that 'it represents ... an advance over Darwin' (CW 42: 327). Lengthy quotations have been necessary here to show that, despite Carver's claims, Marx did not merely argue that Trémaux had established the 'geological limits' of society, but rather saw Trémaux as providing 'a basis in nature' for historical phenomena such as nationality (Carver, 1984b: 255). In this case at least, Marx's 'materialism' involved far more than just an emphasis on the production of the material conditions of life as determinant in history. It becomes a vulgar materialist attempt to derive society from nature, of exactly the type for which Engels so regularly undergoes ritual castigation (Miller, 1979: 7; Cornu: 116; Lichtheim, 1978: 299; Carver, 1984b: 253; Korsch, 1938: 196).

This certainly does not mean that such passages prove that Marx was *simply* a vulgar materialist or a positivist; if this were the case, it is unlikely that we would still be discussing his work today. What they do mean, however, is that the fact that certain texts bear Marx's name is no guarantee of their unity or consistency (Barthes: 46). Thus, despite the apparent social Darwinism of the letters cited above, on other occasions, Marx himself explicitly criticised the direct application of biology to human history. As he wrote to Kugelmann in 1870, it was quite wrong to attempt to bring the whole of history 'under a single great natural law', the Darwinian 'struggle for life.' Engels repeated this point in a letter to Lavrov, of 1875, where he criticised the attempt to apply Darwin's theory as 'eternal laws of human society', and in his lengthy critique of social Darwinism in his *Dialectics of Nature* (SC: 225, 284; DN: 208, 312-

16). Similarly in *Capital*, despite its 'positivist' formulations, Marx also emphasised the differences between human history and natural history: 'we have made the former but not the latter' (Cap. I: 493). Once we accept the existence of such contradictions in Marx's works, it becomes impossible to set up a simple binary opposition between Marx's emphasis on the role of the human subject in history, and Engels' positivist emphasis on history as a process analogous to natural development.

DIALECTICS

The key issue, in assessing the intellectual relationship between Marx and Engels, is whether Marx shared the dialectical ontology propounded in Engels' later works. Inevitably, opinions differ on this issue. For some writers, Marx's writings are in line with Engels' dialectical materialist ontology (Marquitt et al.: 7; Kain: 116); for others they are not (McBride: 58; Hook, 1934: 35-8), or are so only rarely (Colletti, 1975: 18; Levine, 1984: 7, 10). Thus, for Callinicos, it is significant that Marx never explicitly rejected Engels' laws of the dialectic, whereas for Carver the key point is that Marx never specifically agreed with them (Callinicos, 1987a: 62; Carver, 1984b: 249).

Marx certainly does seem to characterise dialectics in ontological, rather than simply in methodological, terms in his comments on Hegel in the 'Postface' to the second edition of *Capital*. Marx argued that, in its 'rational form', Hegel's dialectic was an abomination to the bourgeoisie, 'because it includes in its positive understanding of what exists a simultaneous recognition of its negation, its inevitable destruction; because it regards every historically developed form as being in a fluid state, in motion, and therefore grasps its transient aspect as well.' Thus, in a dialectical perspective, 'the movement of capitalist society is full of contradictions', as witnessed by its periodic crises. Indeed, after citing the lengthy passage from his Russian reviewer quoted above, Marx referred to his 'own dialectical method' as showing 'the necessity of the present order of things and the necessity of another order into which the first must inevitably pass over' (Cap. I: 101-3).

Thus what Marx referred to as his 'dialectical method' was not merely a tool of analysis, but also had inbuilt ontological assumptions about totality, contradiction and process (Wood, 1981: 27, 98, 142, 159, 208-18; Edgley: 293). That Marx did not just have human history in mind, in his dialectical emphasis on change and development, is borne out by his remark that the weakness of the 'abstract materialism of natural science' is that it 'excludes the historical process' (Cap. I: 494). Indeed, as early as *The Poverty of Philosphy*, Marx had claimed that 'All that exists on land and under water, exists and lives only by some kind of movement' (CW 6: 163). Marx and Engels do, therefore, seem to have shared a view of the universe as consisting of matter in motion, and of nature as undergoing its own historical process of development.

However, even if Marx and Engels shared the same broad materialist ontology, this does not necessarily mean that Marx accepted Engels' claims to have identified the dialectical laws at work in nature. Carver's works provide the most lengthy and cogent defence of the view that Marx and Engels fundamentally disagreed on this matter. He argues that the absence of any positive proof that Marx agreed with Engels' views means, since these views conflict with those expressed elsewhere by Marx, that he did not accept them (Carver, 1980: 360). Marx, for some reason, 'found it convenient' to keep quiet about this disagreement, perhaps because he did not feel the need to contradict opinions which were being published under Engels' name. Indeed, he may not even have been aware of Engels' views as the first edition of *Anti-Dühring* (the only one to appear in Marx's lifetime) did not contain Engels' general views on the dialectic (Carver, 1980: 360-1; 1981: ch. 5). There is, Carver argues, no evidence that Marx had even read Engels' work, apart from Engels' claim, two years after Marx's death, that he himself had read *Anti-Dühring* to Marx, on the automatic understanding that his exposition of Marx's outlook 'should not be issued without his knowledge' (AD: 9). Carver asks why Engels did not make this claim when Marx himself was alive and emphasises that Marx himself never explicitly endorsed the views expressed by Engels in *Anti-Dühring* (Carver 1984b: 249). Was there, then, a fundamental disparity between Engels' views and those expressed by Marx?

Marx, Engels and Schorlemmer
A key episode in the debate about whether Marx shared Engels' views is Marx's response to Engels' letter on the dialectics of nature of May 1873 (see p. 101 above). For Carver, this episode shows that, although Marx was aware that Engels was working on the dialectics of nature, when Engels actually sent him his detailed thoughts on dialectics, Marx was 'stand-offish.' Marx replied to Engels by saying 'Have just received your letter which has pleased me greatly. But I do not want to hazard an opinion before I've had time to think the matter over and to consult the "authorities".' These authorities were not, according to Carver, 'very impressed with Engels's insights, though Marx tried to break this to him gently.' Thus, the chemist Schorlemmer, who added marginal comments to Engels' letter after Marx had sent it to him, agreed that the natural sciences studied matter in motion but, Carver argues, was not enthusiastic on the section of Engels' letter on dialectics (Carver, 1980: 358-9; 1981: 52; 1983: 127; 1984b: 252).

Carver's interpretation of this episode is rather remarkable. Firstly, Schorlemmer did *not* merely agree with Engels' natural science but disagree with his dialectics. Engels had described the *entire* contents of his letter as a summary of his 'dialectical ideas on the natural sciences.' Thus, when Schorlemmer wrote 'Very good; my own view', 'Quite true' and 'That's the point' in the margin of Engels' letter, he was agreeing with what Engels saw as his dialectical conception of science. Secondly, Schorlemmer did *not* disagree with Engels' reference to the dialectics of organisms, but merely added 'Neither will I' to Engels' comment that he would not embark on any dialectics in this field 'for the time being' (TORR: 322-3). Thirdly, there was no reason, apart from a lack of technical expertise, why Marx should have been wary in his reception of Engels' letter, as it made no claims about dialectics in society and confined itself solely to a discussion of the character of the natural sciences.

Finally, the significance of Schorlemmer's marginal annotations can only be understood if we see them in the context of his relations with Marx and Engels, and of his own scientific work. Carl Schorlemmer was a German scientist who joined Owen's College, Manchester, in 1859, as assistant to Roscoe, where he became the first professor of organic chemistry in England in 1874. When Schorlemmer first met Engels (probably by 1865, certainly by 1867) he was already a communist, and the latter introduced him to Marx, who corresponded with him about organic chemistry. After Engels' move to London in 1870, Schorlemmer paid him frequent visits, he was one of only half a dozen non-family members to attend Marx's funeral and, in 1892, it was Engels who wrote Schorlemmer's obituary in *Vorwärts* (Henderson, 1976 I: 262-71; Roberts). Thus, when Marx wrote to Schorlemmer for advice he was not writing to an independent authority, but to Engels' close friend with whom Engels had already discussed scientific issues (CW 42: 117, 378, 383, 387-8, 560).

Unfortunately, it is not possible to establish Schorlemmer's philosophy of science prior to Engels' letter on dialectics of 1873. However, many of Schorlemmer's later writings clearly reveal that, far from disagreeing with Engels, there were close parallels between the work of the two men. Thus Schorlemmer and Roscoe's *A Treatise on Chemistry*, published in German in 1876 and in English in 1877, written, according to Engels, 'almost entirely' by Schorlemmer (TORR: 323), praised Lavoisier for being the first to assert distinctly the principle of the indestructibility of matter (Roscoe and Schorlemmer: 25, 47; see AD: 74, 81). Like Engels, Schorlemmer argued that all organic beings are 'constantly undergoing changes' as they assimilate carbon and liberate gas (Roscoe and Schorlemmer: 51; AD: 153).

However, it is in his *The Rise and Development of Organic Chemistry* (1879) that Schorlemmer's philosophical views are most apparent. Here, Schorlemmer followed Engels in his praise for Heraclitus' clear conception of the link between matter and motion; emphasised that atoms 'must be considered as continually in motion'; and, like Engels, adopted Hegel's hierarchy of the forms of motion as the basis of his account of the history of the natural sciences. More specifically, he argued that, in science, 'we must not forget that our present theory is not a dogma but continually changes according to the laws of dialectic' (Schorlemmer, 1879: 6, 75, 94; AD: 24, 70; Wood, 1981: 214). The links between the two men can also be seen in Schorlemmer's claim that the origin of life, the area where neither Engels nor Schorlemmer had attempted any dialectics in 1873, was to be found in the synthesis of an albuminus compound. In 1885, Engels claimed the credit for this hypothesis, even though it was Schorlemmer who had been attacked for it in public. Thus both men assumed that vitalist accounts of the origin of life were mistaken and that 'the same chemical laws rule inanimate and animate nature' (Schorlemmer, 1879: 17, 122; AD: 434; Roberts: 111).

The revised, 1894 edition of Schorlemmer's work made his intellectual ties with Engels even clearer. In his discussion of tautomerism, for example, he argued that there were two opposed views on this subject, but that some compounds contradicted *both* of them. This showed that what was needed was a 'dialectical treatment of the subject', and 'justified even for molecules the axiom of Heraclitus that everything is in eternal flux.' Indeed, in his discussions of the molecular structure of paraffins, he actually quoted *Anti-Dühring* to the effect that 'quantitative change of the molecule produces every time a qualitatively different body' (Schorlemmer, 1894: 142, 183-4; AD: 162).

Thus, far from Schorlemmer being critical of Engels' dialectics, his work defended a view of the universe as a unity consisting of indestructible matter in motion; emphasised the existence of both qualitative, as well as quantitative change; argued that since reality was contradictory, a dialectical treatment of it was needed; and claimed that thought itself develops according to dialectical laws. It would be wrong to pit Schorlemmer against Engels, rather they, along with Marx, should be seen as members of an intellectual circle which developed its views through mutual discussion and co-operation (Stanley and Zimmermann: 236). As Levine has argued, Engels' science was not outdated by contemporary standards (Levine, 1984: 84, 95); it was certainly perfectly in line with Schorlemmer's thought. Indeed, it is likely that Schorlemmer played an important part in the development of Engels' materialist dialectics, even if, as Roberts suggests, this outlook was Engels' own invention (after all, its origins lay as far back as 1858), and Schorlemmer's primary role was in providing the scientific evidence to illustrate it (Roberts: 111).

Marx and Anti-Dühring
The key issue in the discussion of the relationship between the thought of Marx and Engels is not, however, Marx's response to Engels' 1873 letter on the dialectics of nature, but rather whether Marx was aware of the contents of

The return to Hegel: Engels and dialectical materialism

Anti-Dühring. Carver claims that there is no evidence that Marx had read Engels' work, although he admits that Engels did send Marx an inscribed copy of the book (Carver, 1981: 76). Certainly, as Carver emphasises, Engels' letter to Marx of May 1876, in which he summarised his approach to Dühring's work, was couched in very general terms and made no mention of the laws of the dialectic (SC: 287). Nor, despite Welty's claims, does the fact that Marx contributed a chapter on politcal economy to *Anti-Dühring* mean that he was aware of the contents of the rest of the volume. Nor is Marx's letter of January 1877, asking Freud for references to Traube's work on metabolism on Engels' behalf, proof that Marx knew the contents of *Anti-Dühring* even prior to its publication, since Traube's work is also mentioned in *The Dialectics of Nature* (although this letter certainly does imply that Marx had some knowledge of Engels' work on the philosophy of nature) (Welty; AD: 101; DN: 307).

However, it is not true that the first edition of *Anti-Dühring* did not contain Engels' general views on dialectics and that these only appeared in his 'Preface' to the second edition of 1885, two years after Marx's death (Carver, 1980: 361). On the contrary, the first edition of the work contained lengthy defences of the view that nature, history and thought developed dialectically. Indeed, it included a lengthy defence of the dialectical against the metaphysical outlook, which was to be reprinted in *Socialism: Utopian and Scientific*, a work to which, as we shall see, Marx himself was to write a 'Preface' (SW II: 118-25).

Nor is it a mystery that Engels only claimed Marx's endorsement in the 1885 edition of *Anti-Dühring*. After all, Marx's position had not been an issue in the first edition of 1878 when Marx was still alive, since, incredible though it may seem to many modern Marxists, Marx and Engels saw themselves, and were seen by others, as the representatives of a shared political position within the German labour movement. This assumption is apparent in their joint response to the Gotha Programme (1875) of the newly-united Socialist Workers' Party of Germany. As Marx put it: 'Engels and I will publish a short declaration to the effect that our position is altogether remote from the said programme of principles and that we have nothing to do with it' (SC: 272-81; SW II: 13-41). Only with Marx's death, in 1883, did the status of *Anti-Dühring* become an issue which Engels had to clarify in the second edition of his work.

It would be possible to argue *deductively* that it was extremely unlikely that Marx had not read a book which was published in instalments in *Vorwärts* (see SC: 291), of which he possessed a copy and which was intended, and seen, as an explicit defence of his position by his closest friend and intellectual companion at a time when Marx and Engels were trying to establish their influence in the German Socialist Workers' Party. Nevertheless, more positive proof of Marx's knowledge of Engels' views on dialectics and the contents of *Anti-Dühring* is still required.

Perhaps the key text for the question of whether Marx was aware of Engels' views is the 'Preface' which Marx provided for the 1880 French edition of Engels' *Socialism: Utopian and Scientific*, a pamphlet which consisted of three chapters taken from *Anti-Dühring*. In the original manuscript version of this 'Preface', Marx described Engels as 'one of the most eminent representatives of contemporary socialism' and gave a brief biography of his friend from the 1840s to the 1870s. He referred to *Anti-Dühring* itself as written in response to Dühring's theories on 'the sciences in general and socialism in particular', described it as having had a great success amongst German socialists, and offered Engels' pamphlet to its French audience as the most topical part of Engels' work and as 'ce qu'on pourrait appeler une Introduction au socialisme scientifique.' In the printed edition of the 'Preface', Paul Lafargue, over whose initials the text appeared and whom Marx had told to 'clean up the style but leave the matter intact', inserted into Marx's text the claim that *Anti-Dühring* was a 'scholarly and lively critique' of Dühring's theories (MEGA: 27/I 542, 550; MEGA: 27/II: 1249-50).

By providing this 'Preface', Marx not only implicitly endorsed the critique of Utopian socialism contained in Engels' pamphlet, but also a chapter which summarised Engels' claims for the superiority of dialectics over the metaphysical form of reasoning, i.e. that dialectics allows us to see things in their motion, their connection and totality, unlike metaphysics, which sees things in isolation and fixity, and that 'modern materialism is essentially dialectic' (SW II: 118-25). Engels' pamphlet argued that an accurate representation of the development of Nature and of human society could therefore 'only be obtained by the methods of dialectics' (SW II: 121-2). Of Marx's 'Preface' to this work, which describes Engels as one of the most eminent socialists of the day, refers to Engels' critique of Dühring's science, and recommends Engels' text as an introduction to scientific socialism, Carver can say only that it is 'guarded', and that Marx did not sign it with his own name (Carver, 1984b: 252).

The transformation of quantity into quality

However, rather than attempting to *deduce* whether Marx was acquainted with the opinions of a man whom he met virtually every day for years, whether he would have approved of such opinions if he had known of them, or whether he had read the book to which he contributed a preface, it is preferable to examine the content of his own works to see if they reveal any similarities with the dialectical outlook defended in *Anti-Dühring*.

Amazingly, when we do this, we find that it was Marx who *anticipated* Engels in claiming that the same dialectical ontology applies to nature and society alike. Thus, whilst Engels' famous 1873 letter on dialectics confined itself (like that of 1858) to discussing the realm of nature, Marx had already, by this date, referred to 'the law discovered by Hegel that at a certain point merely quantitative differences pass over by a dialectical inversion into qualitative distinctions' and cited as an instance of its validity the case of the master craftsman, who may own money or commodities, but who 'turns into a capitalist only where the minimum sum advanced for production greatly exceeds the known medieval maximum.' Marx concluded: 'Here, as in natural science, is shown the correctness of Hegel's law', indeed, 'the molecular theory of modern chemistry ... rests on no other law' (Cap. I: 423, 4, 438, 448).

Marx also argued that the law of the transformation of quantitative into qualitative change could be seen in the development of large-scale units of production which needed a certain minimum amount of capital to produce the new form of production to convert the 'numerous isolated and independent processes into one combined social process.' Similarly, the productive power generated by such large-scale units of production was itself an instance of Hegel's law of the transformation of quantity into quality: 'Just as the offensive power of a squadron of cavalry, or the defensive power of an infantry regiment, is essentially different from the sum of the offensive or defensive powers of the individual soldiers taken separately, so the sum total of the mechanical forces exerted by isolated workers differs from the social force that is developed when many hands co-operate' (Cap. I: 443, 448).

This example from military history may, given Engels' military interests, suggest that Marx cited the law of the transformation of quantity into quality under Engels' influence; in fact, the two men seem to have come to an awareness of Hegel's law independently, though by a similar route. On 16 June 1867, Engels wrote to Marx praising A. W. Hofmann's *Einleitung in der moderne Chemie* which he praised, despite all its faults, for showing that the molecule, the smallest part of matter, was 'a "nodal point", as Hegel calls it, in the infinite progression of subdivisions, which does not terminate it but marks a qualitative change.' Marx replied, in turn, that Engels was 'quite right about Hofmann', and went on to refer to the section of *Capital* which he had *already* written which outlined the qualitative change of the master of a trade into a capitalist as a result of purely quantitative changes. 'In the text there I quote Hegel's discovery of the law of the transformation of a merely quantitative change into a qualitative one as being attested by history and natural science alike. In the note to the texts (I was attending Hofmann's lectures at the time) I mention the molecular theory, but not Hofmann, who discovered nothing in the matter' (CW 42: 382, 385).

What is most noticeable here is that Marx and Engels' shared return to Hegel, and their common immersion in the natural sciences, led to their independently reaching the same conclusions about the law of the transformation of quantity into quality. However, whilst it was Marx who first made the claim, in print, that this dialectical law applied to both nature and society, it is Engels who has since been cast in the role of scapegoat for it.

The negation of the negation
Just as, when Engels argued the case for the law of the transformation of quantity into quality, he was obliged to defend Marx's prior invocation of it, so, when he upheld the law of the negation of the negation he was explicitly attempting to defend Marx's reference, in *Capital*, to proletarian revolution as 'the negation of the negation'. This reference could perhaps be dismissed as merely an example of Marx 'coquetting' with Hegelian modes of expression, were it not for the fact that it occurs in a chapter which outlines the rise and fall of the capitalist mode of production in terms of the classic Hegelian dialectic of initial unity, separation and higher unity (Cap. I: 103, 928-30).

Anyway, even if we saw Marx's use of Hegelian language as merely metaphorical or rhetorical, we would still need to ask what impression this rhetoric was supposed to convey. Marx's purpose, in referring to proletarian revolution as the negation of the negation, was to show that this revolution had necessarily to occur 'with the inexorability of a natural process.' The analogies between social development, natural processes and Hegelian negations, are used here to convince us of a particular perspective, in which the inevitability of the first negation (the transition to capitalism), provides Marx with the basis from which he could confidently predict the second negation in which the fall of the bourgeoisie and the victory of the proletariat are both 'equally inevitable' (Cap. I: 103, 928-30). Hegelianism was fused here, as in the 'Postface' to *Capital*, with a positivist evolutionism: both discourses were invoked in order to convey the inexorable unfolding of an inevitable process. An appeal to the negation of the negation thus allowed Marx to provide *Capital* with the kind of 'dialectical happy end' which Shanin criticises in Engels' *The Origin of the Family* (Shanin, 1983: 22).

The interpenetration of opposites and contradiction
Marx not only explicitly accepted the dialectical transformation of quantity into quality, and the negation of the negation; he also seems to have accepted the existence of the interpenetration of opposites in both nature and society, and of contradictions in reality. Thus, like Engels he cited the work of Grove, 'the most philosophical of the English (and, indeed German!) scientists' as a proof that 'mechanical motive force, heat, light, elecrticity, magnetism and chemical affinity are all, in effect, simply modifications of the same force and mutually generate, replace, merge into each other etc' (CW 41: 551, 553; CW 42: 138).

For Marx, the constant replacement, merging and mutual generation (i.e. interpenetration) at work in physics were also present in the realm of economics. Thus, in the circulation of money, the velocity of circulation is 'merely a reflection of the rapidity with which commodities change their forms, the continuous interlocking of the series of metamorphoses, the hurried nature of society's metabolic process, the quick disappearance of commodities from the sphere of circulation, and their equally quick replacement by fresh commodities. In the velocity of circulation, therefore, there appears the fluid unity of the the antithetical and complementary phases, i.e. the transformation of the commodities from the form of utility into the form of value and their re-transformation in the reverse direction' (Cap. I: 217).

Such interpenetration can also be seen in the conversion of persons into things, and things into persons, which is inherent in commodity production. There is a similar interpenetration of categories in the process of exchange where 'Commodities as use-values confront money as exchange value', and yet 'both sides of this opposition are commodities, hence themselves unities of use-value and value. But this unity of difference is expressed at two opposite poles and at each pole in an opposite way' (Cap. I: 198-9, 209). Thus, whilst Marx does not explicitly use the term, the concepts he employs in *Capital* are a classic instance of the fluidity stressed by the 'interpenetration' of opposites.

Marx does, however, frequently refer in *Capital* to the dialectical 'unity of opposites'. Commodities are a particularly clear example of this unity of opposites with their inherent 'internal' opposition between their status as use-values and as exchange-values. Indeed, commodities contain a host of antagonisms, and antitheses: between use-value and exchange-value; between private and social labour; and between concrete and abstract labour. Such oppositions form the basis of the 'antithetical phases of the commodity', which constitute the 'real forms of motion' of the process of exchange of commodities for money (Cap. I: 198-9, 209).

Similarly, Marx regarded capitalist society as 'full of contradictions'; although, like Engels, he used the term 'contradiction' to refer to a range of phenomena from logical contradictions and paradoxes, through to examples of real opposition and counterfinality. Such contradictions, or 'dialectical inversions', can be seen in the fact that the constant increases in productivity achieved by capitalism are expressed in increased competition for work; in the outstripping of population by productivity being expressed as the working population always outstripping the requirements of capital; and in the means for the development of production becoming the means of the domination and exploitation of the producers. Such contradictions find their most striking expression in the crises which periodically strike capitalist society (Cap. I: 103, 531, 798-9).

Money, too, is said to contain an 'immanent contradiction' between its function as a measure of value and as a means of actual payments. 'This contradiction bursts forth in that aspect of an industrial and commercial crisis which is known as a monetary crisis.' Similarly, the formula of capital itself is contradictory since 'capital cannot ... arise from circulation and it is equally impossible for it to arise apart from circulation. It must have its origins both in and not in circulation.' The exchange of commodities itself 'implies contradictory and mutually exclusive conditions.' Such contradictions are resolved, as are contradictions 'in general', by a new form of being in which such inconsistencies can exist side by side. 'For instance, it is a contradiction to depict one body as constantly falling toward another and at the same time constantly flying away from it. The ellipse is a form of motion within which this contradiction is both realized and resolved' (Cap. I: 198, 217, 235/6, 268).

Levine has argued that Hegel's dialectic was for Marx an explanation of structure whereas for Engels it was an explantion of process (Levine, 1984: 168). Yet, in fact, for Hegel, for Marx and for Engels, structure and process formed a unity. As Marx put it, 'the development of the contradictions of a given historical form of production is the only way in which it can be dissolved and then reconstructed on a new basis.' Thus working-class revolutionary ferments which oppose the division of labour of capitalist production stand 'in diametrical contradiction' with capitalism. It is the development of such contradictions which will, ultimately, ensure the 'inevitable conquest of power by the working class'; the inevitability of revolution being, like dialectics, another of the concepts to which Marx supposedly did not adhere (Cap. I: 619, 930; Thomas: 8). Thus, in Marx's dialectical outlook, process and movement are generated by inherent structural contradictions.

Conclusion
The philosophy of Hegel offered Marx far more than simply a methodology, or a mode of presenting his critique of political economy. Rather, Hegel's dialectics provided Marx, as they did Engels, with a particular ontological outlook. A classic instance is Marx's discussion of the way in which the apparent exchange of equivalents involved in the purchase of labour-power by capital is 'turned around in such a way that there is only an apparent exchange', where Marx explicitly refers to the 'laws of private property', which 'become changed into their direct opposite through their own internal and inexorable dialectic' (Cap. I: 729).

However, whilst Marx believed that Hegel had established the 'general forms of motion' of the dialectic, in a 'comprehensive and conscious manner', he also argued that, in Hegel's hands, the dialectic had been 'mystified and inverted'. With Hegel, the dialectic was 'standing on its head.

It must be inverted in order to discover the rational kernel within the mystical shell' (Cap. I: 103, 729). Marx's claim to be able to re-invert Hegel, and thus stand him on his feet, has been the source of much debate; indeed whether this operation is even possible has been doubted (Timpanaro: 75; Carver, 1983: 105-6; Vajda).

What Marx meant by this inversion can be seen in his letter to Engels of 25 March 1868 where, in his discussion of Maurer's work, he argued that the progression from communal to private property which had occurred in the real world was not simply, as it was in Hegel, a reflection of the logical unfolding of categories. Rather, the opposite is the case: our logical categories express real, social changes and relations. As Marx put it in *Capital*, 'the ideal is nothing but the material world reflected in the mind of man and translated into forms of thought' (CW 42: 558; Cap. I: 102; see also CW 5: 36; CW 6: 162-3).

Thus, although Marx's ontological outlook is frequently seen as very different from that of Engels, Marx explicitly argued that the dialectical transformation of quantity into quality and the interpenetration of opposites were processes which were to be found in both nature and society. He similarly referred to the negation of the negation as a process which could be seen at work in history, in the progression from the independent, private property of petty commodity production, through capitalism, to socialism. It is not hard to see why, when he defended these dialectical laws in *Anti-Dühring*, Engels believed that he was defending Marx's own outlook.

EPISTEMOLOGY

As we have seen, many writers have argued that Marx and Engels adhered to different epistemological traditions and contrast Engels' allegedly reflectionist and empiricist theory of truth with Marx's emphasis on the active role of socially specific subjects. Having already rejected this characterisation of Engels' thought, there is less need for discussion of Marx's epistemology. All that needs to be stressed here is that Marx, like Engels, was committed to a correspondence theory of truth; insisted on the role of theory in the production of knowledge; and distinguished between reality's forms of appearance and its inner essence.

Marx's method of studying political economy is a classic instance of his theory of knowledge. Naturally, Marx regarded his political economy and his theory of surplus-value as an expression of the proletarian standpoint, the theory which would advance, and rationally express, the interests of the working class. His critique of bourgeois political economy therefore 'represents a class ... the class whose historical task is the overthrow of the capitalist mode of production.' Yet this did not mean that Marx merely thought that his theory was *convenient* for the working class, he also regarded it as scientifically true. He argued that bourgeois political economy had been able to function 'as a science' when the class struggle had been at a low ebb, but that, increasingly, as the struggle between the proletariat and bourgeoisie took on 'more explicit and threatening forms', it had degenerated from genuine science into apologetics for the existing social order.

This ideological function meant that such economists were no longer capable of accurately depicting reality. Instead of revealing the contradictions of capitalism, their aim was now to conceal such contradictions. Only those writers who adopted the epistemologically privileged standpoint of the proletariat could capture reality, as their perceptions were not distorted by the vested interests of the ruling class. In particular, whilst 'vulgar' political economy remained trapped within the notions of the agents of capitalist production, and thus unable to penetrate beyond the realm of misleading outer appearance, Marx believed that his economic theories allowed him to perceive the deeper structures which, in fact, determined appearances. Thus, his political economy was not only revolutionary, it was a project of 'free scientific inquiry', which welcomed counter-arguments 'based on scientific criticism' (Cap. I: 89, 92-3, 96-8, 104-5, 174-5, 194; Cap. III: 441, 956; TSV III: 501).

Thus, despite the empiricist methodology recommended in *The German Ideology*, *Capital* does not begin with a description of, for example, the English economy and society of Marx's day, and then 'sum up' the general results of such observation with the aid of abstractions (CW 5: 37). Rather, as Marx argued in the *Grundrisse*, although concrete reality exists autonomously, outside our heads, it can only be appropriated by means of concepts, categories and abstract determinations which allow us the 'reproduction of the concrete by way of thought.' There is thus a two-fold movement: firstly, from the reality which forms the starting-point for observation towards abstraction; secondly, with the use of such abstractions (such as use-value, exchange-value and so on), back to the concrete, which is now understood as a structured totality, rather than simply in terms of immediate appearances. However, the fact that reality can only be appropriated and reconstituted through thought had given rise to the illusion of those philosophers who believe that reality is *generated* by thought (Gr.: 100-2). Thus Marx, like Engels, could refer to knowledge as 'the material world reflected in the mind of man, and translated into the forms of thought', but this did not mean that such 'reflection' was an automatic or passive process, as this metaphor is often seen to suggest (Cap. I: 102).

However, Marx, like Engels, paid little attention to the issue of how we are to decide between competing theories and paradigms. Whilst he saw both political economy and the natural sciences as establishing the laws of their objects of investigation, in order to make predictive claims about them, he was certainly aware that different forms of validation were appropriate to different branches of knowledge: 'in the analysis of economic forms neither microscopes nor chemical reagents are of assistance. The power of abstraction must replace both' (Cap. I: 90, 100). Yet, of course, this does not, in itself, tell us *which* abstractions are the most useful for understanding economic relations. Thus, if we adopt Marx and Engels' realist epistemology, this does not commit us to the detail of their political economy, such as the labour theory of value, the tendency of the rate of profit to decline and so on.

CONCLUSION

Our attempts to interpret Engels' own attempts to understand Marx's works are a classic example of the difficulties which we, as readers, face in the unavoidable process of ascribing intentions to an author in order to make sense of their 'meaning'. As we have seen, it is Carver's work which provides the most cogent defence of the view that Engels' later works systematically distort Marx's meaning. Inevitably, he is faced with the problem of why Marx did not protest at this distortion of his thought, which, after all, rapidly gained a currency in the German labour movement. In order to answer this question Carver is, like all readers, obliged to ascribe intentions to the two men: either Marx was unaware of the content of Engels' work; or he was too diplomatic to make his disagreement known; or Engels was clever enough to keep their disagreements hidden. In other words, Carver assumes that Marx's works form a consistent whole and can thus *deduce* either that Marx himself must have been conscious of his differences with Engels or that he cannot have been aware of the content of Engels' work. We have explicitly rejected this approach and denied that it is possible to deduce what Marx 'really thought' on the assumption that his works form a unified whole.

Yet, Carver himself suggests an extremely useful alternative approach to the study of the intellectual relationship between Marx and Engels when he says that Marx's work 'makes more sense' when interpreted in a way counter to Engels' dialectic (Carver, 1984b: 250, 256). However, in this case, our attention is turned away from the issue of whether Marx and Engels were *conscious* of their supposed disagreements, and towards the problem of whether Marx *should* have disagreed with Engels' work. However, the fact that *we* may think that the strongest parts of Marx's work 'make more sense' when seen in opposition to Engels' dialectics, does not mean that Marx himself shared our opinions about the meaning and significance of his own work. After all, it would also be equally possible to argue that the strongest parts of *Engels'* work make more sense when seen in opposition to his contradictory and incoherent laws of the dialectic.

Once we abandon the assumption that Marx's works necessarily form a unified and consistent whole from the mid-1840s to the end of his life, we need no longer be surprised that Marx failed to disassociate himself from Engels' *Anti-Dühring*. On the contrary, in the period after 1858, both Marx and Engels had come to characterise their thought in terms of concepts, analogies and vocabularies drawn from Hegelianism and the natural sciences. Yet, in doing so, they created a philosophical basis for their political and social theory which this theory did not require. It would, in fact, have been quite possible for Marx and Engels to have defended their historical materialist claims for the primacy of society's 'economic base' without resorting to a philosophical materialism. Similarly, it would have been perfectly logical (although, as it turns out, empirically incorrect) for them to have argued that the interests of the working class in modern society would 'inevitably' produce socialist revolution without invoking the inexorability of dialectical processes such as the negation of the negation and the transformation of quantity into quality.

Thus, as the Althusserian tradition has rightly insisted, thinkers are *not* the best guide to the significance or originality of their own thought but often attempt to explain their advances in terms of discourses available at the time which actually obscure the implications of their own thought (Jones, 1973: 18). This does not simply mean that thinkers are unaware of the *consequences* to which their theories will lead, as in the case of Maxwell's failure to see that his electromagnetic theory could predict the existence of new phenomena such as radio waves. Rather, it means that the explicit theories with which thinkers attempt to characterise their practice may be very different from the ones which they actually followed, as in the gulf which exists between the poverty of Newton's general theory of scientific achievement and the richness of his own, actual scientific achievement (Chalmers: 117, 132). In other words, Farr was quite wrong to argue that 'authors just are authorities about their work', and thus privileged with respect to its meaning. On the contrary, as Marx himself put it: 'Even in the case of philosophers who give systematic form to their work, Spinoza for instance, the true inner structure if the system is quite unlike the form in which it was consciously presented by him' (Farr: 229; CW 40: 316).

CHAPTER NINE

Historical materialism: an assessment

> There is more to be learned from a major author who is wrong, than a nonentity who is right (Runciman, 1972: 1).

In *Anti-Dühring*, Engels defined historical materialism as the claim that 'all past history, with the exception of its primitive stages, was the history of class struggle; that these classes warring with each other are always the product of the relations of production and exchange – in a word of the *economic* relations of the epoch; and therefore the economic structure of society always forms the real basis, from which, in the last analysis, the whole superstructure of legal and political institutions as well as the religious, philosophical and other ideas of a given historical period is to be explained.' Man's consciousness was thus to be explained by his being, rather than his being by his consciousness (AD: 32-3, 435).

This interpretation of historical materialism, with its three-tier hierarchy of productive forces, class relations and political and ideological superstructure, familiar from *The Condition of the Working Class* and *The German Ideology*, was the one to which Engels remained loyal not only in *Anti-Dühring* but also in his later prefaces to the *Communist Manifesto* and his letters of the 1890s (CM: 57, 62; SC: 397, 441). It was this reading of historical materialism which formed the basis for his *The Origin of the Family, Private Property and the State* (1884), which explained the end of primitive communism and the emergence of new relations of production based on private property in terms of the growth of the productivity of labour. In turn, the state was the product of the emergence of private property and classes and functioned to secure the political domination of the economically dominant class. However, as in the 1840s, Engels argued that, in certain periods, such as that of absolutism, where the warring classes were in balance, the state could acquire an unusual degree of independence (OFPPS: 5-6, 166, 168).

The similarities between the historical materialism of Engels' later writings and that of *The German Ideology* mean that there is no need for us to repeat here the account of Engels' social theory offered above (chapter four). Instead, this chapter will, firstly, offer an assessment of his social theory and, secondly, consider those aspects of Engels' later writings which were not anticipated in his earlier work. In particular, we will examine the defence of historical materialism set out in Engels' letters of the 1890s; look at his development of a 'nomological' conception of historical materialism; ask whether Engels differed from Marx on the multilinear nature of historical development; and, finally, assess Engels' account of the relationship between class and gender.

HISTORICAL MATERIALISM DEFENDED

Ironically, the very originality and scope of Marx and Engels' social theory was also to prove something of a drawback to them, since their theoretical precocity meant that they were rarely confronted with the effective challenges which would have obliged them to justify and to refine their approach. Although they were frequently involved in polemics with Lassalleanism, Proudhonism and Bakuninism, such debates, naturally, centred on political strategy, rather than on the social theory of historical materialism. For this reason, Engels' defence of historical materialism, in particular of the metaphor of 'base and superstructure', offered in a series of letters in the 1890s, are key texts for an assessment of Marxist social theory.

In these letters, Engels wished to make three main points: firstly, that historical materialism was not a philosophy of history of the Hegelian type; secondly, that historical materialism was not a form of economic reductionism but recognised the 'dialectical interaction' between base and superstructure; thirdly, that, despite this interaction, the economic base did have an ultimate primacy in historical explanation. A century after their composition, Engels' letters retain their enduring appeal to Marxist historians keen to reject the familiar accusation of reductionism (Hilton: 178; Thompson, 1978: 261; Delany: 43). How successful was the defence of historical materialism offered in Engels' letters?

Engels' first aim was to reject the criticisms of those who characterised historical materialism as a 'Procustean bed', to which historical evidence had to be adjusted. 'The materialist method turns into its opposite if it is not taken as one's guiding principle in historical investigation but as a ready-made pattern according to which one shapes the facts of history to suit oneself.' Historical materialism was not, he argued, a 'lever' for constructing history 'after the Hegelian manner'; it was 'a guide to study' which 'puts an end to philosophy in the realm of history' and required that 'all history must be studied afresh' (SC: 390-1, 393-4, 443). It should, however, be noted that Hegel himself had also rejected such philosophically-based schema to which the empirical evidence had to conform (Hegel, 1956: 8-9). After all, no thinker is ever likely to admit to writing history on the basis of an *a priori* construction, and all writers of history are obliged to claim that they are respecting the historical evidence.

Secondly, since Engels denied that historical materialism was a 'philosophical schema', to which the historical facts had to be adjusted, he also denied that he and Marx had seen history in monocausal, economic reductionist terms. He argued that it was 'fatuous' for critics of historical materialism to claim that because he and Marx denied an 'independent historical development to the various ideological spheres which play a part in history, we also deny them any effect upon history.' His and Marx's real purpose had been to refute the 'ideological' (i.e. idealist) outlook, which inverted reality and so made the independent development of ideas, or of the state, into the basis of historical reality. To claim that 'the economic factor is the *only* determining one' was to transform the materialist conception of history into 'a meaningless, abstract, absurd phrase.' Those who alleged that historical materialism denied the active historical role of the political and ideological superstructure were thus 'simply tilting at windmills' (SC: 394, 399-401, 435).

Engels himself cited many examples where it was impossible to deny the 'relative independence' and historically active role of the political and ideological superstructure. The state, for example, was not just a product of economic conditions but, in turn, 'reacts ... upon the conditions and course of production' (OFPPS: 166; SC: 398-9). 'It could scarcely be maintained without pedantry' that, of all the many states of North Germany, Brandenburg became the principal power 'because of economic necessity and not also because of other factors (above all its entanglement with Poland and hence with international political relations.' Nor was it possible, 'without making oneself ridiculous, to explain in terms of economics the existence of every small state in Germany, past and present', or to prove that differences between the liberty of testators in France and in England were 'due to economic causes alone.' Yet, such 'accidental factors' (i.e. those whose 'inner interconnection is so remote or so impossible of proof that we can regard it as non-existent and neglect it') could 'exert a very considerable effect on the economic sphere' (SC: 395-6, 400).

In both the realms of law and of ideology, the social superstructure could achieve a degree of independent development. 'In a modern state the law must not only correspond to the general economic condition and be its expression, but must also be an *internally coherent* expression which does not, owing to internal conflicts, contradict itself. And in order to achieve this, the faithful reflection of economic conditions suffers increasingly' (SC: 399 original emphasis). In the sphere of ideology too, the 'economy creates nothing anew, but it determines the way in which the body of thought found in existence is altered and further developed.' The economy's influence thus 'operates within the terms laid down by the particular sphere itself.' In the case of philosophy, the impact of the economy may be particularly indirect, since, in this sphere, 'it is the political, legal and moral reflexes which exert the greatest direct influence.' Thus, 'once an historic element has been brought into the world by other, ultimately economic causes' it 'can react on the environment and even on the causes that have given rise to it' (SC: 401, 435).

Engels thus characterised the relationship between base and superstructure not as a one-way determination by the active base of the passive superstructure, but rather as one of dialectical *'interaction'*. It was 'metaphysical', an empty abstraction to 'see only cause here, effect there.' In practice, the historical process 'goes on in the form of interaction' (SC: 395, 399, 401, 442). As a result he found no difficulty in admitting that 'the various elements of the superstructure' such as political struggles, the state, law and ideologies all 'exercise their influence upon the course of the historical struggles and in many cases determine their *form* in particular.' If historical events are the product of the 'conflicts betwen many individual wills', each of which is determined by 'a host of particular conditions of life', then any particular event is the product of 'innumerable intersecting forces, an infinite series of parallelograms of forces' (SC: 394-5 original emphasis). Nor were such arguments merely a late revision of historical materialism. On the contrary, even at the very genesis of historical materialism, Marx and Engels had explicitly allowed for the 'reciproocal action' of society's productive forces, forms of intercourse, state and ideology (CW 5: 53).

Thirdly, however, Engels did not see the historical process as simply one of interaction between the economy on the one side and and the state and ideology on the other. Rather, as in *The German Ideology* and Marx's '1859 Preface', his letters on historical materialism presented this relationship as one of 'the interaction of two unequal forces.' Thus, once the state arises, there is 'on the one hand, the economic movement, on the other, the new political power.' Although the state 'strives for as much independence as possible' and, once set up, 'is endowed with a movement of its own', nevertheless, 'on the whole, the economic movement prevails'. In the interaction of base and superstructure it is the former which is 'by far the strongest, the most primary and most decisive' element, the one which enjoys an 'ultimate supremacy'. Thus 'interaction takes place on the basis of economic necessity, which *ultimately* always asserts itself.' Amidst the multiplicity of historical causes, economic conditions are 'ultimately the decisive ones', so that, 'in the last resort', it is the economic movement of society which 'is finally bound to assert itself.' It is not that the base is active and the superstructure is passive, rather that the base is the 'prime agent' and the superstructure 'secondary' (SC: 393-6, 399, 401-2, 441-2; OFPPS: 6).

Engels stressed that, since history was the outcome of innumerable conflicting wills and forces, 'what emerges is something that no one intended.' Although 'men make their own history', they do not, as yet, do so 'with a collective will according to a collective plan.' This does not mean, however, that history consists of mere chance. On the contrary, 'all societies are governed by necessity' and, despite the interaction of base and superstructure, it is 'economic necessity which ultimately asserts itself.' Thus, 'the further the particular sphere which we are investigating is removed from the economic sphere and approaches that of pure abstract ideology, the more we shall find it exhibiting accidents in development, the more will its curve run zigzag. But if you plot the average axis of the curve, you will find that this axis will run more and more nearly parallel to the axis of economic development the longer the period considered and the wider the field dealt with' (SC: 395). The problem remains, however, as we shall see below, of why, if base and superstructure interact, we should see this interaction as one of unequal forces. In other words, why should we accept the analogy of 'base' and 'superstructure', with its inherent hierarchy of levels, in the first place?

Whilst Engels rejected an economic reductionist interpretation of historical materialism, he did concede that he and Marx were partly to blame for this interpretation of historical materialism. They had, he admitted, 'laid, and were bound to lay, the main emphasis on the derivation of political, juridical and other ideological notions, and of actions arising through the medium of these notions, from basic economic facts', in order to refute their opponents who denied this derivation. Nevertheless, Engels argued that 'when it came to applying the theory in practice, it was a different matter and there no error was permissible.' As successful examples of the application of the theory Engels cited Marx's *Eighteenth Brumaire* and *Capital*, as well as his own *Anti-Dühring* and *Ludwig Feuerbach* (SC: 396, 401-2, 433-5, 443).

As examples of where he himself had been guilty of lapsing into economic reductionism, Engels could have cited his article, 'Karl Marx' (1877), which argued that, with the help of historical materialism, 'all historical phenomena are explicable in the simplest possible way.' Similarly, in a letter to Schmidt of 1890, he saw historians as being able to 'deduce' society's political and ideological superstructure from its economic base (SW II: 150; SC: 393).

It was, however, in his discussion of the role of force in history in *Anti-Dühring* that polemical overstatement led Engels into some of his most reductionist formulations. Dühring had argued that 'the formation of political relationships is the historically fundamental factor, and instances of economic dependence are consequently always facts of a second order.' The primary historical factor should, therefore, be sought, 'in direct political force and not in any indirect economic power.' For Engels, Dühring's theory possessed little originality. On the contrary, 'the idea that political actions of leaders and states are decisive in history is as old as written history itself'. Against this traditional view, Engels counterposed the claim that 'force only protects exploitation but does not cause it' (AD: 195, 201-3).

Engels thus argued that social relations were by no means the result of force. For example, the replacement of the ancient communal ownership of land with private property, was the outcome of the growth of commodity production and of the peasants' realisation that it was to their own economic advantage. He explained the emergence of private property not by force but rather in terms of its suitability for increased production and the development of trade: 'hence as a result of economic causes. Force plays *no part* in this at all' (AD: 206-7). Similarly, the 'entire process' of the transition to capitalism could be 'explained by purely economic causes, without the necessity for recourse, even in a single instance, to robbery, force, the state, or political interference of any kind' (AD: 206-8).

However, elsewhere in *Anti-Dühring*, Engels himself had argued that the division of society into classes was established 'by violence and robbery, by deception and fraud' (AD: 207, 364). Similarly, whilst *The Origin of the Family* explained the rise of the Athenian state through the pressure of economic development and the rise of private property, 'without the interference of violence, external or internal', its account of the rise of the state amongst the Germans stressed the importance of warfare in the formation of the state and and classes. Through such warfare, with its military commanders and their retinues, the basis for 'hereditary royalty and hereditary nobility' was established. Thus, whilst in Athens, the state 'sprang directly and mainly out of the class antagonism that developed within gentile society', amongst the Germans, 'the state sprang up as a direct result of the conquest of large foreign territories' (OFPPS: 106-7, 118, 142, 160-1, 166).

Sahlins has argued that, far from economic development simply being the basis of the state, it is the primitive state, spurred on by the needs of warfare, which is the key to the advance of the productive forces (Sahlins: ch. 1-3). The problem is not that Engels was unaware of this point. On the contrary, as we have seen, his analysis of Germanic development offered a similar analysis in which state institutions 'could acquire autonomous interests and a vitality of their own' (Hunt II: 21). The problem is rather that, in recognising the active role of 'force' in the origins of class inequalities, Engels undermined his own case for the primacy of the 'economic' and the secondary status of political factors.

However, rather than simply engaging with the detail of Engels' defence of historical materialism, it is more important to offer a broader assessment of his social theory, in particular of his claims for the primacy of the productive forces and his use of the metaphor of base and superstructure. It is to these issues that we now turn.

THE PRIMACY OF THE PRODUCTIVE FORCES: AN ASSESSMENT

As we have seen, the account of historical change offered in *The Origin of the Family*, rested, as it had in *The German Ideology*, on the growth of the productive forces. As I have offered a lengthy critique of such productive force determinism elsewhere, only a summary of this critique need be noted here. Firstly, it is not clear that society's relations of production are determined by or correspond to the level of development of its productive forces. For example, in the cases of ancient world, feudal society and the Asiatic mode of production, production was carried out on the basis of the productive forces characteristic of peasant agriculture. Yet this shared level of development of the productive forces was accompanied by a wide variety of forms of property and class relations: the communal property of the city-state, private feudal property, with free or servile tenants paying feudal rents, the tax-rent of the monopoly state-landlord (Rigby, 1987: 112-13).

Even Gellner, who classifies societies into three main varieties on the basis of their 'mode of production' (in the sense of *The German Ideology*), namely hunter-gathering societies, agrarian society and industrial society, rejects Marx and Engels' claims for the primacy of the productive forces in the explanation of long-term historical development. For Gellner, these three basic forms of material production are accompanied by a 'bewilderingly wide diversity' of social forms, within which it is impossible to make any *a priori* assumption 'as to which sphere of human activity - production, coercion, cognition - is crucial, either in the maintenance and continuity of societies or in bringing forth new forms.' The advent of industrial society, for example, was not the product of any 'obligatory developmental pattern', it was not a 'task' imposed on humanity by the productive forces. Rather, it was a 'miraculous political and ideological balance of power in the non-economic parts of society', a 'uniquely favourable concatenation of cognitive, ideological and political circumstances', which allowed the breakthrough to 'Industria' (Gellner, 1988: 16, 19-20, 131-2).

Secondly, Engels explained both the origins of class society, and the transition from feudalism to capitalism, in terms of the development of the productive forces. Yet, in practice, it is impossible to explain either the crises of specific modes of production, or the transitions between particular modes, in terms of a universally valid law whereby society's expanding productive forces cast off the fetters of the relations of production. On the contrary, in many pre-capitalist societies, where the productive forces tend to stagnate rather than to expand inexorably, the crises of such modes of production (such as the ancient mode or the feudal mode) tend to be the result of the *failure* of the productive forces to grow, rather than of their expansion. Where transitions between modes of production occur, change in the productive forces is often, as in the transition from feudalism to capitalism, the result of prior change in society's relations of production, rather than the cause of such change (Rigby, 1987: 126-33).

Thirdly, Marx and Engels' claims for the social primacy of the productive forces are based on the assumption that such forces are the dynamic social factor which, through their inexorable tendency to develop, produce change in society's forms of intercourse, and thus in its forms of consciousness and political institutions (CW 5: 52-3, 89). Yet, why should we take the growth of the productive forces as a given which can be posited as the universal explanation of social change? After all, Marx and Engels themselves argued that the transition from the ancient world to feudalism was based on the claim that, during this period, the productive forces were *in decline*, as a result of the decay of agriculture, industry and trade and the decrease in population (CW 5: 34, 74-5).

Furthermore, even when Marx and Engels do discuss periods of growth in the productive forces, they present such growth as an an *explanandum* which requires historically specific explanation. They argued, for example, that the adoption of new inventions 'depended on the various empirical conditions' to be found in each country, so that where the growth of the productive forces does occur, it varies in its pace and nature. They thus offered an explanation of the development of manufacturing in the early modern period in terms of the growth of trade and the protectionist policies pursued by the state (CW 5: 32, 52-3, 70-2, 83, 303-4, 518).

Thus, although Marx and Engels argued for the determination of society's relations of production (or 'forms of intercourse') by its productive forces, they themselves were well aware that in all societies, society's forms of intercourse were a factor 'in its turn determining these' (i.e. the productive forces). Similarly, they referred to 'the 'material life of individuals' (their 'mode of production') and society's form of intercourse as two factors which 'mutually determine each other' (CW 5: 50, 329). If production and exchange are the basis of civil society, they are 'in turn determined by it' (i.e. by civil society). Together material production and civil society form the basis for the state and ideology but, nevertheless, 'the whole thing can, of course, be depicted in its totality (and therefore too the reciprocal action of these various sides on one another' (CW 5: 40, 53).

The problem is why, if we can conceive of production and social relations as mutually interacting 'moments' within a totality, should we grant a primacy to the productive forces within this totality? Significantly, Marx and Engels themselves made little attempt to answer this question. Their main argument was that 'men must be in a position to live in order to be able to "make history" and that therefore, since life involves before everything else, eating and drinking, housing, clothing and various other things', the first historical act is 'the production of the means to satisfy these needs, the production of material life itself' (CW 5: 42). Yet, the fact that x is a preconditon of the existence of y does *not* necessarily mean that x is the determinant of the nature of y. For example, grammar is a precondition of our speech, yet this does not mean that grammar therefore determines the content of what we say since 'Engels was right' and 'Engels was wrong' are both grammatical statements.

Not only is Marx and Engels' defence of productive force determinism rather weak, their own writings also contain the seeds of an alternative approach to social change. This alternative rejects any attempt to understand social development in terms of a universally valid philosophy of history. Instead of seeking the 'coherence' or uniformity of historical change, it is historically specific in its explanations. In particular, it allows far more influence to the relations of production in historical change than Marx and Engels' repeated claims for the primacy of the productive forces might lead us to expect. Indeed, Marx and Engels' recognition of the influence of specific class relations over the pace and form of development of the productive forces, and their emphasis on class struggle in historical change, has even led some writers to emphasise the primacy of society's relations of production over its forces of production in explaining long-term historical change (Hilferding, 1981a: 127; Althusser and Balibar: 235; Anderson, 1977: 204; Brenner, 1976, 1982; Rigby, 1987: ch. 8).

Sayer has argued against this alternative approach, on the grounds that it is 'anomalous' with Marx's '1859 Preface', the classic statement of historical materialism (Sayer: 135). However, the fact that such claims, for the primacy of society's relations of production, are 'anomalous' with the '1859 Preface' would only disqualify them as an interpretation of Marx (or, more precisely, of this particular text by Marx). It would still be quite possible for the relations of production to have a social primacy; even Marx, Engels, and the '1859 Preface' were entirely ignorant of the fact (Rigby, 1990). Nevertheless, it is certainly true that, from the time of *The Condition of the Working Class* and *The German Ideology*, through the codification of historical materialism offered by Marx in the '1859 Preface', to Engels' *Anti-Dühring* and *Origin of the Family*, it was their claims for the social primacy of the productive forces to which Marx and Engels gave by far the most emphasis and the most explicit and elaborate formulation (Rigby, 1987: ch. 3).

Callinicos has recently attempted to defend Marx and Engels' claims for the primacy of the productive forces with three main arguments. Firstly, he argues that, 'other things being equal', there is a tendency for the productive forces to grow. Yet, at the same time, he admits that, in practice, 'of course ... other things are often not equal' and that 'there are powerful counter-tendencies which may override this tendency'. This tells us nothing, of course, about the the tendency which will actually emerge as the dominant one in any particular situation.

Secondly, Callinicos adopts Levine's 'compatibility thesis' which usefully reminds us that 'a given level of development of the productive forces is compatible only with a limited range of production relations.' Nevertheless, this compatibility thesis is not, in itself, enough to salvage the primacy of productive forces since, as Cohen has pointed out, 'this argument could equally be turned on its head and made into a claim for the primacy of the relations of production: 'If high technology rules out slavery then slavery rules out high technology' (Cohen, 1978: 158).

Thirdly, Callinicos rightly points out that the fettering of the productive forces by the relations of production will lead to social crisis. Yet he fails to distinguish between Marx's account of the crisis of capitalism (where crisis *is* seen as the result of the growth of the productive forces which leads to a decline in the rate of profit) and the crises characteristic of pre-capitalist modes of production which tend to be caused by the *failure* of the productive forces to grow. Such contrasts point, once more, to the need to explain such crises in terms which are historically specific rather than by setting in motion a universally valid philosophy of history (Callinicos, 1987b: 91-5; Anderson, 1977: 204).

As the need for such modern defences of historical materialism suggests, Marx and Engels' own claims for the social primacy of the productive forces consisted of little more than a number of *assertions*, whether implicit (the productive forces have an inherent tendency to grow) or explicit (society's relations of production correspond to the needs of development of its productive forces) for which they provided little supporting evidence or argument. As a result, such productive forces determinism is now seen, outside the ranks of those concerned to defend orthodox Marxism, as an intellectual 'dead horse' (Berki: 393). Rather, it is Marx and Engels' claims for the determination of society's 'superstructure' of political institutions and forms of consciousness by its economic 'base' which have enjoyed the greatest influence on historians and social scientists. It is these claims that we must now assess.

BASE AND SUPERSTRUCTURE: THREE READINGS

An immediate problem in attempting to assess Engels' social theory is that historical materialism is open to at least three conflicting readings: the 'traditional' reading, defended by G. A. Cohen; the 'dilute' or 'organicist' version of those such as Derek Sayer; and the 'revisionist' interpretation, developed by Maurice Godelier.

'Traditional Marxism' argues that, in analysing social structure, we can conceive of the state and ideology separately from society's relations of production and that there is a hierarchical relationship (i.e. of base and superstructure). between these levels of the social structure (Cohen, 1978: ch. 8; Sayer: 2-3; Rader: 3-10). It was this conception of social structure which lay behind Marx and Engels' frequent accusations that their opponents had inverted reality, and had thus made consciousness and the state into the basis of human history. They criticised Stirner, for instance, for turning reality upside-down in his analysis of ancient philosophy and early Christianity, and so transforming the 'idealist symptom into the material cause'. The metaphor of society as consisting of a base and superstructure is thus not only present when Marx and Engels explicitly invoke it, it also implicitly underlies their critique of Hegelianism for inverting reality and for neglecting the 'empirical basis' of history, of which philosophy was merely the 'ideological, speculative expression (CW 5: 36, 61-2, 88-9, 92, 136-7, 282).

A major problem with this 'strong' formulation of historical materialism is its conception of the levels of the social hierarchy as 'externally related', i.e. as an association of separate elements. It is this aspect of historical materialism which the more sophisticated critics of Marxism have taken as their central target. Their argument is that it is illegitimate for Marx and Engels to claim that society's economic conditions determine the nature of its politics and forms of consciousness since, in practice, politics and forms of consciousness can function as constitutive elements of both the production process and of social relations. If so-called superstructural elements enter into our definiton of the base, then it is illegitimate to derive the former from the latter (Acton: 164-8, 177, 258; Plamenatz: 283-9, 345).

Ironically, Marx and Engels themselves gave a number of examples of such interpenetration of base and superstructure. In *The German Ideology*, for instance, they distinguished between 'classes' of capitalist civil society and the 'estates' of pre-capitalist societies. Used in this specific sense, 'class' refers only to the social relations characteristic of capitalism, where private property has reached its fullest development, freed of the communal constraints and political relations with which it was previously bound up. It is thus only under capitalism that the economy appears as a totally separate sphere and where the relations between classes take a purely economic form: the sale and purchase of wage-labour. Thus, whilst pre-capitalist society was comprised of estates with their legally defined privileges, capitalist society is made up of legally equal individuals who constitute its economically defined classes (CW 5: 69, 73, 89-90; Godelier, 1988: 245-52).

The problem is that if base and superstructure 'interpenetrate', as Marx and Engels claimed they do in pre-capitalist societies, and it is impossible to observe some level of pure 'economic' activity in reality, it follows that the concepts of 'economic base', 'political superstructure' and so on, are analytical abstractions. To abstract a concept (the 'economic level') from reality, and then to invert it and claim that this abstraction is actually the 'basis' of reality, would seem to be a classic instance of the methodology which Marx and Engels themselves rightly condemned as idealist or 'ideological' (SC: 434).

The 'traditional Marxism' model of social structure (which can certainly be supported with quotations from Marx and Engels themselves (CW 5: 329)), with its view of economics, politics and ideology as 'externally related', posits a binary opposition between base and superstructure. Yet, in reality, the terms of this apparent opposition interpenetrate, they inhere within one another. As a result, the model collapses, or, more precisely, inverts itself. Thus, what presents itself as the most materialist analysis of society turns out to be, with true dialectical irony, its exact opposite: pure idealism (Eagleton: 133/4; see, however, Ellis: 78, 90).

Paradoxically, whilst the concept of interpenetration has been used to attack Engels' social theory, Engels himself argued, in general, for a dialectical outlook which saw things 'in their interconnection, in their concatenation, their motion', their 'inseparability' and 'mutual penetration' (AD: 26/7, DN: 17, 63, 214/24, 264). Yet, whilst Engels advocated the concept of dialectical *interpenetration* in his defence of *dialectical* materialism, he advocated the more limited idea of dialectical *interaction*, in his defence of *historical* materialism. In other words the 'dialectical' ontology of Engels' philosophy was in contradiction with the model of social structure explicitly defended in his social theory (Walton and Gamble: 74). We can either retain the hypothesis of the determination of politics and ideology by economics (although we may then disagree with it on empirical grounds), or we can retain the dialectical conception of mutual interpenetration, but we cannot logically retain both of them.

The 'traditional Marxist' response, to the difficulties posed for historical materialism by the problem of interpenetration, is to reassert the claim that we *can* conceive of the economic base separately from the political and ideological superstructure (Cohen, 1988: ch. 2; Lowe). Certainly, we may be able to conceive of relations of production separately from politics, law and ideology in hypothetical examples, or even, perhaps, in specific historical instances. Nevertheless, as Marx and Engels' own claim that pre/capitalist relations of production were based on the extraction of surplus/labour by *extra/*economic forms of compulsion make clear, we cannot maintain this distinction as a universally valid one. Given Marx and Engels' own implicit awareness of the interpenetration of base and superstructure, the reassertion of 'traditional Marxism' nowadays fails to convince few people, even amongst those who are sympathetic to historical materialism.

A second solution to the problems posed for Marxism by the interpenetration of base and superstructure, is simply to deny that any problem exists in the first place. Those writers who adopt this solution thus reject the interpretation of historical materialism offered by 'traditional Marxism', which presents the levels of society as externally related. Instead, they argue that, for historical materialism, society constitutes an organic whole, whose elements are internally related. The productive forces, relations of production, politics, law and ideology are thus seen as interpenetrating and interdependent (Sayer: 145; Rader: ch. 2).

This conception of society as an interpenetrating, organic totality is an attractive one. The problem with it, from a Marxist perspective at least, is that it is difficult to see what is specifically Marxist about it. Such 'dilute' or 'organicist' Marxism consists, in practice, of little more than a *critique* of those thinkers who see the state and ideology as enjoying some separate existence. Thus, whilst the essence of 'traditional Marxism' is to be found in Marx and Engels' critique of the *inversion* of reality performed by Hegelian idealism, the essence of 'organicist Marxism' is to be found in Marx and Engels' repeated criticism of Hegelianism's *abstraction* of ideas, principles, laws and politics from the other social activities of humanity, and its consequent illusion that ideas and the state enjoy independent histories of their own (CW 5: 92-3, 154, 330).

A third solution to the problem of interpenetration is that of Godelier for whom historical materialism is no longer seen as a claim for the primacy of certain institutions ('the economy') over others ('the state' or 'ideology'), but rather as a claim for the primacy of certain social *functions* over others. Thus, as in Marx and Engels' example of the communal property of the ancient city-state, where the state functions as a relation of production through which individuals gain access to its productive forces, the state itself may be characterised as a relation of production. In such cases, political relations are not merely a superstructure of society's forms of intercourse, but are rather a constitutive part of them (Godelier, 1978, 1988).

There is a danger here that, as in the 'organicist' perspective, the mode of production, Marxism's key explanatory concept, 'turns into nothing more than a synonym for the social structure itself, occasionally masquerading as one of its principal parts' (Parkin, 1979: 8). However, this is not necessarily the case. Godelier's analysis does not mean that we must, henceforth, conceive of the state *in its entirety* as part of the base, rather than as part of the superstructure to which it is traditionally assigned. Instead his analysis allows us to distinguish those elements of law or politics which function as constitutive parts of property relations (the 'base'), from other, 'residual' aspects of law, which are a consequence (or 'superstructure'). of such property relations (Wood, E., 1981: 79).

Historical materialism's founding metaphor of 'base and superstructure' has thus been interpreted in very different ways by twentieth-century Marxists. The central weakness of 'traditional' Marxism is that it cannot answer the challenge offered to historical materialism by the problem of interpenetration. The difficulty with 'organicist' Marxism is that whilst it resolves the problem of interpenetration, it does so only at the expense of ceasing to be recognisably Marxist. It is Godelier's analysis which offers the most convincing answer to those critics for whom Marxism founders on the interpenetration of base and superstructure.

However, whilst his functional definition of the relations of production is a necessary logical precondition for Marx and Engels' claims for the primacy of society's 'economic' base, it is not, in itself, sufficient to establish that such primacy actually exists. Ironically, as we shall see in the next section, whilst Godelier's revisionism successfully copes with the complex problem of the interpenetration of base and superstructure, it comes to grief on the far more straightforward problem of the interaction between the two 'levels'.

BASE AND SUPERSTRUCTURE: MILL VERSUS MARX AND ENGELS

As we have seen, the historical materialism of *The German Ideology*, of the '1859 Preface', and of Engels' letters of the 1890s, relies heavily on the metaphor of social 'levels' to express the claim that certain social practices or relations are more fundamental than others. Even if we accept Godelier's redefinition of the economic level to include the relations of production in a broad sense, the problem remains of why, given that Marx and Engels themselves allowed for the existence of a 'reciprocal action' between society's levels, we should accept any *a priori* primacy of the 'economic' (CW 5: 53). If politics and ideology are not historically passive, why should we see them as merely 'superstructural', whilst privileging other social forces as the 'base'?

After all, this ascription of a universal explanatory primacy to certain social practices, which is the claim which gives Marxism its theoretical distinctiveness, would seem to turn historical materialism into a philosophy of history, which *deduces* the results of historical research from *a priori* principles, of the type which Marx and Engels themselves explicitly rejected (SC: 393-4; Croce: 17, 77-8; Lovell: 27-8). The dilemma for Marxism is to maintain a middle course between the perils of an economic reductionist philosophy of history on the one hand and, on the other, an analysis which gives so much autonomy to the social superstructure that it ceases to be recognisably Marxist (Breuilly: 552). It will be argued here, that Marxism has no way out of this dilemma.

It is Weberian theory which, traditionally, is seen as offering the main alternative to historical materialism's claims for the necessary primacy of the economic 'base'. For Weber, society is best conceptualised not as a hierarchy of levels, but rather as a number of 'dimensions' of power and social stratification. Just as it is impossible to claim that one dimension is more important than another in the constitution of an object so, in the social sciences, even in the study of the economic transformations of society, 'it is not possible to enunciate any general formula that will summarize the comparative substantive powers of the various factors involved in such a transformation or will summarize the manner of their accommodation to one another.' Thus, for Weber, it is quite possible that 'the emergence of economic power may be the consequence of power existing on other grounds' (Weber I: 577, II: 926). More recently, writers such as Mann and Runciman have also rejected the necessary primacy of any one form of social power, whether economic, political-military, or ideological in origin (Mann: ch. 1; Runciman 1989: 12-17).

We may thus distinguish two opposed approaches to social structure. In the first approach, which is represented by the historical materialism of Marx and Engels, by Dühring's 'force theory', and by Talcott Parsons' claims for the social primacy of norms and culture, there is a necessary hierarchy of social levels or factors. In the second approach, represented by Mann and Runciman, such hierarchies do exist but are historically specific, rather than universal, in their nature (Mann: 523).

Perhaps a useful alternative to this well-worn opposition is that contained in the account of explanation offered by John Stuart Mill in his *A System of Logic* (1843). Here, Mill argued that the cause of a phenomenon, 'philosophically speaking, is the sum total of the conditions positive and negative taken together; the whole of the contingencies of every description, which, being realised, the consequent [i.e. the *explanandum* – S. R.] invariably follows.' The real cause of a phenomenon 'is the whole of these antecedents', so that, in terms of strict logic, we have 'no right to give the name of cause to one of them exclusively of the others.' Thus, there is no scientific ground 'for the distinction between the cause of a phenomenon and its conditions.' But, if this is the case, it is not possible to claim an explanatory primacy for any one of these conditions (Mill: 214-17). If x, y and z are the conditions needed to bring E about then we cannot claim that x is more important than y or z since each of these conditions is *indispensable* for E to occur.

In practice, of course, we do not, despite Mill's argument, explain a phenomenon by enumerating all the conditions which are necessary for it. Thus, although my being born was a condition of my writing this book, we would not normally refer to it as the 'cause' of my doing so. In our everyday lives, we tend to 'single out one only of the antecedents under the denomination of Cause, calling the others merely Conditions.' In practice, we often distinguish causes from conditions by choosing as the 'cause' of a phenomenon 'the one condition which came last into existence.' We thus tend 'to associate the idea of causation with the proximate antecedent *event*, rather than with any of the antecedent *states* (Mill: 214-15).

However, although we often identify the cause of a phenomenon with that condition which came last into existence, this is not necessarily the case. As Mill pointed out, which condition we refer to as 'the cause' will depend upon the 'purpose of our immediate discourse' and 'there is hardly any of them which may not, according to the purpose of our immediate discourse, obtain that pre-eminence' (Mill: 214-15). In other words, which condition we identify as the primary cause of something will be determined by our own purposes and interests.

A practical example which may clarify Mill's account of explanation is that of a man with pneumonia who is also allergic to penicillin and who thus, after taking the drug, dies rather than being cured. Logically, we have to say, along with Mill, that the 'cause' of his death was all the conditions which were required to bring this consequence about: he was born, possessed an allergy to penicillin, did not know of this allergy, came into contact with pneumonia, went to a doctor and so on. In practice, however, we might say that taking the penicillin, as the 'proximate antecedent event', was the 'real' cause of the patient's death.

Alternatively, given that most people recover from pneumonia when given penicillin, it is quite likely that, in this case, we would see the patient's allergy as the the 'primary' cause of his death. Thus rather than seeing the 'proximate antecedent event' (the taking of penicillin) as the primary condition of the patients's death, we would, for the purposes of our analysis, take this as a given and would instead present the patient's allergy to penicillin as the real 'cause' on the grounds that it is the condition to which our audience needs its attention drawn. Here, what we refer to as the 'cause' of death is not the last condition to come into existence but rather that condition (the allergy) which cannot be taken as a given.

However, if the doctor who was treating our patient had realized that the latter was allergic to penicillin and yet had still insisted on administering the drug to him, we would be quite likely to say that the 'cause' of the patient's death was neither the penicillin, nor his allergy, but rather the fact that his doctor was a homicidal maniac. Here we would take the pneumonia, the allergy, and the properties of penicillin as givens and, for the purposes of enlightening our audience, emphasise the doctor's murderous psychological predisposition.

In other words, which conditions we take as givens, and which we choose to emphasise as 'causes' will very much depend upon our purposes and upon the nature of the audience we are addressing. However, the fact that we present certain conditions as the key variables for the purposes of our argument, does not grant them any ontological primacy. In reality, all of these conditions were necessary to bring about the *explanandum*. As Mill argued, it is only when we take a mass of conditions as given, as 'understood without being expressed', that it is possible to refer to particular conditions as 'causes' (Mill: 215).

However, for the sake of argument, let us assume that in this example we could agree that some particular condition, such as the doctor's psychological state, was the primary 'cause' of the patient's death and that all the other conditions were 'secondary'. Even if such agreement were possible, this psychological state would, of course, in turn require an explanation in terms of the conditions which had produced it: family background, genetics or whatever. Our 'prime cause' would thus cease to be simply an explanation and, would in turn, become an *explanandum*. It is only as long as we take the doctor's pyschological state as a given that it appears to have explanatory primacy. We are thus condemned, logically, to an infinite regression of causation, which excludes any possibility of ascribing explanatory social primacy to any one variable.

In practice, however, we do not need to regress to the Big Bang in order to explain any particular event. Rather, how far we regress down the causal chain which produces each of the conditions needed to bring about a particular event will tend to be determined by what we think can be taken as a given which will, in turn, be determined by our own analytical purposes and by the audience which we have in mind (Anderson, *et al.*: 171). This is not just to say, as do Runciman and Mann, that any explanatory primacy is specific to particular cases and that no factor enjoys a universal primacy. Rather, which factor we emphasise will depend upon our own particular analytical situation and the audience to which our analysis is addressed.

All of these points apply also to the explanation of historical phenomena. As an example we might cite the case of seventeenth-century Bohemia where, following the 40 per cent population decline which occurred in the course of the Thirty Years War, the landlords responded to the threat posed by low rents, high wages and low grain prices by enserfing their peasants to obtain free corvée labour. It could, therefore, be argued that the enserfment of the Bohemian peasantry was caused by its proximate antecedent event: the decline in population (Klima: 52-3).

Yet, very similar conditions in late medieval England had exactly the opposite effect: there the peasants used the shortage of tenants to obtain cheap rents and an end to serfdom. It could thus be argued that the key factor in explaining enserfments, such as that of the Bohemian peasantry, is not to be found in population change but rather in the weakness of the village community which prevented the peasants from resisting the landlords' offensive. Class relations and the outcome of class struggle, not demographic fluctuations, thus have a primacy in explaining social change (Brenner, 1976: 47-60).

In fact, in both cases, it is only by taking certain conditions as given that others appear as primary causes. Thus, *if* we take specific structural conditions (the weakness of the peasant community) as given, then population change will appear as the prime cause of enserfment. On the other hand, if we take warfare and demographic decline as givens, the weakness of the peasantry, will seem to be the key issue. For Mill, however, all of these conditions (the war, population decline, a weak peasantry, etc.) would be the conditions which, taken together, were indispensable if the enserfment was to occur. Any explanatory primacy which we grant to one particular condition is thus the result of analytical convenience (what we think our audience can take for granted) rather than the result of any real causal primacy.

However, for the sake of argument, let us assume that, since population change can 'result' either in peasant freedom (England) or serfdom (Bohemia), we could agree that the outcome of class struggle was the 'key variable' in explaining which social change actually came about. Even if such agreement were possible, the varying outcomes of such struggles would, in turn, require an explanation. We might, for example, see the weakness of particular peasant communities as the result of factors such as their foundation through colonisation, their lack of particular work relations such as co-operative, open field agriculture, or of the absence of a sympathetic state to help guarantee their freedom against seigneurial attack (Brenner, 1976: 56-60, 70). Only so long as we take the weakness of the peasantry as a given does it appear to have an explanatory primacy; in reality, it too has to be explained in terms of its own conditions which will include a host of political, technological and ideological factors. Thus whilst such cases show that historians have in the past been wrong to ignore class and class struggle and that such factors are central to any explanation of long-term social change, they also preclude us from ascribing explanatory primacy to any one variable.

In other words, whilst Marxist historians have often explicitly claimed a primacy for one particular historical factor, such as class struggle, their own analyses have, in order to be convincing, involved an implicit explanatory pluralism. Kitching summarised this situation perfectly: 'Engaging in a professional practice which is more sophisticated than its theorization is in fact very likely to coexist with a trained inability to either recognize or express that sophistication formally or explicitly' (Kitching: 225).

Nor is such pluralism only implicit in those Marxists who emphasise the primacy of class struggle (McLennan: 39-40). On the contrary, since, as Engels rightly insisted, every cause is also an effect, and vice versa, such a pluralism is implicit in *any* attempt to ascribe explanatory primacy, whether to the productive forces, class struggle, politics, ideas or any other variable. Whichever factor we grant explanatory primacy to, its existence must, in turn, be explained by all the conditions which brought it into existence (AD: 27).

To conclude: it is Godelier's reformulation of base and superstructure which provides the most logically coherent account of historical materialism, and it is this version of Marxism with which its critics have to come to terms. Yet, ironically, whilst Godelier's reading of historical materialism effectively deals with the complex problem posed by the interpenetration of base and superstructure, it comes to grief on the more straightforward problem of their interaction, and the consequent infinite regression and pluralism of historical causation. As the deservedly high reputation of Marxist historiography emphasises, Marxists have, in practice, easily avoided the danger of the Scylla of reductionism, upon which Marxism's critics have usually seen it as foundering. Yet, this danger has only been avoided at the expense of being drawn into the Charybdis of pluralism. I have argued here that there is no way in which Marxism can successfully navigate between these two fates.

HISTORICAL MATERIALISM AND FUNCTIONAL EXPLANATION

The two major claims of historical materialism (firstly, that particular relations of production are determined by the needs of development of the productive forces; secondly, that specific state apparatuses or dominant ideologies help secure the survival of particular relations of production) are both examples of 'functional explanation'. A functional explanation is one in which a specific institution or arrangement is accounted for in terms of the benefits, or effects, it produces. Biological explanations of an animal's organs in terms of its advantages for the survival of the animal are an obvious, and classic, example. The key issue, for our purposes, is whether such explanations are valid in the social sciences. If, as Cohen has claimed, historical materialism is dependent upon the use of functional explanation, and if, as writers such as Halfpenny have argued, this form of explanation is invalid, then historical materialism would seem to have little to offer the social scientist (Cohen, 1978: 249; Halfpenny).

Such explanations of an organ or institution in terms of its *effects* would seem to be paradoxical since we normally explain phenomena in terms of their antecedents rather than in terms of their future, and hence, as yet, non-existent, consequences. In biology, however, we are entitled to explain phenomena by the functional effects we have ascribed to them since we have a selection mechanism at work, the 'survival of the fittest', which determines which random genetic variations will survive and which will not. The survival of the fittest thus functions as a 'feedback mechanism' which allows us to explain an animal's form in terms of its functional effects.

The methodological problems involved in using functional explanations in the social sciences can perhaps be most clearly seen in Marx and Engels' functional explanation of society's relations of production in terms of their benefits for the development of the productive forces. Firstly, there is problem of their *ascription* of functionality to the society's relations of production. In fact, Marx and Engels never establish, but merely assert, that particular relations of production are the most suitable for the development of the productive forces at a given time, a claim which is open to historical challenge given the stagnation or even regression produced by particular relations of production (CW 5: 355; Rigby, 1987: ch. 7).

How can we know whether any specific relations of production *are* the most functional for the productive forces at the time they are introduced? After all, even if there was an historical process of 'trial and error' which selected those relations of production most functional for the reproduction of the productive forces, any particular relations of production (such as those of eastern European serfdom which survived for centuries despite their tendency to lead to the stagnation of the productive forces) could have been one of the errors. The difficulty for historians is that, even if serfdom was such an error, they are still faced with the task of explaining precisely *why* serfdom was introduced and why it survived for so long. Far from helping us answer such questions, functional explanations prevent us from asking them in the first place.

However, it could still be claimed that society's relations of production corresponded to the stage of development of the productive forces, *irrespective of whether they were functional or not*. The problem would then be to show why we should grant a primacy to the productive forces, instead of arguing, as Marx and Engels themselves do on other occasions, for the mutual determination of productive forces and forms of intercourse, or the reciprocal interaction of productive forces, forms of intercourse, the state and ideology (CW 5: 53, 329).

Secondly, even if we accepted the functionality of society's relations of production for its productive forces, such a functional ascription would only provide the basis for a functional *explanation* if we could specify the mechanism linking particular forms of intercourse with particular productive forces. One possibility is that conscious human intention was the mechanism through which specific forms of intercourse were brought into being. Yet Marx and Engels seem to reject this possibility and instead emphasise the lack of consciousness involved in the emergence of particular social relations (CW 5: 379, 413). Yet they did not suggest any alternative selection mechanism through which the forms of intercourse most suitable for the development of the productive forces would be brought about. Without such a mechanism, it would be valid to explain the *persistence* of specific relations relations of production through their functionality, once they had come into existence, but their origin would still require explanation on some other basis (Isajiw: 127).

Attempts to defend Marx and Engels' productive force determinism by specifying such a selection mechanism have proved less than convincing.

Cohen's 'scarcity thesis', the claim that human beings would use their rationality to overcome scarcity by developing the productive forces and that society's relations of production would thus eventually be forced to adjust to such new productive forces, was one such attempt. It foundered, however, on historical examples such as the serfdom of early modern eastern Europe, which, it has been argued, existed not because they maximised production, but rather because they maximised the level of surplus labour going to the property-owning class (Cohen, 1978: 152; Rigby, 1987: 117-26).

Torrance attempts to explain the supposed functionality of society's relations of production for its productive forces by suggesting that, whether through a deliberate process of trial and error or by random mutation, those relations of production will emerge and survive which best reproduce the productive forces. The problem with his argument (apart from the fact that at times it seems to involve a confusion of work relations within a unit of production with class-relations of production) is that it assumes exactly what it seeks to prove, i.e. that society's productive forces will inevitably develop, and that its relations of production are, in the long term, explicable through their functionality for the productive forces (Torrance: 388-9; see also van Parijs).

However, whilst historical materialism's reliance upon functional explanation raises massive problems, it does not, *per se* invalidate historical materialism. As Elster has emphasised, functional explanations are valid provided that they specify the 'feedback mechanism' which serves as the explanatory link between an organ, institution or arrangement and its beneficial consequences (Elster, 1985: 28). The fact that functional explanations can legitimately be invoked in certain circumstances means that its use in any particular case must be assessed empirically rather than automatically being dismissed on methodological grounds. The weakness of historical materialism is thus not, *per se*, that it relies upon functional explanation but rather that it fails to specify any feedback mechanism which would allow us to explain the existence of particular relations of production, state institutions or ideologies in terms of their functional effects (Tännsjö; Rigby, 1987: ch. 6).

METHODOLOGICAL INDIVIDUALISM AND PRAGMATOLOGICAL HISTORICAL MATERIALISM

For Elster, Marx and Engels' use of functional explanation is associated with an Hegelian methodological collectivism, holism and teleology. However, he sees this Hegelian causation as, at times, supplemented by their use of a methodological individualism, in which all social phenomena are 'in principle explicable in ways that only involve individuals – their properties, their goals, their beliefs and their actions.' Such methodological individualism, in which statements about social phenomena may, in theory, be reduced down to statements about individuals, is Elster's own preferred sociological approach. He argues that the anti-Hegelian methodological individualism of *The German Ideology*, which distinguishes this work from both Marx's *1844 Manuscripts* and his mature economic writings, may have been the responsibility of Engels, who had 'a more sober attitude towards history than did Marx' (Elster, 1985: 5, 109-10).

The social theory which Elster refers to as 'methodological individualism' does certainly seem to be evident in pragmatological works such as *The Holy Family* and *The German Ideology*, where Marx and Engels criticised Hegelianism for turning the process of history into a subject, which used Man to achieve its aims, so that humanity's activities become the 'tasks' laid down for it by 'History' (CW 4: 93; CW 5: 50). According to Marx and Engels, the only 'tasks' which exist in history are those which are conditional, such as the identification of the strategies which individuals must adopt *if* they are to pursue their own interests' (CW 5: 419).

It may, however, be rather misleading to describe the social theory of *The German Ideology* (of which Elster himself approves) as a form of 'reductionism' or 'individualism'. In fact, as Elster himself admits, 'many properties of individuals, such as "powerful" are inherently relational, so that an accurate description of one individual may involve reference to others' (Elster, 1985: 5-6, 18; Taylor, 1986; Wood, 1986). Perhaps the pragmatological social theory of *The German Ideology* is best characterised as a form of 'structuration' theory' (Giddens, 1984). An analogy which may help to clarify this conception of those human relations which we metaphorically refer to as social 'structure', is that of language. To any specific individual, the language which he or she employs appears as a pre-existent structure with its own vocabulary and rules of grammar. Yet it would be wrong to reify language and to present it as a structure which exists apart from human action. On the contrary, language evolves under the impact of human agency in response to new influences and needs, it is itself a human product (Bennett, 1981: 70). Similarly, social structure is, like language, both the condition *and* the outcome of human agency, both constraining *and* enabling human action. The concept of structuration thus allows us to overcome the traditional dualism of structure and agency in social science, although sceptics may conclude that this insight advances us little beyond Marx's pragmatological claim that 'Men make their own history but ... they do not make it under circumstances chosen by themselves, but under circumstances ... transmitted from the past' (SW I: 247).

Certainly, in *The German Ideology*, Marx and Engels explicitly rejected the concept of 'abstract', non-social individuals whose actions could be explained through the concept of a universal human nature. They argued that the concept of a fixed human nature would necessarily put an end to all specific social analysis by substituting it with a universally valid explanation, such as, for example, the explanation of all human actions in terms of their 'utility'. They argued, therefore, that to invoke, as certain writers did, man's 'natural human affinity' as a justification of socialism was futile since this concept could function equally well as an explanation of slavery or serfdom. Similarly, appeals to 'reason' as a justification of socialism were equally futile, since '"reason" has at all times been an historical product.' Thus, for Marx and Engels, all consciousness is the consciousness of the historically-specific individual 'in his interconnection with the whole of society and about the whole of the society in which they lived.' Even personality is, in this perspective, the product of 'a definite condition', such as one's position as a worker, a social position 'which determines the whole personality' since our personal powers and capacities are the product of material circumstances' (CW 5: 183, 375-6, 378, 410, 465, 479-80).

Thus Marx and Engels counterposed the 'real living individuals', who always exist within 'given historical conditions and relations', upon which they claimed to base their historical materialism, with Feuerbach's abstraction of 'Man', and with Stirner's notion of the 'pure individual', the unique ego which creates itself. Social relations are the mutual relations of particular individuals, but this does not mean that relations between, say, the members of the bourgeoisie and the proletariat are merely personal relations. Rather such relations of individuals to each other are mediated by 'present-day social relations', by the division of labour in which individuals find themselves. These relations, once created, are then confronted by later generations as the conditions of their existence, so that 'the history of a single individual cannot possibly be separated from the history of preceding or contemporary individuals, but is determined by this history.' The social reality with which individuals are confronted is thus 'only a product of the preceding intercourse of individuals', and it is the 'personal, individual behaviours of individuals' which daily reproduces such existing social relations (CW 5: 37, 39, 51-2, 78, 81, 88, 215, 436-8, 442; Elster, 1985: 5-6, 18).

There is, therefore, no need to counterpose the structurationist-pragmatological outlook of *The German Ideology* with Elster's methodological 'individualism' (Callinicos, 1987b: 64-91) since, in practice, the 'individuals' whom Elster claims to take as his starting point are, like those of Marx and Engels, socially-specific individuals who form their beliefs within the framework of their relations with other individuals. Such individuals are both constitutive of the social order yet, in turn, constituted by it. Society and individuals thus co-exist in a dialectical, rather than a reductionist, relationship: it is impossible to conceive of the one without the other.

Historical materialism: an assessment

Marx's presentation, in *Capital*, of individuals as the 'personifications of economic categories, the bearers of particular class relations' which exist independently of them, has led many commentators to see historical materialism as offering an account of social relations which is concerned with objectively existing structures. This structuralism is then contrasted with the methodological individualism of Weberian sociology which sees social relations as 'merely the provisional outcome of contingently reproduced patterns of social action' (Cap. I: 92; Althusser and Balibar: 180; Burris: 69, 71).

Yet, in *The German Ideology*, whilst emphasising that the relations of production exist 'independently of the will' of any one individual who finds them already in existence, Marx and Engels argued against the conception that a class has an existence prior to the individuals who make it up. A class is made up of 'separate individuals' who both compete with each other and with other classes. It is only in so far as they carry on a common battle with another class that they have a common identity. Thus the proletariat is not a single agent, like a club or society which makes decisions. Only by a long process of development do the individuals who constitute the proletariat take shape as an historical subject (CW 5: 51/2, 76/7, 323, 329, 413, 464).

Indeed, in *The German Ideology*, Marx and Engels explicitly rejected the conception of 'society as the subject', a conception which they ascribed to the True Socialists and which they saw as a reflection of a situation in which the products of man's own activity confront him as an alien power. Society is not, even if it appears in this way to the individual, a separate subject but is rather a 'consecutive series of interrelated individuals' and it is through such relations that 'individuals undoubtedly make one another, physically and mentally' (CW 5: 51/2, 76/7, 329, 379, 413, 464).

Marx and Engels' 'structurationist' *German Ideology* thus offers both a critique of and an alternative to the 'structuralist' holism formulated by Althusser on the basis of *Capital*. However, whilst this pragmatological outlook is quite compatible with Weberian sociology in its concepts of agency, the two perspectives remain distinguished from one another by historical materialism's necessary hierarchy of social levels, a conception of social structure which, as we have seen, is rejected by the Weberian tradition.

PRAGMATOLOGICAL/NOMOLOGICAL HISTORICAL MATERIALISM

If, in *The German Ideology*, Marx and Engels employed a pragmatological conception of historical agency, they also, at times, adopted a rather different 'nomological' conception where historical development is seen 'as a natural process taking place in accordance with definite laws' (Fleischer: 13). Thus, as Engels put it in his *Ludwig Feuerbach* (1886), although historical events appear to be governed by chance, in reality they are always governed 'by inner, hidden laws and it is only a matter of discovering these laws' (SW II: 354). For Fleischer, the anthropogenetic, pragmatological and nomological versions of historical materialism involve differences of emphasis, but are not mutually exclusive. Indeed, they 'are legitimate only to the extent that they complement each other' (Fleischer: 13). Yet, as Adamson as pointed out, there is no inherent reason why these approaches should necessarily be compatible (Adamson, 1985: 19-23). To what extent are the anthropogenetic, the pragmatological and the nomological conceptions of historical materialism reconcilable with each other?

At first sight, the nomological view, which sees history as the expression of hidden, inner laws, would seem to reject the centrality of human agency stressed by the pragmatological conception, where 'History is nothing but the activity of man pursuing his aims'. After all, when an apple falls from a tree it is not 'in pursuit of its own aims', but is obeying a law which is external to it, and over which it has no control. As a result, the nomological interpretation version of historical materialism, which Engels offered towards the end of his life, is often distinguished from the views of Marx himself, on the grounds that Engels' invocation of universal 'laws' of history contradicts Marx's realisation that there are no universal covering laws of history (Levine, 1984: 172, 210; Avineri, 1971: 152; Lichtheim, 1971a: 250-1; Jacoby: 55).

However, as we shall see, the problem of the relationship between the pragmatological and the nomological accounts of agency cannot simply be resolved by assigning the pragmatological outlook to Marx and the nomological outlook to Engels. On the contrary, these two different versions of historical materialsm can be identified in the works of both of Engels *and* of Marx. Indeed, as we shall see, it is possible to identify two quite different versions of the nomological outlook itself in the works of both Marx and Engels, one of which is scarcely different from the pragmatolgical outlook (the 'pragmatological-nomological' outlook) whilst the other (the 'positivist-nomological' outlook) is inherently opposed to it.

How does Marx and Engels' nomological conception of history conceive of the relationship between natural laws and the laws of social development? Logically there are three possible positions on this issue. Firstly, there is the reductionist view that *all* social laws are identical with, or can be reduced to, natural laws concerning the motion of matter. Secondly, there is the claim that there are *no* laws which apply to both nature and society. Thirdly, there is the 'emergent evolutionist' proposition that although there may be some laws which apply both to nature and to human society, there are also others which are uniquely applicable to humanity alone.

Historical materialism: an assessment

As we have seen (chapters six and eight, above), it was this third, emergent evolutionist approach which was adopted by Marx and Engels. They thus claimed that the law of the transformation of quantity into quality applied *both* to chemical molecules and to the development of capitalism (Cap. I: 423; AD: 159/63) and yet *also* noted the 'unbridgeable gulf' which could exist between human society and the rest of nature (AD: 34; OFPPS: 34/5). Thus, despite Fleischer's claims, Engels' 'nomological' outlook did *not* commit him to seeing human history as *literally* a 'natural process' (Fleischer: 13). On the contrary, Engels stressed that whilst in nature 'there are only blind, unconscious agencies acting upon one another', the history of society is distinguished by the fact that 'the actors are all endowed with consciousness, are men acting with deliberation or passion, working towards definite goals' (SW II: 354).

Engels did, however, see human history as *analogous* to natural development in two important senses. Firstly, although human history is made by conscious agents, nevertheless, these agents are incapable of exactly achieving their aims. The conflicting individual actions which constitute human history thus 'produce a state of affairs entirely analogous to that prevailing in the realm of unconscious nature', since the path taken by historical development, like that of nature, is not the consciously desired aim of any subjective agent (SW II: 353/4).

If the outcomes of human actions are very different from those intended by their actors, does this mean that historical events are determined by chance? Engels' rejection of this claim led him on to his second analogy between natural and historical development. He argued, as we have seen, that although history may seem to be governed by accident, it is, in fact, 'governed by inner general laws.' History is the product of the actions and motives of human beings but, the nomological Engels argued, historical materialism also allows us to see 'what driving forces in turn stand behind these motives', to understand the real historical causes which 'transform themselves into these motives in the brains of the actors' (SW II: 354/5).

If Engels believed in the existence of laws which were specific to human history, did he see such laws as universally applicable to all societies? Logically, there are three possible views on this issue. Firstly, that all laws of history are universally applicable to all societies. Secondly, that no laws of history are univerally applicable to all societies. Thirdly, that there are some laws of history which are applicable to all societies and some which are applicable only to particular societies. Which of these three positions did Engels adopt?

Engels certainly rejected the claim that *all* laws of history are universally valid. Indeed, at times, he seems to reject the existence of *any* universally valid 'laws' of society and insists instead on the historical specificity of such laws.

The return to Hegel: Engels and dialectical materialism

Thus, in 1865, Engels used the example of Malthus' law of population to argue that 'the so-called "economic laws" are not eternal laws of nature but historical laws that appear and disappear' (CW 42: 136; see also Cap. I: 101; Gr.: 85-7). Similarly, in *Anti-Dühring*, Engels argued that 'anyone who attempted to bring the political economy of Tierra del Fuego under the same laws of poltical economy as are operative in present-day England would obviously produce nothing but the most banal commonplaces. Political economy is therefore essentially an *historical* science' (AD: 187, 192-4, original emphasis).

Yet, in other passages, both Marx and Engels explicitly referrred to the existence of 'the few quite general laws which hold good for production and exchange in all cases' (AD: 187). For instance, in *The German Ideology*, Marx and Engels argued that 'the *whole* development of history' constitutes a '*coherent* series of forms of intercourse' in which '*all* collisions' have their origin in the contradiction between the productive forces and the form of intercourse. Similarly, Marx's '1859 Preface' claimed that '*no* social order is ever destroyed before all the productive forces for which it is sufficient have been developed' (CW 5: 64, 82; CPE: 21, emphases added). Engels repeated these claims in his '1885 Preface' to Marx's *Eighteenth Brumaire* and in his speech at Marx's graveside, as proof that Marx had discovered '*the* great law of motion of history', '*the* law of development of human history' (SW I: 246; SW II: 153, emphases added).

Thus, in practice, Marx and Engels' social theory contains both laws which are historically specific and relate to particular modes of production and others which are universally applicable. It was a belief in such underlying laws of history which provided the basis for Engels' claim that, unlike previous materialist and idealist interpretations of history, historical material-ism had been able to identify the 'real, ultimate driving forces of history' (SW II: 355).

But what, according to Engels, were the 'driving powers' which hold sway in history, the laws which 'lie behind the motives of men who act in history'? (SW II: 355). *In practice*, the so-called historical 'laws' which Engels actually identified in *Ludwig Feuerbach* were simply the constraints on human agency which had previously been set out in *The German Ideology* where Marx and Engels had argued that 'circumstances make men just as much as men make circumstances' (CW 5: 54). Here, at least, there seems to be no contradiction between the pragmatological and the nomological conceptions of historical agency.

Firstly, Engels' *Ludwig Feuerbach* emphasised the role of class struggle as one of the driving forces of history since it determined the motives of the men who make history, even though they themselves are often unconscious of its power. He argued that whilst such conflict was particularly obvious in modern society, where class struggle formed 'the driving force' of history, class struggle was also central to the history of pre-capitalist societies. For instance, the political struggles of the Roman Republic could now be perceived as, in the last resort, about the issue of landed property (SW II: 356-7, 359). Indeed, Engels offered here a far geater emphasis on the role of class struggle in history than did Marx's famous '1859 Preface', although Marx himself elsewhere described such struggle as 'the immediate driving power of history' (SC: 307).

For Engels, class relations and class struggle provided the underlying driving causes of the development of the state and of law: 'In modern history the will of the state is, on the whole, determined by the changing needs of civil society, by the supremacy of this or that class' (SW II: 357-8). Similarly, class relations formed the basis of ideological forms such as philosophy and religion. For example, from Albigensianism until the Reformation, the opposition of the bourgeoisie to feudalism took the 'theological form' of religious heresy which both inherited the traditional theology of Christianity but also transformed this material under the pressure of class interests and relations (SW II: 359-63). Thus, despite their nomological formulations, the social theory of the state and of ideology found in Engels' *Ludwig Feuerbach* involved, in practice, little more than a repetition of the pragmatological claims of *The German Ideology* (CW 5: 59-62, 90, 92).

If classes and class struggle form the basis of the state, politics and ideology, how do such classes come into existence in the first place? Once more, Engels' answer to this question involved little more than a repetition of the claims of *The German Ideology* and the *Communist Manifesto*. Thus, his *Ludwig Feuerbach* argued that capitalism had first appeared within the structure of feudal society but that 'at a certain stage the new productive forces set in motion by the bourgeoisie ... became incompatible with the existing order of production handed down by history and sanctified by law ... The productive forces represented by the bourgeoisie rebelled against the order of production represented by the feudal landlords and the guild-masters. The result is known, the feudal fetters were smashed, gradually in England, at one blow in France' (SW II: 357; CW 5: 64-75; CW 6: 485-90).

Although Engels' later works present history as a process governed by laws, he himself emphasised the differences between the use of laws in the natural and the social sciences. In the former, explanation and prediction exist in a symmetrical relationship: to have explained an event is to have brought it under some predictive covering law. In social science, such prediction is frequently impossible, and explanation and interpretation are often only possible *after* the event. Engels stressed this contrast when he argued that whilst, in organic nature, processes 'recur with fair regularity within very wide limits', in social history, 'the repetition of conditions is the exception and not the rule, once we pass beyond the primitive state of man.' Even when such repetitions do occur in history, 'they never arise under exactly the same circumstances.' As a result, even when the 'inner connections of the social and political forms of existence in an epoch come to be known, this occurs as a rule only when these forms have already half outlived themselves and are nearing their decline' (AD: 111/12). Thus, 'a clear survey of the economic history of a given period can never be obtained contemporaneously, but only subsequently, after a collecting and sifting of the material has taken place' (SW I: 119).

Thus despite the nomological vocabulary of Engels' later writings, much of his social theory was simply a form of interpretive historical sociology. Although in his later works, such as *Ludwig Feuerbach*, *Anti-Dühring* and 'Karl Marx' (1877), Engels refers to the 'underlying laws' or 'driving forces' of history, (AD: 32/3; SW II: 149/50), these simply turn out to be, in practice, the three-tier model of social structure (productive forces, relations of production and political and ideological superstructure) which provided the 'coherence' of historical development identified in *The German Ideology* and Marx's '1859 Preface' (CW 5: 53/4, 74, 82; CPE: 20/2). In this sense, many of Engels' nomological formulations are, as Fleischer has argued, quite compatible with those of Marx and with his own earlier pragmatological writings.

POSITIVIST-NOMOLOGICAL HISTORICAL MATERIALISM

However, if some of Engels' formulations of nomological historical materialism were easily assimilable with the pragmatological outlook, then they could, at times, also lead to a very different form of historical explanation. Engels himself referred to one of the dangers of the nomological outlook when he argued that 'in every department of thought, at a certain stage of development, the laws abstracted from the real world are set over against it as something independent of it, as laws coming from outside, to which the world has to conform.' Such laws are then seen as agents apart, which use humanity to achieve their purposes (AD: 48). Thus, just as the anthropogenetic conception transforms Humanity into an Hegelian principle, whose full realisation is teleologically achieved through the logical unfolding of a series of categories, so, in the nomological conception, it is possible for 'Society' or 'History' to become 'a person apart using man to achieve *its own* aims'. This was, of course, precisely the conception of history which Marx and Engels themselves had criticised in *The Holy Family* and *The German Ideology* (CW 4: 93; CW 5: 50).

In such 'positivist' versions of the nomological outlook, the social processes which, in reality, are produced by 'the conscious will and particular purposes of individuals', are reified into an 'objective interrelation'. As a result, the 'mutual interaction' of human agents is fetishised and becomes seen as an 'alien social power', as a 'process and power independent of them' (Gr.: 196-7). As we shall see, despite his criticisms of such reification, Marx himself was, at times, to fall into this trap.

This 'fetishised' version of the nomological outlook can be seen in Engels' claim that the laws of commodity production asserted themselves 'without the producers and against the producers, as the natural laws of their form of production, working blindly' (AD: 350). Thus, Engels saw the equalisation of the rate of profit between capitalist enterprises, achieved through the redistribution of surplus-value between them, as an outcome which was 'completely foreign to the mind of the individual capitalist', as a process which 'takes place objectively, in the things, unconsciously.' Whilst all capitalists race after the biggest rate of profit, the '*goal* of this race' is the equalisation of this rate. Yet, this argument transforms the unintended *consequences* of human action (the equalisation of the rate of profit) into an objective teleological *purpose* which determines that action. When challenged by Sombart to explain *how* these consequences produced such prior human action, Engels could only lamely reply that more research was necessary (SC: 455).

The nomological conception of historical materialism did not only lead Engels into a reification of social structure but also of historical process. Thus, in a letter of 1894, he argued that the fact that particular individuals, the 'great men' of history such as Napoleon, played a specific historical role was 'pure chance'. Nevertheless, 'if one eliminates him there is a demand for a substitute, and this subsititute will be found, good or bad, but in the long run he will be found'. Thus 'if a Napoleon had been lacking, another would have filled the place', a claim which Engels proved 'by the fact that a man was always found as soon as he became necessary' (SC: 442).

Similarly, in *Anti-Dühring*, Engels refers to revolutionary political force as 'the instrument by means of which *social movement forces its way through* and shatters the dead, fossilized political forms'. In both of these cases, the historical process, the outcome of interacting human agency, is reified and turned into a subject with needs of its own and which uses human agency as its tool. This concept of historical necessity was thus in contradiction with the pragmatological claim, which Engels expressed elsewhere in *Anti-Dühring*, that 'the economic situation does not produce an automatic effect', since 'men make their history themselves', even though they do so 'in a given environ-ment, which conditions them' (AD: 235-6, emphasis added).

A further problem is that the historical 'necessity' identified by Engels was, in practice, an unfalsifiable tautology. After all, the only proof that Napoleon's particular historical role was a 'necessity' of historical development is the fact that he did, in fact, have that particular historical role. As with Hegel's argument that each new philosophy 'must have appeared of necessity at the time of its appearance' (Hegel, 1988: 93), it is difficult to see how Engels' claim could ever be tested.

Finally, history also seems to be converted into a teleological process which uses human agency as a means towards its own ends in those passages where Engels claims that 'the same dialectical laws of motion impose themselves' in both nature and in history so that the unfolding of the dialectic can be seen at work in human history. Marx's claim that communist revolution constituted a dialectical 'negation of the negation', defended at length by Engels in *Anti-Dühring*, was just such an example of the fetishising of the dialectic, transforming it into an agent which used humanity to achieve its purposes (Cap. I: 929; AD: 12, 164-82).

The nomological conception of historical materialism is thus open to two readings. In the first reading, the nomological conception is scarcely different from the pragmatological outlook. Both perspectives claim that men make their own history, even if not under circumstances of their own making, but rather under 'circumstances' which are the outcome of previous, human agency. The so-called 'laws' of history thus turn out to be the constraints on human agency, and the regularities of human action which arise from such constraints, which were set out in the three-tier model of society of *The German Ideology*.

However, in the second version of the nomological outlook, human action is teleologically explained by the agency of some reified process or structure, by the needs of 'History', of 'Society', of the 'Economy', or of the 'dialectical process'. The nomological approach could, therefore, lead Marx and Engels into the kind of fetishism and idealism which they themselves criticised in others. In this 'positivist' version of the nomological approach, Marx and Engels first abstracted the 'laws' of history from the regularities of observed human behaviour, and then, through an inversion of reality, presented such laws as alien powers over humanity, and as the real agents of historical development. Thus, despite Fleischer's claims, the anthropogenetic, pragmatological and nomological versions of historical materialism are by no means always mutually compatible.

It is true that Marx and Engels never abandoned the anthropogenetic, humanist *description* of the course of human history to which they had adhered in their youth. Thus, even in his supposedly 'scientistic', 'positivist' *Anti-Dühring*, Engels praised Hegel for having seen history as not simply 'a wild whirl of senseless deeds', but rather as 'the process of evolution of humanity itself' and claimed that, for 'modern materialism' too, history represented the progress of humanity from an animal-state 'towards freedom' and the 'really human morality' of a classless society (AD: 29, 31, 119, 144, see also CPE: 21-2).

Where the the anthropogenetic, the pragmatological and the nomological conceptions of historical materialism differ is thus not in their *descriptions* of the course of historical change, but rather in their conceptions of the *agency* which brings such change about. In particular, the teleological causation implicit in both the anthropogenetic and the positivist-nomological conceptions of history contradicts the emphasis on human agency which characterises the pragmatological (and the pragmatological-nomological) approach.

It is, therefore, ironic that Marx's '1844 Manuscripts' have been so admired by humanist Marxists since, although they offer an attractive vision of a humanity which has overcome its own alienation, their anthropogenetic account of social development presents this goal as the outcome of a necessary evolution. In effect, it sees history as an inevitable, law-bound progression through stages, of the kind which humanist Marxism usually rejects as 'positivist'. Human agency comes here, as in Engels' own early writings, to be conceived in Hegelian terms as the instrument of the 'cunning of Reason', which governs the process of History and brings about its own aims (Hegel, 1956: 9-10, 21, 32-3). Paradoxically, in both the Hegelian-anthropogenetic and positivist-nomological conceptions, Man achieves his full humanity through a process which is, in a sense, external to him. This was, of course, exactly the mode of explanation whose abandonment constituted the key to Marx and Engels' 'epistemological break' of the mid-1840s (CW 3: 296-7, 305-6; Fleischer: 12-16; CW 4: 93; CW 5: 50, 77, 88-9).

As a result of their teleology, neither the anthropogenetic nor the 'positivist' nomological outlooks sees history as open-ended. However, in the pragmatological outlook (including its nomological inflection), historical development *is*, in theory, open-ended, in the sense that 'History' has no 'goal'. Of course, in practice, even in their most pragmatological works, Marx and Engels assumed that the situation and interests of the proletariat under capitalism would mean that it 'can and *must* emancipate itself' through communist revolution (CW 4: 37; CW 5: 52-3). Nevertheless, the only historical 'necessity' this argument involved was that which depended on human interests and agency.

It is tempting to see Engels' (or Marx's) thought as simply developing chronologically from the anthropogenetic conception of his early Hegelian writings; through the pragmatological conception of *The Holy Family* and *The German Ideology*; to the nomological outlook of his dialectical materialist works. In fact, these three outlooks did not merely succeed one another but could be found sitting uneasily alongside one another within the same texts. Engels did not, in his later writings, simply abandon the pragmatological historical materialism of the mid-1840s. Rather, he retained its central claims, whilst grafting on to them a positivist-nomological conception of historical materialism, which was not only unnecessary for the pragmatological outlook, but was, at times, in open contradiction to it.

MULTILINEAR VERSUS UNILINEAR CONCEPTIONS OF HISTORY

Closely related to the nomological conception of history as a law-bound process of development, is the issue of whether Marx and Engels saw historical change in multilinear terms. Indeed, this is a classic instance where Engels' works are read in order to counterpose them to those of Marx, inevitably to Engels' disadvantage. Thus many writers contrast Marx's awareness of the variety of historical paths taken by particular societies with Engels' alleged adherence to a universal path of development for all societies (Levine, 1984: 121-2, 168; Sawer: 334; Krader: 205). Shanin, for example, claims that Engels did not share Marx's growing awareness of the multilinear nature of historical development. Instead, he permanently abandoned the concept of a specific Asiatic path of development, which he and Marx had adopted in the 1850s, sometime between the publication of *Anti-Dühring* (1878) and *The Origin of the Family* (1884) (Shanin, 1981: 119; Shanin, 1983: 21-5).

Engels must have been familiar with Hegel's view that the 'stationary and fixed' nature of the Orient provided a contrast with the historical path taken by western Europe, from 1840, when he had 'dutifully read' *Hegel's Philosophy of History*.(Hegel, 1956: 116, 139, 173; CW: 2: 490). Nevertheless, it was not until the period after 1853 that he and Marx turned their attention to what Marx's '1859 Preface' referred to as the 'Asiatic mode of production' (CPE: 21). In May 1853, Engels wrote a letter to Marx about his reading of Arabian history, to which Marx replied praising Bernier's claim that the key to the history of the Orient was 'the absence of private landed property.' Engels, in turn, replied that 'the absence of landed property is indeed the key to the whole of the East.' He then explained this absence in terms of the geography of the area, claiming that Oriental agriculture required the provision of irrigation and that such public works were the responsibility either of the local communities or of the provincial and central governments. He argued that it was these institutions which had acted as a restraint on the development of private property rights in land. Engels' letter then provided the basis for much of Marx's article on 'The British Rule in India' (CW 39: 326-8, 332-4, 339-41, 346-8; SFE: 301-7).

Engels was to express very similar views in *Anti-Dühring* where, once more, he linked the lack of progress in the East with its despotism, need for irrigation, absence of private property in land (although, like Marx, Engels was unclear whether it was the village community or the state which owned the land) and the existence of self-sufficent village communities. Far from his permanently abandoning the views on Oriental despotism after 1878, Engels reissued *Anti-Dühring* in 1885 and 1894 and, in 1887-88, planned to publish its chapters on 'the role of force in history', which contained most of this work's references to the Orient, as a separate pamphlet. Finally, it was, of course, Engels who edited *Capital* volume III for publication, with its claim that in Asia, where private property in land was absent, tax and rents coincided. If, with Shanin, we see the concept of Oriental despotism as an example of multilinear historical development (though Lubasz has argued that, for Marx, the Asiatic mode was actually a variant form of the initial stage of primitive communal property), then Engels certainly employed this concept from 1853 until the end of his life (AD: 189, 206, 225, 230/2; RFH: 11/12; Cap. III: 927; Anderson, 1979: 473/83; Shanin, 1983: 5; Lubasz).

Nor is it true that Engels' *Origin of the Family* simply offers a unilinear account of historical development. On the contrary, Engels explicitly stated that it was a lack of space which prevented him from discussing Oriental history. Even within his account of Western history, Engels offered three alternative routes by which the Greeks, Romans and Germans arrived at a form of state organisation and referred to the variety of forms of communal ownership which preceded the emergence of private property (OFPPS: 98, 165/6; AD: 224). Whilst Engels believed that all humanity had experienced a stage of savagery (where it lived by hunting and gathering, formed villages, developed the use of stone and wooden tools and so on), he argued that with the advent of barbarism (where animals were domesticated and agriculture was introduced) the populations of the Old and the New Worlds each 'went on its own special way'. Indeed, in the New World, the lower stage of barbarism 'was nowhere outgrown until the European Conquest' and its higher stages were 'traversed independently only in the eastern hemisphere'(OFPPS: 25/7; EN: 8, 17; Morgan).

Finally, Engels' writings on Russia show that he was far from believing in a universal, unilinear path of historical development. Thus in 1875, Engels argued, as he and Marx had for the past thirty years, that communism could only be built on the basis of 'a certain level of development of the productive forces of society.' The productive forces had reached this level of development 'only in the hands of the bourgeoisie', which meant that this level had not been reached in feudal Russia. Nevertheless, Engels then went on to argue that this did not necessarily mean that Russia would, like western Europe, have to go through a long period of capitalist development before it could reach socialism. On the contrary, although the Russian peasant commune was already past its peak, the possibility did exist of 'raising this form of society to a higher one ... without it being necesary for the Russian peasants to go through the intermediate stage of bourgeois smallholdings.' Yet, Engels continued, this could 'only happen if, before the complete break/up of communal ownership, a proletarian revolution is successfully carried out in western Europe, creating for the Russian peasant the pre/conditions requisite for such a transition.' In turn, however, Engels predicted the imminence of revolution in Russia and argued that the destruction of Tsarism would be a major blow against European reaction (SW II: 46,7, 54,6).

It was this analysis which Marx and Engels adopted in the '1882 Preface' to the *Communist Manifesto*, drafted by Engels, but corrected and signed by Marx (in itself, an interesting illustration of the way in which the two men worked). This 'Preface' argued that, if revolution in Russia proved to be the signal for proletarian revolution in the West, the Russian peasant commune would not have to 'pass through the same process of dissolution' as in the West. Rather, the commune could 'serve as the starting point for a communist development', so that Russia could 'pass directly to the higher form of communist common ownership' (CM: 56; Wada: 70).

Wada sees this 'Preface' as in contradiction with the drafts of Marx's letter to Zasulich, written almost immediately afterwards, which does not postulate the need for a western revolution as a precondition of Russian 'regeneration'. In fact, it would be more accurate to say that Marx's letter to Zasulich simply ignored this issue, as did a similar letter by Marx to the editorial board of *Otechestvennye Zapiski* (1877), a letter which Engels apparently did not see as in contradiction with his own views, since he went to great pains to have it published in Russia (Wada: 41, 71; SC: 291,4). Certainly, it is rather difficult to see any real difference between Marx and Engels' views on the prospects of communism in Russia.

It is thus rather futile to criticise Engels for failing to see that socialist revolutions could be victorious in countries such as Russia and China even without the help of western proletarian revolution (Shanin, 1983: 24). After all, Lenin and Trotsky themselves shared this opinion, even after the October Revolution (Trostsky, 1967: 362,86). Indeed, given the tragic course taken by the 'victorious' Russian and Chinese Revolutions, there may, in fact, be many people who would see these examples as proving, rather than disproving, Engels' arguments about the need for suitable conditions, not just the existence of a revolutionary will, if socialist revolution was to succeed.

CLASS AND PATRIARCHY

In offering an assessment of Engels' social theory, the question of patriarchy is a crucial one since historical materialism is often criticised on the grounds that, with its emphasis on the social relations of production, it is incapable of dealing with non-class forms of inequality and social exclusion, such as race and gender (Parkin, 1979: 4; Giddens, 1981: 242; De Beauvoir: 87; Firestone: 15; Hartmann: 10,11). Traditionally, it is Engels' pioneering work, *The Origin of the Family, Private Property and the State* (1884), which has been seen as 'the definitive Marxist pronouncement on the family and therefore on the so-called woman question' (Vogel, 1983: 75). Here we will look first at Engels' account of the rise of patriarchy and then consider how Engels' analysis of the relationship between gender inequalities and those based on class relates to more recent discussions of this issue.

Perhaps the most enduring aspect of Engels' analysis is his emphasis on the *sociological* origins of women's inequality, and on its socially and historically specific nature and meaning (Sayers et al.: 57-8). For Engels, patriarchy, the social superiority enjoyed by men over women, is not an eternal, *biological* fact, but is rather the product of a certain stage of social development.

As we have seen (p. 197, above), Engels divided social evolution into three main stages: savagery, barbarism and civilisation. Each of these three stages had its own characteristic form of family: group marriage was characteristic of savagery; the pairing family of barbarism; and monogamy of civilisation. For Engels, the idea that 'woman was the slave of man at the commencement of society is one of the most absurd notions that have come down to us from the period of the Enlightenment.' Far from being slaves, women were 'supreme' within the system of communistic households and matrilinear descent which dominated in the *gens* (the kinship system characteristic of barbarism) which gave a 'high esteem' to women. As late as the middle stage of barbarism, and partly even in its upper stage, women held a free and highly respected position. The communistic household was thus the 'material foundation of that predominancy of women which generally obtained in primitive times' (OFPPS: 23-9, 37-42, 46-7, 49, 53, 74-5, 84, 158, 161-4).

However, according to Engels, the development, under barbarism, of new forms of wealth based on agriculture and pastoralism, began to undermine women's social position. At first, these new forms of wealth, had been communal property but, 'at a very early stage', they passed into the private possession of families. Within the pairing family, the existing division of labour had granted women control of the household goods whilst men had controlled 'the procuring of food and the implements necessary thereto.' As a result of this existing sexual division of labour, the ownership of the new forms of wealth, amongst which Engels places emphasis on herds of cattle, 'fell to the man.' Yet, this property, which belonged to the husband within the pairing family, did not pass to his own children, who were seen as members of their mother's gens. Instead, his herds passed to his brothers and sisters, to his sister's children or to the descendants of his mother's children. 'His own children, however, were disinherited.' Thus, the growing wealth in the hands of men gave them an increasing importance within the family and 'created a stimulus to utilize this strengthened position in order to overthrow the traditional order or inheritance' through the female line in favour of his own children. This 'overthrow of mother right was the world-historic defeat of the female sex', through which women lost their supremacy even within the household and became 'mere instrument(s) for breeding children'. (OFPPS: 53/8, 157/9)

Once established, this 'monogamous' family, which Engels distinguishes from the 'pairing' family on the grounds that it was 'based on the supremacy of the man', had, despite variations in its degree of harshness (the Romans having a less oppressive form than the Greeks), persisted up to the present day. Engels thus attempted, explicitly at least, to explain the origin of the subordination of women not in 'natural conditions', but rather in changes in society's productive forces and relations of production. In particular, he emphasised the importance of the 'victory of private property', and the transition to class society (OFPPS: 62, 65, 68, 74/5; Maconachie: 101/2).

Engels' account of the rise of private property and of patriarchy is flawed in a variety of ways. Firstly, it can be criticised in empirical terms. For instance, he wrongly saw matriliny as a universal stage of human development which had preceded patriliny, a claim now rejected by anthropologists. Furthermore, his argument was based on a confusion between matriliny (descent through the female line) with matriarchy (a society where women have a high social status). In fact, there is no necessary correlation between matriliny and a high social status for women, and 'there is no evidence for a matriarchal stage in human history' (Coontz and Henderson: 26; Saliou: 170). Other empirical weaknesses in Engels' account include his attempt to link specific forms of kinship and marriage patterns with particular levels of technological development (Bloch: 66, 75/7). As a result of such empirical errors, it has been said that 'the whole facade of Engels' *The Origin* collapses.' (Godelier, 1977: 103).

Secondly, Engels' analysis can be faulted on theoretical grounds. In particular, despite his attempt to give an historical, rather than a biological, account of the origins of patriarchy, his whole analysis is, implicitly, based on men's inherent desire to pass on their wealth to their own legitimate heirs. As a result, his explanation largely assumes what it purports to explain (De Beauvoir: 86; Gimenez: 40).

Finally, whilst Engels has been praised for perceiving the general correlation between the growth of sexual inequality on the one hand, and the decline of clan/based social organisation on the other, his analysis also suffers from the fundamental problem that 'male dominance has been shown to exist in some pre/class, pre/state societies, lacking true private property.' Indeed, it has even been claimed that, in some cases, the growth of social hierarchy, which Engels saw as leading to patriarchy, 'may increase gender *equality*' (Coontz and Henderson: 32, 108/9). However, despite the importance of such issues, we are more concerned here to assess the general approach within which Engels worked. Engels' anthropology may now be out of date but how useful is his broader, methodological perspective relate in the analysis of the relationship between inequalities of class and those of gender?

At the moment, every possible permutation of class and gender is on offer to us, and no clear resolution of the matter is in sight (Phillips: 21). For some, both types of social inequality form parts of a single, organic system so that, for example, gender inequalities constitute an essential aspect of the inherently patriarchal capitalist mode of production (Young: 64; Vogel, 1981; Middleton, 1974: 198-201). For others, class and gender inequalities constitute two separate structures which, though interacting in practice, can be conceptualised separately (Cockburn: 81).

However, those 'dualists' who adopt this latter approach to the problem can be sub-divided into three, mutually exclusive camps. Firstly, there are those 'strict' dualists who see partnership between the class system and patriarchy as an equal one in which the two hierarchies co-exist in a 'mutually reinforcing dialectical relationship' (Hartmann: 17-19, 29; Eisenstein: 5, 28; Humphries: 16-17). Secondly, there are the 'radical feminists' who grant an analytical primacy to patriarchy as the basis of society's economic, social and political institutions and emphasise the weakness of women's class-links with men (Firestone: 19-21; Millett: 38; Delphy: 38-9, 74-5; Humphries: 16; Bennett, 1987: 6). Finally, there is the 'traditional Marxist' analysis, which claims a primacy for society's relations of production, and which thus sees specific forms of gender inequalities as shaped by, and functional for, particular modes of production (Adamson, *et al.* 1976: 7; McDonough and Harrison: 28, 39; Gimenez: 48; Middleton, 1981: 151-2). How does Engels' work relate to this debate?

In *The Origin of the Family*, Engels defined the materialist conception of history, as he had in *Anti-Dühring*, as the view that 'the determining factor in history is, in the last resort, the production and reproduction of immediate life.' However, he continued, this production and reproduction 'is of a twofold character. On the one hand, the production of the means of subsistence, of food, clothing and shelter and the tools requisite therefore; on the other, the production of human beings themselves, the propagation of the species. The social institutions under which men of a definite historical epoch and of a definite country are conditioned by both kinds of production: by the stage of development of labour, on the one hand, and of the family on the other' (OFPPS: 6).

This much-quoted passage has led many writers to characterise Engels as a 'dualist' who presents production and reproduction as 'two distinct and co-ordinate aspects of production', each of which has an 'equal analytic weight', a dualism which is then equated with that between the realms of class and patriarchy (Hartmann: 17; McDonough and Harrison: 28; Vogel, 1981: 212-13; Vogel, 1983: 31-2, 90). Yet such an equation would be unwise for, despite the fact that women's role in reproduction is vital for an understanding of their social subordination, patriarchal relations are not confined to the sphere of reproduction but permeate all aspects of society, including that of production (Beneria; Hartmann: 14-15).

However, even if we revised Engels' analysis, so that his dualism of production and reproduction was replaced with a dualism of class and patriarchy, it would still be very misleading to portray Engels as a 'strict' dualist, for whom class and patriarchy had an equal weight. On the contrary, Engels' *Origin of the Family* explicitly repeats the argument of *The German Ideology* that, as society's productive forces advanced and private property emerged, social structures 'based on ties of sex', where the family itself functioned as a relation of production, had given way to a social relations in which 'the family system is entirely dominated by the property system' (OFPPS: 6; CW 5: 43). Thus, Engels' analysis gave the family and gender a secondary role, and invoked the growth of society's productive forces, and the emergence of new forms of property, as the primary, dynamic element which explained changes in family and gender relations.

The 'subordinate' status of family and gender relations are particularly apparent in Engels' analysis of patriarchy within the capitalist mode of production. Since Engels associated patriarchy and monogamy with the male desire to ensure the legitimate succession of private property, it followed that male domination continued to flourish within the propertied families of the modern bourgeoisie. However, capitalist society had also created a class stripped of all private property in the means of production: the proletariat. Amongst this class, 'all the foundations of classical monogamy are removed', since 'there is a complete absence of all property, for the safeguarding of which monogamy and male domination were established. Therefore, there is no stimulus whatever here to assert male domination' (OFPPS: 65, 70-2).

Furthermore, since 'large-scale industry has transferred the woman from the house to the labour-market and the factory and makes her, often enough, the bread-winner of the family, the last remnants of male domination in the proletarian home have lost all foundation – except, perhaps, for some of the brutality towards women which became firmly rooted with the establishment of monogamy. Thus, the proletarian family is no longer monogamous in the strict [i.e. patriarchal, S.R.] sense ... The woman has regained, in fact, the right of separation and when the man and the woman cannot get along they prefer to part' (OFPPS: 71-2). Thus Engels offered a 'scientific feminism', which optimistically portrayed capitalism itself as producing a new, non-patriarchal form of family; a form which would provide the basis for the society of the future, when private property, the material basis of male domination, had been fully abolished.

The first problem with Engels' analysis is that, in explaining patriarchy in terms of private property, an institution which is common to a wide variety of class relations, it fails to offer an account of gender relations in terms of their articulation with historically specific relations of production (Vogel, 1983: 87-8). Under capitalism, for instance, even if we confined our analysis simply to the realm of economics, patriarchy must be seen not just in the context of the transmission of private property but also, and more importantly, in terms of the sexual division of labour within paid work (Beechey); of the role of women as a reserve army of labour (Bruegel); and of women's domestic work in reproducing the commodity of labour-power, upon which the capitalist mode of production is based (Seccombe). In particular, we need to see the subordination of women within the working-class family as based upon women's periodic economic dependence upon men, through the 'family wage', and through the lower wages which women receive in the labour market (Hartmann: 25; Land).

Such an analysis would offer an integrated account of the mutual reinforcement which characterises the relationship between capitalism and gender inequalities, rather than merely portraying patriarchy within the working class as an ideological hangover ('brutal attitudes') from a previous era. However, the fact that class and patriarchy form, in practice, two interacting and interdependent systems does *not* mean that gender relations can simply be seen as socially 'subordinate' in the sense that they can be reduced to, or explained by their functionality for, society's relations of production (Barrett: 132-3).

A second problem with Engels' analysis is that, in associating patriarchy with the trans-historical institutions of 'private property' and the monogamous family, he presented patriarchy as an enduring system which seems to lack a history of its own. As in radical feminist accounts of patriarchy, the concept can come to imply 'a structure which is fixed' and 'uniform', thus obscuring the 'kaleidoscope of forms within which men and women have encountered one another' (Millett: 25; Rowbotham: 74). The concept of 'patriarchy' exists as the same level of abstraction as that of 'class society' but whilst we have a classification of forms of class society (feudalism, capitalism, etc.) which allows us to specify the forms taken by society's relations of production, we have, as yet, no equivalent typology of the forms taken by patriarchy. The problem is not just that Engels omitted to produce such a classification; rather, it is that his explanation of patriarchy in terms of the transmission of private property positively prevented him from doing so.

Engels' anthropology may now be outdated and his account of the origins of patriarchy may take for granted exactly what it is seeking to explain, but the main weakness of the analysis offered in *The Origin of the Family* is its equation of patriarchy with the sphere of the family and its correspondence to the institution of private property. Engels was thus unable either to provide an historical typology of the forms taken by patriarchy, or to theorise its relationship to society's successive modes of production. It may be that the conceptual framework and theoretical categories of Marx's *Capital* offer a more fruitful way of achieving an integrated analysis of class and gender than those of Engels' *The Origin of the Family* (Vogel, 1983: 72, 87-8). Nevertheless, Marx himself did not develop such an analysis. As a result of such inadequacies in Marx and Engels' analyses, the relationship between class and gender is one of the few areas where it is more stimulating and instructive to read the works of recent Marxist theoreticians, rather than those of Marx and Engels themselves.

CONCLUSION

To the end of his life, Engels continued to defend the key propositions of historical materialism which he and Marx had first developed in The *German Ideology*, and which Marx had set out in his '1859 Preface', namely, that society's relations of production correspond to the level of development of its productive forces, and that such relations constitute the basis of its political and ideological superstructures. It was this model of social structure and historical evolution (including the possibility of multilinear development) which Engels employed in his *Origin of the Family* and which, despite his emphasis on the dialectical interaction of base and superstructure, he defended in his famous letters of the 1890s. Historical agency was seen here, as in *The Holy Family* and *The German Ideology* in pragmatological terms, where 'men' make their own history, although not under circumstances of their own making. The 'laws' of history which Engels referred to in his later works could, in this perspective, simply be seen as giving an emphasis to those particular 'circumstances' which have always given Marxist social theory its specific character.

Yet, at times Engels lapsed (as did Marx) into a 'positivist-nomological' account of historical agency in which humans are presented as the puppets, or 'bearers', of a fetishised process which seems to exist independently of them. Of course, the fact that no one individual controls historical events and that human actions have unintended consequences certainly makes it *appear* as if 'History' is a process which exists separate from human agency. In reality, however, as Marx and Engels put it in the mid-1840s, 'history is nothing but the activity of man pursuing his aims', within a social context which is itself 'only a product of the preceding intercourse of individuals' (CW 4: 93; CW 5: 81).

However, whilst Marx and Engels' pragmatological concept of agency is superior to that of their anthropogenetic writings (where the agency of historically specific 'men' is replaced by the teleological category of 'Man') and of their positivist-nomological formulations, even this strongest version of historical materialism contains several fatal weaknesses. Firstly, Marx and Engels' claims for the social primacy of the productive forces are unacceptable even to many modern Marxists, who find such claims an embarrassment which has to be 'explained away' (Meyer: 453) or, as we have seen, blamed on Engels.

Secondly, although Marx and Engels' claims for the determination of society's political and ideological 'superstructure' by its economic 'base' are frequently seen as foundering on the issue of the 'interpenetration' of base and superstructure, this problem *can*, as Godelier's work shows, be resolved within the terms of historical materialism. It is rather the problem of the interaction of base and superstructure which provides the crucial stumbling block for those claims for the social primacy of the mode of production, which give Marxist social theory its distinctive character. Only by taking a specific economic situation as the starting point of its analysis, and thus ignoring the previous interaction of economics, politics, law and ideology which Marxism itself recognises as creating that economic situation, do Marx and Engels' claims for the primacy of economic conditions have any credence.

Finally, if we reject Marx and Engels' claims for the primacy of the economic then we need to replace the architectural analogy of 'base and superstructure' with some other metaphor, perhaps that which sees society as composed of a number of 'dimensions', or 'axes', such as class, gender, politics and ideology, which are not articulated in any necessary hierarchy of causality (Davis: xvii). Marxist historiography continues to offer a useful corrective to those historical traditions which have systematically ignored the role of economic change and class struggle in history but, whilst we may welcome historical materialism's emphasis on the *indispensability* of such factors in explaining historical change, there is, nevertheless, no need for us to accept its claims for their necessary *primacy*.

CHAPTER TEN

Scientific and critical Marxism: an assessment

> It is certainly not pleasant to criticize, a hundred years later, the views of a great thinker; views, moreover, that have been irrevocably refuted by the severest of all critics — history (Rosdolsky: 185).

The century since Marx's death has been a disastrous one for the political practice of Marxism. On the one hand, the western working class has consistently failed to carry out the revolutionary tasks which Marxist theory had assigned to it. On the other, in those underdeveloped countries where Marxist parties have been able to take power, the often barbaric results have been little to the liking of western Marxists. Naturally, Marxism's opponents have found the explanation for such barbarities within the theory of Marxism itself, the sins of Stalin being seen as the logical consequence of Marx and Engels' theory. Ironically, instead of questioning the 'idealism' of explaining history in terms of the necessary consequences of ideas, many Marxists have accepted the logic of this sort of argument. If the theory of Marxism was not to be damned by the practice of its exponents, some scapegoat was needed to divert blame away from Marx himself. As always, Friedrich Engels was conveniently at hand to take the blame for Marxism's shortcomings and thus avoid the need for an interrogation of the weaknesses inherent in Marx's own theory.

Thus, it is frequently claimed that, as the founder of dialectical materialism, Engels ignored the role of class consciousness and human agency in revolutionary practice, and saw socialist revolution simply as the outcome of an objective social process. Engels' mechanistic Marxism, his evolutionary outlook and his belief in the possibility of socialism by the ballot-box were directly responsible for the reformism, parliamentarianism and disastrous strategy of the German SPD in the years before 1914. Furthermore, Engels is held to have transformed Marxism from being the expression of the needs and interests of the proletariat, into a supposedly objective science, a position which had then to be refuted by 'critical' Marxists such as Lukács and Korsch. In short, Engels failed to understand Marx's central concept of revolutionary praxis (Callinicos, 1987a: 61; Walton and Gamble: 52, Colletti, 1972: 69; Miller,1979: 99, 109-112; Lichtheim, 1971a: 236-8; Fetscher: 162; Avineri, 1971: 144, 217; Levine, 1984: 21, 49, 55, 165, 172; Timpanaro: 45-8; Thomas: 6; Carver, 1983: 148-50).

Engels differed from Marx, it is claimed, not only on the tactics of socialist revolution but also, and even more fundamentally, about its goals. Whereas Marx had a humanist vision of a socialism, where society would be organised in a way which would allow man's species-being, his true human potential, to be fulfilled, Engels, who lacked the concept of species-being, had a narrow conception of freedom and an impoverished vision of socialism based only on an industrial-puritan glorification of work and productivity. His vision of socialism thus concentrated on the liberation of the productive forces, rather than on the self-liberation of the working class. Unlike Marx, Engels rejected the ethical analysis of capitalism and accounted for the inevitability of socialism without any reference to the values, aims, and purposes of individuals. He thus ignored the critique of the alienation and reification of capitalist society contained not only in Marx's *1844 Manuscripts*, but even in Marx's later works, particularly his discussion of commodity fetishism in *Capital* volume I (Levine, 1975: chs. 4, 11, 13; Fetscher: 165; Colletti, 1973: 178; Easton: 39).

The consequences of Engels' positivist outlook can be seen not only in the reformism of the SPD, but also in the inhumanity of the Bolsheviks' political practice. Indeed, he can be held responsible, at least objectively, for the incarceration of Soviet dissidents in mental asylums, even though Engels himself might have subjectively disagreeed with such practices (Ball: 257-8; Avineri, 1971: 144). Engels was thus responsible both for the reformist timidity of the Second International, and for the voluntarist excesses of the Bolsheviks and Stalin.

Naturally, however, other, less critical assessments of Engels' political philosophy are available (Draper: 25; Berger). The range of views on offer can be seen by the issue of whether Marx and Engels regarded proletarian revolution as inevitable. For some writers, both Marx and Engels were inevitabilists (Eastman: 182; Edgley: 252); for some, neither Marx nor Engels were inevitabilists (Croce: 11); for others, Engels was an inevitabilist but Marx was not (Avineri, 1971: 144; Levine, 1984: 165, 172; Thomas: 8). Only the view that Marx was an inevitabilist, whereas Engels was not, seems to be missing.

Here we will argue that Engels' later writings did not abandon the unity of scientific and critical Marxism which had been set out in his and Marx's joint works of the 1840s. The weakness of his political theory lay not in any alleged divergence from that of Marx, nor in its lack of internal coherence, but rather in its lack of correspondence to reality. As a result, Marx and Engels' communism came to suffer from the same weaknesses as the utopian socialism against which they had originally defined their own outlook.

The return to Hegel: Engels and dialectical materialism

HISTORICAL MATERIALISM AND SCIENTIFIC SOCIALISM

In his *Anti-Dühring*, Engels was to repeat the critique of utopian socialism which the *Communist Manifesto* had outlined thirty years before. Here, once more, Saint-Simon, Fourier and Owen were portrayed as the product of a period when the antagonism between bourgeoisie and proletariat was still in its infancy. Socialism was thus seen as the precondition for a society organised in line with the requirements of universal justice and reason, rather than as the expression of the interests of a particular class. Nevertheless, Engels praised the early Utopians for their 'stupendously grand thoughts', for their critique of the abuses inherent in modern society, and for their vision of an alternative society which was worthy of human beings (CW 6: 514-17; SW II: 107-18).

Against such Utopianism, Engels offered the alternative of 'scientific' socialism. It should, however, immediately be emphasised that Engels did *not* define scientific socialism in terms of philosophical materialism, or of the the laws of the dialectic. He claimed, instead, that 'the two great discoveries' (both made by Marx) through which 'socialism became a science' were 'the materialistic conception of history' and the theory of surplus-value (SW II: 125). What did Engels see as the relationship between these discoveries and scientific socialism?

As we have seen, the definition of historical materialism which Engels offered in his later works was consistent with the social theory which he and Marx had explicitly defended ever since *The German Ideology*: all history, except for its most primitive stages, is the history of class struggles; such struggles have their base in the stage of development of production and of exchange; these economic conditions form the base for society's political, juridical and ideological superstructure. He claimed that, once the materialist conception of history was established, it then became clear that 'socialism was no longer an accidental discovery of this or that ingenious brain but the necessary outcome of the struggle between two historically developed classes – the proletariat and the bourgeoisie' (SW II: 124-5).

Engels argued that, in itself, the moral critique of capitalism's inhumanity was insufficient to bring about communism. Rather, such critiques could only have any practical effect when capitalism 'was already well into its declining phase.' Engels believed in the 1870s, as he had in the 1840s, that capitalism was now reaching the stage where the bourgeoisie 'is increasingly becoming not only socially superfluous, but a social hindrance'. He quoted *Capital* to the effect that, with the growing concentration of capital, 'the monopoly of capital becomes a fetter on the mode of production' and was thus 'being driven to the point at which it makes itself impossible.' As a result of the growth of the productive forces which the bourgeoisie itself had created, bourgeois society was now being driven 'towards ruin or towards revolution', and was increasingly reliant on force in order to safeguard its position in an age of 'impending social revolution'. For Engels, the preconditions for socialism were not merely the will to abolish classes or the idea that capitalism was unjust. Rather, what was required was the development of society's productive forces to a point where the rule of the bourgeoisie had become unnecessary: 'This point has now been reached' (AD: 169, 190/1, 210/11, 248, 364/5).

This does not mean, however, that Engels simply offered an 'objectivist' theory of revolution, which stressed the role of the productive forces, whilst Marx had a 'subjectivist' theory which emphasised the revolutionary agency of the working class. Rather, both men believed that it was the development of capitalism which had produced the proletariat and that, as we shall see, it was the fettering of the productive forces by capitalism which forced the proletariat into a recogniton of its own class/interest: the abolition of capitalist wage/labour (CM: 69; SC: 448; AD: 168/9). It was, after all, this emphasis on the necessity of specific social conditions as the precondition for revolution which distinguished Marx and Engels' outlook from voluntarist Blanquism (Henderson, 1976 II: 580/1).

Since Engels justified his revolutionary politics in terms of his and Marx's account of the relationship between society's productive forces, it seems, at first sight, that Marx and Engels' scientific socialism was based on their historical materialism; their politics and their social science should thus stand or fall together. Yet, in practice, historical materialism as an account of previous social evolution can never be capable of offering a guide to political activity. After all, even if we accepted Marx and Engels' claim that all great social transitions have their roots in the conflict between society's social relations and its expanding productive forces, we could only know whether any particular productive forces had reached their limit of expansion under specific social relations *after* those social relations had been cast aside. In other words, even if Marx and Engels' theory of revolution were true in the abstract, it has no specific practical consequence for political activity (Hodgson: 29). But if this is the case, historical materialism cannot offer a guide to revolutionary action and simply becomes a branch of academic social theory.

A second problem with the theory of revolution set out in *The German Ideology* is that, even if we accepted Marx and Engels' claim that capitalism had now reached the limit of its development of the productive forces (CW 5: 73/5), and thus entered its era of terminal crisis, there is no reason why we should assume that it would necessarily be replaced by communism, rather than by some other form of social relation, such as, for example, state capitalism. Agreement with the broad claims of Engels' social science would then no longer commit us to the specific predictions of his scientific socialism.

We can now see the attraction of the Hegelian 'negation of the negation' for

Marx and Engels' predictions of revolution, since this formula allowed them to emphasise not only the inevitability of historical change, but also seemed to provide a guide to the direction which that change would take (AD: 164-72). Indeed, even in *The German Ideology*, where Marx and Engels' social theory was at its least Hegelian, they seem to have lapsed, in their predictions of the future course of historical development, into the Hegelian, anthropogenetic teleology which had been characteristic of their earlier writings. They argued, for instance, that it was 'an empirical fact' (actually it was a value-judgement by Marx and Engels) that, up to the present, 'separate individuals, with the broadening of their activity into world-historical activity, become more and more enslaved under a power alien to them ... a power which has become more and more enormous and, in the last instance, turns out to be the world market.' Thus, whilst 'individuals *seem* freer under the dominance of the bourgeoisie than before ... in reality, *they are less free*, because they are to a greater extent governed by material forces' (CW 5: 51, 78-9).

With a typically Hegelian logic, Marx and Engels argued that 'only the proletarians ... who are shut off from all self-activity, are in a position to achieve a complete and no longer restricted self-activity.' As a result of historical development, 'the domination of material relations over individuals and the suppression of individuality by fortuitous circumstances, has now assumed its sharpest and most universal form, *thereby setting existing individuals a very definite task*. It has set them the task of replacing the domination of circumstances and chance over individuals by the domination of individuals over chance and circumstances.' This task could only be successfully performed by the social appropriation of the productive forces which would allow the creation of a realm of self-conscious freedom through which the individual and the community would be reunited (CW 5: 51, 78-9, 87, 438).

This conception of 'circumstances' setting individuals 'tasks' would seem, at first sight, to contradict the critique of Hegelian teleology and the hypostatization of 'History' which Marx and Engels had themselves offered in *The Holy Family* and *The German Ideology*. They argued, however, that it *was* permissible to speak of such 'tasks', if we mean by this either 'the revolutionary tasks laid down for an oppressed class by the material conditions' or 'the conscious expression of the necessity which at every moment confronts individuals, classes and nations to assert their position through some quite definite activity' (CW 5: 419). Nevertheless, the problem remains of why individuals or classes should come to see communism as a necessity in the first place.

Marx and Engels' answer to this problem shifted their argument from the realms of Hegelian teleology, to the sociological materialism which formed the basis of *The German Ideology*. They argued that 'at the present time, individuals *must* abolish private property because the productive forces and and the forms of intercourse have developed so far that, under the domination of private property, they have become destructive forces, and because the contradiction between the classes has now reached its extreme limit.' Things have now come to such a pass that 'individuals must appropriate the existing totality of the productive forces', not only to overcome their alienation and to achieve true self-activity, but even to 'safeguard their very existence.' In other words, the 'task' of communist revolution which circumstances had presented to the proletariat was actually a *conditional* task: *if* the proletariat was to overcome alienation, or even to defend its basic material interests, communism was the only means of doing so (CW 5: 87, 439).

In practice, of course, Marx and Engels believed that the proletariat would, through its own rational interest, necessarily arrive at a recognition of the need for communism. Thus, their 'Circular against Kriege' (which may originally have been intended for inclusion in *The German Ideology*) argued that 'as the product of the proletarian movement', the American National Reform Association, a movement advocating land reform, would 'by its own inner logic inevitably press on to communism' (CW 6: 42). As we have seen, even in their writings of 1845-46, when they were at their most pragmatological and saw history as the outcome of conflicting human interests, Marx and Engels' conception of the future was *not*, in practice, open-ended and allowed only one possible outcome from the further development of capitalism.

The revolutionary optimism generated by Marx and Engels' 'organicist' assumption that the crisis of capitalism had the predictable course of a disease, and by their belief the capitalism of the mid-1840s was ripe for proletarian revolution (CW 4: 419; 73-5), can be seen in the letters which Engels wrote to George Julian Harney, the English Chartist leader, in early 1846. Engels' original letters are now lost, indeed he expressly told Harney to destroy at least one of them, but some of their contents can be inferred from Harney's reply to Engels.

Of particular interest is Harney's comment that 'Your speculations as to the speedy coming of a revolution in England, I doubt.' Although revolution was likely to come soon in Germany and France, 'I confess that I cannot see the likelihood of such changes in England, at least until England is moved from without, as well as within.' The extent of Engels' optimism as this time can be seen from Harney's comment that 'Your prediction that we will get the Charter in the course of the present year, and the *abolition of private property within three years* will certainly not be realized; – indeed, as regards the latter, although it may and I hope will come, it is my belief than neither you nor I will see it' (CW 38: 533-4, 536, emphasis added; CW 5: 49, 75).

In practice, of course, Harney's pessimism was to provide a more accurate guide to English development than Engels' revolutionary optimism. But why did the predictions of inevitable proletarian revolution which Marx and Engels made in this period fail to come true? A good starting-point from which to answer this question is provided by Engels' 'Preface' to the 1892 edition of *The Condition of the Working Class in England* where Engels himself admitted that he and Marx had been wrong in the mid-1840s to believe that the contradiction between the productive forces and relations of production of modern society had already reached its extreme limit. On the contrary, the period after 1847 had seen 'the dawn of a new era' of capitalist expansion so that the industrial development of the 1840s had come to look 'comparatively primitive and insignificant' (CW 5: 73; CWCE: 22, 33).

Engels blamed his mistaken predictions of imminent revolution of the 1840s on his 'youthful ardour' (CWCE: 13, 27). The problem is that, as late as 1890, Engels was still predicting the imminent victory of the revolution, his early ardour apparently unchecked (Kapp II: 426). Indeed, his '1892 Preface' retained his 'youthful' optimism and claimed that capitalism had, at last, reached the stage where it could develop society's productive forces no further; a belief in which he was, of course, to be proved as wrong in 1892 as he had been in the 1840s. Thus, Engels' expectations in the 1840s of revolution in the near future cannot merely be passed over as a youthful aberration. Rather, they had much deeper intellectual roots in Marx and Engels' claims that the development of capitalism itself was providing the foundation for communism, claims which were, after all, the aspect of their political philosophy which they themselves believed distinguished them from other 'Utopian' socialists.

A central weakness of Engels' prediction of proletarian revolution, made in *The Condition of the Working Class* and repeated in *Anti-Dühring*, was the assumption that the ruling class would be unable to make the reforms or concessions which would improve working-class living standards and thus avert revolution. If there was 'no prospect of improvement' in the workers' condition, it was logical for Engels to argue that socialism was a rational necessity for the working class, and thus to predict socialist revolution.

Yet, in fact, even in 1845, when Engels wrote *The Condition of the Working Class*, the state had already begun to legislate to ameliorate the effect of the capitalist class's ruthless pursuit of profit. Engels himself noted that 'the power of the state intervened several times' , as in the Apprenticeship Law of 1802 and the Factory Act of 1833, to protect children from 'the money-greed of the bourgeoisie.' He also praised the Truck Act of 1831, which prohibited payment of wages in the form of order usable only at the employer's own store, an Act which, at least in the towns, was 'carried out comparatively efficiently' (CW 4: 442, 462, 470, 561, 581; AD: 200, 354).

In his speeches at Elberfeld in 1845, Engels himself offered his own suggestions for immediate social reforms (including universal education and adequate poor-relief paid for by progressive taxation) on the grounds that they would smooth the way for the eventual victory of communism (CW 4:

254-5, 263-4). What he does not seem to have anticipated is that, in practice, such reforms would not provide a step towards communism, but would rather constitute an alternative to it. In correctly predicting that a Ten Hours Bill would become law, despite the almost unanimous opposition of the employers, Engels contradicted his own claim that the state was merely the bourgeoise organised as a party and that it acted solely to protect the propertied. Similarly, when, in the 1880s and 1890s, he recognised that employers had, in practice, come to accept trade unions, strikes, factory acts and even political democracy, he refuted his own earlier claim that there was no hope of improvement for the workers under capitalism and that they would be compelled, by necessity, to turn towards socialism (CWCE: 29-30; CW 4: 567, 578; OB: 476).

Nevertheless, the significance of political reforms for the failure of Engels' predictions of revolution in England should not be overstated. The Welfare State was, even by 1892, a long way off; the first steps towards a system of social security, for example, were not taken until after the Liberal reforms of 1906.

Perhaps more significant for the failure of Engels' prediction of revolution made in *The Condition of the Working Class* was his claim that capitalism's regular cycle of boom and slump involved crises of ever-increasing intensity. He claimed, therefore, that the slump which he (correctly) predicted for 1847 would be 'more violent and lasting' than that of 1842, which was itself the worst so far experienced (CW 4: 386, 524). In fact, far from each crisis growing in intensity, 'no subsequent slump was ever faintly as catastrophic as the slump of 1841-2.' After 1845, Britain's rapid economic development, its boom in exports and its lead in world industry, resulted in a 'distinct advance' in real incomes and consumption and a marked improvement in the regularity of employment (Hobsbawm, 1972: 94, 160).

Engels himself admitted, in his '1892 Preface', that, since 1845, the English working class had shared in the benefits of England's industrial monopoly and that, even though such benefits had been unevenly distributed, 'even the great mass, had, at least, a temporary share now and then. And that is why, since the dying out of Owenism, there has been no socialism in England' (CWCE: 34). Nevertheless, Engels remained optimistic that the disappearance of the truck system, and of other 'secondary' injustices of the capitalist system in the period since 1845, had created the basis for revealing to the workers that the primary source of their grievances was the capitalist wage-relation itself. The end of Britain's industrial monopoly would put an end also to the 'temporary improvement' in the standards of living of the working class; the 'present dreary stagnation' of the economy would be intensified and become 'the permanent and normal state of English trade.' Thus even the most privileged minority of workers, who had benefited most from the years of prosperity, would find themselves reduced to the level of their fellow workers abroad. 'And that is the reason why there will be socialism again in England' (CWCE: 23-4, 33- 4).

What Engels did not seem to have considered possible is the long-term economic growth which has occurred in the advanced capitalist countries in the century since 1892, a growth which allowed the improvement in working-class living conditions which provided the basis for the reformist strategies adopted by the labour movements of the advanced capitalist countries. Yet, as we shall see, the political economy of Marxism itself had the theoretical space within which to offer a 'materialist' account of the continuing strength of working-class reformism.

SURPLUS VALUE, JUSTICE AND SCIENTIFIC SOCIALISM

If historical materialism's account of the relationship between society's productive forces and its relations of production does not provide a firm foundation for Engels' scientific socialism, can such a foundation be found in the theory of surplus value, Marx's other discovery which, for Engels, had converted socialism into a science? (SW II: 125).

Engels' account of the theory of surplus value followed that offered by Marx in *Capital* volume I. In this analysis, Marx assumes that, in the capitalist mode of production, all commodities, including that of the labour-power sold by the proletarian to the capitalist, exchange at their value, i.e. in terms of the socially-necessary labour-time needed to produce them. The workers sell their labour-power as a commodity to the employers, its value being determined by the labour-time required to produce those commodities which are needed to maintain the labourer. If we assume, for the sake of simplicity, that the commodities needed to reproduce labour- power embody twenty hours a week of labour-power, then the capitalist must pay the worker a sum of money which represents twenty hours of labour. Once the worker has laboured for twenty hours he has 'fully reimbursed' the capitalist for his outlay of money on wages (AD: 262).

Yet, if the capitalist paid out money representing twenty hours of labour and received only twenty hours of labour in return, there would be no incentive to make the outlay in the first place: expenditure and income would balance and there would be no net surplus or profit generated by this exchange of equivalents. In order for the capitalist to make a profit, the commodities produced by his employees must have a greater value than the value of labour-power which constitutes his wages-bill. Thus, although the capitalist may be fully reimbursed after twenty hours labour, he is able, through his employees' inability to maintain themselves without paid-work, to require them to work for, say, forty hours. In this case, the capitalist receives the surplus value of those commodities produced in twenty hours of *surplus* labour time, over and above the twenty hours of labour which is *necessary* for the worker's subsistence (OMC: 38/91; AD: 261/2). It is this 'appropriation of *unpaid* labour' which constitutes the basis of capitalist society, an 'exploitative' relationship which creates the potential for class conflict inherent within capitalism (SW II: 124/5).

For Engels to insist that the capitalist 'extracts labour that he does not pay for' and that such unpaid labour necessarily involves an 'exploitation' of the worker, may seem to imply that Marx and Engels' aim was to offer a critique of capitalism based on some absolute moral concept of justice. Indeed, Engels explicitly claimed that the worker '*correctly* feels that every hour of labour which he performs over and above the replacement of his wage is *unjustly* taken from him'; emphasised the premature exhaustion and death which such labour produces; and compared the 'evil' unpaid labour of capitalism with the exploitation of slaves and serfs in previous modes of production (OMC: 15/20, 23, 40/3; WLC: 11/12; WPP: 38/9; SUS: 74; Negri: 79/80).

Yet Engels was also extremely sceptical about attempts to criticise social relations in terms of any absolute moral criteria, since such criticisms were necessarily based on divergent, historically specific conceptions of truth, justice, reason and so on. 'The conceptions of good and evil have varied so much from nation to nation and from age to age that they have often been in direct contradiction with each other.' Far from being immutable truths which provide a ground from which to criticise modern society, such conceptions are 'the product of the economic conditions of society obtaining at the time.' Against Dühring's claims to have access to eternal moral truths, Engels argued that the three main classes of modern society, the aristocracy, the bourgeoisie, and the proletariat, 'each have a morality of their own.' Thus, 'consciously or unconsciously', people 'derive their ethical ideas in the last resort from the practical relations on which their class position is based' (AD: 22/3, 106/7, 116/19).

In *Capital* volume III, which Engels himself prepared for publication, Marx even argued that, in studying capitalist social relations, it was 'nonsense' to refer to conceptions of 'natural justice'. The relations of capitalism are 'just' so long as they are adequate for it so that, under modern capitalism, slavery and fraud are seen as unjust whilst lending money at interest is not (Cap. III: 460/1).

As Steven Lukes has shown, it can, on the basis of such comments, legitimately be claimed that Marx and Engels regarded the relation between capitalist and worker as just, as unjust, or as neither just nor unjust (Lukes: 48; for a bibliography on this question see Geras, 1985). There are a number of ways of resolving this problem. Perhaps Marx and Engels were not themselves aware of the contradictions implicit in their analysis? Or perhaps their account of capitalism involves an exchange of equivalents in the realm of exchange but not in the sphere of production? (Elster, 1985: 222; Geras, 1985: 55).

However, perhaps the main reason why Marx and Engels' views on the 'justice' of capitalist social relations have created so much debate is that Marx and Engels themselves saw no need to develop a consistent theory on this matter. For them, the issue was largely irrelevant since they believed that the fate of capitalism would *not* be determined by an abstract debate about moral rights and wrongs, but rather by the concrete class struggle inherent within modern society.

This argument had been a central tenet of Marx and Engels' political philosophy ever since *The German Ideology* had claimed that 'Communism is not for us a *state of affairs* which is to be established, an *ideal* to which reality will have to adjust itself', but is rather 'the *real* movement whch abolishes the present state of things' (CW 5: 49, original emphasis). Within this framework, Engels could claim that the capitalist class had enjoyed its power 'at the expense of the working class' whilst, at the same time, arguing that its rule did once have 'a certain historical justification', in the sense that it was the social form 'necessary to develop the productive forces of society to a level which will make possible an equal development worthy of human beings, for all members of society' (SW II: 139; OMC: 20). Only when capitalism reaches the point where it no longer constitutes a form of development of society's productive forces (as Engels believed it had by 1878), 'does the constantly increasing inequality of distribution appear unjust, only then is appeal made from the facts which have had their day to so-called eternal justice' (AD: 190-1).

It is, therefore, ironic that Marxologists have devoted so much attention to the issue of whether Marx offerd a moral critique of capitalism, when, in fact, the whole brilliance of his and Engels' intellectual achievement lay precisely in shifting the critique of capitalism away from the realm of ethics, and on to the ground of material class interests. It was this break with a *purely* moral critique which was expressed by their theoretical progression from alienation to surplus-value as the key *explanatory* concept for the understanding of capitalism; which is not to say that they did not continue to describe, and to condemn, capitalism as a form of human alienation (Wood, A. W., 1981: 7-8).

For Marx and Engels, reality itself, the actual movement of society, not the invective of moralists, was to reveal the historical bankruptcy of capitalism. 'Scientific' and 'Critical' Marxism thus originally formed a unity, since it was Marx and Engels' 'scientific' claims to have identified the developmental tendencies of modern society, which provided the grounds for a 'critique' which would be effected by reality itself, not merely by the works of moralists.

How successful was Engels' attempt to base his 'scientific' predictions of proletarian revolution on the theory of surplus-value? Engels' efforts to connect his predictions of proletarian revolution with the theory of surplus-value can be criticised on a number of grounds. The first, although fundamental, may be briefly expressed: the labour theory of value, which is the starting-point of the theory of surplus value, is fatally flawed and thus cannot provide a reliable foundation for any theory of economics or brand of political philosophy (Rigby, 1987: 239-40).

The second criticism is that Marx and Engels had believed in the inevitability of proletarian revolution long before Marx had worked out his theory of surplus-value; the former was, neither logically nor chronologically prior to the latter. Indeed, the theory of surplus-value merely expressed in more specific terms the conclusion which Marx and Engels had reached as early as the mid-1840s, i.e. that the inherent opposition of interests between the proletariat and the bourgeoisie necessarily 'generated the consciousness of the necessity of a fundamental revolution' amongst the proletariat (CW 5: 52; CW 6; 515). After all, as early as *The Condition of the Working Class*, Engels had characterised the relationship between the propertied and non-propertied classes as one in which the latter were 'exploited'; the theory of surplus-value was not necessary to claim that such relations were exploitative in the sense that 'I derive benefit for myself by doing harm to someone else' (CW 4: 577; CW 5: 409).

Furthermore, whilst commentators on historical materialism often refer to the creation of 'surplus-value' in pre-capitalist modes of production, Marx and Engels themselves emphasised that surplus-*value* was merely the specific form of surplus-*labour* found in the capitalist mode of production. Other modes of production were characterised by other forms of surplus-labour: feudal rent, Asiatic tax-rent and so on. Thus, Marx and Engels' general theory of exploitation did *not* depend on the theory of surplus-value, which they used to analyse the specific nature of the capitalist mode of production (Rigby, 1987: 19-21, 222).

The third criticism which can be made of Engels' grounding of 'scientific socialism' in the theory of surplus-value is that, far from evacuating the ground of moral condemnation, such moral considerations are inherent within the theory of surplus-value itself. As we have seen, Marx and Engels believed that the capitalist mode of production necessarily involved the appropriation of surplus-labour by the bourgeoisie (in the form of surplus-value). For them, 'surplus labour' was not a term of abuse or of subjective moral condemnation. Rather, it was a scientific concept, which allowed them to refer to a feature of capitalism which, like it or not, objectively existed, and which could even be expressed in mathematical terms.

Marx and Engels argued that without the appropriation of surplus-labour, the capitalist would have no incentive to invest in the first place (OMC: 27, 69, 72; Cap. I: 326-7). The problem then emerges of why we should refer to the capitalist' profits as a 'surplus', as the product of 'unpaid' labour which does not benefit the worker. Why not, as in non-Marxist economics, see such profits as a 'cost of production', necessary to tempt the capitalist to invest, which has to be included in the final price of a commodity? After all, as the apologist for the capitalist system could point out, if the capitalists did not receive a return on their investments then they would not employ the worker and the worker would perish (WLC: 31).

The traditional socialist response to this argument has always been, of course, that profits are not a 'necessary' cost of production. It would be possible to organise production so that the workers received the full fruits of their labours *without* the existence of private capital, employers and wage-labourers. But, in this case, the profits which the capitalists receive only constitute an exploitative 'surplus' when seen in the context of alternative social arrangements, i.e. of socialism. Without such an alternative, wage-labourers under capitalism would simply be maximising their benefits by selling their labour-power to the capitalists in order to feed, clothe and house themselves and their families. Thus, as Roemer has recently emphasised, the concept of exploitation necessarily involves an alternative, non-exploitative social arrangement (Roemer, 1989).

But, if this is the case, the concept of surplus-value does not simply refer to something which objectively exists. Rather, whether we see capitalist profits as exploitative is bound up with political and moral judgements about the practicality of establishing a non-exploitative alternative. This is not to say that Roemer's work constitutes a revision of Marx and Engels' theory. On the contrary, it merely makes explicit an assumption which was, as Croce long ago pointed out, implicit in the Marxist theory of exploitation from its first formulation (Croce: 127).

The argument that the concept of surplus-labour contains an implicit moral judgement has profound implications for so-called 'scientific' socialism. Marx and Engels believed that the objective existence of surplus-labour under capitalism would, eventually, generate a socialist consciousness amongst the workers. The workers themselves would thus arrive at socialism not through having Marxism 'forced down their throats', but as a result of their position within capitalist society (SC: 448; AD: 362-3). It was this position which, Marx and Engels argued, made the proletariat 'revolutionary by its innermost nature', and would oblige it not just to resist the 'consequences' of capitalism, such as low pay and long hours, but capitalism itself (CWCE: 23; RFH: 51; WPP: 54-5; OB: 475-7).

Yet, if we accept that capitalism *per se* (as opposed to particularly extreme rates of profit, poor working conditions etc.) only appears exploitative once we have accepted the possibility of alternative social arrangements, then exploitation no longer constitutes an objective *cause* which drives us to a communist consciousness. It becomes, instead, an *effect* of the prior adoption of such a consciousness. Thus, whether we perceive specific social arrangements as 'exploitative' necessarily involves moral and political judgements about the desirability and possibility of alternative social arrangements. In this perspective, we would not become socialists because we see capitalism as exploitative. Rather, we would see capitalism as exploitative because we have become socialists.

The usual reply to such arguments is that the proletariat's position under capitalism will necessarily drive it towards adopting such political judgements. This brings us on to our fourth and final criticism of Engels' claim that the theory of surplus-value provides a theoretical basis for scientific socialism, the problem that, even within the labour-value terms in which they expressed their political economy, Marx and Engels' own theory had the potential to offer an explanation of why reformism has seemed such an attractive choice to the labour movement of the advanced capitalist countries.

As early as *The Condition of the Working Class*, Engels had argued against reformism on the grounds that, as interests of the workers and employers were 'diametrically opposed', the workers could only obtain a better position for themselves by 'attacking the interest of the bourgeoisie' since 'whatever goes into the pockets of the manufacturers comes, of necessity, out of those of the worker' (CW 4: 298, 376, 472, 501-2, 510, 567). Similarly, Marx was to argue, in the 1860s, that the workers' trade union struggles must fail since they limit themselves to a guerrilla war against the effects of the capitalist system, rather than 'the causes of those effects', the system itself which had an inherent tendency 'to push the *value* of labour more or less to its minimum limit' and thus 'to sink the average standard of *wages*' (WPP: 54-5; OTU: 64-5).

In his 1891 'Introduction' to Marx's *Wage Labour and Capital*, Engels was more cautious in his claims, arguing only that the *per capita* share of national wealth falling to the working class 'either increases only very slowly or not at all, and under certain circumstances may even fall.' Nevertheless, he continued to believe that the great mass of the population was 'scarcely, or not even at all, protected from extreme want' (WLC: 12-13). Just as, in the *Communist Manifesto*, Marx and Engels had argued that the workers would, of necessity, be revolutionary because they had nothing to lose but their chains so, thirty years later, Engel was still arguing that since capitalism could not 'secure the individual worker against unemployment and poverty.' The proletariat must carry through the demand for the abolition of classes, 'on pain of sinking to the level of the Chinese coolie' (CM 6: 519; AD: 200, 411; Cap. I: 770, 781-2, 790-4; OTU: 165).

Thus, in 1885, when comparing the standards of living of the contemporary English working class with those of forty years earlier, Engels claimed that whilst the working class, as a whole, had enjoyed temporary improvements, permanent improvements could only be recognised for the 'protected sections' of the working class: the factory workers (who were, paradoxically, supposed to provide the core of the revolutionary proletariat) and the skilled male workers organised into trade unions. For the great mass of workers, however, 'the state of misery and insecurity in which they live is *as low as ever.*' Engels predicted, as we have seen, that the end of Britain's industrial monopoly would mean the development of a socialist movement once more (CWCE: 30/4).

Similarly, in *The Housing Question* (1872), Engels rejected the possibility of solving the housing shortage within capitalism. There was 'only one means' to end this shortage: 'to abolish altogether the exploitation and oppression of the working class by the ruling class', this was the issue 'which really concerns the workers.' The housing shortage was 'a necessary product of the bourgeois social order' and, as Marx and Engels had argued in the *Communist Manifesto*, it was, despite the pious wishes of philanthropists, impossible to abolish it without abolishing capitalism itself. Engels thus concluded that 'as long as the capitalist mode of production continues to exist, it is folly to hope for an isolated settlement of the housing question, *or of any other social question affecting the lot of the workers*' (SW I: 557, 576, 581/2, 588/9, 604/6, 610, emphasis added; CW 6: 513/14). As a result he never seriously considered the possibility that the working class would, by its struggles, be able to achieve substantial, long/term increases in its standard of living within capitalism, and thus seems to have seen no need to develop a theory of reformism.

Yet, Marx's own political economy provided the grounds for just such a theory. Despite the predictions of increasing immiseration which Marx quite explicitly made in *Capital* volume I, his own analysis of the growing productivity of labour inherent to capitalism showed that the commodities which had to be consumed by the workers in order to reproduce their labour/power could be produced in an ever shorter time. As a result, the *value* of labour/power, measured in terms of the labour/time embodied in the commodities needed to maintain it, could be reduced, and the rate of exploitation increased (as necessary labour came to occupy a smaller propertion of the working day) and yet the workers' levels of consumption, their *real wages*, could remain unaltered. Indeed, despite Marx and Engels' attempts to correlate a decline in the value of labour/power with a fall in actual wages, a decline in the value of labour power and an increase in the rate of exploitation were quite compatible with the maintenance, or even with a rise, in the workers' real wages (SW I: 231; 586; WPP: 54; Cap. I: 659, 768/9, 799, 929; SC: 411).

We need not accept the value/terms in which Marx expressed his theory, to see that capitalism's tendency to increased productivity, which, as Marx put it, reduced the 'length and weight of the golden/chain the worker has already forged for himself', could become a long/term tendency of capitalist develop/

ment, rather than merely a phase in the cycle of capital accumulation (Cap. I: 769). This growth in productivity could then create precisely the general prosperity which Marx and Engels saw as a crucial obstacle to proletarian revolution.

What Marx and Engels did not realise was that, far from 'every advance in production' constituting a 'retrogression' in the condition of the great majority of the population (OFPPS: 172), and thus creating a revolutionary consciousness amongst the workers, the effects of the growth of capitalism have been in the opposite direction. The advances in productivity, which Marx and Engels themselves saw as inherent to capitalism, have provided the material basis for the trade unionism and reformism characteristic of the labour movement in the advanced capitalist nations.

A common reply to such arguments is that 'even if the populations of industrialised countries are incomparably better off' in our day than they were in the time of Marx and Engels, the excesses of capitalist exploitation have been transferred to the impoverished populations of the Third World, whose suffering supports our affluence (Harris). The problem with this argument, from a Marxist perspective at least, is that it replaces the 'materialistic basis' of communism, which Marx and Engels believed they had identified in the agency of the proletariat, with a moral appeal to Justice, Equality and so on (SC: 290; AD: 105-6, 112-19). Of course, such an appeal may be successful; Marx and Engels themselves, however, were rather sceptical about this possibility.

To conclude: both of the theoretical bases of 'scientific socialism' offered by Engels are open to dispute. Firstly, even if we agreed that capitalist social relations were only compatible with a certain level of development of society's productive forces, and that capitalism's fettering of the productive forces would provide the basis for communist revolution, this theory would provide us with no means for identifiying this level of development until *after* the revolution had succeeded. Secondly, even if we accepted Marx and Engels' account of the origin of surplus-value, this theory tells us nothing *per se* either about the workers' real levels of consumption or their degree of revolutionary consciousness.

Thus whilst Engels presented his and Marx's predictions of proletarian revolution as the consequence of their historical materialism and political economy, there was, in fact, no logical connection between them. Marx and Engels' purpose was, of course, to change the world rather than simply to interpret it in a new way (CW 5: 5); the problem is that, in the advanced capitalist countries, Marxism has functioned far more successfully as a means of interpreting the world rather than as a means of changing it.

WAS ENGELS A REFORMIST?

Ironically, whilst Engels has been criticised here for *failing* to come to terms with the issue of reformism, and for continuing to adhere to a theory of revolution which social reality itself was fast making redundant, other writers have seen Engels himself as becoming increasingly reformist in his later writings. Thus, he is accused of coming to believe that a peaceful and democratic road to socialism was possible, that socialism could be achieved through the ballot-box and thus did not require revolution and the dictatorship of the proletariat (Thomas: 6; Colletti, 1972: 45/8; Carlton: 169; Fetscher: 216; Mayer: 276). For some, Marx himself shared Engels' belief in a peaceful road to socialism; yet, for others, Engels had never lapsed into reformism in the first place and himself rejected the growing reformism of the German SPD (Henderson, 1976 II: 664, 667; Draper: 25; Callinicos, 1987a: 64).

It is certainly true that, in his later political writings, Engels abandoned the insurrectionary perspective which had modelled its view of proletarian revolution on the revolutions of 1789 and 1830 (Hobsbawm, 1982: 243). In *The Origin of the Family* (1884), Engels had argued that universal suffrage under capitalism could never be anything more than a 'gauge of the maturity of the working class', in its growth as an anti-capitalist force; the metaphor of 'maturity' itself indicating the degree to which Engels regarded this growth as an inevitable one (OFPPS: 170). Yet, in his 1895 'Introduction' to Marx's *The Class Struggles in France* (which was, in effect, Engels' political testament), Engels argued that universal suffrage could have a far more active role as, in Marx's words, 'an instrument of emancipation', which created 'an entirely new method of proletarian struggle' through the formation of a working-class electoral party. As a result, 'rebellion in the old style, street fighting with barricades ... was to a considerable extent obsolete.' After all, 'a real victory of an insurrection over the military in street fighting ... is one of the rarest exceptions' which, even in its classic era in the period before 1848, 'produced more of a moral than a material effect' on the military forces which supported the revolution's opponents.

Since 1848, developments had been 'all in favour of the military', making the chances of an outright military success for the forces of the revolution even more unlikely. Even in France, where the conditions for insurrection were more favourable than in Germany, socialists were realising more and more that 'slow propaganda work and parliamentary activity' were the immediate tasks facing the working-class party. Thus, whilst Engels by no means renounced the 'right to revolution', he described the two million voters who supported German Social-Democracy as the 'decisive "shock-force" of the international proletarian army'. To throw this force into a premature military confrontation with the government would be suicidal; the revolutionary party was 'thriving far better on legal methods than on illegal methods' (SW I: 129-36; FIA: 377).

Engels claimed that his view, that social revolution could, in England at least, be effected by peaceful means, had been the view of Marx himself (Cap. I: 112-113). Certainly, in 1872, in his 'Speech on the Hague Congress', Marx had argued that, in the light of its institutions and history, the proletariat of each country would have to find its own road to taking power: 'There are countries, such as America and England, and if I was familiar with its institutions I might include Holland, where the workers may attain their goal by peaceful means'. However, Marx continued, in the majority of continental countries, which lacked democratic institutions, 'the lever of the revolution will have to be force.' Moreover, Marx argued that even where proletarian revolution took a peaceful form, it would inevitably meet violent resistance from those whose interests it threatened (FIA: 324; Rubel and Manale: 267, 277, 311; see also SC: 313-14).

Similarly, in 1895, Engels himself argued that, confronted with the ever-growing strength of the German socialist movement, the party of 'Order' would resort increasingly to dictatorship and absolutism (SW I: 137). As Engels' 'Preface' to the English edition of *Capital* put it, Marx never forgot to add, when predicting peaceful revolution in England, that he hardly expected the English ruling classes to submit to a peaceful and legal revolution without a 'pro-slavery rebellion', the phrase Marx and Engels used to refer to the American slaveowners' defence of their interests in the American Civil War (FIA: 163; Cap. I: 113).

This perhaps explains why, three years *after* allowing for the possibility of peaceful revolution in England, Engels told Gerson Trier that, whilst he disagreed with the latter's strategy of rejecting all collaboration with radical-bourgeois parties, 'we are agreed on this: that the proletariat cannot conquer political power, the only door to the new society, without violent revolution' (SC: 386). Similarly, when the German Social-Democrats published Engels' '1895 Introduction' in a censored form, Engels wrote bitterly to complain that he had been 'misrepresented' and made to look like 'a peaceful worshipper of legality at any price', the policy favoured by Liebknecht. Yet, said Engels, the policy of opposition to violent tactics was applicable 'only for the Germany of today and even then with an important proviso. In France, Belgium, Italy and Austria, these tactics could not be followed in their entirety and in Germany may become inapplicable tomorrow' (SC: 461).

Just as Marx and Engels argued that it was wrong for socialists in the present to come up with blueprints outlining the detail of social arrangements in a future socialist society (SW I: 571), so, whilst continuing to defend the general perspective of the *Communist Manifesto*, they argued that the practical application of its principles would 'depend, as the *Manifesto* itself states, everywhere and at all times, on the historical conditions for the time being existing' (CM: 53, 63). They thus devoted little attention to the detail of how the proletariat would bring about the revolution through which it would transform the means of production into public property (AD: 369). Indeed, Engels dismissed as Utopian even the attempt to predict whether the proletariat, 'when it comes to power, will simply seize by force the instruments of production, the raw materials and the means of subsistence, whether it will pay immediate compensation for them or whether it will redeem the property therein by small instalment payments' (SW I: 629-30).

It was, as Berger has shown, Engels, rather than Marx, who devoted the most attention to the question of revolutionary tactics. He argues that, as early as the 1850s, Engels had realised that a regular army would, in a pure contest of military strength, overcome a popular insurrection. Engels' answer to this problem developed through a number of stages until he eventually reached 'classical Marxism's solution to the great tactical problem of how the revolution was to be made': the theory of the vanishing army. As Engels told Bebel in 1884, the revolution could not succeed whilst the army was against it. The dissolution of the state's military power, through internal discord or through the refusal of working-class conscripts to fire on their brothers, was thus a precondition of revolutionary success. Engels seems not to have considered other tactics such as Lenin's revolutionary seizure of power or a Sorelian general strike. All he could offer was the assurance (in other words, the hope) that the working class would achieve a revolutionary consciousness and that it would choose a propitious moment for its seizure of power (Berger: ch. 9).

Engels may have had more to say about the tactics of revolution than Marx; nevertheless a huge gap remained between his general perspective, where the revolution was presented as the 'world-emancipating act' which constituted the 'historical mission' of the proletariat, and the actual guidance which he offered on how this mission was to be brought to a successful conclusion. As a result, it is far easier to say which political tactics Engels did *not* favour (Blanquist or Bakuninist voluntarism, Bernsteinian revisionism), rather than to specify those which he and did, in practice, advocate.

CRITICAL MARXISM: THE STANDPOINT OF THE
PROLETARIAT AS THE GROUNDS OF CRITIQUE

Many readers will not be too dismayed at the critique of the grounds of Engels' scientific socialism offered above since this outlook now finds favour in few quarters. Such readers will doubtless see an alternative to scientific socialism in the 'critical Marxism' tradition which has dominated western Marxism in the twentieth century. Yet, in fact, far from critical Marxism offering an alternative to scientific socialism, it stands or falls with it. Why should this be the case?

As we have seen, any claim to offer a critique of social and political institutions must provide itself with some ground from which such a critique can be mounted if it is to elevate itself above mere opinion. But what grounds of critique are open to the Marxist tradition? The classic answer to this question is that provided by Lukács in *History and Class Consciousness* (1923), which makes explicit the argument already implicit in *The German Ideology*, that capitalism can be criticised from the class standpoint of the proletariat because it does not meet the needs and interests of the working class. We can thus criticise capitalism in the name of a future where the proletariat's needs are met: 'the proletariat cannot liberate itself as a class without simultaneously abolishing class society as such.' However, for Lukács, the class standpoint of the proletariat could not be identified with the the consciousness which any particular workers had at any particular time since the proletariat is not, at all times and in all places, aware of its own class-interest (Lukács: 51, 70)

More recently, Lukács' position has been restated by Callinicos who claims that 'classical Marxism is the theoretically clarified experience of the international working class movement.' Yet Callinicos himself admits that 'experience is never self-interpreting. Workers will interpret their experience of struggle in the light of their existing beliefs' (Callinicos, 1987b: 224, 227). The problem, however, is *how* we are to decide between conflicting interpretations of working-class experience. After all, in 1862, Marx condemned the 'servile Christian nature' of the English workers whilst, in the following year, Engels claimed that 'the English proletariat's revolutionary energy has all but completely evaporated and the English proletarian has declared himself in full agreement with the dominancey of the bourgeoisie' (CW 41: 430, 466; Henderson, 1976 II: 677, 682). Why, then, should Lukács' (or Callinicos') communism be equated with the 'real' standpoint of the proletariat? Why should we not, for example, argue that the strategy which expresses the class standpoint of the proletariat is the pursuit of its material interests within capitalist society through trade unions, political reforms and so on?

Lukács' answer to this question is, in practice, the one which has traditionally been offered by 'scientific' Marxism since 1845-46: capitalism has now reached an impasse and entered an era of decay when it can no longer play an historically progressive role; the interests of the working class thus require its abolition (Lukács: 51, 65, 67, 70). It may, at first, seem as though critical Marxism's emphasis on the crucial importance of the class-consciousness of the proletariat in the communist revolution, and its acknowledgement of the role of contingency in historical development, provide a contrast with the 'inevitabilism' of scientific socialism (Lukács: 70). Yet, ironically, only a faith in the inevitability of the proletariat achieving a particular standpoint (revolutionary class consciousness) in the future allows critical Marxism to claim to be able to identify what this standpoint of the proletariat consists of in the first place.

Without such an ability to predict the future consciousness of the proletariat, the supposed 'class standpoint of the proletariat' would simply be a claim about the consciousness which the proletariat 'should' have, i.e. it would be merely an expression of moral preference. It was to avoid this conclusion that Lukács was obliged to argue that the proletariat's development of a revolutionary consciousness is a process in which 'the proletariat is not given any choice ... The only question at issue is how much it has to suffer before it achieves ideological maturity, before it acquires a true understanding of its class situation and a true class consciousness' (Lukács: 76).

Thus, in practice, Lukács' critical Marxism rests, just as scientific socialism does, on the prediction that the proletariat must, because of its position in modern society, eventually develop a revolutionary, communist class-consciousness. This was the position which Marx and Engels adopted when they argued that capitalism 'transforms the great majority of the population into proletarians' and thus 'creates the power which, under penalty of its own destruction, is forced to accomplish' the communist revolution. (SW II: 107, 124/5, 137/8).

After all, the *Communist Manifesto* itself had concluded, in a passage which Marx cited at the end of *Capital*, that the victory of the proletariat and the fall of the bourgeoisie were 'equally inevitable'. The communists were thus the most 'advanced' section of the working class; the section which understands 'the line of march, the conditions and ultimate general results of the proletarian movement.' Given this conception of a 'line of march' which the proletariat would, by its own social position and interests, be obliged to undertake, Marx and Engels did not see trade unions simply as ends in themselves but rather as 'schools for socialism', 'military schools' which prepared the workers for the decisive battle with the bourgeoise which was approaching (CW 4: 512; CW 6: 492/7, 502/3; Rubel and Manale: 249; Cap. I: 930).

Marx and Engels continued to see the perspective of the *Manifesto* as the basis of their political philosophy. Thus, in his 'Preface' to the 1888 English edition of the *Manifesto*, Engels argued that, for the development of a communist class-consciousness, Marx had 'entirely trusted to the intellectual development of the working class, which was sure to result from combined action and mutual discussion.' As he put it two years later, 'for the ultimate triumph of the ideas set forth in the *Manifesto*, Marx relied solely and exclusively upon the intellectual development of the working class, as it necessarily had to ensure from united action and discussion' (CM: 53, 60, 69).

Thus, even though Marx and Engels recognised that actual working classes might be deferential and, for the moment, accept the rule of capital, they could easily explain away such a lack of revolutionary spirit in terms of short-term factors, such as the effect of the Irish Question on the English workers, the inadequacies or corruption of their leaders, the 'temporary' prosperity resulting from periods of economic boom or 'bourgeois contamination' (CW 41: 468; Johnson, C., 1980: 80-1, 88-9). Engels never abandoned the predictions of communist revolution which he and Marx had arrived at in the 1840s. Thus, as late as 1892, he was still repeating the claim, which he had made as early as 1845, and which had been repeated in the *Manifesto*, that, 'in proportion as large-scale industry expands in a given country', so a communist consciousness develops amongst the proletariat (CW 4: 324; CM: 72; CW 6: 490-94).

It was for this reason that, despite his own recognition of the failure of his youthful predictions of proletarian revolution, Engels still expressed indignation when he found that it was rumoured that he had come to see *The Condition of the Working Class* as a piece of 'immature juvenilia'. Similarly, whilst Marx later referred to the Engels' youthful 'illusion' that the proletarian revolution would occur 'tomorrow or the day after', he also expressed his admiration for the youthful optimism Engels displayed in *The Condition of the Working Class*, rather than feeling the need to reconsider the basis tenets of his political philosophy (CW 41: 465, 469, 646).

Similarly, Engels conceded, in his 1895 'Introduction' to Marx's *Class Struggles in France*, that his and Marx's earlier revolutionary optimism had been an 'illusion', and that they had overestimated the ease with which it would be possible to win the support of the masses for ideas 'which were the truest reflection of their economic condition, which were nothing but the clear, rational expression of their needs.' In fact, as Engels admitted, 'the state of economic development on the Continent at that time [i.e. 1850, S.R.] was not, by a long way, ripe for the elimination of capitalist production', as was proved by the massive degree of development of the productive forces which had taken place since that date (SW I: 124).

Yet, Engels continued to offer a 'sure confidence' in the victory of socialism on the grounds that the European-wide development of capitalism and industry was sweeping away the remnants of previous modes of production and simplifying class relations so that, increasingly, a 'genuine bourgeoisie' confronted a 'genuine large-scale proletariat.' In this situation, the communist call for the abolition of classes 'takes hold of one country after another in the same order and the same degree of intensity that large-scale industry develops in each country.' Thus, Engels continued to hold on to the optimistic belief that the very development of capitalism itself was creating the grounds for a class-conscious proletariat, whose development would overcome local and national differences, and which would eventually form 'one great army of socialists' (AD: 200-1; SW I: 125). It does not seem to have occurred to Engels that, in identifying such grounds for optimism, he could have been as mistaken in 1878 or 1895 as he had been in the 1840s.

CRITICAL MARXISM: HUMAN ALIENATION AS THE GROUNDS OF CRITIQUE

Given the failure of the proletariat to fulfil its role as the agent of communist revolution which was assigned to it by both scientific and critical Marxism, the 'class standpoint of the proletariat' now seems, to many, to offer a rather flimsy basis from which to criticise capitalist society. Those who wish to mount such a critique have thus frequently turned to the alternative grounds of the human 'species-being' which formed the basis for Marx's critique of capitalism in the *1844 Manuscripts*. This humanist critique is often contrasted with Engels' writings which are said to reject the ethical critique of the alienating effects of capitalist society in favour of a positivist scientism. In particular, as we have seen, Engels is said to have ignored the importance of Marx's concept of commodity fetishism (the ideological mechanism through which the 'social relations between men' assume 'the fantastic form of a relation between things') in his analysis of capitalism (Cap. I: 165; Levine, 1975: chs 4, 11, 13; Fetscher: 165; Colletti, 1973: 178; Easton: 39).

Of all the accusations made against Engels in order to contrast his works with those of Marx, this is perhaps the most amazing. Far from Engels abandoning the humanist critique of capitalism which he himself had put forward as early as 1843-44, when he had argued that, under capitalism, men had become the 'slaves of things' (CW 3: 480), even his most 'positivist' works contain a humanist condemnation of the alienation produced by the capitalist mode of production. Far from Engels being a reductionist who was guilty of equating human society with the natural world, Engels himself repeatedly *condemned* capitalism for reducing humanity to an animal-like state in which it lacked control of its own destiny.

He argued that under the 'anarchy of social production' of capitalism, 'the forces operating in society work exactly like the forces of nature - blindly, violently and destructively'. As a result, 'the very product of the worker is turned into an instrument for his enslavement', by the laws of commodity production which 'assert themselves without the producers and against the producers, as the natural laws of their forms of production working blindly.' Thus, 'to this day, the product is the master of the producer' and, in the struggle for survival characteristic of modern society, 'the brutish state of nature appears as the peak of human development.' In this perspective, it is capitalism which is 'reductionist', not Engels' analysis of it (AD: 350, 352-3, 361-2; OFPPS: 172; SC: 356).

Against these 'animal conditions of existence', Engels counter-posed a 'really human' society in which 'the anarchy within social production is replaced by consciously planned organisation' and 'the conditions of existence ... hitherto dominating humanity now pass under the dominion and control of humanity ... The laws of man's own social activity which have hitherto confronted him as extraneous laws of nature dominating him, will then be applied by man with full knowledge and hence be dominated by him.' As a result, the way is opened up not only for 'security for every member of society ... an existence which is not only perfectly adequate materially', but which also 'guarantees him the completely free development and exercise of his physical and mental faculties' (AD: 365-6; OFPPS: 110-11, 171-5).

Marx and Engels were thus in agreement that, as Engels put it, directly quoting *Capital* volume I, the forces of capitalism work as if through an 'over-powering natural law'. With the evermore specialised division of labour, 'man is also divided ... the stunting of man grows in the same measure as the division of labour' until, with the development of large-scale industry, man is degraded 'to the mere appendage of a machine.' In such a system, even the exploiting classes are 'enslaved by the instruments of their activity' (AD: 362, 379-80, 383). It was this critique of the crippling effects of the social division of labour, a critique which wernt back to his writings of the 1840s, which Engels used to criticise Dühring's 'puerile' notion that socialism would perpetuate such specialisation and that its freedom of the producer would consist merely of 'the choice of which means of production is to enslave him' (CW 5: 47; AD: 386-7). That such elementary points still have to be made speaks volumes about the wishful thinking which passes for much current Marxology.

Whether readers are persuaded by Engels' critique of capitalism, and the alternative he offered to it, will, in the end, be determined by their subjective moral preferences. We are not, therefore, concerned here to criticise Engels' condemntation of capitalism on 'external' grounds, for instance, by questioning the practicality of his Utopian belief that society could do away with a specialised division of labour. Rather we will offer an immanent critique of Engels' humanism on the grounds that, at times, his and Marx's *own* analysis calls into question *all* concepts of a human 'essence', and thus removes the possibility of producing an Archimedean point from which to mount any critique of capitalism.

In *The German Ideology*, Marx and Engels argued that concepts of what is 'human' or 'inhuman' are, like all other concepts, the product of certain social relations; far from being eternal categories they are historically specific. The

Christian concept of the human essence, for example, based itself on the 'autonomy of the spirit' and thus inevitably saw nature, even our own flesh, as 'something foreign to us'. Christianity therefore regarded our own natural desires as an external constraint which should be resisted rather than, as in Feuerbach, an essence which was to be realised (CW 5: 254). Similarly, in his letter to Marx of November 1844, Engels had criticised Stirner for not seeing that his concept of the egoistic 'unique one' was merely a reflection of the atomism of modern society. It was impossible for Stirner to begin his analysis with 'abstract' individuals; he was thus obliged, in practice, to base his concept of the egoist on the real individuals found in a specific society (CW 38: 11).

Yet, if we are confronted with conflicting concepts of what constitutes the human essence, how are we to choose between them? How do we know, for instance, whether the atomism of modern society is the fullest expression of the human essence or its complete negation? Marx and Engels' answer to this question was that it would not be resolved in the abstract, in philosophical debate, but in practice, as individuals pursued their class interests and sought the fullest expression of their own essence.

Thus, as Engels argued in November 1844, even if we allowed Stirner's egoism as the starting point of our analysis, 'it would be a simple matter to prove to Stirner that his egoistic man is bound to become communist out of sheer egoism.' He thus agreed with Stirner that 'we must first make a cause our own, egoistic cause before we can do anything to further it.' Thus 'we are communists out of egoism' and 'it is out of egoism that we wish to be *human beings*, not mere individuals' of the sort produced by modern society. Communism was, in this perspective, not a matter of moralistic self-sacrifice, as Hess seemed to argue, but rather constituted an 'egoism of the heart', an egoism which 'is the point of departure for our love of humanity which is other wise left hanging in the air.' Communism was not just another moral scheme, although it would have moral effects. Communism was the expression of the real interests of individuals, and it was through the pursuit of such interests that the individual and the community would be fused since the individuals's interests could only be realised through communal co-operation (CW 38: 11-12, original emphasis).

These arguments were developed in *The German Ideology*: 'the communists do not preach morality at all ... they do not put to people the demand: love one another, do not be egoists etc; on the contrary they are very well aware that egoism, just as much as selfishness, is in definite circumstances, a necessary form of the self-assertion of individuals.' Communism was not merely a new morality. Rather, it was the expression of the dissatisfaction of a class of individuals with the concrete social relations within which they existed; relations which did not meet their needs and interests. Without the existence of a revolutionary agent, an agency brought into being by the growth of the productive forces of capitalism, then the description of the social conditions of modern society as 'inhuman' would be a mere phrase (CW 5: 247, 355, 431-2).

Such arguments are repeated, as we have seen, in Engels' later writings where moral condemnations of capitalism, 'however justifiable' they may be, were, in themselves, incapable of ending the 'misery' of capitalism. Instead, capitalism would be abolished because capitalism itself had brought into being the proletariat, the class which 'under penalty of its own destruction is compelled to accomplish' the revolutionary abolition of private property (AD: 190, 200, 362; see also Rubel and Manale: 266, 315, for similar claims by Marx).

Thus, Marx and Engels' critique of capitalism as inhuman was based on their predictions of the fully human communist society of the future. The present could, once more, be criticised in the name of the future which rational necessity (in the form of the class interests of the proletariat) would bring about. It was this identification of the proletariat as the material basis for their critique of capitalism which represented the brilliance of their intellectual achievement. Communism, in this perspective, was not merely an external moral system, or philosophical scheme worked out in the minds of philosophers to which the proletariat had to ally itself. Rather, communism was the activity through which the proletariat expressed its interests and and its world-historical existence. Capitalism would not be negated merely in the realm of thought but, more importantly, by the movement of social reality itself (CW 5: 49; CW 6: 177, 498).

Armed with such predictions, Marx and Engels were able to avoid the political and theoretical pitfalls of voluntarism, with its one-sided emphasis on agency); of fatalism, with its neglect of the human agency needed for the transition to communism; and of moralism, which criticised capitalism in terms of a subjective or arbitrary ethical schema. Marx and Engels thus claimed to have grounded their theory on the movement of reality itself. The problem was, of course, that once reality developed in ways which they had not anticipated, their theory was left hanging in mid-air. It is with this issue that we will conclude our assessment of Marx and Engels' political theory.

CONCLUSION

Paradoxically, whilst Marx and Engels' identification of communism with the class interest of the proletariat represented a brilliant *theoretical* solution to the problem of how criticism could be made into an effective force within the world, it also constituted in practice, as Avineri has emphasised, the weak point of their entire political thought. (Cornu: 71-2; Avineri, 1971: 250-2).

The return to Hegel: Engels and dialectical materialism

As in their earlier works, Marx and Engels continued to base their politics on an abstraction but now, instead of appealing to 'reason' or to the 'human essence' as the explicit grounds of their critique, they appealed to the 'class interests of the proletariat'. Yet, in practice, just as they and other thinkers had previously been obliged to give a specific content to the abstraction of 'Reason', so Marx and Engels had to specify what constituted the class interest of the proletariat. Their solution was, of course, that communism represented the true interests of the proletariat and that, as *The Holy Family* and *The Condition of the Working Class* argued, the workers would, of necessity come to realise this (CW 4: 37, 507, 581/2).

The problem with this approach, as we have seen, is that the class which Marx and Engels expected to bring about the communist revolution has been rather unwilling to carry out its revolutionary task and has, instead, concentrated on improving its position within capitalist society. As a result, the material grounds of critique, which Marx and Engels had identified in the praxis arising from the class-existence of the proletariat, has been cut from under the feet of modern Marxism. As a result, Marx and Engels' 'scientifc' socialism became, in its own terms, simply another form of Utopianism.

Engels himself failed to confront this problem, continuing to rehearse the political battles of the 1840s against Utopian socialism, when what was really needed was a response to the phenomenon of working-class reformism which Marx and Engels continued to see simply in terms of 'steps' on the journey to the 'goal' of communism, preliminary stages of a 'larger movement' (CM: 70/1; SW I: 125; WPP: 54). This belief that the working class would necesarily arrive at a revolutonary consciousness through its own rational interests meant that, for Marx and Engels, 'inevitability' was not the oppposite of 'freedom', nor did it exclude the role of working-class agency (Rubel and Manale: 204, 255, 266, 314/15; Wood A. W., 1981: 115; Miller, 1979: 64/95).

More importantly for our purposes, it also meant that, as Fernbach perceptively put it, Marx and Engels had 'no theoretical space for the possibility of a workers' movement that is organized politically as a class and yet struggles for reforms solely within the capitalist system.' Where Fernbach seems mistaken, however, is his belief that *if* Marx and Engels had developed such a theory, they would have been able to take the 'decisive steps necesary', through the power of their ideas, to combat the consciousness which, as we have seen, has its roots deep within the social being of the working class under capitalism (FIA: 59).

When later Marxists attempted to fill this gap and to account for the strength of reformism, they usually, as we saw in chapter four, sought an explanation in the realm of ideas, in the power of some 'dominant ideology' rather than in the social position of the working class. This solution was not simply a 'mistake' on their part. Rather, it was a necessity if the fundamental basis of Marxism's theory of revolution, the claim that, as Marx put it, the modern class struggle 'necessarily leads to the dictatorship of the proletariat', was not to be abandoned (SC: 64).

If we abandon the necessary revolutionary development of the proletariat as the grounds for a critique of capitalism, as the Frankfurt School did as a result of the failure of the western proletariat to bring about communism, or even to prevent fascism, then, as Bernstein long ago pointed out, capitalism can only be criticised in moral terms (Bernstein: 222-4; Bottomore, 1984: 81). In effect, critique, shorn of its grounding in social reality, comes merely to constitute yet another ethical ideal (the modern preference is for 'the full development of human potential') to which society should adjust itself.

This poses us with the problem, of course, of why we should prefer one set of morals (the humanist Marxist one) to any other, and why we should expect people to act in accordance with this set of morals, so that it has an effect in the real world. It was precisely as a means of side-stepping this problem that Marx and Engels presented their politics as not merely another moral scheme, but rather as the expression of the real movement of modern society. They correctly saw that mere moralising would not produce socialism, that socialism would not emerge because it was an ethically attractive idea. Rather, *if* socialism was to come about it must be linked to the real interests of a class in modern society which would provide the agency to bring it into being.

It was Marx and Engels' claim to possess a scientific knowledge of the future which provided the basis upon which they mounted their critique of capitalist society; criticism was thus dependent upon their 'scientific' prediction of proletarian revolution. Yet, in turn, the need for such a ground from which to criticise capitalism was dependent upon Marx and Engels' outrage at the alienation, oppression and exploitation which they saw as inherent to capitalism, an outrage nowhere more apparent than in Engels' *The Condition of the Working Class in England*. As Marx put it in 1867, he had sacrificed his health, happiness and family to completing *Capital*: only if he had chosen to be 'an ox' could he have turned his back on 'the sufferings of mankind' and looked after his own skin (SC: 173).

Thus, Marx and Engels' critique of capitalism was not merely the *result* of their 'scientific' analysis of modern society, and of the predictions they drew from it. On the contrary, such predictions were employed to bolster a moral critique of capitalism which Marx and Engels had *already* arrived at: both men were, after all, communist in their politics before they formulated the historical materialism of *The Holy Family*, *The Condition of the Working Class* and *The German Ideology*. Yet, instead of explicitly justifying their politics in terms of their moral outrage (a justification which would raise the problem of how we choose between competing moral values and of how to determine the best means of implementing particular values), Marx and Engels legitimated their political outlook by claiming that it was merely the expression of the interests of the proletariat within modern society (CW 6: 177, 498). In effect, they produced a moral-philosophical critique of capitalism whose explicit rhetoric denied its own moral-philosophical nature by claiming not to be an ideal to which reality had to adjust itself but simply the expression of the 'real movement' of society (CW 5: 49).

Finally, it should be emphasised that to criticise Marx and Engels on the grounds that their predictions of proletarian revolution have not proved correct, is not simply, with the advantage of hindsight, to criticise them for having failed to predict the future correctly. The point is rather that, by basing their theory of revolution on the claim that the proletariat would 'historically be compelled' towards revolution since communism represented the 'real movement' of history (CW 4: 37; CW: 5: 49), Marx and Engels themselves invited judgement on these grounds.

The German Ideology fused the scientific and the critical aspects of Marxism into a dialectical unity, within which each was dependent upon the other, a unity to which Marx and Engels remained loyal in their later works such as *Capital* and *Anti-Dühring* (Gouldner: 53-8). It is precisely this interdependence of the two outlooks which has, given the failure of proletarian revolution to occur, undermined not only the inevitabilism of scientific Marxism but also all those critiques of capitalism which, implicitly or explicitly, depend upon the prediction of proletarian revolution in order to establish their right to criticise. Thus the major weakness of Engels' revolutionary theory is not, as his critics maintain, that he abandoned the outlook which he and Marx had arrived at in the 1840s, but rather that he remained loyal to it in circumstances where reality itself was evolving in new directions. Once we abandon a faith in his and Marx's predictions of proletarian revolution, the only fate which awaits Marxism is either to become a form of humanistic moralising or a variety of academic social theory.

CONCLUSION

Engels without myth

> The [Hegelian] system appeared quite unassailable from without, and so it was; it has been overthrown from within only, by those who were Hegelians themselves' (Engels, 1843. CW 3: 404, original emphasis).

Even more than is the case with the works of Marx, Engels' philosophical, sociological and historical writings are open to a bewildering range of interpretations and evaluations as particular readers construct specific 'Engelses' from his texts. This does not mean, however, that these conflicting interpretations of Engels' works are entirely imaginary or arbitrary constructs. On the contrary, whilst such interpretations are sometimes the product of pure projection on their author's part, they usually ground themselves in one of the number of different discourses present within Engels' texts. The problem is that this particular discourse is then privileged as Engels' 'real meaning', which has to be accepted or rejected by the critic. Yet, once we recognise that Engels' works contain a host of contradictory discourses, it becomes futile to accuse him of simply being a positivist and a mechanical materialist. Such a recognition enables us to realise that Engels himself offered powerful critiques of positivism and mechanical materialism. Engaging with Engels' contradictions, and thus identifying the strongest aspect of his thought, is likely to be more intellectually productive than parodying it through one-sided quotation.

As we have seen, this process of selective quotation is usually carried out in order to contrast Engels' work with that of Marx. Such contrasts are occasionally justified, often foolish, and always motivated, chiefly by a desire to forestall criticism of Marx himself. Yet, if we so desired, we could, through selective quotation, argue that it was Marx who saw proletarian revolution as an inevitable, 'natural' process and Engels who stressed the role of working-class agency. We could portray Marx's social theory as reductionist and emphasise Engels' awareness of the active role of society's superstructure. We could present Marx's epistemology as 'reflectionist' and contrast it with Engels' awareness of the active role of the subject in the production of knowledge. We could counterpose Marx's rejection of the criticism of capitalism in moral terms with the critique of the alienating effects of capitalist society which Engels offered from 1843 onwards. Such an exercise would, of course, be as sterile as that which has traditionally been performed on Engels' works. It is pointless to counterpose Marx against Engels when the individual works of each of the two men are so internally contradictory.

It is the existence of such contradictions which allows the critic of Marxism to enter into a positive dialogue with it, to criticise Marxism from within. After all, just as Christians are unlikely to be swayed by criticism based on the outlook of, for example, Hinduism, so Marxists are likely to be immune to criticism which bases itself on grounds which are external to its own theory. Thus, we have here attempted to offer an *immanent* critique of Marxism. We have argued, for example, that far from Marx and Engels' political economy providing a firm basis for 'scientific socialism', it also offers a powerful materialist explanation of working-class reformism, and have criticised 'traditional' historical materialism on the grounds that, in its hypostatisation of the concept of the 'economy', it is actually a form of pure idealism.

Norman Geras has recently attacked those writers who criticise Marxism from within until nothing is left of the original theory (Geras, 1990a: xi). Yet, as we have seen, criticising Marxism from the outside is unlikely to have any impact on Marxists themselves, and serves merely to confirm such critics in their own prior opinions. The only other alternatives to criticising Marxism from within would seem to be the increasingly desperate defence of it as orthodoxy offered by the fundamentalists; the denunciation of Marxism as 'The God that Failed' adopted by its apostates (Deutscher: 341-51); or the ever more sophisticated exegesis of its founding texts preferred by scholastic Marxists. Almost a century after Engels' death, none of these alternatives offers much prospect of developing a social theory or political philosophy adequate for our current needs.

In general, despite the contradictory discourses which are present within each of his texts, it is useful to divide Engels' works into three main periods. In the first, anthropogenetic period, prior to *The Holy Family*, Engels wrote as an Hegelian socialist for whom history consisted of the teleological unfolding of the principle of Humanity. In the second, pragmatological period, including *The Condition of the Working Class*, *The German Ideology*, the *Communist Manifesto* and his writings on the Reformation and the German Revolution of 1848, Engels retained his anthropogenetic conception of the course of history but now expected a fully human society to be brought into being by the material interests and agency of the proletariat. As the frequent later reissues of the *Manifesto* emphasise, Engels never consciously abandoned this outlook.

Yet, as Korsch has argued, whilst the basic principles of Marxism remained 'essentially unaltered', Marx and Engels' works did undergo a shift of emphasis. In the 'quite unrevolutionary' second half of the nineteenth century, the unity of theory and practice was broken, and Marxism came to be seen increasingly as an objective science, a nomological outlook which had established the laws of social evolution. Korsch dates this new era from June 1848 when, with the crushing of the French workers' movement, reaction emerged triumphant and the short-term hopes of revolution faded (Korsch, 1972: 50-7).

However, if this new epoch of reaction began in June 1848, Marx and Engels did not immediately change their outlook in accordance with it. On the contrary, even though by November 1850 they had recognised the reality of the defeat of the 1848 Revolution (RE: 284, 321, 323, 330, 343; PWG: 115), Marx and Engels continued to anticipate economic crisis and revolution throughout the early 1850s. Only with the failure of the depression of 1857 to result in economic collapse do Marx and Engels seem to have altered their political outlook, although Hobsbawm has argued that Engels remained more optimistic about the prospects of revolution than Marx (Henderson, 1976: 200; Hobsbawm, 1982: 241).

In 1846, Engels had predicted the abolition of private property within three years; by the mid-1860s, he was obliged to wonder how long it would take for the English workers to free themselves from their 'apparent bourgeois infection'. At the same time, despite the founding of the First International, Marx was arguing that the 'present standpoint of the workers' movement' did not permit 'the old boldness of speech'. In a political climate where the proletariat of the most economically developed nation in the world, was the 'demoralised' 'tail' of the Liberal party, a 'political nullity', the revolutionary optimism generated by the assumption that it would be easy to win the great mass of the people to ideas which 'were nothing but the clear, rational expression of their needs', was quite inappropriate (CW 38: 534; SC: 131, 139-40, 295, 344; SW I: 124).

Such conditions made an appeal to working-class 'interest' into a rather insecure foundation for Marx and Engels' political philosophy. The pragmatological outlook, with its historical open-endedness, was hardly suited to an age where the working class seemed incapable of recognising where its own 'real' interests lay. After all, what if the workers continued to fail to realise their own real interests? Or what if they pursued their interests by non-revolutionary or inappropriate means? How could Marx and Engels then claim to speak in the name of the 'future' of the labour movement (CW 6: 497, 518)?

The nomological outlook 'tamed' these dangerous implications of Marx and Engels' own earlier pragmatological perspective. Like the pragmatological perspective, the nomological outlook explicitly rejected idealism and teleology. Yet, through its invocation of Hegelian and scientific vocabulary, the nomological outlook was able, despite the immediate lack of revolutionary spirit amongst the working class, to speak in the name of an inevitable future which the 'laws' of economic development or the 'negation of the negation' would bring about (Cap. I: 102, 929). In this sense, the nomological outlook involved little more than a shift of time-scale; it was the pragmatologiocal outlook adapted to an era of reaction.

The danger was that such 'laws' of historical development and dialectical solutions to the 'contradictions' of capitalism (Cap. I: 102-3, 929-30) could come to be presented by Marx and Engels as processes which are 'divorced from the real world and are set over against it as something independent.' They could be seen as 'laws coming from outside, to which the world has to conform', a conception which they themselves had criticised (AD: 48). Social processes then *appear* as if they are natural phenomena, which exist apart from the 'conscious will and particular purposes of individuals' which gave birth to them. (Gr.: 196-7). The result, as we have seen, was a positivist Hegelianism, which came to exist alongside the pragmatological historical materialist outlook which Marx and Engels had first set out in *The German Ideology*.

It was in this political climate that 'dialectics' came to have such an importance for Marx and Engels' own conception of their intellectual achievement. Such 'materialist dialectics' were not simply an analytical tool or a method of presenting material. Rather, Marx and Engels attempted, through the vocabulary of dialectics, to express their natural and social ontology, an outlook which they both saw as being in harmony with contemporary developments in the natural sciences. Yet, at best, the language of dialectics was redundant in Marx and Engels' thought, since it merely allowed them to redescribe, in Hegelian language, developments in nature or society which they had already analysed in non-Hegelian terms. Thus, to say that capitalism had replaced petty commodity production was a useful contribution to social history; to claim that this development represented the first negation in the process of the negation of the negation added nothing to their analysis.

At worst, however, the return to the vocabulary of dialectics was positively harmful, undermining the sociological insights of Marx and Engels' own pragmatological outlook. One purpose of this vocabulary was, of course, to provide the basis from which Marx and Engels could predict the forthcoming negation of the negation: the expropriation of the expropriators. Yet, to present historical development in these terms was to convert it into a rational process in which the contradictions of one stage are necessarily resolved by the emergence of a new stage of development. This perspective was open to Hegel who, as an ontological idealist, saw history as the unfolding of Reason or Spirit, although even he argued that it was only possible to see what was 'rational' in history *after* the event. But this alternative was *not* open to two materialist thinkers who had already argued that 'History' was not the reified subject of its own process but was simply the activities of humanity in pursuit of its aims.

To say that communist revolution would be the inevitable result of the the proletariat coming to perceive its true interests was logically legitimate, if empirically incorrect. To claim that communist revolution was the negation of the negation was, as *The German Ideology* had pointed out, at best, redundant and, at worst, misleading (CW 5: 247, 305). Similarly, Marx and Engels' dialectics of nature were either banal, since they were so vague that they could be applied to anything, or became positively harmful, in that they offered the prospect of a 'philosophy standing above the other sciences' of the type which Engels himself had criticised (AD: 31).

Just as every generation comes up with its own interpretation of Marx and Engels' works, so every generation requires its own critique of Marxism. It is the works of the period from *The Holy Family* and *The Condition of the Working Class* to *The Peasant War*, *The Eighteenth Brumaire* and *Germany: Revolution and Counter-Revolution*, rather than their earlier anthropogenetic writings or the dead-end of their later dialectics of nature and political economy, which represent the peak of Marx and Engels' intellectual achievement. It is, therefore, the heritage of this period, with its pragmatological historical materialism and synthesis of 'critical' and 'scientific' Marxism, with which the critic of Marxism has to come to terms. Paradoxically, it is only now, when 'the time of mass-based socialist movements which conceived themselves as specifically Marxist may well be up' (Geras, 1990b: 32), and when the need to offer a critique of Marxism is thus actually less pressing, that we are free to perform this task. Through such a critique, Marxism 'cannot be rejuvenated but only understood. The owl of Minerva spreads its wings only with the falling of the dusk …'

BIBLIOGRAPHY OF WORKS CITED
All works published in London unless otherwise specified

WORKS BY MARX AND ENGELS

F. Engels, *The Condition of the Working Class in England* (ed. W. O. Henderson and W. H. Chaloner; Oxford, 1958).

F. Engels, *The Condition of the Working Class in England* (Introduction by E. J. Hobsbawm; 1972).

F. Engels, *The Peasant War in Germany* (Moscow, 1977).

F. Engels. *The German Revolutions* (ed. L. Krieger; Chicago, 1967).

F. Engels, *Germany: Revolution and Counter-Revolution* (1969).

F. Engels, *On Marx's Capital* (Moscow, 1972).

F. Engels, *Anti-Dühring* (Peking, 1976).

F. Engels, *The Role of Force in History* (1968).

F. Engels, *Dialectics of Nature* (Moscow, 1964).

F. Engels, *The Origin of the Family, Private Property and the State* (Moscow, 1968).

F. Engels, *Engels: Selected Writings* (ed. W. O. Henderson; Harmondsworth, 1967).

W. H. Chaloner and W. O. Henderson, eds, *Engels as a Military Critic* (Manchester, 1959).

K. Marx and F. Engels, *Collected Works* volumes 1-42, (1975-87, Lawrence and Wishart).

K. Marx and F. Engels, *Gesamtausgabe*, volumes 1- (Berlin, 1975-).

K. Marx and F. Engels, *The Communist Manifesto* (Harmondsworth, 1970).

K. Marx and F. Engels, *Correspondence 1846-1895* (ed. D. Torr; 1936).

K. Marx and F. Engels, *Selected Correspondence* (Moscow, 1975).

K. Marx and F. Engels, *Selected Works* volume I (Moscow, 1962); volume II (Moscow, 1949).

K. Lapides, ed., *Marx and Engels on the Trade Unions* (New York, 1987).

K. Marx and F. Engels, *On Britain* (Moscow, 1953).

K. Marx, *Wage Labour and Capital* (Moscow, 1970).

K. Marx, *Surveys From Exile* (ed. D. Fernbach; Harmondsworth, 1973).

K. Marx, *Pre-capitalist Economic Formations* (ed. E. J. Hobsbawm, 1975).

K. Marx, *A Contribution to the Critique of Political Economy* (1971).

K. Marx, *Capital* volumes I-III (Harmondsworth, 1976-81).

K. Marx, *The First International and After* (ed. D. Fernbach; Harmondsworth, 1974).

K. Marx, *Wages, Prices and Profit* (Moscow, 1970).

K. Marx, *The Ethnological Notebooks of Karl Marx* (ed. L. Krader; Assen, 1972).

Bibliography

OTHER WORKS

Abercrombie, N., Hill, S., Turner, B. S., 1980. *The Dominant Ideology Thesis.*

Abrams, P., 1982. *Historical Sociology* (Shepton Mallet).

Acton, H. B., 1962. *The Illusion of the Epoch.*

Adams, H. P., 1965. *Karl Marx in his Earlier Writings.*

Adamson, O., et al., 1976. 'Women's oppression under capitalism', *Revolutionary Communist*, no. 5.

Adamson, W. L., 1981. 'Marx's four histories: an approach to his intellectual development', *History and Theory*, vol. 20.

Adamson, W. L., 1985. *Marx and the Disillusionment of Marxism* (Berkeley).

Aers, D., 1986. *Chaucer* (Brighton).

Althusser, L., 1971. *Lenin and Philosophy and Other Essays.*

Althusser, L., 1977. *For Marx.*

Althusser, L. and Balibar, E., 1975. *Reading Capital.*

Andler, C., 1901. *Le Manifeste Communiste de Karl Marx et F. Engels* (Paris).

Anderson, P., 1977. *Passages from Antiquity to Feudalism.*

Anderson, P., 1979. *Lineages of the Absolutist State.*

Anderson, P., 1980. *Arguments Within English Marxism.*

Anderson, R. J., Hughes, J.A. and Sharrock, W.A., 1986. *Philosophy and the Human Sciences* (Beckenham).

Arthur, C. J., 1986 *Dialectics of Labour* (Oxford).

Avineri, S., 1971. *The Social and Political Thought of Karl Marx* (Cambridge).

Avineri, S., 1985. *Moses Hess: Prophet of Communism and Zionism.* (New York).

Bak, J. ed., 1976. *The German Peasant War of 1525.*

Ball, T. 1984. '*Marxian science and positivist politics*', in Ball, T. and Farr, J., *After Marx* (Cambridge).

Barrett, M., 1984. *Women's Oppression Today.*

Barthes, R., 1982. *Image-Music-Text.*

Beechey, V., 1982. 'Some notes on female wage labour in capitalist production' in Evans, M., ed., *The Woman Question: Readings on the Subordination of Women.*

Beneria, L., 1979. 'Reproduction, production and the sexual division of labour', *Cambridge Journal of Economics*, vol. 3.

Bennett, J. M., 1987. *Women in the Medieval English Countryside* (Oxford).

Bennett, T., 1981. *Formalism and Marxism.*

Benton, T., 1977. *Philosophical Foundations of the Three Sociologies.*

Benton, T., 1979. 'Natural science and cultural struggle: Engels on philosophy and the natural sciences', in Mepham, J. and Hillel-Ruben, D., *Issues in Marxist Philosophy*, vol. II (Brighton).

Berger, M., 1977. *Engels, Armies and Revolution* (Hamden).

Berki, R. N., 1988. Review of Rigby, 1987, in *Political Studies*, vol. 36.

Bernstein, E., 1972. *Evolutionary Socialism*.

Bertrand, M., 1979. *Le Marxisme et L'Histoire* (Paris).

Bloch, M., 1983. *Marxism and Anthropology* (Oxford).

Bottomore, T., 1984. *The Frankfurt School*.

Brazill, W. J., 1970. *The Young Hegelians* (New Haven).

Breuilly, J., 1987. 'The making of the German working class', *Archiv fur Sozial geschichte*, vol. 27.

Brenner, R., 1976. 'Agrarian class structure and economic development in pre-industrial Europe', *Past and Present*, no. 70.

Brenner, R., 1978. 'Dobb on the transition from feudalism to capitalism', *Cambridge Journal of Economics*, vol. 2.

Brenner, R., 1982. 'The agrarian roots of European capitalism', *Past and Present*, no. 97.

Bruegel, I., 1982. 'Women as a reserve army of labour: a note on recent British experience', in Evans, M., ed. *The Woman Question: Readings on the Subordination of Women*.

Burke, T. E., 1983. *The Philosophy of Popper* (Manchester).

Burris, V., 1987. 'The neo-Marxist synthesis of Marx and Weber on class', in Wiley, N., ed., *The Marx-Weber Debate* (Newbury Park).

Callinicos, A., 1987a. *Marxism and Philosophy* (Oxford).

Callinicos, A., 1987b. *Making History: Agency, Structure and Change in Social Theory* (Cambridge).

Carew-Hunt, R. N., 1969. *The Theory and Practice of Communism* (Harmondsworth).

Carlton, G., 1965. *Friedrich Engels: the Shadow Prophet*.

Carver, T., 1976. 'Marx and Hegel's *Logic*', *Political Studies*, vol. 24.

Carver, T., 1980. 'Marx, Engels and dialectics', *Political Studies* vol. 28.

Carver, T., 1981. *Engels* (Oxford).

Carver, T., 1983. *Marx and Engels: the Intellectual Relationship* (Brighton)

Carver, T., 1984a. 'Marxism as method', in Ball, T. and Farr, J. 1984. (Cambridge).

Carver, T., 1984b. 'Marx, Engels and scholarship', *Political Studies*, vol. 32.

Carver, T., 1985. Review of Levine, 1984, in *Political Studies*, vol. 33.

Carver, T., 1988. 'Communism for critical critics: *The German Ideology* and the problem of technology', *History of Political Thought*, vol. 9.

Carver, T., 1989. *Friedrich Engels: His Life and Thought*.

Chalmers, A. F., 1986. *What Is This Thing Called Science?* (Milton Keynes)

Cockburn, C., 1986. 'The relations of technology' in Crompton, R. and Mann, M., eds, *Gender and Stratification* (Cambridge).

Cohen, G. A., 1978. *Karl Marx's Theory of History: A Defence* (Oxford).

Cohen, G. A., 1988. *History, Labour and Freedom: Themes from Marx* (Oxford).

Bibliography

Colletti, L., 1972. *From Rousseau to Lenin.*

Colletti, L., 1973. *Marxism and Hegel.*

Colletti, L.,1975. 'Marx and the dialectic', *New Left Review,* no. 93.

Collier, A., 1979. 'Materialism and explanation in the human sciences', in Mepham, J. and Hillel-Ruben, D., *Issues in Marxist Philosophy,* Vol. II (Brighton).

Coontz, S., and Henderson, P., eds, 1986. *Women's Work, Men's Property.*

Cornforth, M., 1968. *The Open Philosophy and the Open Society.*

Cornu, A., 1957. *The Origins of Marxian Thought* (Springfield).

Croce, B., 1981. *Historical Materialism and the Economics of Karl* Marx (New Brunswick).

Davis, N. Z., 1975. *Society and Culture in Early Modern France* (Stanford).

De Beauvoir, S., 1974. *The Second Sex* (Harmondsworth).

Delany, S., 1990. *Medieval Literary Politics* (Manchester).

Delphy, C., 1984. *Close to Home.*

Descartes, R., 1974. *Discourse on Method and The Meditations* (Harmondsworth).

Deutscher, I., 1969 'The ex-communist's conscience', in Mills, C., *The Marxists* (Harmondsworth).

Draper, H., 1977. *Karl Marx's Theory of Revolution. Book I: State and Bureaucracy* (New York).

Eagleton, T., 1983. *Literary Theory* (Oxford).

Eastman, M., 1970. 'Against the Marxian dialectic', in Curtis, M., ed., *Marxism* (New York).

Easton, S. M., 1983. *Humanist Marxism and Wittgensteinian Social Philosophy* (Manchester).

Edgley, R., 1983. 'Philosophy', in McLellan, D., ed., *Marx: the First Hundred Years.*

Eisenstein, Z. R., ed., 1979. *Capitalist Patriarchy and the Case for Socialist Feminism* (New York).

Ellis, R. M., 1989. *Against Deconstruction* (Princeton).

Elster, J., 1985. *Making Sense of Marx* (Cambridge).

Evans, M., 1975. *Karl Marx.*

Farr, J., 1987. 'Marx, science and the dialectical method', *Philosophy of the Social Sciences,* vol. 17.

Fetscher, I., 1971. *Marx and Marxism* (New York).

Findlay, J. N., 1958. *Hegel: A Re-examination.*

Firestone, S., 1979. *The Dialectic of Sex.*

Fischer, E., 1975. *Marx In His Own Words* (Harmondsworth).

Fleischer, H., 1973. *Marxism and History.*

Flinn, M., 1984. 'English workers' living standards during the Industrial Revolution: a comment', *Economic History Review,* second series, vol. 37.

Fromm, E., 1963. *Marx's Concept of Man* (New York).

Gaskell, E., 1979. *North and South* (Harmondsworth).

Gaskell, P., 1833. *The Manufacturing Population of England: its Moral, Social and Physical Condition and the Changes Which Have Arisen from the Use of Steam Machinery.*

Gaskell, P., 1836. *Artisans and Machinery: the Moral and Physical Condition of the Manufacturing Population Considered with Reference to Mechanical Substitutes for Human Labour.*

Geary, D., 1987. *Karl Kautsky* (Manchester).

Gellner, E., 1986. *Relativism and the Social Sciences* (Cambridge).

Gellner, E. 1988. *Plough, Sword and Book: the Structure of Human History.*

Gemkow, H. et al., 1972. *Friedrich Engels: a Biography* (Dresden).

George, M., 1987. 'Marx's Hegelianism: an exposition', in Lamb, D., ed., *Hegel and Modern Philosophy.*

Gerratana, V., 1977. 'Marx and Darwin', *New Left Review,* no. 82.

Geras. N., 1985. 'The controversy about Marx and justice', *New Left Review,* no. 150.

Geras, N., 1990a. *Discourses of Extremity.*

Geras. N., 1990b. 'Seven types of obloquy: travesties of Marxism', in Miliband, R., Pantich, L. and Saville, J., eds, *The Socialist Register* 1990.

Giddens, A. ed. 1974. *Positivism and Sociology.*

Giddens, A., 1981. *A Contemporary Critique of Historical Materialism.*

Giddens, A., 1984. *The Constitution of Society* (Cambridge).

Gimenez, M., 1987. 'Marxist and non-Marxist elements in Engels' views on the oppression of women', in Sayers, Evans and Redclift, *Engels Revisited.*

Godelier, M., 1977. *Perspectives in Marxist Anthropology* (Cambridge).

Godelier, M., 1978. 'Infrastructures, society and history', *New Left Review* no. 112.

Godelier, M., 1988. *The Mental and the Material.*

Gorman, R. A., 1981. 'Empirical Marxism', *History and Theory,* vol. 20.

Gouldner, A., 1980. *The Two Marxisms.*

Gramsci, A., 1971. *Selections from the Prison Notebooks* (ed. by Q. Hoare and G. N. Smith).

Gregory, F., 1977. *Scientific Materialism in Nineteenth Century Germany* (Dordrecht).

Gunn, R., 1977. 'Is nature dialectical?', *Marxism Today,* vol. 21.

Halfpenny, P., 1983. 'A refutation of historical materialism?', *Social Science Information,* vol. 22.

Harris, L., 1990. 'Why I remain a small 'c' communist', *The Guardian,* 4 January 1990.

Hartmann, H., 1981. 'The unhappy marriage of Marxism and feminism: towards a more progressive union' in Sargent, L. ed., *Women and Revolution: A Discussion of the Unhappy Marriage of Marxism and Feminism.*

Heath, S., 1981. *Questions of Cinema.*

Hegel, G. W. F., 1956. *The Philosophy of History* (New York).

Hegel, G. W. F., 1969. *Hegel's Science of Logic.*

Hegel, G. W. F., 1970. *Hegel's Philosophy of Nature* (three volumes).

Hegel, G. W. F., 1971. *The Phenomenology of Mind.*

Hegel, G. W. F., 1979. *The Philosophy of Right* (Oxford).

Bibliography

Hegel, G. W. F., 1987. *Hegel's Logic* (Oxford).

Hegel, G. W. F., 1988. *Introduction to the Lectures on the History of Philosophy* (Oxford).

Henderson, W. O. and Chaloner, W., eds, 1958. *The Condition of the Working Class in England* (Oxford).

Henderson, W. O., 1976 *The Life of Engels* (two volumes).

Henderson, W. O., 1983. *Friedrich List: Economist and Visionary 1789-1846.*

Hilferding, R., 1981a. 'The materialist conception of history', in Bottomore, T., *Modern Interpretations of Marx* (Oxford).

Hill, C., ed., 1940. *The English Revolution of 1640.*

Hill, C., 1969. *Society and Puritanism.*

Hillel Ruben, D., 1979. 'Marxism and dialectics', in Mepham J. and Hillel Ruben, D., eds, *Issues in Marxist Philosophy*, volume II.

Hilton, R. H., 1990. 'Unjust taxation and popular resistance', *New Left Review*, no. 180.

Hindess, B. and Hirst, P. Q., 1977. *Mode of Production and Social Formation.*

Hirst, P. Q., 1985. *Marxism and Historical Writing.*

Hobsbawm, E. J., 1972. *Industry and Empire* (Harmondsworth).

Hobsbawm, E. J., 1973. 'Karl Marx's contribution to historiography', in Blackburn, R., ed., *Ideology in Social Science.*

Hobsbawm, E. J., 1979. *Labouring Men: Studies in the History of Labour.*

Hobsbawm, E. J., ed., 1982. *The History of Marxism*, vol. I (Brighton).

Hodges, D. C., 1965. 'Engels' contribution to Marxism', *The Socialist Register.*

Hodgson, G., 1975. *Trotsky and Fatalistic Marxism* (Nottingham).

Hook, S., 1934. *Towards the Understanding of Karl Marx.*

Hook, S., 1936 *From Hegel to Marx.*

Hook, S., 1950. *Reason, Social Myths and Democracy* (New York).

Hook, S., 1955. 'Dialectical materialism and scientific method', *Bulletin of the Committee on Science and Freedom*, no. I.

Howard, D., 1972. *The Development of the Marxian Dialectic* (Cambridge).

Howard, D., and Klare, K. E., eds, 1972. *The Unknown Dimension: European Marxism since Lenin* (New York)

Humphries, J., 1987. 'The origin of the family: born out of scarcity not wealth', in Sayers, Evans and Redclift, *Engels Revisited.*

Hunt, R. N., 1974/84. *The Political Ideas of Marx and Engels*, (two volumes) (Pittsburgh).

Hyppolite, J., 1969. *Studies on Marx and Hegel.*

Ilyichov, L. F., et al., 1976. *Frederick Engels: a Biography* (Moscow).

Inwood, M. J., 1983. *Hegel.*

Isajiw, W. W., 1968. *Causation and Functionalism in Sociology.*

Jacoby, R., 1981. *Dialectic of Defeat: Contours of Western Marxism* (Cambridge).

Johnson, C., 1980. 'The problem of reformism and Marx's theory of fetishism', *New Left Review*, no. 119.

Johnson, R.,1982. 'Reading for the best Marx: history and historical abstraction' in Johnson, R. and McLennan, G., *Making Histories*.

Jones, E. L., 1976. *Agriculture and the Industrial Revolution* (Oxford).

Jones, G. S., 1973. 'Engels and the end of classical German philosophy', *New Left Review*, no. 79.

Jones, G. S., 1977. 'Engels and the genesis of Marxism', *New Left Review, no.* 106.

Jones, G. S.,1982 'Engels and the history of Marxism', in Hobsbawm, *The History of Marxism*, vol. I.

Jordan, Z. A., 1967. *The Evolution of Dilaectical Materialism*.

Kain, P. J., 1986. 'Marx's method, epistemology and humanism', *Sovietica* , vol. 48, 1969.

Kapp, Y., 1979. *Eleanor Marx* (two volumes).

Kitching, G., 1988. *Karl Marx and the Philosophy of Praxis*.

Klein, M., 1980. *Envy and Gratitude and Other Works 1946-63*.

Klein, M., 1981. *Love, Guilt, and Reparation and Other Works 1921- 45*.

Klima, A., 1979. 'Agrarian class structure and economic development in pre-industrial Bohemia', *Past and Present*, no. 85.

Kolakowski, L., 1978 *Main Currents of Marxism*, volumes I - III (Oxford).

Korsch, K., 1938. *Karl Marx*.

Korsch, K., 1972. *Marxism and Philosophy*.

Krader, L., 1982. 'Theory of evolution, revolution and the state: the vital relation of Marx to his contemporraries Darwin, Carlyle, Morgan, Maine and Kovalevsky', in Hobsbawm, *The History of Marxism*, vol. I.

Krieger, L., 1953. 'Marx and Engels as historians', *Journal of the History of Ideas*, vol. 14.

Krieger, L., ed., 1967. *F. Engels: The German Revolutions* (Chicago).

Kuhn, A. and Wolpe, A., eds, 1978. *Feminism and Materialism*.

Kuhn, T., 1962. *The Structure of Scientific Revolutions* (Chicago).

Lamb, D., 1980. *Hegel: From Foundation to System* (The Hague).

Land, H., 1982. 'The family wage' in Evans, M., ed., *The Woman Question: Readings on the Subordination of Women*.

Lapsley, R., and Westlake, M., 1988. *Film Theory: an Introduction* (Manchester)

Lawler, J., 1982. 'Hegel on logical and dialectical contradiction and misinterpretation from Bertrand Russell to Lucio Colletti', in Marquitt, Moran and Truitt, *Dialectical Contradictions*

Leff, G., 1961. *The Tyranny of Concepts*.

Lenin, V. I., 1969. 'Friedrich Engels', in *The Three Sources and Component Parts of Marxism* (Moscow).

Levine, N., 1975. *The Tragic Deception: Marx contra Engels* (Santa Barbara).

Bibliography

Levine, N., 1984. *Dialogue Within the Dialectic.*

Levine, N., 1987. 'The German historical school of law and the origins of historical materialism', *Journal of the History of Ideas* vol. 48.

Lewis, J., ed. (no date). *A Textbook of Marxist Philosophy.*

Lichtheim, G., 1971a. *Marxism: an Historical and Critical Study.*

Lichtheim, G., 1971b. *From Marx to Hegel and Other Essays.*

Lichtheim, G., 1978. 'On the interpretation of Marx's thought', in McQuarie, D., ed., *Marx: Sociology/Social Change/Capitalism.*

Lindert, P. H. and Williamson, J. G., 1983. 'English workers' living standards during the Industrial Revolution: a new look', *Economic History Review*, second series, vol. 36.

Lindert, P. H. and Williamson, J. G., 1984. 'Reply to Michael Flinn', *Economic History Review*, second series, vol. 37.

Loewenstein, J., 1980. *Marx Against Marxism.*

Lovell, T., 1980. *Pictures of Reality.*

Lowe, C. 1985. 'Cohen and Lukes on rights and powers', *Political Studies* vol. 33.

Lowith, K., 1965. *From Hegel to Nietzsche.*

Lubasz, H., 1984. 'Marx's concept of the Asiatic mode of production', *Economy and Society*, vol. 13.

Lukács, G., 1971. *History and Class Consciousness.*

Lukes, S., 1985. *Marxism and Morality* (Oxford).

McBride, W. L., 1977. *The Philosophy of Marx.*

McDonough, R. and Harrison, R., 1978. 'Patriarchy and relations of production', in Kuhn and Wolpe, *Feminism and Materialism.*

Macfarlane, A., 1978. *The Origins of English Individualism* (Oxford).

MacGregor, D., 1984. *The Communist Ideal in Hegel and Marx* (Toronto).

MacIntyre, A., 1988. *Whose Jusice? Which Rationality?* (Notre Dame).

McLellan, D., 1976. *Karl Marx: his Life and Thought* (St Albans).

McLellan, D., 1977a. *Engels* (Hassocks).

McLellan, D., 1977b. *The Thought of Karl Marx.*

McLellan, D., 1980. *The Young Hegelians and Karl Marx.*

McLennan, G. 1988. 'The historical materialism debate', *Radical Philosophy*, no. 50.

McMurtry, J., 1978. *The Structure of Marx's World View* (Princeton).

Maconachie, M., 1987. 'Engels, sexual divisions and the family' in Sayers, Evans and Redclift, *Engels Revisited.*

Maguire, D., 1972. *Marx's Paris Writings: an Analysis* (Dublin).

Mann, M., 1986. *The Sources of Social Power*, volume I (Cambridge)

Marcus, S., 1979. *Engels, Manchester and the Working Class.*

Marcuse, H., 1941. *Reason and Revolution* (New York).

Marquitt, E., 1982. 'Contradictions in dialectical and formal logic', in Marquitt, Moran and Truitt, *Dialectical Contradictions*.

Marquitt, E., Moran, P. and Truitt, W. H., 1982. *Dialectical Contradictions: Contemporary Marxist Discussions* (Minneapolis).

Mayer, G., 1936. *Friedrich Engels: a Biography*.

Meikle, S., 1983. 'Marxism and the necessity of essentialism', *Critique*, no. 16.

Meikle, S., 1985. *Essentialism in the Thought of Karl Marx*.

Meikle, S., 1986. 'Making nonsense of Marx', *Inquiry*, vol. 29.

Mepham, J., 1979. 'From the *Grundrisse* to *Capital*', in Mepham, J. and Hillel-Ruben, D., *Issues in Marxist Philosophy*, volume I.

Meyer, A. G., 1990. Review of Rigby, 1987, in *American Historical Review*, vol. 95.

Middleton, C., 1974. 'Sexual inequality and stratification theory', in Parkin, F., ed., *The Social Analysis of Class Structure*.

Middleton, C., 1981. 'Peasants, patriarchy and the feudal mode of production in England', *Sociological Review*, vol. 29.

Mill, J. S., 1970. *A System of Logic*.

Miller, D., ed. 1983. *A Pocket Popper*.

Miller, J., 1979. *History and Human Existence: From Marx to Merleau-Ponty* (Berkeley).

Miller, R. W., 1984. *Analyzing Marx* (Princeton).

Millett. K., 1985. *Sexual Politics*.

Mishra, R., 1979. 'Technology and social structure in Marx's theory: an exploratory analysis', *Science and Society*, vol. 43.

Monod, J., 1974. *Chance and Necessity*.

Morgan, L. H., 1963. *Ancient Society* (Cleveland).

Negri, A., 1984. *Marx Beyond Marx* (South Hadley).

Norman, R., and Sayers, S., 1980. *Hegel, Marx and Dialectic: a Debate* (Brighton).

Nova, F., 1968. *Friedrich Engels; his Contribution to Political Theory*.

Parkin, F., 1979. *Marxism and Class Theory: a Bourgeois Critique*.

Paterson, R. W. K., 1971. *The Nihilistic Egoist: Max Stirner* (Oxford).

Paul, D., 1981. '"In the interests of civilization": Marxist views of race and culture in the nineteenth century', *Journal of the History of Ideas* vol. 42.

Phillips, A., 1987. *Divided Loyalties: Dilemmas of Sex and Class*.

Plekhanov, G. V., 1969. *Fundamental Problems of Marxism*.

Plamenatz, J., 1984. *Man and Society*, volume II.

Pomper, P., ed., 1986. *Trotsky's Notebooks 1933-35* (New York).

Popper, K. R., 1940. 'What is dialectic?', *Mind*, new series, vol. 49.

Pundt, A, G., 1935. *Arndt and the Nationalist Awakening in Germany* (New York).

Rader, M., 1979. *Marx's Interpretation of History* (New York).

Bibliography

Razi, Z., 1979. 'The Toronto School's reconstitution of medieval peasant society: a critical view', *Past and Present*, no. 85.

Razi, Z., 1983. 'The struggles between the abbots of Halesowen and their tenants in the thirteenth and fourteenth centuries', in Aston, T. H., Coss, P., Dyer, C. and Thirsk, J., eds, *Social Relations and Ideas* (Cambridge).

Rex, J., 1969. 'Friedrich Engels', in Raison, T., ed., *The Founding Fathers of Sociology* (Harmondsworth).

Riazanov, D., 1973. *Karl Marx and Friedrich Engels* (New York).

Rigby, S. H., 1987. *Marxism and History: a Critical Introduction* (Manchester).

Rigby, S. H., 1990. 'Making history', *History of European Ideas*, vol. 12.

Roberts, J. K., 1972. *The Life and Work of Carl Schorlemmer* (unpublished University of Manchester M.Sc. thesis).

Roemer, J., 1989. 'What is exploitation? Reply to Jeffrey Reima', *Philosophy and Public Affairs*, vol. 18.

Roscoe, H. E., and Schorlemmer, C., 1877. *A Treatise on Chemistry*, volume I.

Rosdolsky, R., 1986. 'Engels and the "non-historic" peoples: the national question in the revolution of 1848', *Critique*, no. 18-19.

Rosenberg, N., 1981. 'Marx as a student of technology', in Levidow, L. and Young, B., eds, *Science, Technology and the Labour Process*.

Ross Gandy, D., 1979. *Marx and History* (Austin).

Rowbotham, S., 1982. 'The trouble with "patriarchy"', in Evans, M. ed., *The Woman Question: Readings on the Subordination of Women*.

Rubel, M., 1977. 'Friedrich Engels – Marxism's founding father', in Avineri, S., ed., *Varieties of Marxism* (The Hague).

Rubel, M. and Manale, M., 1975. *Marx Without Myth* (Oxford).

Runciman, W. G., 1972. *A Critique of Max Weber's Philosophy of Social Science* (Cambridge).

Runciman, W. G., 1989. *A Treatise of Social Theory volume II: Substantive Social Theory* (Cambridge).

Sahlins, M., 1983. *Stone Age Economics* (Cambridge).

Saliou, M., 'The processes of women's subordination in primitive and archaic Greece', in Coontz and Henderson, *Women's Work, Men's Property*.

Salvadori, M., 1979. *Karl Kautsky and the Socialist Revolution 1880-1938*.

Sartre, J-P., 1976. *Critique of Dialectical Reason*.

Sawer, M., 1977. 'The concept of the Asiatic mode of production and contemporary Marxism' in Avineri, S., ed., *Varieties of Marxism*. (The Hague).

Sayer, D., 1987. *The Violence of Abstraction: the Analytical Foundations of Historical Materialism* (Oxford).

Sayers, J., Evans, M., and Redclift, N., eds, 1987. *Engels Revisited: New Feminist Essays*.

Sayers, S., 1985. *Reality and Reason: Dialectic and the Theory of Knowledge* (Oxford).

Sayers, S., 1987, 'The actual and the real' in Lamb, D., ed., *Hegel and Modern Philosophy*.

Schmidt. A., 1971. *The Concept of Nature in Marx*.

Schmidt, A., 1972. 'Henri Lefebvre and contemporary interpretations of Marx', in Howard and Klare, *The Unknown Dimension.*.

Schorlemmer, C., 1879, *The Rise and Development of Organic Chemistry* (Manchester).

Schorlemmer, C., 1894. *The Rise and Development of Organic Chemistry* (revised edition).

Schram, S. R., 1969. *The Political Thought of Mao Tse-tung* (Harmondsworth).

Seccombe, W., 1974. 'The housewife and her labour under capitalism', *New Left Review*, no. 83.

Segal, H., 1974. *Klein* (Brighton).

Shanin, T., 1981. 'Marx and the peasant commune', *History Workshop*, vol. 12.

Shanin, T., ed., 1983. *Late Marx and the Russian Road*.

Shaw, W. H., 1978. *Marx's Theory of History*.

Sheehan, J. J., 1978. *German Liberalism in the Nineteenth Century* (Chicago).

Shepherd, D., 1989. 'Bakhtin and the reader', in Hirschkop, K. and Shepherd, D. *Bakhtin and Cultural Theory* (Manchester).

Singer, P., 1985. *Hegel* (Oxford).

Skocpol, T., 1979. *States and Social Revolutions* (Cambridge).

Slaughter, C., 1986. 'Making sense of Elster', *Inquiry*, vol. 29.

Snyder, L. C., 1978. *Roots of German Nationalism* (Bloomington).

Somerville, J., 1981. *The Philosophy of Marxism* (Minneapolis).

Stalin, J. V., 1951. *Dialectical and Historical Materialism* (Moscow).

Stanley, Z. L. and Zimmermann, E., 1984. 'On the alleged differences between Marx and Engels', *Political Studies*, vol. 32.

Stepelevich, L. S., ed., 1983. *The Young Hegelians: an Anthology* (Cambridge).

Stirner, M., 1971. *The Ego and His Own* (ed. J. Carroll).

Struik, D. J., 1971. *Birth of the Communist Manifesto* (New York).

Tännsjö, T., 1990. 'Methodological individualism', *Inquiry*, vol. 33.

Taylor, C., 1975. *Hegel* (Cambridge).

Taylor, C., 1979. *Hegel and Modern Society* (Cambridge).

Taylor, M., 1986. 'Elster's Marx' *Inquiry* vol. 29.

Thomas, P., 1976. 'Marx and science', *Political Studies*, vol. 24.

Thompson, E. P., 1972. *The Making of the English Working Class* (Harmondsworth).

Thompson, E. P., 1978. *The Poverty of Theory*.

Timpanaro, S., 1975. *On Materialism*.

Toews, J. E., 1980. *Hegelianism: the Path Towards Dialectical Humanism* (Cambridge).

Torrance, J., 1985. 'Reproduction and development: a case for a Darwinian mechanism in Marx's theory of history', *Political Studies* vol. 33.

Trotsky, L., 1967. *The History of the Russian Revolution* (three volumes).

Bibliography

Vajda, M., 1972. 'Karl Korsch's Marxism' in Howard and Klare, *The Unknown Dimension.*

van Parijs, P., 1982. 'Functionalist Marxism rehabilitated', *Theory and Society*, vol. 11.

Vogel, L., 1981. 'Marxism and feminism: unhappy marriage, trial separation or something else', in Sargent, L., ed., *Women and Revolution: A Discussion of the Unhappy Marriage of Marxism and Feminism.*

Vogel, L., 1983. *Marxism and the Oppression of Women.*

Wada, H., 1983. 'Marx and revolutionary Russia' in Shanin, *Late Marx and the Russian Road..*

Walton, P. and Gamble, A., 1972. *From Alienation to Surplus Value.*

Weber, M., 1978. *Economy and Society* (Berkeley).

Weiss, D. D., 1977. 'The philosophy of Engels vindicated', *Monthly Review*, vol. 28 (8).

Welty, G., 1983. 'Marx, Engels and *Anti-Dühring*', *Political Studies,* vol. 31.

Whitehead, A. N., 1964. *Science and the Modern World* (New York).

Whitfield, R., 1988. *Frederick Engels in Manchester* (Salford).

Winch, P., 1977. *The Idea of a Social Science and its Relation to Philosophy.*

Wood, A. W., 1981. *Karl Marx.*

Wood, A. W., 1986. 'Historical materialism and functional explanation', *Inquiry,* vol. 29.

Wood, E. M., 1981. 'The separation of the economic and the political in capitalism', *New Left Review*, no. 127.

Woolfson, C., 1982. *The Labour Theory of Culture.*

Young, I., 1981. 'Beyond the unhapppy marriage: a critique of the dual systems theory', in Sargent, L., ed., *Women and Revolution: A Discussion of the Unhappy Marriage of Marxism and Feminism.*

NAME INDEX

Abrams, P., 64
Acton, H. B., 127
Adams, H. P., 64, 93
Adamson, W. L., 188
Adorno, T., 96
Althusser, L., 9, 47, 62, 139
Anderson, P., 7
Andler, C., 4, 89
Avineri, S., 7, 144-5, 231

Bauer, B., 16-17, 25, 47, 64, 68
Bebel, A., 102
Beck, K., 19
Bentham, J., 41-2
Benton, T., 37
Bernier, F., 196
Bernstein, E., 2, 4, 102, 224, 233
Börne, L., 19, 21
Brzozowski, S., 4
Büchner, L., 101

Callinicos, A., 172, 225
Carlyle, T., 35, 41
Carver, T., 5, 6-7, 8, 100, 150-1, 154-5, 162
Cohen, G. A., 7, 173, 184
Colletti, L., 5, 7, 118, 134-5, 143
Comte, A., 147
Croce, B., 137

Darwin, C., 99, 107, 109, 113, 121, 145-6, 148-9
Della Volpe, G., 96
Descartes, R., 104, 125, 131
Draper, H., 63, 144
Dühring, E., 96, 102, 103, 104, 115, 130, 154, 168, 178, 229

Eastman, M., 134
Einstein, A., 122, 123, 143
Elster, J., 184, 186
Evans, M., 4, 7

Farr, J., 163
Fernbach, D., 232
Fetscher, I. 5, 121, 145
Feuerbach, L., 16, 17, 24, 25-6, 30, 32, 47, 48-9, 62, 64, 67-8, 78, 88, 100, 103, 186, 230
Fischer, E., 4
Fleischer, H. 36, 48, 64, 88, 188, 189, 194
Fock, V., 143

Fourier, C., 35, 36, 47, 65, 208
Freund, W., 154

Galileo, G., 123, 125
Gamble, A., 107, 145
Gaskell, P., 52
Gellner, E., 170
Gentile, G., 4
Geras, N., 236
Godelier, M., 173, 176-7, 181-2, 205
Graeber, F., 19, 22-3
Gramsci, A., 4, 7, 96
Grove, W., 99, 113, 157
Grün, K., 89
Gunn, R., 134
Gutzkow, K., 19, 21, 23

Harney, J., 65, 211
Halfpenny, P., 182
Hegel, G. W. F. 12-18, 20, 23, 24-8, 30-1, 35, 36, 66, 88, 99-100, 103, 104, 106, 109, 110, 111, 112, 114, 115, 131, 134-5, 150, 156-7, 159, 165, 194, 195, 196, 238
Heine, H., 19, 21
Herwegh, G., 45
Heraclitus, 152
Hess, M., 29-30, 29, 45, 52, 90
Hindess, B., 139
Hirst, P. Q., 139, 140
Hobbes, T., 125
Hofmann, A., 99, 156
Holbach, P., 78
Hook, S., 134

Immermann, K., 21

Jones, G. S., 105
Jordan, Z. A. 122, 144
Joule, J., 113

Kain, P. J., 7
Kant, I., 24, 109, 120, 125, 140
Kautsky, K., 4, 86, 134, 146
Kepler, J., 125
Kitching, G., 71, 181
Kolakowski, L., 103, 135
Korsch, K. 4, 236-7
Krieger, L., 4, 82
Kugelmann, L., 149
Kuhn, T., 138-9, 142

Name index

Kühne, F., 21

Labriola, A., 4
Lafargue, P., 155
Lange, F., 100
Laplace, P. 124, 125
Lassalle, F., 98, 99, 146
Laube, H., 19
Lavoisier, A. L., 119, 139, 152
Lavrov, P., 107, 149
Leff, G., 124
Lenin, V. I., 4, 113, 198, 224
Levine, A., 173
Levine, N. 5/6, 72, 117, 153, 159
Lichtheim, G., 7, 12, 90-2, 147, 148
Liebknecht, W., 101, 102, 223
List, F., 69
Locke, J., 125
Lovell, T., 141
Lubasz, H., 197
Lukács, G., 4, 96, 225/6
Lukes, S., 215

Macfarlane, A., 124/5
McLellan, D., 7, 90/1, 147
Malthus, T., 34, 121, 190
Manale, M., 64/5
Mann, M., 178, 180
Mao Tse-tung, 4, 96
Marcuse, H., 96
Masaryk, T., 4
Maskimov, A., 143
Mayer, J., 113
Mayer, K., 146
Maxwell, J. C., 163
Meikle, S., 129
Mill, J. S., 178-81
Miller, J., 147
Moleschott, J., 101
Mondolfo, R., 4
Monod, J., 129
Mundt, T., 19

Newton, I., 109, 125, 163
Norman, R., 112, 115, 135

Owen, R., 35, 208

Parsons, T., 136, 178
Paul, D., 148
Planck, M., 122
Plekhanov, G. V., 4, 96
Popper, K. R., 115, 123, 140
Priestley, J., 119/20, 139
Proudhon, P. J., 35, 65, 97, 98, 99, 100

Roberts, J. K., 153
Roemer, J., 218
Roscoe, H. E., 119, 152
Rubel, M., 64/5
Ruge, A., 18, 45
Runciman, W. G., 178, 180
Rutherford, E., 122

Sahlins, M., 169
Saint-Simon, H., 35, 147, 208
Sartre, J-P., 5, 96
Sayer, D. 172, 173,
Sayers, S., 139
Scheele, K., 119
Schelling, F., 24/6
Schiller, J., 21
Schmidt. A., 5, 7, 145
Schmidt, C., 104, 112
Schorlemmer, C., 119, 151-3
Schücking, L., 19
Shanin, T., 157, 196, 197
Shelley, P., 21
Sombart, W., 193
Spinoza, B., 125, 163
Sorel, G., 4, 224
Stalin, J., 96, 206, 207
Stein, L. von, 29
Stirner, M., 49, 62, 64, 66/7, 68, 174, 186, 230
Strauss, D., 16, 23-4
Struik, D. J., 89, 93
Sue, E., 29
Szabó, E., 4

Thompson, E. P., 60, 138, 140
Timpanaro, S., 105
Torrance, J., 184
Traube, M., 154
Trémaux, P., 148/9
Trier, G., 223
Trotsky, L., 96, 198

Vogt, K., 101

Wada, H., 198
Wallace, A., 108
Walton, P., 107, 145
Weber, M., 177/8, 197
Weiss, D. D., 4
Weitling, W., 29, 32
Welty, G., 154
Winch, P., 138
Wood, A. W., 4, 118, 138

Zasulich, V., 198

SUBJECT INDEX

alienation, 5, 17, 18, 26, 29, 31-7, 39, 41-2, 46, 54-5, 87, 207, 210, 228-31
ancient mode of production, 71, 170, 171
anthropogenetic outlook, 36-7, 46, 48, 194-5, 204, 210, 236
Asiatic mode of production, 170, 196-7, 217
atheism, 24, 104, 108, 122, 123-4

bad breast, Engels' function as, 3-9, 72, 73, 74, 89-90, 91-3, 96-7, 104-8, 117-8, 120-1, 144-63, 196-8, 206-7, 222, 228, 235-6
barbarism, 197, 199-200
base and superstructure, 7-8, 72-4, 164, 166-8, 177-82, 204, 205, 208
  interpenetration of, 174-7, 205

capitalist mode of production, 53-9, 71, 87-9, 91-2, 158-9, 202-203, 208-9, 211, 213-14, 214-16, 220-1, 228-31
  see also commodity fetishism; industrialisation; surplus-value; working class
Chartism, 30, 44, 57, 211
class, see class struggle; estates; relations of production
class struggle and class-consciousness, 30, 44, 51-2, 56-9, 72, 77-81, 85-6, 88, 93, 116, 136, 164, 180-1, 187, 190-1, 206, 208-14, 215, 219-20, 222-4, 225-8, 230-3, 237-9, see also exploitation; ideology; socialism; state
commodity fetishism, 37, 207, 228-9
Communist League, 90
communist society, predicted nature of, 6, 29, 35, 87-8, 90, 92 207, 229
contradiction, dialectical, 14, 33-5, 42-3, 113-16, 128, 134-6, 142-3, 153, 158-9, 238
conventionalism, 137, 139, 141-2
Critical Marxism, 4, 87, 207, 224-34
critique, grounds of, 18, 26-8, 37-8, 41-2, 67, 87-8, see also Critical Marxism; socialism

dialectic, idealist, 13-16, 29, 33, see also principles
dialectical materialism, 96-163, 238-9
  minimalist and maximalist readings of, 122-4, 128-9, 132, 143 relationship to historical materialism, 6, 116-17, 136-7 see also contradiction; epistemology; interpenetration of opposites; materialism; motion; negation of the negation; quantitative and qualitative change
dialectics of nature, 97-116, 150-7, see also dialectical materialism

emergent evolutionsism, 105-6, 110

empiricism, 119, 137-9, 141, 160
epistemological break, 38-41, 47-50, 62
epistemology, 117-21, 137-42, 160-2, see also conventionalism; empiricism, realism; reflection
essentialism, 109-10, 129
estates, distinguished from classes, 174
evolution, biological, 99, 109-10, 113, 145-6, 148-9
exploitation, 214-19, see also surplus value
family, 54, 69, 70-1, 199-204
fetishism, 192-5, 204, 238, see also commodity fetishism
feudal mode of production, 71, 170, 171
formal logic, 14-15, 114-15, 134-5
forms of intercourse, 70, see also relations of production
Frankfurt School, 233
functional explanation, 182-4

gender, see family; patriarchy

hindsight, political and historical, 17-18, 27-8, 234, 239
historical development, multilinear nature of, 7, 129, 196-8, 204
historical materialism, 47-83, 116-17, 136-7, 164-205, 239
  idealism of 'traditional' interpretation of, 174-5, 236 see also anthropogenetic outlook; base and superstructure; dialectical materialism; historical development; ideology; methodological individualism; mode of production; nomological outlook; patriarchy; pluralism; pragmatological outlook; productive forces; reductionism; relations of production; state; structuration theory; work relations
holism, 105-7, 113, 184
humanism, 2, 5, 19-37, 41-3, 54-5, 81, 87-9, 106, 228-32, see also alienation; Critical Marxism; critique; Man; utopian socialism

idealism, philosophical, 12-16, 17, 24-6, 30-1, 38-50, 65-6, 77, 79, 100, 104, 108, 111, 123, 134-5, 166, 174-5, 238, see also dialectic; principles
ideology, social basis of, 40-1, 58-9, 73, 77-81, 164, 166-7
industrialisation, 19, 29, 40, 52-3, 59-60, 71
interpenetration of opposites, 14-15, 99, 101, 110, 112-13, 126-7, 132-4, 142, 157-9, 160, 175

[255]

Subject index

liberalism, 19-22, 27-8

Man, abstraction of, 49, 51, 67-8, 89, *see also* humanism
materialism, 2, 6, 17, 24-5, 30, 68-9, 100, 101, 103-8, 111, 122-4, 136-7, 145-50, *see also* atheism; dialectical materialism; historical materialism
metaphysical world-view, 109, 112, 114-15, 124-5, 154, 167
methodological individualism, 184-7
mode of production, 69-70, *see also* ancient; Asiatic; capitalist; feudal; primitive communist
moralising, futility of, 51-2, 57, 84, 88, 108-9, 215-18, 226, 230-31, 233-4, *see also* Scientific Marxism
motion, as property of matter, 108-10, 124-5, 146, 150-1, 152-3

national characteristics, 21-2, 39-40, 44-5, 62-3
nationalism, 21-2
negation of the negation, 67, 97, 105, 110-11, 113, 116, 128-32, 142, 143, 157, 160, 209-10, 238-9
nomological outlook, 82-3, 187-95, 204, 236-8

optimism, Engels' political, 20-1, 28, 33, 211-12, 227-8, 237, *see also* socialism, inevitability of

patriarchy, 19, 54, 198-204
Pietism, 18-19, 22-3, 28
pluralism, explanatory, 178-82
political economy, 'bourgeois', 32, 24, 40, 58-9, 84
positivism, 2, 3, 104-5, 147, 192-5, *see also* nomological outlook; reductionism
pragmatological outlook, 48, 62, 81-2, 185-92, 194-5, 204, 210-11, 236, 238
praxis, 5, 6, 107
primitive communist mode of production, 70-1, 164, 169, 197, 199-200, *see also* barbarism; savagery
principles, dialectical self-development of, 27, 29, 30-1, 33-4, 38-40, 42-3, 44, 46, 37, 62, 65-6, *see also* idealism
private property, as a form of alienation, 31-2, 36, 37, 39
productive forces, social primacy of, 6, 7, 52-4, 69-72, 90-3, 117, 164, 170-3, 182-4, 191, 204, 205, 208, *see also* socialism

quantitative and qualitative change, 99, 101, 105, 110, 125-7, 133-4, 142, 153, 155-7, 160

realism, philosophical, 137, 139-42, 160-2
readings, of Marx and Engels, 1-9, 96-7, 235-6, *see also* bad breast
Reason, 12-13, 17-18, 27-8, 33, 35-6, 41, 43, 232
reductionism, of social phenomena to material, 104-7, 110, 145-50, 188-9, *see also* dialectical materialism; relationship to historical materialism
reflection, knowledge as a, 118, 138, 160-1
reforms and reformism, 3, 6, 58, 92-3, 206, 212-14, 220-1, 222-4, 225, 232-3
relations of production, 70, 72, 172, 180-1, 185-7, *see also* ancient mode of production, Asiatic mode; capitalist mode; class; estates; feudal mode; forms of intercourse; primitive communist mode; productive forces
religion, 12-13, 15, 16-17, 18-19, 22-5, 26, 32, 34, 43, *see also* atheism
reproduction, 201-2
revolution, *see* class struggle; Russia; socialism
Russia, possibility of communism in, 197-8

savagery, 197, 199-200
Scientific Marxism and socialism, 3, 4, 84, 106-21, 231-4, 236-9
socialism
    as class interest of workers, 43-4, 91, 225-6, 230-1, 233-4 as an ideal, 44-5, 49-50, 51, 91, 208, 230, *see also* communist society; moralising; Scientific Marxism; utopian socialism
    growth of productive forces as basis of 70, 84-6, 197-8, 208-11, 216, 221, 227
    inevitability of, 33-1, 36, 42-3, 57-8, 84-6, 130-1, 132, 157, 159, 195, 226-7, 239, *see also* anthropogenetic outlook; Scientific Marxism
    violence needed to achieve?, 222-4
state
    as a form of alienation, 32-3
    Hegel on, 15-17
    origin of, 164, 197
    social basis of, 40-1, 58, 73, 74-5, 164, 166-7
structuration theory, 185-7
surplus-value, 119, 141, 214-21

teleology, 12-16, 18, 27-8, 33, 42-3, 44, 46, 48, 81-2, 109, 114, 193-5, 210, *see also* anthropogenetic outlook
Toronto School, 136
trade unions, 56-7, 226
True Socialism, 88-9, 187

utopian socialism, 44-5, 49-50, 51-2, 57, 84, 88-9, 91, 208
    Marxism as a form of, 232, *see also* socialism

women, *see* family; patriarchy
work relations, 69-70
working class, social condition of, 19, 21, 31-2, 43-44, 55-6, 60-1, 219-20
    golden chains of, 220-1

Young Germany, 18-23
Young Hegelians, 16-18, 23-81, 47, 65-7

[256]

EU authorised representative for GPSR:
Easy Access System Europe, Mustamäe tee 50,
10621 Tallinn, Estonia
gpsr.requests@easproject.com

www.ingramcontent.com/pod-product-compliance
Ingram Content Group UK Ltd.
Pitfield, Milton Keynes, MK11 3LW, UK
UKHW021836140426
5217IPUK00021B/1476